Weeded

MASTERS *of* MYSTERY

ALSO BY CHRISTOPHER SANDFORD

Fiction
Feasting with Panthers

Arcadian

We Don't Do Dogs

Sport
The Cornhill Centenary Test

Godfrey Evans

Tom Graveney

Imran Khan

Film
Steve McQueen

Roman Polanski

Music
Mick Jagger

Eric Clapton

Kurt Cobain

David Bowie

Sting

Bruce Springsteen

Keith Richards

Paul McCartney

MASTERS *of* MYSTERY

*The Strange Friendship of
Arthur Conan Doyle
and Harry Houdini*

CHRISTOPHER SANDFORD

palgrave
macmillan

MASTERS OF MYSTERY
Copyright © S. E. Sandford, 2011
All rights reserved.

First published in 2011 by PALGRAVE MACMILLAN® in the United States—a
division of St. Martin's Press LLC, 175 Fifth Avenue, New York, NY 10010.

Where this book is distributed in the United Kingdom, Europe, and the rest of the
world, this is by Palgrave Macmillan, a division of Macmillan Publishers Limited,
registered in England, company number 785998, of Houndmills, Basingstoke,
Hampshire RG21 6XS.

Palgrave Macmillan is the global academic imprint of the above companies and has
companies and representatives throughout the world.

Palgrave® and Macmillan® are registered trademarks in the United States, the United
Kingdom, Europe, and other countries.

ISBN: 978-0-230-61950-0

Library of Congress Cataloging-in-Publication Data
Sandford, Christopher, 1956–
    Masters of mystery : the strange friendship of Arthur Conan Doyle and Harry
Houdini / Christopher Sandford.
        p. cm.
    Includes bibliographical references and index.
    ISBN 978-0-230-61950-0 (hardback)
    1. Houdini, Harry, 1874–1926—Friends and associates.   2. Magicians—
United States—Biography.   3. Doyle, Arthur Conan, Sir,
1859–1930—Friends and associates.   4. Authors, Scottish—20th century—
Biography.   5. Spiritualism.   I. Title.
GV1545.H8S26   2011
793.8092'2—dc23

                                                                          2011022076

A catalogue record of the book is available from the British Library.

Design by Letra Libre

First edition: December 2011

10 9 8 7 6 5 4 3 2 1

Printed in the United States of America.

To WHG, GAK, and St. Aubyns,
where I discovered the characters

"Body and spirit are twins: God only knows which is which."
— Algernon Charles Swinburne

"If matter mute and inanimate, though changed by the forces of Nature into a multitude of forms, can never die, will the spirit of man suffer annihilation when it has paid a brief visit, like a royal guest, to this tenement of clay? No. I am as sure that there is another life as I am that I live to-day."
— William Jennings Bryan

"When I walked into the séance room and saw that beautiful blonde, her applesauce meant nothing to me. I have been through apple orchards."
— Harry Houdini, speaking of the medium
Mina Crandon, or "Margery"

CONTENTS

Ten pages of black-and-white photographs
appear between pages 152 and 153.

ACKNOWLEDGMENTS

T his is not a biography of Arthur Conan Doyle, or of Harry Houdini. Anyone interested in reading more about either one will find some suggestions in the bibliography at the end of the book. Although one or two of Conan Doyle's or Houdini's more partisan admirers declined the offer to help, occasionally after venting at me, the research process generally was productive and tantrum-free. I tried to pursue it in a spirit of honest inquiry. Writing this book after doing various biographies of rock and film stars was refreshing; nobody threatened me with violence, or promised that I'd never work again (although I did receive an enigmatic late-night phone message each Halloween, the anniversary of Houdini's death). I only wish I could blame someone listed below for the shortcomings of the text. They are mine alone.

For archive material, input, or advice I should thank, institutionally: Abacus; the American Society for Psychical Research; *Atlantic Monthly*; Bookcase; Bookends; Bookfinder; the British Library; the British Newspaper Library; Cambridge University Library; *Chronicles*; CricketArchive; the Cricket Society; the *Daily Mail*; the *Daily Telegraph*; FBI—Freedom of Information Division; General Register Office; the Harry Ransom Center of the University of Texas at Austin; the History Museum at the Castle of Appleton, Wisconsin; the Houdini Museum of Scranton, Pennsylvania; the Library of Congress; Longton Spiritualist Church; the Magic Circle; Magicus; Michigan State Department of Health; the National Portrait Gallery; the *New York Times*; New York University; Old Renton Book Exchange; Orbis; Palgrave Macmillan; Portsmouth City Council; Public Record Office; Renton Public Library; Seattle Police Department; Seattle Public Library; the Seeley Library; the *Spectator*; Spiritualists' National Union; SPR; *The Times*; Undershaw; University of Montana; University of Puget Sound; Vital Records; Windlesham's Manor.

Professionally: Glenn Alai, Rev. Maynard Atik, Tony Bill, Jeff Blood, Paul Bradley, Paul Brooke, Dick Brooks, Curtis Brown, Joan Brown, the late William Burroughs, Susan Carey, Matt Carpenter, Jean Cazes, Julia Cerelli, Charles Champlin, Anna Chen, Dan Chernow, Paul Clements, Gary Cotton, Gemma Cox, the Cricket Writers Club, Bud Crowe, the late Tony Curtis, Paul Darlow, Dorothy Dietrich, Richard Dysart, Rex Evans, Mike Fargo, Judy Flanders, Tom Fleming, Focus Fine Arts, Rachel Foss, John Fraser, Toni Gahl, Brenda Galang, George Galloway, Corinne Garcia, Duncan Gascoyne, Jim Geller, the late W. H. Gervis, Tony Gill, Golem, Herman Graf, Michael Gunton, Nigel Hancock, Polly Harris, Alan Hazen, Michael Heath, Paul Hogroian, the Houdini family, Jim Hoven, Emily Hunt, Inca, Jon Jackson, David Jacobs, the Jaggers, David Kelly, John M. Kelso, the late Alan Kennington, Alan Lane, Christopher Lee, Jon Lellenberg, Rev. John-Otto Liljenstolpe, Cindy Link, Claire Looney, Robert Mann, Kathy Marsh, MCC, Peter Meadows, Colin Midson, Andrew Miller, Linda Morris, Tiffany Niederwerfer, Barry Norman, Maureen O'Donnell, Caroline O'Shea, Max Paley, John Pavlik, Penn and Teller, the late Harold Pinter, Katharina Rae, Neil Rand, PNB, Jim Repard, Suzannah Rich, Scott Richert, Paul Shelley, Dennis Silk, Peter Smith, Connie Sopocy, Alex Stacey, Nina Stefani, Ed Strauss, Airie Stuart, Eli Wallach, Adele Warlow, Rick Watson, Rusty West, Alan Weyer, Mary Wilson, Tom Wolfe, Dora Yanni, Tony Yeo.

Personally: Adis, Air Canada, Arvid Anderson, Sam and Barbara Banner, Pete Barnes, the late Charles Benjamin, Ann Bevan, Clare Bevan, the late Terry Bland, Stanley Booth, Ian Botham, Hilary and Robert Bruce, Cocina, Common Ground, Complete Line, Ken Crabtrey, CricInfo, Celia Culpan, Deb K. Das, the Davenport, Mark Demos, Monty Dennison, Devil's Punchbowl Hotel, Karen Dowdall-Sandford, the Dowdall family, John and Barbara Dungee, Ednorog, Mary Evans, Malcolm Galfe, the Gay Hussar, the Gees, Gethsemane Lutheran Church, Audrey Godwin, Colleen Graffy, James Graham, Tom Graveney, Peter Griffin, Grumbles, Dacia Hanson, Charles Hillman, Alex Holmes, Hotel Vancouver, Paul Huelin, Jo Jacobius, Jamieson family, Lincoln Kamell, Betty and Joan Keylock, the late Tom Keylock, Aslam Khan, Imran Khan, Kidd Valley, Kinko's, Stephen Lacey, Terry Lambert, Belinda Lawson, Robert Lethbridge, Barbara Levy, Vince Lorimer, the late Jackie McBride, Les McBride, Ruth and Angie McCartney, Mackenzie River Pizza, the Macris, Lee Mattson, Jim and Rana Meyersahm, Missoula Doubletree, Sheila Mohn, the Morgans, Colleen Murray, John Murray, National Gallery Sackler Room, Rev. Jonathan Naumann, Chuck Ogmund, Valya Page, Robin Parish, Peter Perchard, Greg Phillips, Chris Pickrell, Roman Polanski, the late Dr. John Prins, Prins family, the late Navaal Ramdin, Renton Computers, Keith Richards, Katalina

Sabeva, Debbie Saks, Sam, Delia Sandford, my son and heir Nicholas Sandford, Sefton Sandford, Sue Sandford, Peter Scaramanga, Seattle C.C., Rev. Kempton Segerhammar, the late Cat Sinclair, Fred and Cindy Smith, Rev. and Mrs. Harry Smith, Spruce Street School, the Stanleys, Thaddeus Stuart, Jack Surendranath, Dave Thomas, the Travel Team, Ben and Mary Tyvand, William Underhill, Syra Vahidy, Di Villar, the late Roger Villar, Lisbeth Vogl, John and Mary Wainwright, Walgreens, Charlie Watts, Chris West, Richard Wigmore, the Willis Fleming family, Heng and Lange Woon, the Yukawas.

C. S.

2011

1
PARALLEL LIVES

The lights were low, the music soft as the audience settled into their seats in the largest building in Garnett, Kansas, that cold Sunday night in November 1897. They were there to see a traveling variety show whose star attraction the local *Evening Review* had hailed as "the World Famous Medium" who, the paper noted, "has been prevailed upon by popular request of the public to give a Spiritualistic séance . . . Pianos will float over the head of the audience, tables will be levitated by unseen hands, messages will appear," the report added, a prospect sufficient for 1,034 customers to pack the plush, vaguely Romanesque Opera House to the rafters—an impressive turnout in a farm town of only 6,000 inhabitants.

Harry Houdini did not disappoint them. Bounding on stage, the wiry, tousle-haired twenty-three-year-old, dressed in ill-fitting tails, was able both to produce the promised psychic phenomena, and to reveal certain disquieting personal details about members of the audience, including the news that one well-known businessman who was present was "cruelly neglecting to tend his own mother's grave" despite enjoying "many merry excursions with [his] lovely secretary," a charge that led the man to make a hurried departure from the hall amid some mirth from the crowd. Houdini went on to state that a young mother who was in the theater was undoubtedly thinking of her deceased baby Louise, "whom the Lord has been pleased to call at an early age." Shielding his eyes as though squinting into the heavens, he added that "Louise and many others are here with us tonight." The remark was greeted by "audible gasps," the paper reported. After more in this vein, Houdini announced that he would conclude the performance by unmasking the murderer of a local woman named Sadie Timmins. "We propose to contact our friends and ancestors on the other side," he went on. "You cannot hide a nefarious deed from the spirits, and Mademoiselle Beatrice, a trained psychometric clairvoyant, will assist me." At that Houdini was joined on stage by Mlle Beatrice, in reality his twenty-one-year-old wife Bess, a petite brunette from Brooklyn who was clad in a lace wedding dress. Bess sat down in a chair and Houdini tied a blindfold around her head, the better "to concentrate her energy and filter out extraneous vibrations."

As the orchestra struck up the mournful chords of "Nearer My God to Thee," Bess suddenly groaned and slumped forward in her chair. "She is in a trance state," Houdini explained, always conscientious about informing his audience of exactly what they were witnessing on stage. After appealing for silence, he then began to question his wife, who answered him in an unusually low, moaning voice.

"Was Sadie Timmins murdered in her own home?"

"Yes."

"Where did the deed occur?"

"In her kitchen."

"With what instrumentality?"

"She was hacked . . . seventeen times . . . with a butcher knife."

"Did she know her killer?"

"Yes."

By this time there was something approaching a small riot in the hall. The murder of Sadie Timmins had been an especially brutal one, even by the standards of turn-of-the-century Kansas, and local emotions ran high. Suspicion had fallen on several prominent Garnett citizens, including the town's hot-headed young lawman, Sheriff Keeney. Hysterical denunciations, screams, and sobbing drowned out Houdini's next few remarks, and a minute or more passed before he once again turned to his wife.

"What is the killer's name?" Houdini said it so softly that everybody fell quiet. "Answer. Now. *What is his name?*" he asked, ever more insistently.

But neither Bess, nor the spirits possessing her, would ever solve the terrible mystery of Garnett, Kansas. As Houdini repeated the question, now all but shouting in his wife's face, Bess dramatically swooned sideways in her chair, her chin lolling onto her chest. "She's fainted!" Houdini announced in a quavering voice, before stepping forward to the footlights with the time-honored inquiry: "Is there a doctor in the house?" The curtain fell. The next minute saw a steady crescendo in the sort of rowdy chanting and whistling normally associated in Garnett with burlesque shows, although the audience acclaim was now unmistakably tinged with the renewed sound of women crying. Some thirty years later, Houdini was still able to vividly remember the events of that night, and even willing to reveal some of his methods. His shaming of the local businessman had owed more to diligent research than to spiritual guidance. "That Sunday morning," Houdini recalled, "accompanied by the sexton and the oldest inhabitant of the town, we walked out to the village cemetery, and I had a notebook, and what was not [apparent] from the tombstones—any information that was lacking, the sexton would tell me the missing data, and the old Uncle Rufus would give me the scandals of everyone sleeping in God's acre. And you can imagine my going out there and retailing that terrible stuff." There had never been a serious prospect of Bess exposing the murderer of poor Sadie Timmins. It was "all humbug and a good presentation mixed together." The presentation came with a mythic penumbra, too, of the sort of fictional "whodunit" epitomized by the hugely popular cases of Sherlock Holmes. By 1900, Houdini was sometimes billed as "Sherlock Holmes Eclipsed," and the critics and public alike routinely compared him to the legendary detective.

By the time Houdini looked back on his youthful performance in Garnett, he had long since abandoned any pretense to mystical powers. In the first paragraph of his 1924 book *A Magician among the Spirits*, he wrote, "I associated myself with mediums, joining the rank and file and hold[ing] séances as an independent medium to fathom the truth of it all. At the time I appreciated the fact that I surprised my clients, but while aware of the fact that I was *deceiving* them I did not see or understand the seriousness of trifling with such sacred sentimentality and the baneful result which inevitably followed. To me it was a lark." A bit later in the text, Houdini added, "Spiritualism is nothing more or less than mental intoxication; Intoxication of any sort when it becomes a habit is injurious to the body, but intoxication of the mind is always fatal to the mind," before calling for a law that would "prevent these human leeches from sucking every bit of reason and common sense from their victims."

People pretending to enjoy occult powers, if not actual communion with the dead, is a theatrical trick as old as storytelling. But in Houdini's case there may have been more to his early Spiritualistic revues than merely a desire to separate the public from their money. In December 1885, his beloved half brother Herman had died of tuberculosis, at the age of twenty-two. Houdini, who was eleven, attended a series of séances, or at least what were described as "perfumed conclaves," in a failed attempt to communicate with Herman's spirit. Three years later, he went to the home of a medium in Beloit, Wisconsin, where a voice purporting to be that of Abraham Lincoln could be heard echoing from a trumpet that swung across the room. The astute fourteen-year-old soon realized that the voice was produced by a hidden gramophone player, and that the trumpet was flying around on an invisible wire.

Even then, Houdini was prepared to suspend his disbelief. Two nearly identical, walrus-mustached brothers from Buffalo, New York, Ira and William Davenport, had toured the world in the 1860s and 1870s with a show whose most famous effect saw them lashed together inside a packing crate—the so-called "spirit cabinet"—that also contained musical instruments such as a tambourine, a trumpet, and a violin. Once the box was locked, the instruments would sound. When it was unlocked, the deadpan-faced brothers were found to be still securely tied in place. When the lid went down, the music started again. Sometimes the whole pantomime lasted as long as an hour. There were those who believed that supernatural forces were at play, and when reading the news reports the young Houdini declared himself "enthralled" by this "truly wonderful business." Houdini's brother Theo remembered him as being "a great worshipper of the Davenports" for several years into his early adulthood. Their ability to inhabit even a large wooden box while under restraint was to be the starting point for a number of Harry's own illusions. In July 1910, Houdini made a 900-mile journey to visit Ira, by then the only surviving Davenport brother, who at this time finally felt able to reveal the secret of the "Davenport Rope-Tie" that had allowed the brothers to slip in and out of their bonds. Poignantly, the seventy-year-old Ira, although ravaged by throat cancer, wanted Houdini to join him on a new worldwide tour in which they would present the old trick, but with added twentieth-century props such as the latest police-issue steel handcuffs. Ira died before plans could be made, but, even then, Houdini was reluctant to "out" the Davenports, writing somewhat ambiguously only that "I can make the positive assertion that [they] never were exposed."

In October 1892, Houdini's father Rabbi Mayer Weiss died in New York at the age of sixty-three. His eighteen-year-old son sold his own watch in order to pay for a "professional psychic reunion" with the deceased, who had left behind various debts. The medium was apparently able to materialize Rabbi Weiss, who was reluctant to dwell on earthly or financial matters, but instead assured his son that he was "very happy." "It seemed strange to me that my father, knowing our pinched circumstances, would say any such thing," Houdini remarked. But even then he held to the view that there were legitimate "sensitives" who could bring word from the beyond. While Houdini's purely theatrical use of Spiritualism over the next few years gave way to what he called "a realisation of the seriousness of toying" with the occult, he never abandoned his attempts at paranormal communication. On a six-month tour of Europe in 1920, Houdini attended more than a hundred séances, and two years later was ready to sit in a darkened Atlantic City hotel room where he was rewarded by a fifteen-page letter, channeled through a medium, apparently dictated by his late mother.

Few in Houdini's audience that night in Garnett could have known how deeply his father and others had impressed him with their advocacy of what Rabbi Weiss called a "strict and strenuous"—and deeply traditional—Judaism. Though somewhat fitful as a breadwinner, the rabbi was widely respected as a man of letters, whom the *Volksfreund,* the weekly German-language paper in his adopted home of Appleton, Wisconsin, called "gebildeter"—"very cultured." After he had become a global celebrity, Houdini informed a reporter that his proudest achievement was to have on file "records for five generations that my direct forefathers were students and teachers of the Bible, and recognised as among the leading scholars of their times." Always a bibliophile, he frequently reminded audiences that his father "bequeathed me all of his texts," before adding, "and I have read every one." As a child, Houdini also came to appreciate that Rabbi Weiss, with his four-cornered miter and black, floor-length cassock, cut an exotic and, to some, sinister figure in rural Wisconsin, and he would encounter more virulent displays of anti-Semitism throughout his own career. When visiting Russia in 1903, for example, Houdini learned that "Hebrews" were allowed in "only with a licence, like a dog, and even then no Jews are allowed to sleep in Moscow or St Petersburg." Despite this and numerous other cases of harassment over the years, he kept a faith that was "profound and unquestioning," he once remarked, if not always based on complex theological arguments. As a middle-aged man, Houdini was to tell an interviewer that he had the "utmost reverence" for the biblical texts, which he followed like a "good, willing child." Asked by the reporter who his favorite author was, he replied, "My dad."

While in Appleton, Houdini would also have been aware of a popular philosophy that already had a long history, some of it quite reputable, by the time he came to trifle with it professionally. Spiritualism, the premise that man's physical shell disintegrates at death, but that his soul survives exactly as it was, only on another plane, could be traced back at least as far as the writings of the Swedish mystic-philosopher Emanuel Swedenborg (1688–1772), who claimed to have had a vision one night while dining in a London tavern. According to Swedenborg, who was fifty-six at the time, "a darkness fell upon [my] eyes and the room changed character," at which point a luminous figure appeared in the gloom and announced, "Do not eat too much!" The same apparition then came to Swedenborg later that night in a dream and proclaimed that he was the "Lord Jesus Christ [who] had selected me to reveal the spiritual truth of the Bible." The result was Swedenborg's *Arcana Coelestia* ("Heavenly Secrets"), which appeared in eight volumes between 1749 and 1756, and whose closely argued central thesis defeated all but the most agile minds of the day. In 1766, Immanuel Kant published his own considered opinion that Swedenborg's accounts were "nothing but illusions," although even he allowed that there seemed to be "a strain of divine inspiration" to some of his writings.

Showmanship first came to pervade Spiritualism in 1848, when the Fox sisters, Margaret, aged fourteen, and Kate, aged twelve, apparently began to hear nocturnal "bumps and raps" in the bedroom of their small farmhouse in Hydesville, New York. The girls' mother became convinced that an unseen force she named "Mr. Splitfoot" was communicating with them, and that "distinct manifestations of an intelligent life" continued even when she and the children moved home. Within a year, the sisters and their mother had become a popular attraction in theaters up and down the American east coast. The author James Fenimore Cooper, the anti-slavery campaigner and journalist William Lloyd Garrison, and George Bancroft, recently retired as Secretary of the US Navy, were among the many eminently respectable figures to endorse the demonstrations as genuine. In 1850, Horace Greeley, a Whig politician, editor of the influential *New York Tribune* (and widely credited with having coined the phrase "Go west, young man"), took up the girls' cause in a series of front-page articles, though privately he came to express regret that even as teenagers Margaret and Kate had "taken a sip," the beginning of a serious drinking problem in their later days.

Perhaps inspired by the Foxes' example, a variety of late-nineteenth-century public figures and other citizens on both sides of the Atlantic, some of them already veterans of the vaudeville stage, began to speak of their religious or extrasensory encounters. "A mystical feeling about oneself comes easily to performers in the spotlight," the author Gary Wills has said, and significant numbers of the political, scientific, or artistic elite now came to express their own strong sense of communion with worlds unseen. Many of these contacts took place under the stressful conditions of the illness or death of a family member. In 1849, Charles Dickens began to attempt "mesmeric cures" of his young sister-in-law Georgina Hogarth, who was said to be suffering from "intestinal evil." The novelist reported that his performances of "animal magnetism," as hypnotism was then called, also afforded him clairvoyant power. Personalities as diverse as Queen Victoria, the poet W. B. Yeats, and the Norwegian Symbolist painter Edvard Munch all later engaged in Spiritualistic efforts to reach a departed loved one. There was a dramatic surge of interest in the paranormal in the immediate aftermath of the American Civil War, with its 620,000 military casualties and undetermined number of civilian deaths. In the White House, Abraham Lincoln and his wife held a series of candlelit séances following the death of their eleven-year-old son William of typhoid fever in 1862, by no means the last time a US President was to engage in the occult. On the public stage, meanwhile, a long parade of mesmerists, table-tappers, furniture-levitators, speakers-in-tongues, yogic fliers, healers, and seers held paid demonstrations of their apparent ability to invoke the spirits. There was a particular vogue for the "automatic writing" pioneered by the American medium Henry Slade, who claimed to receive paranormal messages on a small slate blackboard he held in his hands. Some of these performers bore scientific scrutiny better than others, but there was no denying the influence of the movement as a whole. By the time the young Houdini arrived in the country in 1878, more than 11 million Americans admitted to being Spiritualists. According to Greeley's *New York Tribune*, there were 742 Spiritualistic churches established in the United States and "upwards of 30,000 Trained Ministers," meaning mediums or clairvoyants, dedicated to "furthering the New Revelation."

In late-Victorian Britain, the fashion for Spiritualism often came with a feminist subtext. Women were thought to be uniquely qualified to communicate with spirits of the dead, and in the séance room, at least, a medium could enjoy a degree of independence and authority not readily available to her elsewhere. There are no reliable figures on actual attendance at séances or services, although it was widely believed at the time that an increasing number of the nominally respectable were dabbling in psychic affairs. When reviewing the history of Spiritualism in the United Kingdom, Houdini would remark that "[b]y the 1870s an invitation to tea amongst London's gentility would often conclude with a candlelit course in which the spirits would be asked to reveal themselves by rotating or lifting the table, among other manifestations, to the delight of the audience." At the end of that decade there would be three regularly published British magazines dedicated to the paranormal, as well as a growing amount of hardcover literature. By 1882, the British movement as a whole was sufficiently widespread to bring about the creation of the Society for Psychical Research (SPR), with a committee of largely Cambridge-based academics promising "to approach [Spiritualist] issues without prejudice or prepossession of any kind, and in the same spirit of exact and unimpassioned en-quiry which has enabled Science to solve so many problems, once not less obscure nor less hotly debated." The SPR initially set up five subcommittees, to variously investigate Mesmerism, Mediumship, Reichenbach Phenomena [electromagnetic forces], Apparitions and Haunted Houses, and Séances, as well as a Literary Panel to study psychic history and conduct surveys. In one early census, the SPR asked 17,000 adults whether they had ever experienced a "spiritual hallucination" while fully awake and in good health. Of the 1,684 who said they had, there were those who insisted that they had been physically "embraced" or "kissed" by an unseen force, among several other less conventional liaisons.

In 1893, a thirty-four-year-old Scots-Irish doctor, lecturer, seafarer, sportsman, pamphleteer—and globally renowned author of the Sherlock Holmes stories—named Arthur Ignatius Conan Doyle applied to join the SPR. Although striking, this wasn't the abrupt leap from the famously rational world of Holmes to the shadowy one of Ouija boards and ghosts some have suggested. The president of the SPR who approved Conan Doyle's application was no less solid a figure than Arthur Balfour, a former Conservative leader of the House of Commons and future prime minister, whose friend Annie Marshall regularly brought him letters written to him from the Other Side. Among the society's other prominent members were the naturalist Alfred Russel Wallace, Darwin's peer in the theory of natural selection; the physicist Oliver Lodge, one of the developers of wireless telegraphy; Lodge's fellow scientist William Crookes, a commercially successful inventor and founding editor of *Chemical News;* and the pioneering Fabian author Frank Podmore. The list isn't exhaustive. In its prospectus, the SPR made it clear that it sought to bring what it called "coldly scientific logic" to its investigations, which then ranged from its meticulous census work to a perhaps more engrossing paper on a Holmes-like case filed under the name of "the Spectre Dog of Peel Castle." It was an approach that would have commended itself to a young medical man with an open mind on basic theological issues.

His SPR membership, in fact, was only the most recent—if the most public—sign that Conan Doyle was something more than the parodically stuffy relic of God and Empire sometimes portrayed. To some later detractors, even his appear-ance was held against him. Doyle was tall, squarely built, heavily mustached, with plastered-down brown hair. He carried his umbrella at the furl; his bearing was military; and he lived in a large, red-bricked suburban villa stuffed with mahogany tables, marble busts, and hunting prints. On the surface, he was the epitome of a late-Victorian clubman. His exquisite manners were proverbial, and he was unfailingly courteous even in the most trying of circumstances. Some thirty years later, Conan Doyle received the disturbing news from a "spirit guide" named Pheneas that the world would soon suffer a cataclysmic event in which "there will be great loss of life. It will be terrific. All humanity will be shaken to the core," although, Pheneas added, "No one will suffer who should be spared. It will be like a great sieve passing through all that is worthless, retaining only the fruit." "I am greatly obliged to you," Doyle replied urbanely. Houdini would once remark that his future opponent struck him as the "very perfect specimen of an Englishman." Somewhat belying his young-fogey image, the Conan Doyle who joined the SPR was also a lapsed Roman Catholic, an inquisitive student of practices such as mesmerism and telepathy, and increasingly receptive to the possibility of a wide range of other psychic phenomena.

Even so, Conan Doyle's full-scale conversion to Spiritualism was an unusually protracted one. In January 1880, when he was twenty and struggling as a medical assistant in Birmingham, he attended a public lecture with the title "Does Death End All?," writing afterward that it was "a very clever thing . . . though not convincing to me." He later reported that he had "had the usual contempt which the young educated man feels towards the whole subject which has been covered by the clumsy name of Spiritualism," a subject he then saw as a litany of fraudulent mediums, spurious phenomena, and other "bogus happenings" that had duped the public.

As early as July 1882, Conan Doyle wrote a story (published a year later in *Bow Bells*) entitled "The Winning Shot." Squarely in the Gothic tradition, it dabbles in the world of mesmerism and thought-transference before building to a vaguely supernatural climax in which a young man taking part in a rifle contest is unnerved to see a vision of himself standing immediately in front of the target. Conan Doyle's contemporaneous account of the story to his mother as "a very ghastly Animal Magnetic vampirey sort of tale" suggests that he was still using the paranormal primarily for its narrative potential rather than to change people's hearts and minds. Among Doyle's next efforts was "The Captain of the 'Polestar,'" in which he allowed his fictional hero, like him a young doctor, to refer mockingly to "the impostures of Slade," the American slate-writer. Later in 1883 came a story he called "Selecting a Ghost," in which a wealthy shopkeeper seeks to audition spooks to haunt his mansion. In his early twenties, the age at which Houdini was staging his own Spiritualist revues in America, Conan Doyle still took an essentially lighthearted, if not comic view of the supernatural, a subject not only rich in its own right, but with the added commercial advantage of being topical. Both men would grow noticeably more earnest on the issue in years ahead.

In late 1883, Conan Doyle made the acquaintance of one of those faintly eccentric polymathic figures so prevalent in Victorian public life. Alfred Drayson, a fellow member of the Portsmouth Literary and Scientific Society, was a distinguished former soldier and prolific author on everything from the game of billiards to the rotation of the earth, on which he wrote a sophisticated, if controversial monograph. Physically, Drayson was the epitome of a retired major general, with a richly tinted complexion and a luxuriant waxed mustache. He was also a practicing Spiritualist who believed not only that ghosts could be summoned by a medium, but that they were frequently accompanied by the "apport," or materialization, of everyday household objects. Drayson reported that he had once been present at a séance where a dozen fresh eggs appeared on the table in front of him. By some arcane process of deduction, these were said to have been beamed into the room from suburban New York. Conan Doyle may not immediately have been converted by Drayson, but it was said in a private report of the Society's proceedings that he "always Loved the distinguished Member's speeches." Doyle later dedicated a collection of short stories to "my friend Major-Gen A. W. Drayson," although in doing so he cited only his admiration for his "great and as yet unrecognised services to astronomy."

In 1884, Drayson introduced Conan Doyle to the teachings of Madame Helena Blavatsky, a stout, middle-aged Russian-born Spiritualist who had immigrated to New York and co-founded the Theosophical Society there. The Theosophists propounded various unorthodox views on reincarnation and time travel, and came to be identified by some with the idea of Aryan supremacy. Madame Blavatsky later moved on to India and eventually England, where her apparent demonstrations of mental psychic feats including levitation, clairvoyance, and telepathy attracted widespread comment. In December 1885, the Australian lawyer Richard Hodgson published a report in the *Proceedings* of the Society for Psychical Research charging Blavatsky and the Theosophists with persistent fraud. We know that Conan Doyle followed both the debate, and the furious Theosophist response to the SPR, but, again, kept the paranormal firmly in check in his own writings.

When Conan Doyle started his first Sherlock Holmes story, *A Study in Scarlet*, in March 1886, he had several goals, avowed and secret, but psychic instruction was not among them. Some thirty-five years later, he was still at pains to keep his personal beliefs separate from those of his fictional detective. "This agency stands flat-footed upon the ground, and there it must remain," Holmes remarks in the somewhat macabre story of "The Sussex Vampire." "The world is big enough for us. No ghosts need apply."

In November 1886, Conan Doyle signed over the rights of *A Study in Scarlet* in perpetuity to Ward, Lock and Company, a publisher of pulp fiction, for the unpromising sum of £25. "I never at any time received another penny for it," he recalled in his memoirs. At the same time, he was conducting a series of experiments in which he and an architect friend named Henry Ball would sit in adjoining rooms and attempt to project their thoughts to one another, apparently with some success. On January 24, 1887, Conan Doyle, Ball, and a small group of like-minded researchers met in the darkened dining room of a house in the north end of Portsmouth. The initial results of their séance were disappointing, although after half an hour of silence the dining table itself began to tap up and down in a kind of Morse code they interpreted as "You are going too slowly. How long are you going to take?" Some time later, the group made contact with a local professional medium named Horstead, "a small bald grey man with a pleasant expression," who was seemingly able to levitate the table in front of them, as well as to channel the spirits of the ancients. At a sitting on June 16, Horstead began to speak in a low, tremulous voice and, turning to Conan Doyle, remarked that his was "a great brain" that was "full of magnetism." Horstead then passed him a scrap of paper on which he had written, "This gentleman is a healer. Tell him not to read Leigh Hunt's book." As Doyle had recently been thinking of buying that critic's 1840 *The Comic Dramatists of the Restoration,* it appeared to be a notable feat of prediction. He would later conclude that "this message mark[ed] in my spiritual career the change of 'I believe' into 'I know.'"*

Less than a month later, Conan Doyle published a letter in *Light,* one of the now half-dozen popular British psychic magazines. Acknowledging that he was a "novice and inquirer" in the field, he noted, nonetheless, it was "absolutely certain that intelligence [can] exist apart from the body." The message from the Portsmouth medium had apparently convinced him of life's ultimate meaning. With his characteristic gift for the lucid phrase, Doyle assured the readers of *Light* of the unimpeachable logic of his position. "After weighing the evidence," he wrote, "I could no more doubt the existence of the phenomena than I could doubt the

---

*Horstead's insights should be set against the fact that Conan Doyle had already been practicing medicine locally for five years, and that he was known to share his reading habits with friends and colleagues.

existence of lions in Africa, though I have been to that continent and have never chanced to see one."

It may be relevant, even so, to bear Conan Doyle's personal circumstances in mind alongside his more stringently analytical powers at the time he made his later public commitment to psychic exploration. In the autumn of 1893, what one observer called "Conan Doyle's unfailing optimism [and] schoolboy high spirits" were sorely tested by two family tragedies. On October 10, his father Charles died at the age of sixty-one at Crichton Royal Institution, a Scottish mental hospital. The older Doyle (who never used the compound surname) was a gentle, unworldly man whose undoubted artistic talent rarely met with commercial success. From around the age of thirty he began, instead, to drink heavily. Toward the end of his life, Charles Doyle kept an illustrated journal on whose front page he wrote, "Keep steadily in view that this Book is ascribed wholly to the produce of a MADMAN. Whereabouts would you say was the deficiency of intellect? Or depraved taste? If in the whole Book you can find a single Evidence of either, mark it and record it against me." The drawings within reveal a fascination with sprites and fairies, along with piercing jolts of insight into the artist's own deteriorating mental condition. One picture shows Doyle being swallowed alive by a ferocious-looking Sphinx, over the caption, "When I was drawing the Royal Institution, Edinburgh, I was a good deal worried by sphinxes." Arthur had done his best for Charles and, poignantly, even commissioned him to illustrate an early reprint of *A Study in Scarlet,* but the full horror of his father's descent into alcoholism and mental turmoil was a tale for which he clearly felt his public wasn't yet ready. Charles himself called his condition his son's "dreadful secret." Rather than travel to Scotland to help with the arrangements for his father's funeral, Conan Doyle chose to stay home and attend a lecture entitled "Recent Evidences as to Man's Survival of Death."

Conan Doyle was thirty-four years old at the time his father died. One journalist has said that as a result "he sank into a deep, impenetrable silence, stun[ned] by the supreme tragedy of his life to date." But another, perhaps even greater blow would follow almost immediately. That same month, Conan Doyle's thirty-six-year-old wife Louisa was diagnosed with tuberculosis, and given only a few months to live. "I am afraid we must reconcile ourselves to [it]," Doyle wrote to his mother. "I had Douglas Powell, who is one of the first men in London out on Saturday and he confirmed it."

It may not be coincidental that Conan Doyle made his application to join the SPR within a month of both his father's death and his wife's diagnosis. Both events, with an emphasis on "bodily life's fragility [and] decay," would seem to have accelerated his researches in the supernatural. Conan Doyle might have argued, too, that he was really doing no more than refining the fundamentals he'd learned at home and at school—Spiritualism, as he often reminded people, essentially being just the scientific extension of orthodox religion. Even so, Doyle wouldn't yet allow the intellectual attractions of the paranormal to affect his writing. His fiction was unabashedly mass-market art, and his frequent literary allusions to the mystic were often comic, never didactic, and always in the interests of the story. Some of the true flavor comes through in an 1893 letter from Robert Louis Stevenson, who greets Conan Doyle with the genial salutation, "O! Frolic fellow Spookist."

Who, then, were these two men who were to leave such an indelible impression on the debate about life after death?

In some ways they were almost comically different. They were born fifteen years apart, Conan Doyle on May 22, 1859, into a Roman Catholic family largely composed of artists, in Edinburgh; Houdini on March 24, 1874, in Budapest, where his father made a living as an itinerant soap salesman and lawyer before practicing as a rabbi. As an eight-year-old, Doyle went away to boarding school and eventually earned a medical degree at Edinburgh University. Houdini's formal education ended at the age of twelve when he ran away from home, and he spent much of his adult life compensating by compiling what, with typical restraint, he called "the world's most expensive private collection of books," rich both in the classics and in texts on comparative religion, Spiritualism, and above all, magic. Houdini, of course, was a showman, and as such never a victim to false modesty—he "makes an introductory speech telling how good he is," the *New York Telegraph* noted of one performance, "and you wonder why he doesn't get on about his business of breaking out of handcuffs." Conan Doyle, though not free of authorial vanity, was rather more of the genial, self-effacing Scot who remarked of his early struggles as a writer, "My dear, I am continually sending things to the *Cornhill* and they send them back with a perseverance worthy of a better cause." Even physically, the two cut a sharp contrast. Houdini was short and lean, with the physique of a flyweight boxer, and was often described as "wound up like a coiled spring"; Doyle was big and raw-boned, and is remembered as once playing in a match (with some distinction, it should be said) at Lord's cricket ground, "breath[ing] heavily, the sweat beading his thick moustache, while he lumbered amiably around the outfield." One modern journalist has made the facetious but not wholly inapt comment that when standing together, Conan Doyle and Houdini "looked like Pooh and Piglet."

In some other ways, they were astonishingly similar. Neither belonged to the traditional ruling class, and it's difficult to imagine either succeeding without having taken real risks with his life and work. Detective fiction barely existed at the time Conan Doyle introduced Sherlock Holmes in *A Study in Scarlet,* and a lesser man might have been discouraged by the initially lukewarm reaction to it. As it was, the young author was compelled to take whatever commissions came his way (including his translation of a German article submitted to the *Gas and Water Gazette*) while persevering with the stories that made Holmes, and himself, famous. Houdini, too, overcame almost insuperable odds, which included not only the constant and very real threat of his injury or death, but also the material challenges of surviving in the shark-filled waters of the late-nineteenth-century American vaudeville circuit, before emerging as the world's highest paid public performer.

Conan Doyle and Houdini shared certain other broad patterns and personal characteristics. Both were the sons of kindly but commercially failed fathers. Both had a particular lifelong aversion to alcohol. Both formed deep sentimental attachments to their mothers, whose influence over them was evident even as they became rich and famous men. Both were self-invented in the sense that Doyle, the model of an English gentleman, was really part of a colorful Scots and Irish tapestry, while Houdini, who later billed himself as "the greatest of all American stars," was born Hungarian. In time, each man became the financial prop of a large extended family. There was barely a relative they didn't support or help to support, although in Houdini's case there was also the paradox of a man who would blow $35,000 (around $1.2 million today) to buy a film-processing laboratory in the somewhat whimsical hope that it would help make him a movie mogul, while still fretting over a $1 dry-cleaning bill. Sometimes the parallel between the two men was more material, even comically so. In 1908, Houdini appeared as a character in a German dime novel with the title *Auf den spuren Houdinis* in which he is rescued by Holmes, "his great admirer," from a gang of rivals who seek to murder him by pouring sulfuric acid into his escape apparatus.

Conan Doyle was solicitous about his first wife, nursing her through what became a thirteen-year physical decline, even if the marriage was based more on mutual respect and fondness than any grand passion. He was also fiercely loyal to the former Jean Leckie, whom he married a year after Louisa's death, all part of an elaborate etiquette of correct behavior toward women. For years, Houdini, too, was sometimes thought "excessively uxorious," at least according to the Los Angeles *Call*, which noted that "he held [Bess's] hand, kissed her, put his arm around her, and in many other ways showed how much he loved her," though by the same token he seems not to have been above a brief affair with the widow of the novelist Jack London. In public, Houdini referred to Bess as his "Sweet Wifey," among other endearments, and for thirty-two years issued her with a nearly daily stream of love notes and trinkets. One of the last acts of Conan Doyle's life was to struggle into his garden and pick the first wildflower of the spring for his wife. By a mild coincidence, both Jean Conan Doyle and Bess Houdini were trained singers, though Bess's repertoire later inclined more to the popular music-hall fare of the day. Conan Doyle advocated a muscular approach to life that in his case included cricket, soccer, bicycling, boxing, equestrianism, mountain-climbing, surfing, skiing, and golf (in the last two he was something of a pioneer); was long intrigued by classical displays of virile or gymnastic ability; and was once a judge of an Albert Hall competition to find the strongest man in the world, in which the contestants paraded by clad in Roman sandals, black tights, and leopard skins. Such a man can hardly have failed to appreciate what Houdini called his own "gospel of strenuosity," and the sheer physical prowess he brought to his public escapes.

"The more I reflect on Houdini [and] Doyle," wrote Walter Prince, an ordained minister and a member of the American Society for Psychical Research in the 1920s, "the more it seems that the two men resembled each other. Each was a fascinating companion, each big-hearted and generous, yet each was capable of bitter and emotional denunciation, each was devoted to his home and family, each felt himself an apostle of good to men, the one to rid them of certain beliefs, the other to inculcate in them those beliefs." Both Conan Doyle and Houdini brought a religious zeal to bear in their bitter clash about Spiritualism, and it's arguable that this was a substitute for the religion of their youth. Part of the historical image Houdini sought to cultivate was that of the original thinker as well as the man of action, while Doyle gave early evidence that he had more to offer the world than merely the fictional detective of whom he once said, "He is becoming such a burden to me that it makes my life unbearable." When two supremely intelligent and ambitious public propagandists meet and they are, like Conan Doyle and Houdini, men of private religious intensity, the stage is set for real drama.

2

DR. CONAN DOYLE AND THE PRINCE OF THE AIR

He was the ultimate self-made man, or so it seemed, a creative artist who not only became world famous, which might have been enough for another author, but was also a tireless campaigner for social and criminal justice, a historian, essayist, practicing doctor, pioneer amateur photographer, parliamentary candidate, paleontologist, motorist, athlete, spirited banjo player, and the de facto head of a new religion. He was of modest origins. His parents were poor and his nomadic boyhood was darkly shadowed by his father's drinking and premature retirement. Quite apart from the stigma involved, there were obvious practical household concerns as a result. As he later noted, his father was "of little help" to the family, "for his thoughts were always in the clouds and he had no appreciation of the realities of life." He worked his way through a Roman Catholic boarding school, and the expense of travel meant that he sometimes spent even the Christmas holidays there. At age ten, he wrote home to inform his mother that two other boys at the school had just died from croup, casually adding some time later that "we have had a great commotion here, [from] the fact that our third prefect has gone stark, staring mad." Many of his classmates went on to become priests or soldiers while he privately renounced Catholicism, and his own ambition to be a doctor owed as much to circumstances—the situation demanded "energy and application," he wrote—as to any burning vocation. When he eventually graduated from university he had no firm plans or prospects, and despite lacking these he found himself "practically the head of a large struggling family," his father having finally been institutionalized for alcoholism.

But the world was one vast opportunity for Arthur Conan Doyle. He had faith in the future of "God's country"—Britain—and in his own future, and his unfailing optimism consistently prevailed over the darkest circumstances. Personal adversity was just another challenge to him. In 1891, when he was thirty-two, Conan Doyle came down with an attack of the sort of virulent influenza that had killed his elder sister Annette just a year earlier. For a week he was in mortal danger, suffered acute pain, and described himself as being as weak and emotional as a child. Even when the crisis passed there was a question of whether he could resume an active life. Typically, Conan Doyle turned the problem to his advantage. As he reviewed his options, he realized that he was wasting time trying to establish himself as a doctor, and "determined with a wild rush of joy to cut the painter" and trust to his power of writing. From that moment on, he never gave the impression that he could consider any course but a "fully robust" life and a successful literary career, to be delayed only briefly while he regained the use of his limbs. He came to this decision at a time when he was flat on his back in bed, and barely able to lift a spoon to his mouth.

Conan Doyle had grown up in and around Edinburgh, the third of nine children, two of whom died in infancy, to Charles Altamont Doyle and the former Mary Josephine Elizabeth Foley. Conan Doyle's mother was of Anglo-Irish stock, and was later affectionately described by her son as having a "sweet face [with] peering, short sighted eyes [and a] general suggestion of a plump little hen, who is still on the alert about her chickens." "The Mam," as he called her, single-minded in her maternal devotion, would remain Arthur's close confidant up to the time of her death in December 1920, when he was sixty-one. Among her many enthusiasms were the dual subjects of heraldry and her family's illustrious fighting history, and her elder son grew up thrilled by tales of the Foleys' heroism at the battles of the Nile and Waterloo. Being both precocious and male, when society generally still favored the latter, he seems to have been doted on as a small boy. Without wishing to delve too far into the realm of psychiatry, biographers always seem to recall Sigmund Freud's line on these occasions: the dictum that "a man who has been the indisputable favourite of his mother keeps for life the feeling of a conqueror" was undoubtedly true here. Unsurprisingly, perhaps, the young Conan Doyle would also become something of a storyteller. At the age of five he impressed the family with a one-paragraph essay about a big-game hunter armed with "a knife, gun and pistle" on the trail of a ferocious tiger.

Conan Doyle's father does not make an immediately sympathetic figure. Various accounts have accused him of being a "chronic, violent drunk," a "bearded madman" who neglected his large family, and who, as his wife noted years later, would steal from both her and the children to buy drink or, failing that, resort to imbibing furniture varnish. The familiar-sounding theme of a cruel or ineffectual man and a saintly woman would recur in Conan Doyle's fiction, not least in the Sherlock Holmes story "The Abbey Grange." Well into his own middle age, Arthur worried that he might have inherited his father's "great fraility." Conan Doyle would refer to the matter even on his deathbed, when he advised his children to "for my sake continue to avoid alcohol, all of you. That way safety lies."

There is little evidence, even so, that Charles Doyle was ever physically violent or in any way "abusive" in the modern sense. He was, perhaps, emotionally distant and selfish, showing little concern for the feelings of his young wife (just seventeen when he married her) and little understanding of his children. But this was no more than could be said of most mid-Victorian men. Charles held down a respectable if dreary position as a surveyor in Scotland's Board of Works for some twenty-five years, when he was pensioned off at the age of forty-four. After that he was frequently institutionalized (though not finally confined for another four years), telling one of his admitting doctors that he was "get[ting] messages from the unseen world," and turned increasingly to his ever-present sketchbook for comfort. In later years he experienced violent epileptic fits. Charles Doyle is now thought by some to have been suffering from Korsakoff's Syndrome, a brain disorder characterized by memory loss, blackouts, and general apathy.

Conan Doyle's paternal ancestry was important not only because of the "dreadful secret" of Charles's alcoholism, but for the vein of artistic ability that ran through that side of the family. The uniting theme seems to have been one of staunch faith in the teachings of the Catholic Church, coupled with a broad streak of individual creative endeavor and, on occasion, mild eccentricity. Arthur's grandfather John Doyle moved from Ireland to London in the early 1820s, and became a successful portrait painter and political caricaturist working under the *nom de crayon* "H. B." Three of John's four surviving sons went on to make a mark in the art world. In 1864, James Doyle published *A Chronicle of England*, which he copiously illustrated himself. The next son, the foppishly dressed Richard or "Dicky" Doyle, became the in-house artist for *Punch* magazine and designed its long-running cover, while his younger brother Henry was also a cartoonist, who went on to the Chairmanship of the National Gallery of Ireland. Material success, as we've seen, eluded the youngest son Charles, born in 1832, who went to

Edinburgh as a seventeen-year-old in search of work and took rooms with the Foley family at 27 Clyde Street, a small, red brick house next to the town's main veterinary college (in whose windows "skeletons of all descriptions, from a horse to an ape, [were] ranged higglety-pigglety for the amusement or discomfiture of the populace," it was reported), where they had advertised for a lodger. "Very pleasant people and very Irish," Charles remarked genially. His marriage to Mary Foley took place in Edinburgh on July 31, 1855, the feast day of St. Ignatius, which accounts for their son Arthur's second name. Charles's maternal uncle Michael Conan, born in 1803, eventually a Paris-based correspondent for the *Art Journal,* was godfather to Arthur and his sister Annette, who alone of the nine Doyle siblings took the compound surname.

In September 1867, the unaccompanied and "bitterly crying" Conan Doyle left Edinburgh for England and spent two years at Hodder House, the prep school for Stonyhurst College near Clitheroe in Lancashire, before moving up. It must have been a daunting prospect for a hitherto cossetted eight-year-old, and all the more so as he would generally return home for only two months of each of the next seven years. Doyle would long remember his first sight, from the top of its mile-long approach avenue, of the senior school's imposing late-sixteenth-century facade, with its pale-green domes topped by golden eagles. Despite its architectural splendors, his five years at Stonyhurst don't appear to have been happy ones. Apart from the cold and the institutional food, there was the matter of corporal punishment. Conan Doyle later wrote that the preferred instrument for this had been a thick, india-rubber rod that was used to beat the victim's hands up to eighteen times, leaving him unable to turn the handle of the door of the room in which he had suffered. Doyle also recalled, with some feeling, the "bigotry" of the uncompromising Catholic curriculum. The emphasis was on physical and moral vigor in the pursuit of religious and civic duty. Many of Conan Doyle's letters home to the Mam have survived and, for the most part, read like the relentlessly cheerful assurances of a teenage boy trying hard to be brave, full of detailed accounts of his diet and various, perhaps related, illnesses, as well as his more successful exploits on the games field. Doyle showed some talent at history, but for most of his time at Stonyhurst he was considered as possessing only average mental prowess, with one scathing report calling him "uncouth—noisy—scatterbrain." It seems fair to say that few of his Jesuit masters could have realized they had a future internationally famous man of letters in their midst.

Whatever Conan Doyle's academic deficiencies at Stonyhurst, he began to emerge as a storyteller, ready and willing to entertain his classmates at a price.

"Sometimes," he wrote, "I would stop dead in the very thrill of a crisis, and could only be set a-going again by apples. When I got as far as 'With his left hand in her glossy locks, he was waving the blood-stained knife above her head, when—' I knew I had my audience in my power." He spent the Christmas holidays of 1874 with his aunt and uncles in London, where among other things he saw the young Henry Irving play the title role in *Hamlet,* and visited Madame Tussaud's waxworks—reporting that he was "delighted with the room of Horrors"—then located, perhaps significantly, above the market in Baker Street. We can assume Conan Doyle's eventual emergence as a dramatic writer owed little to the classroom and more to seminal experiences like these. He left Stonyhurst the following summer, and spent a civilized year at a Jesuit school in Feldkirch, Austria. By now, however, he increasingly fretted about money in his letters home, a concern that was to resonate in his diaries and private conversations for the next fifteen years. Although Doyle had been shielded from the full enormity of his father's decline, Charles had now lost his job and begun his long descent into alcoholism and mental illness. In these straitened circumstances, the Mam had again resorted to taking in lodgers, among whom was a twenty-two-year-old qualifying doctor and occasional published poet named Bryan Waller. Mary Doyle's ambiguous relationship with the dashing and ambitious Waller has intrigued generations of Conan Doyle's biographers; it's known that Waller took over paying the rent on the Doyles' Edinburgh flat, and that in time Mary went to live in a cottage on Waller's family estate in Thornton, West Yorkshire. One of Conan Doyle's American friends declared years later that at some point in the mid-1880s there had been a "great family hullabaloo" at which the two young doctors, only six years apart in age, quarreled bitterly over which of them was better qualified to provide for Mary's financial welfare. The evidence, the friend said, was in a "wild letter" written by Dr. Waller. Whatever the merit of the story, there is no mention of any "hullabaloo" in Conan Doyle's own correspondence, which, after initially welcoming Waller's role in the family, then falls conspicuously silent on the subject.

In 1876, when he went up to Edinburgh University, Conan Doyle was "a trifle reckless," he later admitted, a big-chested, shambling seventeen-year-old whose clothes always seemed a size too tight. He was also unpretentious, sporty, and affable, "a trier," in one account, who thrived in the perhaps underdeveloped world of Scottish college cricket (with a core batting technique recalled as "well-meant but rustic"), and liked nothing more than to sit over a lunchtime glass of beer and an improving book. A particular favorite was Thomas Macaulay's three-volume *Essays,* an instant bestseller on its appearance in 1848, and significant not only as historical literature but as what's been called a "moral route-map" to the impressionable Conan Doyle. As a young man, Macaulay had turned against his father's "sentimental religiosity" and become an atheist. "Morality should be based solely on regard to the well-being of mankind in the present life, to the exclusion of all considerations drawn from belief in God, or in a future state," he wrote. This "rather chimed" with the Jesuit-educated Doyle, who combined his more cerebral reading with the works of Walter Scott, Charles Dickens, and Edgar Allan Poe.

To his many disciples, Macaulay was clearly saying the right things at the right time, with the ease and facility of expression natural to the writer. A rationalist, or increasingly scientific, view of the world (Darwin had published his *Origin of Species* in 1859, the year Conan Doyle was born) now seemed to some to call into doubt the literalist interpretation of the Bible. Doyle's own faith had been severely shaken at his Catholic school. He would later write of hearing "a great fierce Irish priest" with the name of Father Murphy declare that eternal damnation awaited anyone outside the Church, "and to that moment I trace the first rift [between] me and those who were my guides." At Edinburgh, Conan Doyle increasingly began to speak of his personal religious beliefs, always a subject of some importance to college students and especially so, perhaps, to one whose daily academic life was devoted to scientific inquiry. For all that, Doyle was never an "atheist" in the absolute sense of the word. He was a "birthright Catholic," he later noted, raised to accept the "infallibility and literal correctness of the Bible." In time, this gave way to a broadly Unitarian faith which held that there was a "wonderful poise" to the universe and "tremendous power of conception" behind it, but which renounced some of the more dogmatic Christian ideals. To his credit, he had the courage of his convictions. At something of a crisis point in his early medical career, Conan Doyle was invited to London to visit his "wealthy and devout" paternal aunt and uncles in order to discuss his future. By all accounts, the ensuing interview was not a success. The family's basic offer was that Doyle should find somewhere to practice medicine, and that once there they would make introductions for him to various prominent friends who would bring him their business. The idea appealed to him on a commercial basis, but it came with an important condition. In order to enjoy the sort of patronage his family had in mind, Conan Doyle would need to return to the Catholic Church and accept the "literal and utter infallibility" of the Word. He politely declined the offer. His uncle "Dicky" Doyle, shortly before suffering a fatal apoplectic fit, made a final effort to change Arthur's mind over lunch at the Athenaeum Club, but this, too, ended unsatisfactorily. "When I first came out of the faith in which I had been reared, I certainly did feel for a time as if my life-belt had burst," Conan Doyle wrote in his autobiographical *The Stark Munro Letters*.

In 1877, a notable character called Dr. Joseph Bell came into Arthur's life at Edinburgh. The frock-coated Bell was thirty-nine years old when Conan Doyle first attended one of his lectures, a thin, white-haired Scot with the look of a prematurely hatched bird, whose Adam's apple danced up and down his narrow neck. Bell is said to have spoken in a piping voice and to have walked with a jerky, scuttling gait suggestive of his considerable reserves of nervous energy. He was "practically in perpetual motion," an Edinburgh student recalled. "He was always in a hurry to get to the next whatever-it-was." Bell was also a keen observer of his patients' mental and physical characteristics, which he used as an aid to diagnosis. A lecture in the Royal Infirmary's gaslit amphitheater might begin with Bell informing his packed, male-only audience that the man standing beside him in the well of the auditorium had obviously served, at some time, as a noncommissioned officer in a Highland regiment in the West Indies—a deduction based on the man's failure to remove his hat (a Scottish military custom) and telltale signs of tropical illness, among other minutiae. At the end of Doyle's second year at Edinburgh, Bell picked him out to serve as his clerk, the beginning of a relationship between the brilliant man of reason and his somewhat stolid accomplice that would foreshadow that between Sherlock Holmes and Dr. Watson.

The mythology that has grown up around Conan Doyle and his creations is as massive and imposing as any in literature. Although Doyle was eventually to be the commercially successful author of some twenty-five books, quite apart from the Holmes canon, in a career spanning over forty years, neither he nor his best-known characters burst on the scene overnight. He did his first adult creative writing in the summer of 1879, when he had just turned twenty. Edgar Allan Poe's darkly atmospheric *Tales of Mystery and Imagination* provided a thematic starting point, even a format, but the impoverished medical student initially put pen to paper chiefly as a way to supplement his income. A South African adventure story Conan Doyle called "The Mystery of Sasassa Valley" soon sold to the Edinburgh-based *Chambers's Journal* for a princely three guineas, but Doyle's first flush of success wasn't to be entirely representative of his early literary career. In the autumn of 1880 he sent off his thriller "The Haunted Grange of Goresthorpe" to *Blackwoods* magazine, which either rejected or lost the manuscript. Fortunately the author retained a copy, though it was to be 120 years before the Arthur Conan Doyle Society finally published it.

Psychologically, the importance of this period of apprenticeship lies in two things. The first is that, despite the inevitable blows, Conan Doyle didn't abandon his nascent literary ambitions. While outwardly the most he achieved was a steady flow of stories that, broadly speaking, remained pastiches of Poe, the fact that he persevered with his craft over a testing period of seven or eight years shows the latent strength of will without which any budding writer inevitably sinks. The second important development was Conan Doyle's willingness to work twice as hard as most of his fellow students. Starting in the spring of 1878, he took a series of paid assistantships with doctors in the midlands and north of England, which he managed to combine with his studies in Edinburgh. "I suffer from laziness," Arthur more than once informed the Mam, although the exact opposite seems to have been true. In June 1879 he took a junior position with a Dr. Reginald Hoare in Aston Road, Birmingham. Hoare's was a "five-horse practice," said Doyle, whose hands-on duties exposed him for the first time to the full depth of urban slum life and its attendant miseries. While this was grist for his later career, there was a more immediately obvious benefit to his Birmingham job. Arthur was doubtless attracted by wages of £2 a month, particularly as his letters home to the Mam show that he was constantly concerned for, if not obsessed with, his finances, ruefully dwelling on such disasters as a lost umbrella or a broken one-penny pipe. It was in this atmosphere that Conan Doyle began to think seriously about the possibility of making money as a writer. It was also now that he walked in out of the rain one evening to attend the public lecture entitled "Does Death End All?"

Harry Houdini was not born in Appleton, Wisconsin, on April 6, 1874. The date and place were almost universally accepted during his lifetime, and perhaps form an appropriately deceptive basis for a career dedicated to the art of illusion. He certainly never went out of his way to correct the misconception, which arose out of a combination of clerical error and his own reluctance to dwell on his immigrant past. On the very day Houdini fell fatally ill in 1926, he signed a sketch of himself with the inscription ". . . b April 6 '74/Appleton, Wisc," and those details duly appear on his death certificate, filed just over a week later.

Houdini wasn't even his real name, of course. He was born Erik Weisz on March 24, 1874, in the family home at Rákosárok utca 1. SZ. in Budapest. The newly consolidated city was then spread out around a number of bustling squares in a haphazard jumble of shops, bazaars, tenements, bungalows, bridges, and soaring, baroque spires. From their front windows the Weisz family could glimpse the river Danube, while at the back the main Pest steel mill blasted night and day; the clanging of plates made a thought-annihilating thunder, and sewage ran raw and braided in the gutter. In a rare moment of reflection, the adult Houdini once remarked that this had been a "fearful place" to come into the world—"almost an omen." Coincidentally, March 24 was also celebrated in ancient Rome as the Day of Blood. It was believed that any child born that day would be punished by an early death.

The boy's parents seemed to share his reservations about the place, because in 1876 the forty-seven-year-old Mayer Weisz took the train from Budapest to Hamburg and from there sailed to a new life in America. His thirty-five-year-old wife Cecilia, their four young sons, and a fourteen-year-old son, Herman, from a previous marriage would eventually join him there in July 1878. Considerable speculation has been expended by Houdini's biographers on Mayer Weisz's activities during those two years of separation, but too little data is available to persuasively color the story. It's known that the family name was changed by immigration officials to Weiss and that by the autumn of 1878 they had relocated to Appleton, a typical Midwestern farm community of its time, with a population of 7,000, but also with three newspapers and both a busy pulp mill and a university nearby, built up among the marshes of the Fox River 100 miles north of Milwaukee. In time Mayer Weiss became the town rabbi, a job he's thought to have assumed without undue professional qualifications, and took the lease on a one-story timber home set next to Appleton's main drainage canal—a "major boon" to the children. The ditch's slippery dirt banks made it dangerous for small boys, but its two or three feet of "icy, rank water" made it tempting on a hot day. Cecilia banned her children from it, but Ehrich, as the young Houdini was now known, was a spirited youth, eager for fun and adventure, and he jumped in often. Every account of his childhood stresses his irrepressible nature—"it made him what he became," one brother recalled. When Ehrich was eight he saw a traveling circus that pitched its tents for the night in Appleton's Memorial Park. Enthralled by the tightrope walking, he promptly strung up a length of Cecilia's washing line between two trees and began to practice the act, an enthusiasm that ran right through his adolescence and survived several bruises and the loss of his front teeth.

That same year, 1882, the Weiss family became American citizens, prompting the Rabbi to write back to friends in Budapest noting proudly that he had learned "to sit up, then to crawl, and finally to walk unassisted" in the new world. The assessment was premature. Within six months, he had lost his job, latterly conducted in an improvised temple located over Appleton's Heckert's saloon, apparently too old, at fifty-three, for the needs of the town's small Jewish community. In December 1882, Mayer took Cecilia and their now seven children to live in Milwaukee, where he conducted a few impromptu services but failed to excite any interest among the city's five established synagogues. The records show that the family was forced to appeal to the Milwaukee Hebrew Relief Society for coal to see them through the winter. Ehrich appears to have adapted to the situation, and went out onto the main street to sell newspapers. He worked hard, not only commercially, but around the tiny Weiss homestead as well. He had to hoe weeds for his mother, and help plant the vegetables that were the family's staple diet. Although small for his age, he developed a strong set of shoulders and a tough physique. His hair was dark, wooly, and obviously home cut, a curl of it falling down nearly to his eye, but neatly parted. He was constantly hyperactive, with a "fidgety, nervous energy" and the burning conviction, he recalled, "that in America, with hard work and determination a man can get anything." Around his tenth birthday, few children worked harder, or were more determined, than Ehrich, although the family circumstances were, he wrote, "pinched . . . Still," he added, "I *believed*."

Legend insists that Ehrich opened his first lock while in pursuit of a piece of pie secured in Cecilia's kitchen cupboard. It's known that one afternoon in October 1883, when he was nine, he earned 35¢ by making his debut as a trapeze artist called "The Prince of the Air" in a Milwaukee circus, and that he later gave a series of impromptu performances around town in which he demonstrated his ability to bend over backward and pick up a pin from the floor with his teeth, among other feats of physical agility. He was also experimenting with some of the tools of the trade that later made him famous. When his other activities allowed, he liked to loiter in Hanauer's, the neighborhood hardware store, where he would become familiar with a range of padlocks and bolts. Ehrich was on the premises one day in the summer of 1885 when a policeman came through the door escorting a fearsome-looking man in shackles. The man had just been found not guilty in a court hearing, but somehow the key had broken off in the lock of his handcuffs, "and judging from his language, which was ripe, he wasn't happy about it." Seizing the moment, the eleven-year-old produced a thumbnail-sized metal buttonhook from his pocket, worked it around inside the lock, and snapped open the cuffs within a minute.

Houdini's psychobiographers have speculated on the effect of his half brother Herman's death from tuberculosis in greater detail than on any other event of his childhood. The assumption is that it had a major impact on his developing character, apparently making him "neurotically guilty" and "determined to do even better," to "make up the loss to his parents." In fact, just three months later Ehrich ran away from home and lived for the better part of a year with a middle-aged couple in rural Wisconsin, where he somehow supported himself as a shoeshine boy. The Weiss family also soon gave up on Milwaukee and moved to New York City, where they took a small flat on East 75th Street, underneath the elevated railroad line. Tiring of his exile, Ehrich joined them there in September 1887. Whatever his recent traumas, he outwardly maintained a semblance of well-being, becoming a passionate swimmer, runner, and boxer as a teen, and occasionally reprising his role as "The Prince of the Air," clad for the occasion in a pair of red woolen tights and a cape fashioned from a bedsheet. His relative lack of education seems not to have impaired either his commercial prospects or his self-confidence. As a fifteen-year-old he was regularly holding down three part-time jobs at once, and added a fourth, as a necktie cutter, by confidently walking up and down the line of other applicants standing on the street outside the hiring office, telling them that the position had been filled, and then presenting himself inside as the only candidate.

In November 1890, Ehrich saw a small newspaper article about the pioneering French magician Jean Eugène Robert-Houdin (1805–71). He was sufficiently intrigued to buy Robert-Houdin's autobiography, which he then read "five or six times," developing an admiration for the author close to hero worship. Here was the seminal adolescent influence that steered Ehrich away from a career of "civilian happiness, mercantile respectability and religious duty" and onto the stage. As a performer, Robert-Houdin had rejected the conventional separation of the entertainer from the audience, and the tendency of most mid-Victorian conjurers to conduct themselves "as though engaged in a pious office." "I felt being an illusionist was a very lonely business," he wrote in an 1870 letter. To counter this, Robert-Houdin had begun to develop a more flamboyant style, culminating in a series of exhibitions he called the *Soirées Fantastiques,* held in Paris in 1845. These revolutionized the art and practice of magic at a stroke, giving it something close to its modern flavor of gaudily packaged sorcery as performed by a stand-up comedian. Instead of the traditional, "rather solemn" presentation, Robert-Houdin would prowl up and down the always brilliantly lit stage, calling audience members up to assist in a variety of sensational tricks, including one in which his young son would apparently levitate in front of their eyes.

After devouring Robert-Houdin's book, Ehrich began to work on various coin and card effects, which he presented in the more modest settings of the local park or, once, the small back room of the Young Men's Hebrew Association building. Even here, he gave evidence of his burgeoning self-confidence by billing himself for the occasion as "Eric the Great." It was a panache that extended to his other extracurricular activities.

One contemporary report has him parading up and down the street dressed in shorts and a running vest, with "a long row of shiny ribbons and medals" pinned to his chest. While some of these were undoubtedly won legitimately, others appeared to be home-made. In either case, he was widely known as a tough competitor. After reading the list of entrants for a long-distance running event some miles outside of New York in 1890, another young athlete is said to have sprinted home, shouting along the way, "My God! Weiss is in the race! We're screwed!"

In the summer of 1891, Ehrich and a work colleague named Jacob Hyman gave a series of semi-professional magic shows around New York, for which they billed themselves as the Brothers Houdini. When Hyman went back to his more stable job in the tie-cutting factory, it became a solo turn. At one lower Manhattan hall, the remaining performer modified his family nickname of "Ehrie" and appeared for the first time as Harry Houdini. His real-life younger brother Theo later joined the act, which they advertised as "Oriental Juggling & Prestidigitation," though sometimes announcing themselves by the more fluid "The Modern Monarchs of Mystery." The highlight of the show, which they performed as many as fifteen times a day (while earning only a dollar a week, after expenses), was an effect they called "Metamorphosis." The basic idea was that Harry would be tied in a sack and securely locked in a steamer trunk, which members of the audience would be invited on stage to padlock and truss with heavy ropes. Theo would then stand at the front of the stage, count to three, and clap his hands, at which point the curtain would swiftly fall, hiding both brothers from view. When it opened again only two or three seconds later, Harry himself would be standing at the front of the stage. The trunk was still there, roped and padlocked. When it was opened, Theo would emerge from it to a standing ovation from the crowd.

On October 5, 1892, the brothers hurriedly canceled their act and rushed to New York's Presbyterian Hospital, where their father died that night following surgery for cancer. Mayer Weiss was sixty-three and left behind a widow and six surviving children, the youngest of whom was just ten. Harry is said to have taken his mother aside and tearfully promised her that one day he would shower her in gold. He was eighteen years old and, for a ferociously driven individual, not getting very far very fast. He seemed headed for a hard, ill-paid life as a shop worker and occasional magician.

Adolescence proved a stormy period for Conan Doyle as well as Houdini, not least because of each man's obvious reservations about the personal example, and legacy, of his father. According to conventional psychological wisdom, the affection their mothers lavished on them in the same period was to encourage a sense of their own uniqueness, one that, at least in Houdini's case, bordered on narcissism. The third common element of their early adulthood was a bracing degree of poverty, and the matching realization that it was up to them both to make their own way in the world and to provide for a large family. It was to take Conan Doyle several years longer than it took Houdini to acquire a comparable sense of direction, but neither one can have doubted the full extent of the challenge in front of him.

Partly because of their fathers' experience, both young men underwent something of a spiritual crisis. As we've seen, Conan Doyle came to identify the Catholic faith with the sort of hellfire orations epitomized by the likes of Father Murphy, as well as with its "non-progressive" and "suicidal" refusal to accept that a 1,900-year-old religion might wish to adapt to, or at least acknowledge, recent scientific developments. It may be significant, too, that while Charles Doyle took his beliefs with him into a series of mental institutions, his wife Mary renounced the Catholic Church and in time became an Anglican. The child of such parents might reasonably be felt receptive to the sort of plausible, ecumenical figures and charismatic psychic pioneers he encountered when he set out on his own in his early twenties.

Houdini, it's true, never did renounce his father's faith, although he gave some observers the impression that he had. His friend and future co-researcher of the paranormal, Walter Franklin Prince, wrote, "He gave up Judaism, but the fervor with which he carried on his anti-Spiritalistic propaganda, not publicly only but in private conversation, was to me so striking, that I once told him that the preaching zeal of his fathers had descended to him, only it was turned in another direction. It was his religion." A journalist named Alan Kennington who knew Houdini in London formed broadly the same view of "a man on a crusade . . . His somewhat martial approach to life always struck me. I have a vivid picture of him . . . standing in a crowded room and saying in his guttural voice of his experiences with a famous medium: 'If the British people understood the real character of Miss Carrière, they would boil her in oil.'"

In their different ways, neither Conan Doyle nor Houdini was free of a touch of the evangelical. The latter was more of an agitator, of whom it was cleverly—but untruthfully—said that he was so lacking in largeness of views that "he cannot conceive of a tempest outside of a teapot." Dozens of irresponsible utterances can be combed out of Houdini's speeches. Conan Doyle, he once remarked from the Montreal stage, was "just a big school boy . . . If he was here in front of me, I would tear him to ribbons." On another occasion, he spoke of the distinguished British psychic researcher Dr. Hereward Carrington as "the famous cigarette smoker, whose wild spiritistic trash has had so much prominence in our newspapers and magazines," while Carrington's colleague Malcolm Bird became "the celebrated authority on pre-historic fly-specks." Intemperate as this was, Houdini's adversaries could be just as robust when it came to advancing the claims of the New Revelation. To Conan Doyle, a particularly histrionic séance conducted for him by a Toledo, Ohio, woman seemed to be in the "highest degree evidential." Some time later, he reported that a spirit voice had been heard whispering at his home in England. "Now is that not final?" he asked. "What possible loophole is there in that for deception?" Asked for a testimonial by a controversial American medium, Doyle stated "beyond all question" that her powers were genuine. These were not entirely isolated lapses of judgment by an author famous for the reasoning powers of his most celebrated fictional creation. In time, Conan Doyle seemed to become not only increasingly convinced of his cause, but obsessed with the idea that there was a well-organized conspiracy among his enemies to suppress the truth. It was all a "very deadly plot," he wrote of one case, before complaining that Houdini was somehow being used by the Catholic Church to obstruct him.

In February 1880, Conan Doyle again took a leave of absence from Edinburgh University and set sail as the ship's surgeon on the steam-driven whaler S.S. *Hope,* bound for the Arctic sea off Greenland. The six months that followed, though arduous, were a "glorious" interlude he spoke of nostalgically for the rest of his life. "I've got a strong Bohemian element in me, I'm afraid, and the life just seems to suit me," he wrote back to the Mam. The rough-hewn but "splendid" crew addressed him as "Doc," fed his imagination with pirate yarns and tales of improbable hurricanes, and engaged him in reasonably friendly boxing matches staged in an improvised ring on the foredeck. He also had the opportunity to pulverize 55 seals out of a total of 3,614 scored by the ship's company, among several other such character-forming exploits. On May 22, the "Doc" turned twenty-one years old while, as he wrote, "at 80 degrees north latitude." It's arguable that Conan Doyle also came of age as a writer while at sea, drawing on the experience for semi-fictional material, including the Holmes adventure "Black Peter," throughout his career.

In June 1881, Conan Doyle took his Bachelor of Medicine and Master of Surgery degree, an event he celebrated by drawing a cartoon of himself dancing with glee, above the caption: "Licensed to Kill." His immediate prospects were less rosy than the high-spirited sketch suggested. "We have packed papa off to a health resort," Conan Doyle euphemistically wrote his sister Lottie, referring to an alcoholics' sanitarium in Aberdeenshire. For her part, the Mam was now being openly subsidized by the young Dr. Waller, an arrangement Conan Doyle would later concede had brought both temporary relief and also numerous complications. The impoverished graduate—now engaged in a platonic but somewhat strained affair with a pretty Irish girl named Elmore Weldon—seems to have considered immigrating to South America, but instead settled for a second commission as a ship's surgeon, setting sail that October on the dilapidated passenger-and-cargo freighter *Mayumba*, bound for west Africa. On the whole, it proved a less congenial experience than his previous outing. The tropical heat would have commended itself to Dante's *Inferno*, Doyle reported, and several of the ship's company, including him, came down with malaria. No sea voyage on which there is at least one fatality from disease can be thought entirely satisfactory from the surgeon's point of view. Prescribing himself some recuperative exercise, Conan Doyle then narrowly avoided a shark while swimming alongside the ship at anchor in the bay off Lagos. "I don't intend to go to Africa again," he was left to conclude, admitting that, his father's example notwithstanding, he had drunk freely enough at this stage of his life. To compound a generally unhappy cruise, the *Mayumba* then somehow caught fire on its return journey, though eventually straggled back to Liverpool in January 1882.

At yet another professional standstill, Conan Doyle heard from a fellow Edinburgh graduate named George Budd, enthusing about the colossal success and unlimited opportunities of his recently opened practice in Plymouth. In response to Arthur's cautious letter of interest, Budd cabled back: "WHY NOT CALL ME A LIAR AT ONCE? I TELL YOU I HAVE SEEN THIRTY THOUSAND PATIENTS IN THE LAST YEAR . . . ALL PATIENTS COME TO ME. WOULD NOT CROSS THE STREET TO SEE QUEEN VICTORIA . . . WILL GUARANTEE YOU THREE HUNDRED POUNDS THE FIRST YEAR." It seemed almost too good an offer to be true, Conan Doyle wrote, and in fact it was. The high-strung Budd and he quarreled almost immediately, with the established doctor claiming to have suffered a catastrophic loss of business as a result of his friend's "intrusion." When Budd then took a hammer to Doyle's brass nameplate displayed on the surgery wall, the latter elected to leave Plymouth and move some 130 miles along the coast to the Portsmouth suburb of Southsea.

Conan Doyle's eight years in residence at No. 1, Bush Villas, Elm Grove—a sooty, three-story brick house located between a church and a pub—proved to be the turning point of his life. Arriving as a "feckless" bachelor GP with less than £10 to his name, he left again as a well-received author and man of affairs, with a wife and young daughter in tow. What distinguished him in his long climb to first fame and then respectability was his sheer perseverance toward his goals. For all Conan Doyle's amiability, he could be egotistical and a touch devious in pursuing these goals, a trait often found among adult children of alcoholics. When a man fell from a horse and fractured his skull on the street immediately outside Bush Villas, Doyle was able to report back to the Mam that he had received two guineas and a lavish write-up in the *Portsmouth Evening News* as a result. He failed to mention that, after treating his patient, it was he himself who had raced across town to the newspaper offices in order to plant the story.

Conan Doyle frequently admitted to being lonely in his early days in Southsea, and often remarked that what he really needed was a wife. He could buoy himself up in a letter home to his mother, but then fall into a "dark Irish depression" later, full of self-doubt and criticism. Having failed to persuade the Mam to allow his fourteen-year-old sister Connie to live with him, he successfully asked her to send his nine-year-old brother Innes instead. With the eventual addition of a house-keeper, Bush Villas would come to assume at least some of the characteristics of the fictional ménage at 221B Baker Street. Although Conan Doyle's practice took time to build—he was to barter medical treatment for butter and tea from a neighboring grocer who suffered from epileptic fits—he was able to report income of £260 in his second year in Southsea and close to £300 the year after that. "It was not a significant sum," he later insisted, remarking truthfully that he was still barely covering expenses. Nor, however, was it an insignificant sum, especially when combined with the proceeds from his literary work. In June 1883, the prestigious *Cornhill* magazine paid Conan Doyle a handsome 29 guineas for his story "J. Habakuk Jephson's Statement," a chiller inspired by the real-life case of the *Mary Celeste,* the American brig found floating unmanned off Gibraltar ten years earlier. "It is going to make a sensation," Doyle predicted, though this was mitigated by the fact that *Cornhill* published it without a by-line, leading many reviewers to speculate that it had been written by Robert Louis Stevenson.*

Conan Doyle struck his young brother as intensely driven and excessively mature. By 7:00 each morning, he was "up and scribbling away" in his downstairs consulting room. Although this was furnished by a "possibly tenth-hand" table and

---

*Despite some imaginative press coverage on the subject, the epileptic shopkeeper wasn't the young H. G. Wells, who was then working as a drapery salesman's apprentice about a mile from Elm Grove. Rudyard Kipling had recently spent a large and unhappy portion of his own childhood in Portsmouth, which he later described as being "unchanged in most particulars since Trafalgar." Even now, the city is largely defined by the Royal Navy, the soccer team, and the apparently incessant rain.

a few equally ancient chairs, it was almost luxurious compared to the rest of the house. After a full day's surgery, Doyle was back at his desk until approaching midnight, at which time he might step outside to furtively polish the new brass plate at the door. From 1883, he became an active member of the Portsmouth Literary & Scientific Society, where he would develop into an accomplished public speaker. Alongside his more bookish activities, he was now a keen photographer; played competitive rugby, golf, and billiards; was one of the early organizers of Portsmouth Football Club; and captained the town's cricket team. All this co-existed with his growing interest in the paranormal, though an 1883 exchange of letters in the *British Journal of Photography* suggests that he remained more of a materialist on the issue than would be the case later. In reply to a W. Harding Warner, who wrote to advance his claim that certain men have "radiating from them a light [that] can be photographed," Conan Doyle replied, "Will Mr Harding Warner consent to throw a 'photosphere or luminous halo' round this Delphic utterance of his? From so-called facts he draws inference which, even if they were facts indeed, would be illogical, and upon these illogical inferences draws deductions which, once more, no amount of concession would render tenable."

Shortly after arriving in Portsmouth, Conan Doyle bowed to the wishes of the Mam, who had never quite taken to her prospective daughter-in-law, and ended his friendship with Elmore Weldon. It seems not to have been his only romantic stirring to meet essentially the same fate. Not long before that, Conan Doyle had met another young woman in Edinburgh, where she happened to be rehearsing for a part in an amateur production of *HMS Pinafore*. Arthur insisted that both his mother and favorite younger sister Lottie go with him to the opening night. Following the performance, he took the woman to the Doyle-Waller house to introduce her. After then escorting her home, Arthur returned and asked what the family had thought of her. The Mam gave a careful mother's reply: "I told him she did her turn nicely."

Conan Doyle's romantic frustrations came to an end in the spring of 1885, when he met a handsome and soft-spoken twenty-seven-year-old woman named Louisa Hawkins. With her round face and brown-red hair, which she often wore in a bun, she bore a passing resemblance to a younger version of the Mam. Around March 15, Conan Doyle agreed to take in Louisa's brother Jack as a resident patient at Bush Villas, where he would comfort him as best he could through the advanced stages of cerebral meningitis. Although Jack died just ten days later, an affection formed between his doctor and bereaved sister (who now enjoyed a legacy of £100 a year from her late father's estate), circumstances broadly similar to those contained in the 1890 Holmes novel *The Sign of Four*. The sweet-natured Louisa was duly presented to the Mam, who approved. That April, Conan Doyle submitted a thesis to the Edinburgh examiners on sensory-neuron degeneration (as occasioned by untreated syphilis), which allowed him to finally add the letters "MD" to his name, although by then he had already been practicing medicine for seven years. On August 5, he and "Touie," as he called her, were married near the Wallers' estate in Yorkshire, where the Mam had gone to live some time before. Three years earlier, in April 1882, Conan Doyle had written to his sister Lottie that he had "nearly frightened the immortal soul" out of Waller in some way, and that his fellow doctor had been unable to leave the house for almost a month as a result. The relationship seems to have survived, because Waller apparently stood as best man at the wedding. Charles Doyle was currently detained at the Montrose Royal Lunatic Asylum, and so unable to attend. The newlyweds honeymooned in Ireland, where Conan Doyle largely occupied himself by playing cricket in a series of matches for the Stonyhurst old boys' team. There is some question of whether Touie even accompanied him throughout the visit. Back in Southsea, Doyle's medical practice continued to grow, although his night job still met with only mixed commercial success. A novel he submitted "everywhere" with the title of *The Firm of Girdlestone* failed to arouse any offers, while a story called "Uncle Jeremy's Household" went on a similarly circular tour before eventually appearing some two years later in *Boy's Own Paper*. The fact that Doyle, for all his efforts, conspicuously didn't have the means to keep his new wife in the lap of luxury presumably contributed to his decision to strike out in a new literary direction in the spring of 1886. Making a name for himself, achieving a piece of work that the world would recognize, supporting the Mam and his extended family, marginalizing Dr. Waller, proving himself a worthy and active partner to Touie—these ambitions showed beneath Conan Doyle's surface indolence and conviviality.

This was also the period in which the seemingly conventional provincial GP was attending his first séances and following the reincarnation and time-travel theories of Madame Blavatsky and her fellow Theosophists. As a doctor, Conan Doyle made no secret of his interest in the uncharted potential of the human mind. In fact, a degree of Spiritualistic belief seemed *de rigueur* for many late-Victorian scientists, prominent among them, as we've seen, Darwin's colleagues Alfred Russel Wallace and Thomas Huxley, and the groundbreaking physical chemist William Crookes, the last of whom "unequivocally endorsed" several mediums. The idea that such men somehow deliberately threatened the established Christian Church, which promptly saw its theological authority replaced by a blancmange of panthe-

ism, mysticism, and greeting-card sentimentality, hasn't stood the test of historical inquiry. Even the writings of a self-confessed "Spookist" like Crookes contain
affirmations of the "palatable" and "universal" aspects of religion, such as divine
protection, infallible justice, and, of course, life after death. The later nineteenth-
century obsession with angels, which influences Christmas cards to this day, seems
to have broadly satisfied both religious traditionalists and those seeking a more
occult meaning of life.

Conan Doyle's early researches into the paranormal weren't, then, an unheard-
of or illogical activity for a young doctor whose recent family history seemed to
imply a distressing association between religious fervor and insanity. Nor, under
Touie's "gentle and amiable" influence, as he put it, would he abandon himself to
the more intense Spiritualistic practices. The idea of Conan Doyle babbling incan-
tations as part of a robed coven, of the sort popularized a few years later by the
occultist Aleister Crowley, needs correction. As he was frequently at pains to point
out, there was "nothing remotely discordant" between a degree of psychic belief
and Christianity in its purest form. "Test the spirits to see whether they be of God,"
the New Testament urges, and Conan Doyle did so, at least to his own satisfaction,
by profusely thanking the Almighty and making the sign of the cross at the beginning of each séance. "There are many beautiful passages in the Bible which linger in
my mind," he wrote to an inquiring correspondent, recommending the Acts of the
Apostles and St. Paul's letters for their "intellectual pleasure." His strongest conviction was "in favor of complete liberty of conscience [and] against hard-and-fast
dogma [of an] unjustifiable and essentially irreligious kind," he later informed *The
Scotsman*. Still, the question arises of how a man steeped in empirical reasoning,
the author of "An essay upon the vasomotor changes in tabes dorsalis and on the
influence which is exerted by the sympathetic nervous system in that disease" (to
give Conan Doyle's 1885 thesis its full title)—and, for that matter, a Scot who had
won bare-knuckled boxing matches staged on the deck of an Arctic whaler—could,
within a relatively few years, come out publicly as a believer in fairies.

Psychologists can and do theorize about the reasons for Conan Doyle's extreme
persistence, his intensity, the way he worked so hard to convince people he was right
in every argument, even, in later years, to the point of seemingly abasing himself
in order to advance his claims for the paranormal. Was it all because of the depth
of his shame, because, as at least one biographer speculates, "he was embarrassed
by his father," and thus acted out of an insecurity that at one time had included

continual worry about whether the very house in which the Doyles lived was going to be taken away from them? Or was it something deeper? Something not just in his circumstances, but in his nature? Charles Doyle had not, after all, cracked up at the time Arthur first discovered he could hold an audience by the power of his storytelling. Whatever it was that made Conan Doyle the indefatigable man he was, heredity as well as humiliation plays a role in the explanation. Both these factors had seemed to combine in the summer of 1878, when the nineteen-year-old Edinburgh undergraduate somehow found time between his medical studies and assistantships to write a long essay on "The intemperance of our country—the cause of its prevalence and the means of suppressing it," which he submitted, anonymously, for a £5 prize contest.

Current literature offers numerous insights into the behavior of adult children of alcoholics, even if this tends to be focused on those who have not, as the experts say, "recovered" from their early ordeals. It's been suggested that children who overcome the adversity of their upbringing to live successful, well-adjusted lives share certain common characteristics, including, perhaps not surprisingly, a strong belief in the importance of self-help. In Conan Doyle's case, there was also to be a lifelong sympathy for the sufferers of social, economic, or even criminal injustice—a category that prominently included those persecuted for their Spiritualist beliefs—a profound code of personal honor, often seen in chivalrous displays toward women, and an intense patriotism. At least two of these qualities surfaced when, in July 1900, on the voyage home from performing field-hospital duty in the Boer War, Doyle encountered a French army officer who insisted, at a dinner party "that included ladies," that the British forces had used the particularly destructive "dumdum" bullets when firing on the enemy. In the words of his biographer John Dickson Carr, Doyle "turned beetroot-red and called him a liar. The officer tendered a written apology."

At age twenty-seven, Conan Doyle was "a most extraordinary being," in one account, a superficially respectable figure who was in reality "that strangely English combination of serious-frivolous, which he passed off as Irish." His writing career was a similar study in contradictions. Although Conan Doyle's "J. Habakuk Jephson's Statement" had been warmly received when it appeared in *Cornhill,* a subsequent Christmas story of which he was inordinately proud failed to impress even the editor of *Tit-bits* magazine, who then declined to enter into a correspondence when the aggrieved author wrote to complain about his treatment. His early "socio-political" novel *The Narrative of John Smith* suffered what Doyle later admitted was the not unkind fate of being lost in the post, while his semi-autobiographical

The Firm of Girdlestone took six years to find a publisher, and even then avoided any significant sales. The increasingly busy doctor appeared to be embarked on a secondary career that was unlikely to bring him either popular success or literary esteem. Apart from placing a selection of stories with the down-market firm of George Redway in a digest called "Dreamland and Ghostland: an Original Collection of Tales and Warnings from the Borderland of Substance and Shadow," he was now rarely to see his name in print. The odds, at this stage, were that he would have gone on to write perhaps one or two more unpublished novels. Then a long and modestly successful medical practice, possibly graduating from Portsmouth to London; the occasional paper for a small paranormal or occult society; retirement; death; appreciative but not long obituaries, followed by a footnote in the Victorian literary anthologies—that would have been it. As it was, Conan Doyle chose to persevere with more contemporary subject matter, in which his specialist scientific knowledge would be applied to the commercially evergreen crime genre. Soon crossing out his working title of "A Tangled Skein," he called his new effort *A Study in Scarlet.*

At nineteen, the same age at which Conan Doyle was responding to his family circumstances by writing his essay on alcoholism, Houdini was picking up the pieces left by his own father's death and the resulting financial woes. "*Weiss, Weiss, du hast mich verlassen mit keinder—Was hast du gethan?*" ("Weiss, Weiss, you've left me with your children—what have you done?"), he recorded his mother loudly complaining at the funeral. Houdini's immediate move was to take a booth at the 1893 World's Columbian Exposition in Chicago, where, twelve times a day, dressed in a loincloth as a Hindu fakir, he performed tricks such as apparently causing a handful of seeds to sprout into a full-size mango tree in front of the audience's eyes. It was by no means the least elevated of his various money-making efforts before he eventually hit on the persona that made his fortune. Meanwhile, as well as the sixteen-year-old Theo, there was his youngest brother Leopold, thirteen, and his sister Gladys, ten, to feed, while at fifty-two the semi-literate Cecilia's commercial prospects were limited. It was largely by watching the other sideshow attractions on hand in Chicago that Houdini now learned how to "put over" not only a trick, but also himself. The result was a typically robust all-round display. There was the little harlequinade when Harry would hop up and down, chanting "*Goly, goly, chelly gol,*" accompanied by Theo on a lyre, to encourage the mango tree to bud. There was the invitation to members of the audience to step up and participate in the magic, sometimes offering them a monetary prize if they could successfully explain it, a practice later to be a staple of Houdini's performances. Above all, there was the tireless promotional zeal that would see him hype the act in dozens of press interviews and advertisements, as well as in more ad-hoc activities that included paying a variety of circus freaks to jump out in the Exposition's public walkways and shoo pedestrians his way.

On June 22, 1894, Houdini married an eighteen-year-old Brooklyn girl named Wilhelmina Beatrice Rahner, or Bess, after knowing her about a week. A former seamstress, she had gone on to join a female song-and-dance troupe that moved in the same professional circles he did. There was to be some lingering difficulty arising from the fact that Bess was from a strict German Roman Catholic family who, in her words, regarded "a Jew [as] a person of doubtful human attributes." Although Cecilia Weiss graciously accepted the arrangement, it was to be twelve years before the bride's mother spoke to her again. There was no money to spare, and the couple honeymooned in a rooming house on Coney Island. On their return, Bess replaced Theo in the Houdinis' act, and, at only 5 feet and 90 pounds, soon proved herself adept at getting in and out of the trunk in the "Metamorphosis" effect.

A few days after his wedding, Houdini led Bess and Theo out onto a lonely rural bridge at midnight. As the church clock struck behind them, he solemnly raised their hands in the air and told them to "swear to heaven that both of you will be true to me. Never betray me in any way, so help you God." It was an act of striking self-belief for a struggling carnival performer whose day-to-day working life took place among a parade of singing clowns, performing monkeys, morbidly obese women, tattooed babies, limbless violin players, and a seemingly conventional New York housewife with the stage name Thardo who subjected herself to repeated rattlesnake bites. To augment his income, Houdini published a 5¢ booklet revealing such everyday tricks as how to hurl a flaming tomahawk at a confederate's head, and reported in his diary that this had "sold big."

So nondescript on New York's streets—one early interviewer said that he looked "like a bellhop in a flop hotel"—Harry suddenly came into focus when he mounted a stage to confront a crowd. A Brooklyn man named Dewey Cutler, attending his first Houdini performance, was struck by a sudden lifelong impression of the performer's "small, pleading hands." And there was his "vital disposition" as a whole, expressed in his "hopped-up pacing from side to side of the hall" and a "constant stream of barked-out boasts, challenges and exclamations . . . a force of personality that was overpowering." Although a naturally energetic man, Houdini's mannerisms perhaps owed something to the fact that he was existing on no more than four hours sleep a night, and a diet largely consisting of cakes and coffee, over both of which, Cutler recorded, "I once watched him pour the contents of a full can of rich honey." This was eclipsed by the experience of the young sons of a family Houdini was visiting, who saw him put seven spoonfuls of sugar into a steaming mug at his elbow on the breakfast table.

In March 1895, Harry and Bess were taken on by the Welsh Brothers Circus where, for $25 a week, they performed a twice-nightly routine of conjuring tricks, mind-reading feats, song-and-dance numbers, and the climactic Metamorphosis trunk effect. When even that program proved insufficiently potent at the box office, Harry gamely agreed to don a caveman's suit and a disheveled wig to appear as "Projea, the Wild Man of Mexico," a role that called for him to do little more than hop around a cage vigorously scratching himself and grunting at the audience. He also began to experiment with a so-called "Hindu trick" where he would swallow a handful of sewing needles and then apparently regurgitate them, now neatly threaded together. Although the needle effect became a staple part of his act throughout his career, Houdini evidently worried that it, too, might not convey the family-friendly image he wanted—"Uncooth [sic]?" he asked himself in a note. In November 1895, Houdini announced from the stage of a dime-museum in Manchester, New Hampshire, that he would be secured in the steamer trunk that night not with rope, but with two pairs of tempered steel handcuffs. Much like Conan Doyle's introduction of scientific reasoning to the crime story, his new show-stopper deftly brought a modern touch to a time-honored entertainment.

Meanwhile, Houdini persevered first in the circus, and then as player-manager of a traveling burlesque group called the American Gaiety Girls. This outfit seems to have had little artistic pretension beyond performing an energetic dance known as the "hoochy-koochy," followed by some spirited all-female wrestling. The Boston *Daily Advertiser* deplored that "much of the ensuing stage business [was] vulgar" and some of it "positively indecent in tenor and allusion." After the Gaiety Girls disbanded, Houdini briefly teamed up with another performer to present a mentalism act. This legendary turn is poorly documented, but apparently involved Harry using a pocket watch to put his partner in a "deathly sleep," to gauge which members of the audience would be invited up to jab needles into his arms and legs. As the dominant half of the act Houdini took the stage name "Professor Moran," which suggests he may have been familiar with Conan Doyle's sinister creation Professor Moriarty, who had made such a splash in the Holmes story "The Final Problem" two years earlier.

After an impoverished spell playing the straight man to Marco the Magician, Houdini went back to work on his most promising illusion so far. Increasingly, the Metamorphosis act (which he actually called his "ghost box") came to resemble the Davenport brothers' pioneering blend of Spiritualism and escapology. To give the effect a more mediumistic twist, Houdini sometimes resorted to lowering his voice and letting out a series of hoarse moans once locked inside the trunk—proof, to some, that he wasn't alone in his confinement. Or he might rap out a series of Morse-code messages while he lay with his hands and feet seemingly securely bound in his coffin-like retreat. It was enough to convince many in the audience that they were witnessing a genuine feat of dematerialization when Harry and Bess then appeared to suddenly switch places. Houdini's own claims both for the trick and for himself weren't small: "It has created a sensation in Europe, Australia and the United States," he noted in an 1895 promotional flyer, at a time when he was still performing Metamorphosis to vocal but small music-hall audiences in a narrow corridor of the American east coast.

In the summer of 1896, Houdini and an invited audience of newspapermen witnessed a New York insane-asylum patient struggling dementedly to free himself from a straitjacket as part of a demonstration of its uses. The unfortunate man repeatedly rolled around on the floor of his cell, banging his head against the brick wall and "letting out a pitiful cry . . . calling to his God to end his ordeal." Houdini was observed to "watch closely, but comment little" on this spectacle, a variant of which he soon added to his routine. Yet his desperation for a good effect still couldn't get him whatever it was he wanted. Later in 1896, Houdini undertook a cash-strapped tour of the Midwest, billed as "Cardo, the King of Cards." The poverty format continued back in New York, where he tried to open a magic school, but attracted only one student, an elderly escaped convict who was soon returned to the authorities.

Now facing destitution, with Bess suffering from pneumonia, Houdini walked into the offices of each of the five New York daily newspapers and offered there and then to sell them the secrets of "all his tricks," including Metamorphosis, for $25. In vain. Meeting his fan Dewey Cutler in the lobby of their mutual boardinghouse, he admitted to being "terribly blue" about both his career prospects and the hardships being suffered by Bess. This was honest and considerate, but it was also one of the last times in his life when Houdini was to feel that humility was a worthwhile option. Later that year, he presented himself at a police station in suburban Boston and challenged the amused desk-sergeant to slap his best pair of handcuffs on him. The reports of what happened next vary, but all agree on the essential fact that Houdini retired to a corner and returned between 1 and 5 minutes later, a free man. Having had the foresight to invite the press for the occasion, he couldn't have asked for better coverage than what appeared the next morning in the *Boston Advertiser*—"the king of handcuffs," it now called him.

The modest origins of the act that made Houdini Houdini are still apparent in the surviving posters and playbills of the 1896–97 season. One remarks that a $100 prize will "be given to any SHERIFF, CONSTABLE, OFFICER, or private individual who can bring Prof. Houdini any Handcuffs or Leg-Fetters from which he cannot escape," but another reported only that the "Wizard of Shackles" would appear second on the bill to a pair of apparently "grotesque" female contortionists. Real indignity would befall Houdini's subsequent efforts in Halifax, Nova Scotia, to escape from the back of a young racehorse named Drumlin, to which volunteers strapped him, while a crowd of reporters and photographers stood by. Apparently excited by all the fuss, the colt had gone "completely loco," the *Mail-Star* reported, "buck[ing] up and down with its human cargo still intact, but now slung precariously under the animal's belly." Drumlin was then seen to bolt down a country lane, "Professor Houdini frantically gesticulating [and] attempting to right himself" as he and his mount disappeared from view. Mortifying as it was, this actually represented the public-relations pinnacle of his Canadian tour, since the press ignored him from then on. Houdini had better luck escaping from the "maniac cuff and belt" at the local police station, but by then his stock in Halifax was beyond repair. Back in the Midwest, a theatrical agent booked Harry and Bess as a double act to perform Metamorphosis, but then himself vanished, owing them a week's wages. In an attempt to make good the shortfall, Houdini, "the King of Cards," joined in some poker and craps tournaments in a downtown Chicago hotel. He lost a further $60.

In 1897, the Houdinis teamed up with a traveling medicine show named Doctor Hill's California Concert Company—low, if not the absolute dregs of theatrical entertainment, with a basic roster of mildly risqué song-and-dance men, implausibly buxom, bloomer-clad strongwomen, and pathetically deformed children, usually interspersed with some amusingly prehensile monkeys. At intervals, the fast-talking Dr. Hill himself would take the stage to promote the benefits of patent remedies like his Mokeena ("the Mokeena you drink, the mokeena you feel"), which generally consisted of heavily sugared water with a few added drops of dynamite-strength whiskey. Among the Houdinis' colleagues was a fellow husband-and-wife vaudeville act named Keaton, whose two-year-old son Joe went on to some success under the nickname Buster. Hill and his company also had a marked fondness for the kind of flamboyant "Spiritualist" displays then in vogue in North

America. In a typical 10-minute "bit," pots and pans would apparently fly across the darkened room, unseen musical instruments would play, and the face of a departed celebrity like George Washington would loom out of the shadows to address a few words to the audience—an overall effect not unlike the ghost ride at a modern-day carnival. It did not take Houdini long to grasp the commercial potential of the occult. In one Kansas City performance he promised to "materialise tables and instruments, [which would] float in midair when conditions are favorable," as well as to receive and transmit "messages from dead and departed friends." "Broke the record for paid admissions," Houdini contentedly noted in his diary. It was the same in Omaha, St. Louis, and Milwaukee, where crowds flocked to see the pale, thin Hungarian mystic with his pretty, clairvoyant wife.

Still, Houdini was enough of a rabbi's son to worry about the "sad effect" of his mediumistic hoaxes on the public. When the California Company folded, he quit the world of Spiritualism for all professional purposes for the next twenty years. Apparently guilt-stricken that he had "taken the sponduliks" for his deceptions, Houdini would go out of his way to set the record straight in a series of interviews in 1898 and 1899. "Whenever any of these alleged spiritual mediums tell you that they have supernatural aid," he told one reporter, "you may safely set them down as frauds. [My] trick is merely a matter of sleight-of-hand." It's rather to Houdini's credit that he was prepared to publicly renounce his most popular act to date, particularly when this led to renewed hardship for him and his wife. Not long after their experience of packing the Opera House in Garnett, Kansas, Harry and Bess were back for a second season with the Welsh Brothers Circus. "Rottenest business," Houdini recorded in his diary one night in Pennsylvania. "No dinner . . . I slept on side-walk," he wrote, adding that he had gotten into a tussle there with "Bill the Dog-Boy," and bought himself a gun as a result.

3
METAMORPHOSIS

Houdini never traveled light. As well as his and Bess's personal effects, he carried around an assortment of professional props that even in the late 1890s was sufficient to fill nine steamer trunks and two large hampers. A few years later, Houdini was to remark matter-of-factly that he never left home without forty pieces of luggage. Eventually he hired builders to break down the front wall of his house in New York and install a steel trap door, so that his equipment could be hoisted off the street by crane and lowered into his cellar. By the time he performed in Russia in 1903, Houdini had acquired a well-stocked—perhaps overstocked—mobile kitchen; half a dozen large crates and barrels, among other escape apparatus; a jointed flagstaff and Stars and Stripes; several boxes of press cuttings and advertising material; a dressmaker's dummy; six hatboxes for Bess; a portable 248-piece toolkit; two parrot cages; and a working electric chair. Only resistance from the shipping line brought a temporary end to his procurements. Toward the end of his life, Houdini was also able to boast a collection of books and manuscripts that required the services of a full-time librarian. The magician Charles Carter visited him in New York and wrote that he was "perfectly amazed at the profoundity of erudition you are the justly proud possessor of, both in the countless tomes and papers of your library, and that which is stored away in your brain." A photograph at London's Charing Cross station in November 1909 shows Houdini and his assistants posing nonchalantly with eighteen pieces of luggage arranged on two rubber-tired trollies; porters had already removed the heavier equipment to a special baggage car before the picture was taken.

Houdini's traveling accessories were also the indirect cause of his flamboyant stage presentation. In 1897, he and Bess had found themselves changing trains in the dead of night at Chicago's Union Station to begin their sixteen-week engagement with the California Concert Company. There had been no porters available at that hour, and as a result much of their mountainous pile of luggage remained on the platform at the scheduled departure time. Houdini had rapidly assessed the situation, walked to the front of the locomotive, and thrown himself flat onto the tracks, to which he clung in a grip that defied the efforts of several railway officials to remove him. "The human limpet would not relinquish his hold," according to one newspaper report, "until or unless his possessions accompanied him in their entirety . . . The standoff lasted some five minutes, and attracted a vocal crowd, before eventually being settled in the passenger's favor." The US national transportation system was not then troubled, as it was later, by Health and Safety officials, so, having made his point, Houdini and his luggage were allowed to continue on their way. "I told you it would work," he remarked quietly to Bess. Houdini later described the incident as "the turning point in my career . . . That was the first time I realized the public wanted drama. Give 'em a hint of danger, perhaps of death—and you'll have 'em packing in to see you!"

A *Daily Mirror* report of the young Houdini on stage in London gives some idea of his partly innate, partly acquired showmanship. When the small, bow-legged man stepped forward on the platform, "there was initially almost no applause. He stood silent for a moment. Then he began to speak, quietly and ingratiatingly at first. But before long his voice had risen to a hoarse cry that gave an extraordinary effect of an intensity of feeling . . . Consistently pacing and gesticulating, he was a mass of pent-up energy. Leaning forward as if he were trying to compel his inner self into the consciousness of all these thousands, he soon held us under a spell by the sheer force of his personality." This was *before* Houdini had so much as picked a lock, it should be noted. By the end of the 90-minute performance, "the 'house' went frantic with delight," the *Mirror* added. "Cheer after cheer burst from the rapturous spectators . . . it was left for Houdini to take a protracted series of curtain-calls, while the orchestra repeatedly struck up a chorus of 'See the Conquering Hero.'"

No one would claim Conan Doyle possessed quite the same degree of histrionic skill, but in his own quiet way he knew how to command an audience. Several accounts have been given of him as a schoolboy orator and of the hypnotic effect he had on a crowd. His early efforts were crude by comparison to his public lectures of the 1920s, with their elaborate stage-management and the confidence that came from years of experience. But the elements on which he built were there from the beginning. Doyle, whom a British reporter once compared to "two stolid policemen rolled into one," conspicuously lacked both Houdini's febrile stage presence and raw energy, and is sometimes said to have been "throaty" or "hesitant" when addressing a large meeting. It would be a mistake, however, to discount him because of any supposed "genius for self-effacement" of the kind the *New York World* saw in him in 1922. Conan Doyle had begun lecturing to such august bodies as the Edinburgh Philosophical Institution while still in his late twenties, and would hardly have survived as a public speaker for the next forty years without a degree of confidence in his own abilities. A Seattle *Facts* reporter watched an "ill-bred heckler" repeatedly interrupt Doyle's talk on Spiritualism in that town. "On the third or fourth occasion . . . Sir Arthur raised his right hand, as if catching a ball, and with one or two smart words brought the audience over to his side. His technique resembled the thrusts and parries of a fencer, [and] he was merciless in dispatching an opponent." Conan Doyle typically spoke with a large red handkerchief balled in his hand and "used this to good effect, wav[ing] and fluttering it aloft as he wound up into his final oratorical crescendo," leaving the audience to begin "a cannonade of clapping and foot-pounding which sounded like a demonical roar of thunder."

Conan Doyle and Houdini shared not only certain professional characteristics, but also some key experiences. Both, in their mid-twenties, were at a career crossroads. Houdini clearly aspired to something better than a life in a traveling freak show, while Conan Doyle had ambitions beyond those he could ever hope to satisfy as a provincial doctor. Each man had a young wife and, just as important, a widowed (or effectively widowed) mother and large family to keep. Both had watched their fathers go to pieces, an experience that many psychologists believe can lead to "the basic anxiety"—the sense of being adrift in a hostile world—which, the theory goes, causes the child to form an idealized image of himself and then to adopt this as his true identity. From then on, his energies are invested in aggressively projecting this self-image, which typically has a self-confident, virile, or even heroic aspect to it. Such individuals tend not to take well to opposition.

Twenty-five years later, when rebuking a critic who had accused him of drawing on the works of Edgar Allan Poe and Émile Gaboriau, to whose fictional detectives Sherlock

Holmes was rude, Conan Doyle ended with the lines: "So please grip this fact with your cerebral tentacle/The doll and its maker are never identical." It was an elegant rebuttal, and one that goes some way to answering the question of how an author with an interest in the paranormal but of otherwise irreproachable personal habits could have created English literature's ultimate rationalist, who just also happens to be a bipolar drug addict given to shooting up cocaine three times a day to overcome his lassitude. Writing, to Conan Doyle, was an imaginative or moral exercise, not a parlor game where the intellectual elite would try to identify "real-life" models for his characters. Holmes, therefore, was a composite of several historical, living, or invented personalities. He was also very much a creature of his times. Conan Doyle later noted, "About the year '86 I had read several detective stories which had interested me," but at the same time had also irritated him by the haphazard way in which the detective got his man. "It seemed to me that it might be possible to construct a systematic and scientific method of thought and observation which would attain results which at first sight might appear impossible," he wrote. Although there is a certain amount of period detail to the stories, with their soupy miles of gaslit streets, Holmes is essentially a modern, even mildly futuristic human calculating machine who takes full advantage of such emerging disciplines as psychiatry, forensics, toxicology, ballistics, analytical chemistry, and anthropometrics—the use of precise body measurements to "profile" criminals—to complement his legendary powers of observation.

A *Study in Scarlet* did not prove easy to place, and even its eventual appearance in *Beeton's Christmas Annual* of 1887 was little cause for celebration. It brought Conan Doyle neither fame nor fortune. By the time the story was reprinted in a modest hardback edition the following year, its author's attention was elsewhere. He spent the winter of 1887–88 writing a historical novel, *Micah Clarke,* set at the time of the Monmouth Rebellion against King James II 200 years earlier. Once again the initial reaction was mixed. One publisher rejected the manuscript with the scathing verdict that it lacked "the one great necessary point for fiction, i.e., interest." Despite its unpromising start, *Micah Clarke* was published to some acclaim early in 1889, around the same time as the new edition of *A Study in Scarlet.* The Holmes story "will pave the way for Micah nicely," Conan Doyle wrote to the Mam. At that stage he had few plans to revive the inhabitants of 221B Baker Street, and, in common with the reading public, clearly had no idea that they were bound for immortality. Doyle remarked at the time that his life consisted of his medical practice, his paranormal interests, and his writing, in that order, "with a little cricket as a corrective." Holmes might have been forgotten but for the arrival in London of Joseph Stoddart, the editor of the influential *Lippincott's Monthly Magazine* in Philadelphia. On August 30, 1889, Stoddart invited Conan Doyle and Oscar Wilde to dinner at the Langham Hotel. They left with commissions for, respectively, *The Sign of Four* and *The Picture of Dorian Gray.* The second Holmes novella, with its potent mixture of oriental treasure, revenge, romance, and a blowgun-firing pygmy, appeared to warm notices on both sides of the Atlantic early in 1890. Although Doyle had already embarked on what he called "better things"—including another historical adventure, *The White Company,* set to the backdrop of the Hundred Years War, and full of necessarily archaic but energetically sustained idiom like "quotha" and "windage" and "by the holy Dicon of Hampole"—he would clearly have to persevere with his eccentric sleuth. There would be two more novels and fifty-six short stories featuring Holmes over the next thirty-seven years.

Long before then, connoisseurs and the general reading public alike had agreed that Conan Doyle was a master of the highest order. The first-person, multi-story crime narrative, in which the forces of darkness are painted with gothic panache, may not have been a literary breakthrough, but few authors brought it off with less fuss and more attention to character, and to telling detail, than he did. The unvarnished style was ideal for its subject. In the spring of 1891, Conan Doyle sent two Holmes stories, "A Scandal in Bohemia" and "The Red-headed League," to Herbert Greenhough Smith, the thirty-six-year-old editor of the mass-market *Strand Magazine.* "He liked them from the first," Doyle recalled, an understatement to rank alongside his casual remark to the Mam, as the global Sherlock Holmes publishing phenomenon got under way, that "He seems to have caught on." Some thirty years later, Greenhough Smith vividly remembered his first reaction to Conan Doyle. "I at once realised that he was the greatest short story writer since Edgar Allan Poe . . . Here was a new and gifted story-teller: there was no mistaking the ingenuity of the plot, the limpid clearness of the style, the perfect art of telling a story."

Since some 300 books, not to mention the scholarly articles, PhD theses, and a lively exchange among a cult of followers known as Sherlockians are all available on the subject, it's perhaps best to be brief on Holmes's origins. As we've seen, the basic template for the character was Conan Doyle's old professor Dr. Joseph Bell. Bell himself came to enjoy the association, and went on to offer his services as a consultant in several police investigations, including, apparently, the case of Jack the Ripper. The surname was probably an homage to the American poet-physician Oliver Wendell Holmes, while Conan Doyle was friends at Stonyhurst with a Patrick Sherlock. (Although Doyle himself is often thought of as an oversized Dr. Watson figure, the author's own powers of forensic deduction, as we'll see, raise the legitimate question of how much of himself he put in Holmes.) Nowhere in his sixty published appearances is there any mention of the character specifically wearing a deerstalker cap or an Inverness cape, or smoking a calabash pipe. Sidney Paget, the illustrator of the Holmes stories for *The Strand,* seems to be responsible for the first two accessories, while the American actor William Gillette, who first brought the character to the stage in 1899, found the curved stem of the calabash to be less of a strain on his jaw muscles than that of a conventional pipe. Gillette and his successors Clive Brook and Basil Rathbone were equally fond of the line "Elementary, my dear Watson," a phrase Conan Doyle never used. Gillette also brought a novel twist to the character when, as Holmes, he gazed into a female client's eyes and purred, "Your powers of observation are somewhat remarkable, Miss Faulkner . . . I suppose—indeed I know—that I love you!" Gillette would still be playing the role on stage at the age of seventy-eight, taking Holmes up to an era when fictional detectives were dealing with pushy leading ladies and rogue Nazis. Holmes's accomplice was surely inspired by Conan Doyle's near-neighbor and fellow Edinburgh-trained GP in Southsea, Dr. James Watson. The notorious Professor Moriarty bears some affinity to a German-born safecracker named Adam Worth, who enjoyed a brief career as a "gentleman thief" in London in the early 1880s; others have bestowed the honor on Sir Robert Christison, another of Conan Doyle's professors at Edinburgh, or on Christison's successor, Thomas Fraser, an austere Scot chiefly remembered today as a tireless advocate of vivisection. When Doyle began writing the Holmes stories, he had little personal experience of London, and had to rely on a post office map for much of the physical action. Toward the end of his life he told a suitably shocked American audience that he had never so much as set foot in Baker Street, though this was to forget that he had visited the wax museum there in 1874, and had enthused long afterward about "the images of the murderers" he drew while in the Chamber of Horrors.

To review the books, monographs, films, and other, more ad-hoc projects inspired by Holmes today is not to note a revival of interest, but simply to let down a bucket into a bottomless well. Nearly a century after his creator's death, the character has become a one-man entertainment complex. He's been the subject of at least a hundred plays and as many television or radio dramas, and spawned countless literary sequels and knockoffs—including one, with the title *A Samba for Sherlock,* in which a nearly blind detective gropes his way around the barrios of Rio de Janeiro, and another, *The Beekeeper's Apprentice,* which outs him as a feminist. There are Sherlockians who devote themselves to solving the riddle of "the great hiatus" between Holmes's apparent watery death at the hands of Professor Moriarty, set in May 1891, and his reappearance in the guise of a hunchbacked London bookseller three years later. "I travelled for two years in Tibet . . . then passed through Persia, looked in at Mecca, and paid a short but interesting visit to the Khalifa at Khartoum," the character himself somewhat cryptically remarks. Thanks to the Internet, there are enjoyably spirited long-distance discussions that try to resolve discrepancies in the canon, for instance how many times Dr. Watson was married and the exact location of the wound he suffered in the Afghan War. Was Conan Doyle merely a literary agent, and a real-life Watson the author of the stories? Was Holmes actually a woman? There may be no other characters in English literature, not excluding those of P. G. Wodehouse, who continue to excite such fanatical and, at times, slightly batty devotion.

Part of the appeal, surely, lies in Conan Doyle's skillful creation not just of a memorable leading man, but also of a dramatis personae that could sustain interest in the series for more than thirty years. The pairing of Holmes and Watson, in particular, was a brilliant stroke that went on to become the prototype of a whole raft of comically mismatched yet interdependent double acts, from Jeeves and Wooster to Morse and Lewis. That "Napoleon of crime" Professor Moriarty, though only directly appearing in two stories, is clearly one of the great literary fiends of an era that was no stranger to episodes of monstrous violence. As Conan Doyle was among the first authors to realize, the reading public can be simultaneously appalled and fascinated by the most grotesque breakdowns of civil order. It's the intellectual game of solving the crime that vicariously delights and excites us. Holmes brought that irresistible shudder, midway between joy and terror, to the millions who allowed him to rationalize for them what was otherwise the inexplicable, macabre, or horrific: at the end of each story, however outlandish its plot, affairs are successfully returned to their rightful, late-Victorian or Edwardian order. The central character also had the added advantage of being not only brilliant, but troubled as well, thus making for another staple of the crime genre ever since. It might be going too far, but not going entirely in the wrong direction, to say that Holmes's appeal cut across all considerations of nationality, background, or intellect. To give just two examples of the many available: James Joyce wrote of his character Leopold Bloom in *Ulysses* "taking stock of the individual in front of him and Sherlock-holmesing him up," a use that won the author a place in the *Oxford English Dictionary;* while a young escape artist on tour of Germany in 1905 sat down to write a letter addressed to "Mr Homes" of Baker Street, in which he complained, "Characterless men [are] stealing the fruits of my brain work. They are trying to get rid of me, by either crippling me for life or even going to the extreme of taking my life in cold blood." There is no evidence that Houdini actually posted this letter, or that he was one of the countless readers around the world who thought that Holmes and Watson were real people (in 1968, the Chinese government formally condemned the detective as "bourgeois"), but it perhaps illustrates the depth of the cult.

Conan Doyle was also fortunate in his timing. The 1890s saw the birth or rapid growth of a number of British retail businesses like John Lewis, Marks and Spencer, Sainsbury's, and Boot's that remain familiar today. Appealing to broadly the same, increasingly urbanized middle class, it was also a golden era of mass-circulation family periodicals like the new *Strand Magazine*—at sixpence, half the price of most monthlies of the day—where Holmes found an immediately receptive audience. "A Scandal in Bohemia" appeared in *The Strand*'s July 1891 issue, which enjoyed a total subscription of 485,000, meaning perhaps 2 million readers out of a literate English population of some 17 million men, women, and children: a story today would have to be read by roughly 6 million people, which is more than the combined circulation of *The Times*, the *Daily Telegraph*, the *Guardian*, the *Independent*, the *Daily Mail,* and the *Daily Express* to claim a similar hold on the public. The year 1892 marked Holmes's *annus mirabilis* in *The Strand.* January and February saw the publication of "The Adventure of the Blue Carbuncle" and "The Adventure of the Speckled Band" respectively, and Conan Doyle was soon able to command a fee of £50—twice his total income from *A Study in Scarlet*—for each future submission. Following that, his rate rose to £1,000 for a group of twelve stories, a J. K. Rowling–like sum at the time. The surviving manuscripts show that Doyle made minimal revisions to the neatly handwritten text ("always as clear as print," Greenhough Smith remarked appreciatively), and suggest that he already knew his characters well enough to write with something approaching conversational ease. One early highlight of the series was "Silver Blaze," which appeared in December 1892, and is still widely quoted today for its episode of "the curious incident of the dog in the night-time." Confronted by what was now a publishing phenomenon, certain reviewers became tetchy, making it a point of honor to show their independence by carping (and, it has to be said, the author's all-important grasp of the world of horse-racing in "Silver Blaze" is only fair). Although Conan Doyle earned himself some of the critical yappings and shin-bitings that inevitably greet a British literary triumph, most notices, let alone the reaction of the reading public, were everything he could have hoped for.

While the rewards were immense, Conan Doyle would grow increasingly ambivalent about his "small creation." It reflected the conflict between what he clearly saw as his serious historical work and what he called the "different and humbler plane" of crime fiction, to which he returned in later years chiefly to pay his bills.

It's possible to speculate that by the time, in 1926, when he was able to write a complete Holmes story and play two rounds of golf all in the same day, Conan Doyle's feelings on the subject were also tinged with guilt that he seemed to be making so much for so little out of his "poor hero of the anemic printed page," as he once referred to him. "I have grave doubts," Conan Doyle wrote at the time a first theatrical production was being mooted, "about putting Holmes on the stage at all. It is drawing attention to my weaker work which has unduly obscured my better." He went on to inform William Gillette, who asked if Holmes might get married for the "dramatic integrity" of the play, "You may marry him, murder him, or do anything you like to him." Holmes's seeming death in "The Final Problem," published in the December 1893 *Strand,* just over two years after his debut there in "A Scandal in Bohemia," triggered the perhaps apocryphal story that bereaved readers had walked around the streets of London wearing black arm-bands. Conan Doyle himself was more stoical, jotting only the words "Killed Holmes" in his notebook. He took a similarly laconic approach when the American *Collier's Weekly* offered him the astronomic sum of $25,000, or roughly £6,000, to revive Holmes in a series of six stories. "Very well, A.C.D.," he scribbled back on a postcard. Although obviously fond of the "old fellow," as he later allowed, Doyle also never quite escaped the feeling that Holmes took him from more important things. At least once he remarked that he was weary of his name, adding that he had had such an overdose of the detective, "I feel towards him as I do towards paté de foie gras, of which I once ate too much, so that the name of it gives me a sickly feeling to this day."

On January 28, 1889, Louisa Conan Doyle gave birth to a daughter, Mary, whom her father delivered at home. The baby arrived at 6:15 AM and Conan Doyle recorded that he was back at his desk three hours later to put in a full day correcting the proofs of *Micah Clarke.* A son would follow on November 15, 1892, in the midst of Conan Doyle's first flush of success with Sherlock Holmes. Some discussion ensued with the Mam and others about the boy's name, which was eventually given as Arthur Alleyne Kingsley Conan Doyle, to be called Kingsley. No one considered christening him Sherlock. Between these two events the family left Southsea, in December 1890, after a farewell dinner presided over by Dr. James Watson. Conan Doyle then traveled on the continent, where he seems to have had some idea that he might study if not actively practice eye surgery. In the event, he perhaps facetiously recalled, he chiefly spent the time "enjoy[ing] a little of gay Viennese society" and writing a novel, *The Doings of Raffles Haw,* which even its author conceded was not a major achievement. In the spring of 1891, Conan Doyle went back to London, took rooms behind the British Museum, and set up a surgery at 2 Upper Wimpole Street, about a mile east of Holmes's fictional lodgings, where he advertised himself as an oculist. That didn't work out either, as Doyle was to ruefully acknowledge when recalling that his practice had consisted of a consulting room and the shared use of a waiting room. "I was soon to find that they were both waiting rooms," he admitted.

In April 1891, Conan Doyle submitted "A Scandal in Bohemia," with the results noted, soon followed by "The Red-headed League" and "A Case of Identity." That summer, after falling gravely ill, he had the epiphany that resulted in his tossing his handkerchief to the ceiling and deciding to strike out full-time as a writer. As always when he settled on a course of action, he threw himself into it body and soul. At that stage of his career Doyle typically wrote a prolific 2,000 to 3,000 words a day, often working six days a week. As a result, he was able to produce not only the first quota of Holmes stories, but also what he called a "Puritan" (or Huguenot) novel, *The Refugees: A Tale of Two Continents,* as well as a 65,000-word Napoleonic saga, *The Great Shadow;* its historical companion piece, "A Straggler of '15," a story that Conan Doyle later turned into a one-act play; and a somewhat untypical comedy of manners called *Beyond the City,* all of which followed in a single, eighteen-month creative rush. Although Doyle's medical career had ultimately failed, he kept a hectic and increasingly well-remunerated schedule as a thirty-two-year-old professional author. The exact total is hard to establish, but it's likely that he wrote over a third of a million words in 1891, not including his voluminous correspondence with his family, friends, and the large number of curious or obsessed fans who typically addressed him as Holmes. Conan Doyle earned £1,616 in the same period, the bulk of it from his pen, which was roughly five times his annual income in Southsea.

Much of this frantic activity went on in a large, red-bricked house at 12 Tennison Road, South Norwood (close to some of the action depicted in *The Sign of Four,* and opposite the Priory School, which gave its name to a later Holmes story), where Conan Doyle and his family moved in the summer of 1891. The sixteen-room suburban villa reflected his growing prosperity. Much of Conan Doyle's natural exuberance, and unsuitability for the role of a monastic writer, were on show. As well as several military prints, and more whimsical paintings by Charles Doyle, there was a muscular atmosphere symbolized by the prominent display of a harpoon, a bear's skull, and a seal's paw, among other souvenirs of the S.S. *Hope,* and what one visitor called a "virtual pavilion" of sporting goods littering the hall, including cricket bats, tennis rackets, and a tandem bicycle on which, Doyle told an interviewer, he was never happier than when taking his wife on a 30-mile spin. He earned the significant sum of £2,279 in 1892. Some of it went on investments, but he was also notably generous to the Mam, to whom he provided a monthly allowance, as well as to other friends and relatives. Beyond that, he had the satisfaction of putting up funds for a variety of old acquaintances. When his mercurial colleague George Budd died in his early thirties, Conan Doyle quietly contributed to Budd's widow and four young daughters for years to come.

As if his own deluge of stories and novels wasn't enough, Conan Doyle also found time to collaborate with his fellow Scots-born author James Barrie. The short and mustachioed Barrie, a pocket version of the older man, would go on to enjoy some acclaim with *Peter Pan*, but was chiefly known at the time for a series of modestly successful novels of parochial Scotland, as well as a play about the eighteenth-century poet Richard Savage, which had closed after one matinee performance. The two writers shared an affinity for cricket and played in a team under Barrie's captaincy called the "Allahakbarries," which they translated as "Lord help us." Both had an almost messianic belief in the importance of play in general and cricket in particular, for Doyle "an idea of the gods" that was a revolt against the soul-destroying uniformity to which much of the rest of the world seemed to be headed. Regrettably, the Allahakbarries' actual performances only rarely lived up to this ideal. Their first fixture did not bode well: one player turned up wearing pajamas, another extended the idea by falling asleep in the outfield, while a third—a Belgian—thought the game had finished every time the umpire called "Over." The Allahakbarries managed a total of just 11 runs on that occasion. Years later, Conan Doyle achieved the unusual distinction of managing to set himself on fire when batting in a cricket match. A ball struck him on the outside of his thigh and ignited the box of matches that he kept in his pocket. "We played in the old style," Doyle reflected of his time in the Allahakbarries, "caring little about the game and a good deal about a jolly time and pleasant scenery," though this perhaps downplays the competitive spirit that steadily crept into the proceedings.

Unfortunately, the two men's exercise in communal writing proved considerably less agreeable. Late in 1892, Barrie had accepted a commission to write the libretto for a comic opera produced by Richard D'Oyly Carte, the impresario behind Gilbert and Sullivan, whose own partnership was then showing signs of creative strain. The resulting project became one of those theatrical disasters that remain largely ignored at the box office, but attain a sort of glamour for the sheer enormity of their failure. By January 1893, the high-strung Barrie was able to complete the first draft of a story with the mild comic potential of a girls' school being invaded by male students, but then succumbed to a mystery illness that was probably a nervous breakdown. On hearing the news, Conan Doyle loyally put aside his own work and went to Barrie's home in Suffolk to help. He was later to admit to certain misgivings after having read the script his friend presented him. "Ideas and wit were there in abundance," Conan Doyle recalled. "But the plot itself was not strong." On May 13, 1893, the curtain went up on the joint piece they called *Jane Annie, or The Good Conduct Prize* at D'Oyly Carte's Savoy Theatre. A sign had been fixed over the door there as a result of Gilbert and Sullivan's successes that urged patrons to leave quietly, but on this occasion there was no trouble—most of the subdued audience didn't linger, although one reviewer would note that "some dissentient noises" were heard. George Bernard Shaw, a critic with whom Conan Doyle would cross swords more than once in the years ahead, thought it "the most unblushing outburst of tomfoolery that two responsible citizens could conceivably indulge in publicly." *Jane Annie* went on to run for seven weeks, if only because D'Oyly Carte had nothing to immediately put on in its place. Conan Doyle was philosophical about the flop, particularly after his one-act play *A Story of Waterloo*, which opened in London in May 1895, went on to become a staple of late-Victorian theater. Both he and Barrie liked to tell the story of a friend joining them for supper at the Athenaeum Club following the first performance of *Jane Annie* and replying, when asked why he hadn't cheered, "I didn't like to, when no one else was doing it."

Back in South Norwood, a succession of frustrations and sorrows that eclipsed any professional disappointment began to unfold for Conan Doyle. Following his sister Annette's loss to pneumonia at just thirty-three, and his father's lonely death at the Crichton asylum came confirmation that Louisa was infected with tuberculosis, from which there was scant hope of recovery. It was a chain of events that even the constitutionally optimistic Arthur admitted was "a little overwhelming." After completing a nationwide lecture tour he installed his sister-in-law at Tennison Road with the two small children and took Louisa to Davos, Switzerland, where it was hoped that the mountain air would at least delay the inevitable. Doyle was there, dealing with these real-life issues, when the furor about Sherlock Holmes's supposed death erupted in London, which means he is unlikely to have been "assaulted by an irate *Strand* reader, while out strolling in Piccadilly," as has been suggested. He was, however, able both to complete his autobiographical novel *The Stark Munro Letters* and to become a pioneer of alpine skiing, which he later wrote about at some length. Anyone watching his early exploits on the Davos slopes would have seen only a stout, ruddy-faced thirty-four-year-old man dressed in tweed knickerbockers, boasting a pair of rudimentary elm-wood skis. He must have seemed like the last person to strike the local instructor, Tobias Branger, as "a veritable Mozart" of the sport, but Doyle threw himself into his new hobby in typically robust fashion. "It is as near to flying as any earth-bound man can come," he informed the readers of *The Strand*, before boldly predicting that the time would come when "hundreds of Englishmen will go to Switzerland for the 'ski'-ing season, in March and April."

⛎   ⛎

"There was nothing lynx-eyed, nothing 'detective' about Conan Doyle," wrote the journalist Harry How, who visited South Norwood in August 1892. "He [was] just a happy, genial, homely man; tall, broad-shouldered, with a hand that grips you heartily, and, in its sincerity of welcome, hurts." But later events were to magnify and dramatize the paradoxes implicit in Conan Doyle's character from the time, in his early twenties, when he had begun to dabble in telepathy and other forms of non-verbal communication. It in no way detracts from his obvious and enduring achievements to note that, within thirty years, profilers of Doyle would be dealing with the problem of psychiatric imbalance.

When, in the summer of 1893, Conan Doyle happened to pick up a story by Guy de Maupassant with a plot broadly similar to one he had in mind, the coincidence struck him as a "spiritual interposition by a beneficent force" he conjectured to be his guardian angel, among a host of other such entities actively communicating with him. It was by no means his only experience at the time of the otherworldly, in its broadest form. Earlier that year, Doyle had managed to work his interest in mesmerism into even as unlikely a vehicle as *Jane Annie*. Early in the proceedings, the title character shows a somewhat incongruous talent for hypnotism, which she demonstrates to a bloomer-clad chorus of her fellow inmates. Later that winter, Conan Doyle wrote from Switzerland to thank the physicist Oliver Lodge for a paper that was probably a report on the American mentalist Leonara Piper, who appeared to be able to reveal personal details about her clients' lives by supernatural means. Although Doyle later wrote that "there [was] no possible doubt that the lady's powers were genuine," he admitted to Lodge that his curiosity in the matter still exceeded his knowledge. (Lodge was already convinced, as an expert in the field, that "certain high individuals" like Mrs. Piper could communicate by electromagnetic waves.) Early in 1894, Conan Doyle began work on a novella he called *The Parasite*, which featured several more episodes of hypnotism. That he still reserved judgment on the paranormal as a whole can be seen when a character in the book attends an obviously rigged séance. "I like none of these mystery-mongers," he remarks, before going on to denounce the sort of medium who gulls her customers by "slapping a surreptitious banjo."

In June 1894, Conan Doyle accompanied two fellow members of the Society for Psychical Research on a mission to the remote coastal village of Charmouth, Dorset. They were there to investigate an allegedly haunted house occupied by an Irish family and their mute, elderly maid—"a gothic ménage," Doyle noted. On their first night there, the three men sat up with a specially modified camera and other equipment with which to capture any spirits that appeared. None did. On the second night, Conan Doyle reported that he had been startled to hear a series of loud bangs coming from the kitchen, but that nothing looked out of place there when he and his colleagues ran downstairs to investigate. He seems to have suspected at the time that they were the victims of a hoax, perhaps perpetrated by the family's twenty-year-old son in league with the maid. When he wrote about the incident some thirty-five years later in his book *The Edge of the Unknown,* Conan Doyle added that the house in question had burned down a short time later, and that the skeleton of a young boy was discovered buried in the garden. The inference was that the child's spirit had somehow been responsible for all the commotion.

Conan Doyle the materialist and skeptic also recognized a strain of mysticism in himself that often imbued his writing. What gave the early Holmes stories the ring of truth was their combination of human warmth and scientific spirit. Their author seems to have remained unconvinced about the claims of the occult at this stage, because, following his experience at the haunted house of Charmouth, he rarely returned to the subject for the next twenty-two years.

At twenty-five, the age at which Conan Doyle married and formally qualified to practice medicine, Houdini was still eking out a living on the racy burlesque and medicine-show circuit. He and Bess now divided their act between escape or "submission" effects like Metamorphosis and, as he put it, "more basic" turns as "freak clowns" or "hoofers," with occasional forays into the paranormal. The last were the best paid, Houdini remarked, noting that after a well-attended winter's-night séance he was able to buy a $15 "fine red dress" for Bess and a $10 fur overcoat for himself. But he had increasing doubts about his career as a Spiritualist, particularly after a young, grief-stricken couple "broke down" and "went nuts" when he purportedly brought them a message from their dead infant son. Perhaps to assuage his guilt, Houdini revealed that his "Silent Second Sight" spot with Bess was less about genuine telepathy than a series of codes between husband and wife. "I have even trained my right ear to move up and down, and to thus give my assistant the tip," he told the magic journal *Mahatma*.

Houdini's fortunes changed dramatically when, in the spring of 1899, he met a rotund, thirty-two-year-old Chicago impresario named Martin Beck. Beck challenged him on the spot to escape from three sets of supposedly foolproof handcuffs, which Houdini did within a minute. He then made twenty-five playing cards vanish at his fingertips and brought a dove out of a top hat, for good measure. The next day, Beck cabled: "You can open Omaha March twenty-sixth sixty dollars. Will see act [and] probably make you proposition for all next season." As Houdini later wrote across it, "This wire changed my whole life's journey."

With Beck booking them into his nationwide chain of Orpheum theaters, the Houdinis soon refined their act into a tightly scripted package of handcuff escapes and effects like the "Hindoo needle shocker," with Metamorphosis closing the show. The exact bill of fare varied from town to town and, as Beck announced, with only a touch of hyperbole, "You could come on ten straight nights and never see the same act twice." Houdini's new creative rush was in some ways comparable to Conan Doyle's of eight years earlier. He began to add ever more intricate or bizarre escapes to his repertoire—in San Francisco, a group of policemen came on stage to secure him in four pairs of handcuffs and two pairs of leg-irons, leaving him "trussed like a turkey at a Thanksgiving shoot," a reporter said. Houdini was free again inside six minutes. Within only a season at the Orpheum, he was earning the fabulous sum of $400 a week, or only some $300 less than his entire annual salary as a circus performer. With certain rare exceptions, Houdini's interest in the paranormal would now pass from the active phase for years to come. Although he fell out with Beck (who soon wrote to warn his protégé against "get[ting] a swelled head, as we are cutting heads off every day"), he would remain what he called with typical modesty "the all-in star of world stage entertainment" for the rest of his career.

With a flair for publicity, Houdini again began appearing at police stations wherever he performed and challenging the nearest officer to lock him up. Whatever the restraint, he was free again within minutes, leaving the press he had invited for the occasion to write about "The Czar of Shackles," or "The Man of Marvels," among other equally effusive headlines. On the evening of April 5, 1900, he strolled into Chicago police headquarters, where he was stripped naked, chained, and gagged, and then, in this "grotesque human package," pushed into a cell that had two apparently tamper-proof locks. Three minutes later he was back at the front desk, strategically cupping his hands in front of him but otherwise free, to calmly ask for a cigar. About his only failure of the time came when a traveling salesman staying in the same Kansas City hotel managed to jam "the King of Escape" into the lobby telephone box, while an amused crowd looked on. The next morning's headline in the *Star* read, "Houdini Detained."

How did he do it? A locksmith named Charles Courtney who worked with Houdini later remarked that it was largely a matter of "diligent homework . . . he had a remarkable knowledge of locks and other devices." In other words, he knew just where and how to apply the steel pick he generally secreted in his hair, between his toes, or elsewhere on his body. Sometimes he equipped himself with an artificial sixth finger attached to one hand, which also acted as a discreet hiding-place. Houdini himself observed that his secret was his "photographic eyes," and that by looking at a handcuff he could get a "vision of the key, [which] was of much importance to me in preparing for the opening" of the lock. It should be remembered that in the early 1900s there were still only a relatively few variants in the design of American mass-produced handcuffs. Houdini may not have been above offering the occasional bribe to a policeman or other confidant. ("Superintendent Hoy again to hand," he wrote of one British officer. "Very touching man. Touched me for five Quidlest.") As several newspapers remarked when praising his good manners, Houdini invariably paused before attempting a jail escape to shake the hands of the assembled witnesses, which as well as being sporting on his part would have allowed an accomplice to palm him a key. Some of the milk cans, crates, and other containers in which he was confined were later found to be "gimmicked" with false panels or some other means of egress. It was also known that he could manipulate a small lock-picking device called a Mattatuck tool with his fingertips, his toes, or even his mouth. When Houdini called for volunteers to come on stage and tie him up, the *Star* wrote, "he took care to first dilate his chest, [which] he could do to abnormal degree, without ever seeming to alert the audience." When the volunteers retired, he would shrink back to normal size and wriggle free from the now slack restraints. Along with practice, dexterity, and brute physical force, there was also a degree of old-fashioned showmanship at work, often sufficient to distract the audience's attention from the mechanics of the trick. Scantily clad female or garishly uniformed male assistants abounded. Some years later, crowds in New York flocked to see Houdini apparently make an elephant disappear in front of their eyes, an effect which perhaps owed more to a subtle arrangement of mirrors and lighting than to the "psychic dematerialization" advertised. A subsequent "thrilling aeronautical crash" as part of a film called *The Grim Game* was in fact performed by a stunt double.

But none of these skills or ruses, which only partly explain his ever more flamboyant escapes, matched the mesmerizing self-confidence Houdini brought to his public performances. One reporter in Boston wrote that, after his first successful trick of the night, "it was clear that the Master Mystifier was feeling the exaltation of the emotional response now surging up toward him from his thousands of admirers. His voice rising to passionate climaxes, he denounced the many 'fake Harrys' trespassing on his turf, and continued with a pledge of undying love for his audience. 'I, the true Houdini, will never fail you' was his final slogan. There was thunderous applause."

On June 9, 1900, the Houdinis arrived in England for what would effectively become a five-year overseas tour, and took lodgings at 10 Keppel Street, a narrow thoroughfare overshadowed today by the Senate House of the University of London. Their initial working environment was the more sumptuous Alhambra Theatre in Leicester Square. Built along the lines of a Moorish palace, the Alhambra was the preferred venue for royal variety performances of the day. Houdini sold out the 800-seat hall for five weeks and returned for an equally well-subscribed Christmas engagement, which, the *Evening Globe* predicted, "would make the mystifier serious coin." Just to be on the safe side, Houdini hired men to walk up and down outside the doors of the theater with sandwich boards announcing, "The Sensation of London," and distributed several thousand promotional flyers that included the testimonial of a Sergeant Bush, Chief Gaoler of Bow Street, who noted it was "A very smart Show, and certainly requires a bit of doing." Houdini was also to make his first professional appearances on the continent, where by and large he stuck to the proven formula. "Most of my success in Europe," he wrote, "was due to the fact that I lost no time in stirring up local interest in every town I played. The first thing I did was to break out of jail."

During the course of a show, Houdini not only would present his standard tricks like Metamorphosis, but also encouraged local challenges. At the Hippodrome, Glasgow, the audience watched as a team of nine carpenters hammered together a platform at the front of the stage, pausing occasionally to demonstrate that it was "solid [and] not part of any hocus-pocus." The same crew then assembled a square wooden packing crate. It, too, was shown off to the audience's satisfaction. Houdini was then secured inside the crate, which was lowered onto the platform. The carpenters nailed the whole thing in place, and crisscrossed it with a chain and heavy rope, which was topped off by a Sailor's Knot. "We were left staring at something that resemble[d] a monstrously ribboned birthday present," the *Globe* wrote. The curtain was then lowered in front of the stage, while the orchestra struck up a selection of popular tunes. Even denied a view of the performer, "the audience was transfixed by the unfolding drama." Fifteen minutes later, to the strains of "Rule, Britannia," a barefoot and panting Houdini burst through the curtain. The platform and box were still in place behind him, roped and nailed together. "Mobs waited for me," Houdini noted of his subsequent departure from the theater. "They took me shoulder high, carried me home and upstairs. Had to make a speech from the window."

A highlight of Houdini's early European success was his return to Budapest, where he sent for his mother to join him. At a reception at the ornate Regal Hotel, he watched "everyone kneel and pay homage [to Cecilia], every inch a queen, as she sat enthroned in her heavily carved and gilded chair." Less agreeable was an appearance in Cologne, where the *Rheinische Zeitung* greeted him with an article entitled "Die Entlarvung Houdinis" ("Houdini Exposed") that accused him of bribing various parties to effect his escapes. Houdini sued for slander and eventually won 200 marks from a local police officer named Graff, who had told the paper a complicated story about his providing a skeleton key that "the so-called Man of Marvels" had then concealed in a bodily cavity. The paper itself was fined 50 marks. The modest size of the total award, the equivalent of some $150, or £40, was perhaps the least significant part of the trial for Houdini. "The case has filled the press," he noted with satisfaction, "and has given me a great deal of prominence." Never one to conceal his good fortune, he took out an advertisement in papers throughout Germany and Britain, noting that the case had given him "the singular pleasure of defeating the Police in their own court . . . I made them look like a lot of DIRTY MEN." The verdict was "the greatest feat I ever accomplished," he added.

Although Houdini was making "serious coin," and enjoyed lavishing gifts on both his mother and wife, he was personally frugal and admitted he was "awkward and naive" in society. Even as a world-famous headline act, he preferred to keep the company of the sort of circus artists he had known on the way up. Houdini once told a London *Times* reporter that he felt more at home with "strong-arm men and bear wrestlers" than with "The Blue-Bloods of the land." One of his best friends at home in New York was a magician named Bill Robinson, who worked under the alias Chung Ling Soo. The heavyset Soo, resplendent in an oriental mustache and kimono, was known for breathing "lightning" over the heads of the audience, at least until the magnesium he used for the effect burned out his teeth. Houdini remarked that he and the dentally challenged Robinson sometimes liked to take a third-class train ride into the countryside to feast on a picnic of "soda pop and jelly." One of the weaknesses of a "mother's boy" is the lifelong need for a female presence. Houdini was helpless around the house, unable to perform even such simple chores as making breakfast, choosing a suitable lamp, or hanging a picture on the wall. He admitted to being "hagridden" without a woman to look after him. His "really ideal" companions, he told a London reporter conducting a sort of prototype *Desert Island Discs* interview, were his "two sweethearts [Cecilia and Bess] and those sound and manly souls whose acquaintance I made under the big top."

Houdini's finest moment as an escape artist probably came at the Hippodrome theater in March 1904, when a journalist named Frank Parker of the *London Daily Illustrated Mirror* challenged him to break free of a pair of handcuffs specially made for the occasion by an irreproachable English blacksmith. "They are locks within locks and there is not a similar pair in the world," the paper promised. Working in a tight frock coat that left his shirt collar and cuffs exposed like a surplice, Houdini was to spend fully an hour and a quarter writhing and groaning behind a thin screen set at the front of the stage. The orchestra was able to play a full program of waltzes. The audience, Parker noted, "yelled themselves frantic" when Houdini eventually appeared, dangling the cuffs from a finger. The next day's press outdid themselves, writing in almost biblical terms about "the inexplicable riddle" of "the miracle worker" in their midst. When the initial furor began to die down, Houdini stoked it up again by offering to pay 100 guineas to anyone who could duplicate his feat.

At the beginning of the twentieth century, Russia was the largest and most backward of the Great Powers. Heavily dependent on the land, the bulk of its people were poor, unskilled, and uneducated: some two-thirds of the men and nearly 90 percent of the women in European Russia could neither read nor write. The general atmosphere of ethnic hatred and contempt encouraged by the central government gave local officials a mandate to treat Russia's Jews as little more than animals, though "on the whole, even livestock were better fed," according to the Ukrainian schoolteacher and diarist Pytor Shachin. The officially tolerated anti-Semitism included a litany of robberies, beatings, shootings, and humiliations of Jews scarcely less barbaric than that inflicted on Europe by Hitler's shock troops a generation later. In May 1901, Czarist police fired on Jews who took to the streets in Tiflis, Georgia, to demand a minimum wage, killing some forty-five men, women, and children and wounding two hundred more, to give just one example. Theft of property was often followed by arson and wanton destruction, in which local people, their prejudices fed by years of anti-Semitic propaganda and dire poverty, participated with enthusiasm. Jewish girls and women who strayed outside of their home communities were liable to be manhandled and raped, or to suffer innumerable other acts of sadism. While all this was going on, as Shachin recorded, a government crew armed with an early box film camera regularly toured the regions, staging scenes for cinema audiences back home in St. Petersburg or Moscow in which kindly Russian soldiers appeared with gifts of food and clothing for the "louse-ridden, haggard [Jews] who stared back at them with sunken eyes."

This was the "Godforsaken, medieval spot" where Houdini spent some five months in the summer and early autumn of 1903. The tour contributed significantly to his burgeoning legend. Despite having most of his personal possessions pilfered by Russian border guards on entering the country, Houdini was able to give a series of well-attended theater performances in the larger towns. Even there, the superstitious audiences were apparently convinced they were witnessing a supernatural feat when they saw the Metamorphosis effect—the crowd "in turn gasped [and] crossed themselves," the Moscow *Gazeta* wrote of the climax of one show. Houdini referred to them in his diary as "200-years-behind-the-time folks." No one else would believe quite as strongly that "I [was] dematerializing like a spook" until Arthur Conan Doyle did so twenty years later.

The highlight of Houdini's extended visit came with his escape from a "Siberian transport cell," or "carette," a forbidding-looking armored van used for conveying prisoners into long-term exile. Working stark naked, Houdini was confronted by a variety of supposedly impregnable locks and bolts, as well as being personally bound hand and foot, with 20-pound iron weights dangling from each wrist. He was free again within 45 minutes. While between engagements, Houdini visited the scene of various recent pogroms, including one in Kishinev, Bessarabia, that had left fifty-two dead and nearly five hundred injured—an "awful state of affairs," he later told a journalist, adding that he was "prouder than ever to be an American." It's worth dwelling on Houdini's overall reaction, if only because he was rarely again to express any larger social or religious views until the time of his clash with Conan Doyle. He may also have taken the opportunity to telegraph back information on the Russian state security services to a contact at Scotland Yard. Houdini was to remark that his eventual departure from Moscow had been a full-scale escape in itself. He was able to leave only after parting with close to half his arduously negotiated performance fees to pay local "taxes." For years afterward, the main Russian newspapers referred to him with the back-handed compliment of the "Hebrew miracle man."

There is some similarity in the way to which Houdini and Conan Doyle reacted to fame. Certainly both men grew tired of their best-loved creations long before the public did. By late 1904, perhaps influenced by his treatment in Russia, Houdini was already speaking of retiring the "Handcuff King" and devoting himself to a more sedentary life researching and writing books. The following July, he made a speech from the stage of the Gaiety Theatre in Leith in which he announced that he would make a final European tour and "quit the escape business while I can." He was then thirty-one, and had been performing at that level less than five years. Apart from the physical and mental strain involved, he was plagued by a growing army of imitators on both sides of the Atlantic, passing themselves off as "Harry Rudini" or "Harry Blondini," among other close variants of his name. In 1905, the list of those trespassing on his act had come to include his younger brother Theo, or "Dash," who now called himself Hardeen. "I was very much alarmed to learn that he was coming," Houdini told reporters when Theo arrived to begin a theatrical engagement in New York. "He says that he will not antagonize me . . . I guess the country is big enough for both of us."

But Houdini didn't quit. Perhaps he was sensitive to the likely sharp loss of income had he retreated to his library, or perhaps he was addicted to the applause of the crowd. He rarely met an audience he didn't like. When Houdini left London to sail home to New York at the end of his prolonged first European tour, a "wildly cheering mob" had lifted him onto their shoulders and begun to sing, "And when you go, will you no come back?" It was a "powerful appeal," Houdini admitted, and one he responded to by a series of ever more elaborate, or spectacular, public escapes. In January 1906, he broke free of the Washington, DC, condemned cell that had held Charles Guiteau, the assassin of President Garfield some twenty-five years earlier. In November of that year, Houdini executed the first of his "free escapes" by leaping off the Belle Isle Bridge into the frigid Detroit River thirty feet below while wearing two pairs of handcuffs. Before long he was accepting challenges to get out of everything from a 10-foot-high sealed manila envelope to a similarly outsized leather football that players from the University of Pennsylvania team stitched him into on the stage of a Philadelphia theater. In time, he would also break free of a cast-iron boiler, a "crazy-crib" bed of the sort used to restrain mental patients, and a full keg of beer, from which he emerged wet but smiling.

Unlike the more credulous of his admirers, Houdini knew well enough that his series of electrifying escapes owed more to sleight-of-hand than to the supernatural. But while rejecting all "the hocus-pocus explanations" of Metamorphosis and the other illusions, he seems to have been in two minds about the possibility of actually making contact with the dead. On an October 1907 train journey across the American Midwest, Houdini wrote an adaptation of Elizabeth Chase Allen's poem "Rock Me to Sleep," in which the author imagines being visited by her late mother appearing in human form. In Houdini's version the returning parent was Mayer Weisz, who had passed away exactly fifteen years earlier.

There was a certain professional and personal symmetry between Conan Doyle in the early 1890s and Houdini a decade later. As we've seen, both were ambivalent about the primary source of their fame, but persevered with it for years to come. Each man yearned for respectability. Conan Doyle clearly invested greater hopes in a historical novel like *The White Company* than in Sherlock Holmes, and complained bitterly when the critics treated the former "too much as a mere book of adventure." Houdini, for his part, was inordinately proud of his own occasional writings, as well as of the fact that he could "entertain folks in five languages," even if his monologue on stage in Copenhagen had led the audience there to conclude they must be watching a comedy act.

Whether he expressed it well or not, Conan Doyle was "warmly fond" of his family. In later years, he enjoyed telling Mary and Kingsley long stories of his courtship of their mother, even though this necessarily touched on the distressing fate of Louisa's brother. Without any conclusive evidence to go on, there is a strong likelihood that Conan Doyle was flagrantly unfashionable in terms of today's morality and remained faithful to his wife throughout her long physical ordeal. He was also a man of the world. In 1899, six years into Louisa's decline, he published a novel called *A Duet with an Occasional Chorus,* in which the hero is blackmailed by a woman with whom he has previously enjoyed a "prematrimonial experience." Conan Doyle's unusually frank treatment of the affair suggests at least theoretical familiarity with such activities on his part, while his subsequent work on behalf of divorce law reform similarly implies some degree of empathy with those "confined to a loveless union." Both Conan Doyle and Houdini were prone to sentimental gestures toward their wives, the latter continuing to shower Bess with perhaps over-florid love poems, among other endearments, until his death. Conan Doyle is remembered as a genial if somewhat distant father who, like many men of his era, took a restrained approach to showing his emotions. The Houdinis remained childless, though they seem to have been affable and generous to other people's offspring. Both Bess Houdini and Louisa Conan Doyle knew that they shared their husbands' affections with their formidable mothers-in-law. In Doyle's case, adolescence had also left him with a "sour" view of organized religion and a dread of alcoholic beverages.

By his early thirties, each man had come to modify his position on the supernatural. Conan Doyle continued to attend occasional séances throughout the 1890s, even if unconvinced by their results. He also gave money to *Light,* the journal of the London Spiritual Alliance, and showed a marked taste for the ghoulish even in his mature stories. But despite a semi-professional curiosity in phenomena like telepathy or levitation (in later years, Doyle was to write enthusiastically of a Mrs. Guppy who, on June 3, 1871, "was floated from her house in Highbury and appeared upon the table of a room at 61 Lambs Conduit Street"), he was rarely an active participant in the occult. His experience at the house in Charmouth seems to have satisfied his interest in direct psychical research, at least for now. In 1897, a fellow doctor offered to initiate him into the Order of the Golden Dawn, a magic society that advanced the claims of alchemy, tarot divination, and astral travel, among other esoteric practices, but Doyle found that his diary was "too full to allow [him] to join." Similarly, by 1898 and 1899 Houdini had renounced his previous fondness for theatrically staged séances. "I got disgusted with myself when Bessie and I were doing our psychic act . . . The poor fools wept and believed we were in touch with the spirit world," he remarked. Some twelve years later he made a pilgrimage to visit Ira Davenport, whose mixture of showmanship and presumed occult powers had foreshadowed his own. Although Davenport told him in parting that he wanted them to jointly undertake a global "mystery entertainment" tour, Houdini politely evaded the offer; the two men never met again.

If Arthur Conan Doyle was in any doubt of the worldwide impact made by the "humbler plane" of his detective fiction, it would have been dispelled the moment he set foot in New York on October 2, 1894. He was met at the quayside not only by a "lively mob" of reporters shouting questions to him about Sherlock Holmes, but by a variety of ordinary citizens dressed for the occasion in a collection of capes, deerstalkers, and other supposed Holmes regalia, some of whom also took the opportunity to extemporize a favorite scene or two from the canon for the author's benefit. He was not to be entirely free of this sort of "well-meaning but invasive" tribute throughout the ten-week lecture tour that followed. Keeping what he called a "considerable programme" of appearances up and down the East Coast, Conan Doyle gave a set speech he entitled "Readings and Reminiscences," using "a melodious, hearty, welcoming voice," wrote the *New York World*, "with none of the tricks of elocutionists." A high point of the trip came at Thanksgiving, which he spent in Brattleboro, Vermont, playing golf—then almost unknown across the Atlantic—with Rudyard Kipling, who had settled there with his American wife. In the new year, Conan Doyle was back in Davos with Louisa. He took the opportunity to write the first batch of his well-received "Brigadier Gerard" stories, which happily combined his love of early-nineteenth-century historical romance with some of the narrative fizz of Holmes. Another, less successful Napoleonic saga, *Uncle Bernac,* followed in 1897. Never one to rest on his laurels, Conan Doyle also began work on a Regency prizefighting novel he called *Rodney Stone,* followed in turn by *The Tragedy of the Korosko*—a "book of sensation" he admitted, if somewhat visionary in dealing with the subject of Islamic terrorism. Were that not enough, the "cheerfully gamut-running" author produced both a series of paranormal tales that became known as the *Round the Fire Stories* and a volume of poems, *Songs of Action,* in the same two-year period.

After an extended Egyptian tour, Conan Doyle and his family settled in a house in the elevated village of Hindhead, Surrey, which Doyle perhaps optimistically called the "English Switzerland." After a winter of monsoon-like rain, he was soon forced to revise his estimate of its benefits to Louisa's health. Despite that, Doyle was to make Hindhead his home for the next eleven years, and only disposed of his property there in 1921. The house he built, Undershaw, craned out over the spectacular gorge known as the Devil's Punchbowl, the "loveliest spot in England," he wrote, even if allegedly haunted by the ghosts of highwaymen who had once been hung from a gibbet there. In 1851, a Celtic cross was erected on the site of the executions in response to public unease about it. To one visitor, the view from Undershaw was "like a scene from a Wagnerian tale," with an equally impressive "palatial interior, reach[ed] by an entrance hall emblazoned with a stained-glass window of Cathedral dimensions." The house also featured twelve bedrooms, a gatekeeper's lodge, a stable, and a tennis court. Curiously, Conan Doyle asked the architect for internal doors that would open both ways and also, apparently, for a secret den built behind a bookcase in his library.

Around the time Conan Doyle moved into the property, he also engaged in two brief but typically spirited literary feuds, both arising from an affront to his code of ethics. In the first, he crossed swords with the popular novelist Hall Caine, author of the prototype-feminist novel *The Christian,* whose talent for self-advertisement

Doyle addressed in a letter to the *Daily Chronicle.* "I think it unworthy of the dignity of our common profession that one should pick up paper after paper and read Mr Caine's own comments on the gigantic task and the colossal work which he has just brought to a conclusion . . . It is for others to say these things." In 1897, it was already brazenly unfashionable for an author to show any such restraint. The following year, Doyle was similarly incensed to learn that many of the worst reviews of his new novel were the work of a single critic, William Nicoll, and again wrote to the *Chronicle* to denounce this "growing scandal" of the trade.

On March 15, 1897, Conan Doyle met a twenty-three-year-old Blackheath woman named Jean Leckie. He would celebrate the anniversary each year for the rest of his life by presenting her with a spring flower, suggesting that he associated her with an act of renewal, or rebirth. Ironically, Conan Doyle had also met his wife Louisa on or around the same date—the Ides of March—twelve years earlier. The lively and attractive Jean, said to have possessed a "chatty" manner and "dazzling" green eyes, was both an expert horsewoman and a budding opera singer. She was also descended from an ancient Scottish family that had shown various signs of artistic and literary ability over the years. Conan Doyle, who was then just short of his thirty-eighth birthday and the father of two children, fell in love with her "immediately, desperately, and for all time," his biographer has written. Whatever the exact nature of the relationship—and all accounts are based heavily upon guesswork and hearsay—it seems certain both that Jean was introduced to the Mam early in the proceedings, and that Doyle himself long struggled to reconcile the affair with his responsibility to Louisa. Strikingly, just five months after meeting Jean he wrote a story called "The Confession," in which a Catholic woman speaks of her feelings of guilt over a youthful love affair. Doyle's novel *A Duet with an Occasional Chorus* followed in 1899. It, too, touches on sexual infidelity.

In November 1899, at the age of forty, Conan Doyle felt duty bound to volunteer to serve with the British forces fighting the Boers in South Africa. The Mam was not pleased, rather tactlessly noting that her son's "very height and breadth" would make him an easy target for the enemy. Although the army declined his services, he was eventually to spend four months working as a surgeon in a field hospital in Bloemfontein, where he arrived in March 1900.

Initially, this seems not to have been too arduous. The hospital was set up on the grounds of the Ramblers Cricket Club, in whose pavilion Conan Doyle continued to enjoy meals served to him by his butler Cleeve, whom he paid to accompany him on the journey. But when, on April 14, the Boers managed to sever the town's water supply, he and his fellow doctors were confronted by the "hellish vista" of a typhoid epidemic. The artist Mortimer Menpes, covering the war for the *Illustrated London News,* later wrote of Conan Doyle "throw[ing] open the door of one of the wards . . . The only thing I can liken it to is a slaughter-house. The place was saturated with enteric fever, and patients were swarming in at such a rate that it was impossible to attend them all." Even in the midst of this horror, Conan Doyle remained characteristically cheerful, organizing a series of football matches where players "slithered around on a field deep in blood and waste." Returning to Britain, he ran, and lost, as the Liberal Unionist candidate for Edinburgh Central in the so-called "khaki election" of October 1900. That same month saw his premature history, *The Great Boer War* (as it turned out, hostilities continued for another nineteen months), both stoutly defending the British position and calling for the creation of a more modern, less class-ridden army where the premium would be on technology rather than on tactics and attitudes largely unchanged since Waterloo. Some of the same points were made in his book-length 6d pamphlet *The War in South Africa: Its Causes and Conduct,* which quickly went through eighteen editions. In April 1902 the new King Edward VII wrote to inquire whether Conan Doyle would accept a knighthood. Acknowledging that there were those in his profession, like Kipling, who thought such honors unseemly, he promised to "think long" about his reply, which turned out to be yes. The Mam was delighted.

Meanwhile, the actor-manager William Gillette had come to Undershaw to secure Conan Doyle's approval for the American stage adaptation of Sherlock Holmes. The play's eventual transfer to London, in September 1901, was a roaring success. It marked the beginning of a continuing cottage industry that was to spawn upwards of 1,400 professional theatrical performances, as well as numerous amateur productions and readings, and at least one unauthorized book "homage" in the next decade alone. In August 1901, Conan Doyle himself overcame his scruples about Holmes to revive the detective in *The Hound of the Baskervilles.* The story of the infernal dog haunting the Devon moors was initially brought to him by a *Daily Express* correspondent, Fletcher Robinson, who had been on the same boat returning from South Africa. Conan Doyle negotiated an unheard-of fee of £100 per 1,000 words for first-publication rights in *The Strand.* Since the magazine sold 33,000 more copies than usual that month, neither Greenhough Smith nor his proprietors can have been too unhappy with the arrangement. Conan Doyle appears to have paid roughly a third of his fee to Fletcher Robinson, though there is some doubt about their future relationship; like Dr. Watson's first name, or the exact number of his marriages, it's one of those insoluble Holmes riddles to have excited a lively exchange of views over the years. More than a century later, a team led by the author Rodger Garrick-Steele applied unsuccessfully for permission to exhume Robinson, who died in 1907 at the age of thirty-six. Their initiative followed years of speculation that Conan Doyle had somehow "arranged to have his unacknowledged collaborator poisoned in order to avoid exposure as a fraud," a charge that seems fanciful even by the most acute Sherlockian standards. Robinson (who was credited in full under the first column of text of the story's appearance in *The Strand*) almost certainly succumbed to typhoid fever, like an estimated 32,000 other Britons that year. Following the success of the book version, *Collier's Weekly* magazine made its irresistible offer for Conan Doyle to bring Holmes out of his eight-year retirement for a further round of adventures. Having argued in 1891 against her son's wish to kill the detective, now the Mam was worried that he might disappoint his public. It was left to Conan Doyle to assure her that he was "not conscious of any failing powers," a claim richly sustained by the story "The Empty House" in which Holmes foils a would-be assassin by tricking the man into firing at a wax dummy of him.

Jean Leckie had been among those anonymously waving from the quayside when, in March 1900, Conan Doyle's ship departed for South Africa. Two years later, there was to be no such discretion when she came on board to kiss him off as he embarked on another voyage, bound for Italy. In between these two events, Jean and he had enjoyed at least one weekend retreat at the Ashdown Forest Hotel in Sussex, where they were chaperoned by the Mam. Whether the lovers' involvement was explicitly sexual cannot be known beyond doubt. But it was evidently enough to scandalize Conan Doyle's younger sister Connie and her husband, the author "Willie" Hornung, whose *Raffles: The Amateur Cracksman,* a bestseller in 1899, owed something to the Holmes model. In August 1900, Conan Doyle was able to indulge his love of cricket by appearing for the MCC side in a series of matches at Lord's.* Strolling around the ground arm-in-arm with Jean one afternoon, he encountered his sister and brother-in-law, who were not amused. A subsequent clear-the-air interview at the Hornungs' flat ended acrimoniously. Conan Doyle was left to write to the Mam protesting that his own family had behaved "monstrously" in the matter.

---

*On August 25, in a fixture played at Crystal Palace, Conan Doyle succeeded in dismissing the venerable W. G. Grace, the titan of Victorian cricket (who admittedly had scored 110), an achievement he ranked above any prize the literary world could confer on him.

The ensuing coolness with his beloved sister was a "disagreeable and unfamiliar" experience for Conan Doyle, who by then was either financially or in some other way supporting as many as fifteen relatives. Now in his mid-forties, he was to report feeling at the "absolute top" of his energies and earning power. There had once been a time when he had been floundering around as an "impoverished young scribe" and there was to come a moment when that same writer metamorphosed into an elderly occult propagandist, querulous and dogmatic and open to widespread ridicule. But in between there was a wonderful golden late summer. Conan Doyle was not a man who, having found a winning formula, was content to practice it with little or no variation for the rest of his life, any more than he could stand to be idle for more than a few minutes at a time. By now his correspondence averaged some 400 letters a week, most of which he dealt with personally. He was not only a knight of the realm but Deputy Lieutenant of Surrey, and the organizer of a 300-strong militia he called the Undershaw Rifle Club. He continued to play competitive tennis, golf, and billiards; enthusiastically strummed the banjo; and in 1902, when he was forty-three, ascended some 6,000 feet in a hot-air balloon, an experience that "thrilled" him and in turn led to his taking to the air in a rickety biplane. He was also something of a pioneer motorist, paying 400 guineas for a 10-horsepower navy blue Wolseley, in which he bowled around the Surrey countryside dressed in tweed plus-fours and a yachting cap, collecting various speeding tickets and once overturning the car as he rounded the corner into Undershaw, leaving his brother Innes and him pinned to the ground until help could arrive.

On top of his other civic duties, Conan Doyle was to make the acquaintance of Scotland Yard's Superintendent William Melville, the same contact to whom Houdini had cabled back information from Russia. Melville went on to head the security service MO5 (subsequently MI5) and continued to receive occasional reports from both men of their experiences on the continent in the run-up to the First World War. A more public political gesture by Conan Doyle ended poorly when he stood as a Liberal Unionist (or de facto Conservative) in the January 1906 general election, once again losing tidily to his Liberal opponent. That concluded his direct involvement in party politics, an experience he privately compared to an "utter hell." With the royalties flowing in, Conan Doyle could certainly get by without an MP's income, and his chief financial challenge in these years seems to have been in selecting suitable investment opportunities: an organization he chaired called the Automatic Sculpture Company went bust when its machinery persistently destroyed the marble statues it was designed to reproduce; both a rustproofing concern and various sunken-treasure recovery syndicates proved similarly disappointing, although his marketing of a motorized bicycle he called the Autowheel eventually returned a small profit.

Meanwhile, Conan Doyle had revived Sherlock Holmes (with a plot apparently suggested to him by Jean Leckie), though for once Greenhough Smith at *The Strand* had editorial reservations about the new stories, two of which, "The Norwood Builder" and "The Solitary Cyclist," got by with no actual crime for Holmes to solve. Certain critics would later carp that Jean had assumed a creative role in her partner's work not wholly dissimilar to that played by Yoko Ono some sixty years later. "The Priory School" (the name of Doyle's real-life neighbor on Tennison Road) brought its author a sack of indignant letters about its cavalier technical descriptions of bicycle wheels and other esoteric details. In April 1904, Doyle was once again to apparently call "time" on the Holmes franchise. "I am tired of [the detective]," he told the *New York Times*. "I want to do some more solid work again. Sherlock and Gerard are all right in their way, but after all, one gets very little satisfaction from such work afterward. Nor do I think I shall write any more short stories for some time to come." Conan Doyle's most ambitious work of the period was his historical novel *Sir Nigel,* a prelude to *The White Company,* which won him mixed reviews but a handsome $25,000 for American serialization rights. The money would have been welcome, because in May 1906 Conan Doyle's theatrical agent Addison Bright shot himself after it was discovered that he had systematically embezzled some £27,000, most of it from Doyle and James Barrie.

Shortly afterward, Conan Doyle was given a second and still greater jolt by the news that his wife Louisa was dying. It was nearly thirteen years since she had been diagnosed with a "hopeless" case of tuberculosis. The couple had continued to move restlessly about in search of the best possible climates to curb the disease, including a return trip to Southsea, where they found that the old surgery had become a corsetry shop named Doyle House. By the spring of 1906 Louisa was permanently bedridden, pitifully frail, and could speak only in a whisper. Toward the end, she is said to have summoned her seventeen-year-old daughter Mary and told her "not to be shocked or surprised if my father married again, but to know that it was with her understanding and blessing." Louisa died peacefully at home on Wednesday, July 4. She was forty-nine. "I tried never to give Touie a moment's unhappiness," Conan Doyle later wrote to his mother, among many such assurances. Not surprisingly, he fell into a period of introspection and depression in the months ahead, but emerged from it to marry Jean Leckie on September 18, 1907, at St. Margaret's Church, Westminster.

Over the past fifteen years, Conan Doyle had grown accustomed to fielding a steady stream of letters or direct representations by members of the public, many of them addressing him as "Sherlock Holmes" and soliciting his help in everything from locating a missing loved one to predicting the winner of the Grand National. None of these mysteries was quite as profound as the one involving a thirty-year-old Anglo-Indian solicitor named George Edalji, a parson's son, whose case Doyle took up with typical zeal in January 1907. Well regarded in his profession, Edalji had attracted attention by publishing a book on railway law for the ordinary passenger. He had also distinguished himself by establishing a monthly free legal service for anyone requiring a consultation. Precociously intelligent, if somewhat retiring and soft-spoken, he appeared to be both a model professional and an outstanding early case of Asian assimilation into British society. So there had been some little consternation when, in 1903, Edalji had been arrested for a series of particularly gruesome cattle mutilations that had taken place near his family home in Great Wyrley, Staffordshire. Despite protesting his innocence, he was swiftly convicted and spent three years in prison for the offense. As a half-caste foreigner whose crime carried the imputation of sexual dysfunction, his time in custody had exposed him to the full venom of the Edwardian penal system. Newly freed, he had sent Conan Doyle some newspaper reports of the case and was swiftly invited to meet the author in London. Striding through the lobby of the Grand Hotel, Charing Cross, for their appointment, the onetime oculist extended a "bear-like hand" and greeted his guest with the Holmesian observation, "You suffer from astigmatic myopia, I see." Subsequent independent tests confirmed that Edalji would have struggled to make his way out of his house and across muddy fields to surgically molest livestock in the dead of night. Convinced that "I was in the presence of an appalling tragedy" which perhaps owed more to the victim's race than any compelling evidence against him, Conan Doyle went public in the *Daily Telegraph* with an 18,000-word dialectical blast called "The Story of Mr George Edalji."

Confronted by this unexpected broadside, which both the domestic and international press took up on their front pages, the British Home Office hurriedly convened an Edalji Committee, which concluded the "complaining party" was innocent of the physical woundings but, bizarrely, guilty of having written a series of childishly formed, unsigned letters boasting of the attacks that the police had made a centerpiece of their case. As a result, Edalji was given a post-facto pardon but no financial compensation. Conan Doyle refused to let the matter lie there, and continued to lobby successive governments over the next five years, frequently comparing this "outrageous breakdown of British justice" to the Dreyfus Case in France and at one time leading him to clash with the new Home Secretary, his friend Winston Churchill. The Court of Criminal Appeal was established in August 1907 at least partly as a result of his protests. Edalji was a guest of honor at Conan Doyle's wedding reception that September, and was exonerated many years later when a Birmingham day-laborer named Enoch Knowles confessed to having sent the anonymous letters.

Edalji's wasn't to be the only case that the creator of Sherlock Holmes, and as such himself widely regarded as a consulting detective, was called upon to solve. In August 1912, Doyle published another 18,000-word diatribe, "The Case of Oscar Slater," whose more lurid details rivaled any of his fictional mystery. It began in the wintry, fog-ridden streets of Glasgow, where an elderly spinster named Marion Gilchrist was found bludgeoned to death in her home one night in December 1908. Suspicion had quickly fallen on the thirty-six-year-old Slater, a German-Jewish immigrant and petty thief, who had pawned a brooch similar to one stolen from the victim's house before leaving the country under an assumed name aboard the RMS *Lusitania*. Arrested in New York, he was returned to Scotland, convicted on largely circumstantial evidence and sentenced to death, later commuted to life in prison. Conan Doyle's pamphlet on the case forcefully rebutted much of the police evidence, and led to an eventual admission by Helen Lambie, the murdered woman's maid, that she had seen a man fleeing the scene of the crime and that this individual was "probably not" Slater. Even that bombshell failed to move the authorities, and Slater remained in custody until November 1927, when it emerged that the original investigating detective had reported that the case against the accused was "very much less strong" than against several other suspects, a phrase that had been changed to read only "no stronger" when read out at the trial. Slater's conviction was subsequently overturned by the High Court and he was awarded £6,000 compensation, or roughly £330 for each year of his wrongful imprisonment. Conan Doyle was adamant that it had been a "miscarriage of justice even [more] brazen" than the Edalji case, though there was one other critical distinction. While Edalji had been an "utterly blameless and forlorn" young man, Slater was a morally dubious character who responded "in the most churlish terms" when Conan Doyle suggested that he might refund him the out-of-pocket expenses incurred on his behalf. Their relationship then deteriorated to the extent that Doyle threatened to sue his onetime beneficiary, writing to him that he was "the most ungrateful as well as the most foolish person whom I have ever known." Slater at first attempted to placate Doyle with the gift of a (possibly stolen) silver cigar cutter, but eventually agreed to contribute £250 toward his defense costs. The author was left to conclude sadly that the man he had done so much to help "seem[ed] to have taken complete leave of his senses."

Conan Doyle was to participate in several other high-profile cases over the years, showing at least some of the forensic abilities of his fictional detective. In January 1925, he took up the cause of an acquaintance named Norman Thorne, a Sussex chicken farmer who had been convicted of strangling his fiancée. On this occasion he was unsuccessful, and Thorne was executed in Wandsworth jail that April 22. When the mystery writer Agatha Christie went missing in December of the following year, Conan Doyle favored a more paranormal approach to the affair. Having acquired one of Christie's gloves, he gave this to a psychic named Horace Leaf. Leaf immediately reported that it belonged to someone called Agatha who was "not dead, but half dazed and half purposeful," and would "be heard of next Wednesday" in a location "with connection to water." This proved to be a notable feat of what Doyle called "mediumistic prophecy"—Christie was found not on Wednesday, but on Tuesday, staying at a spa hotel in Yorkshire—although as the vanished author's name and possible hiding place were already splashed over every British newspaper by the time Leaf made his prediction, there may also have been more material means at work.

Conan Doyle also spoke out on a range of wider issues that engaged his finely honed senses of honor and justice. In October 1909 he published a 60,000-word booklet called *The Crime of the Congo,* railing at conditions in that slave state. Although not free of occasionally insensitive ethnic remarks in the Slater case, Doyle was a friend of the Zionist movement and sat on the London committee of the General Jewish Colonising Organisation. In 1912, he reversed his lifelong view and declared himself in favor of partial Irish home rule, impressed, he wrote, that similar steps toward self-government in South Africa had actively improved that country's relations with Britain. But while Conan Doyle was prepared to embrace a number of controversial and often deeply unpopular causes—including a campaign against the execution of Roger Casement, his onetime ally in the Congo debate, who, in 1916, attempted to raise a somewhat ramshackle pro-German insurrection in Ireland—he remained a cultural and social conservative, raging, for instance, against the "intellectual insanity" of modern art and coming out strongly against female suffrage, particularly after a group of women saw fit to burn down Tunbridge Wells's cricket pavilion.

ᔕ ᔕᵔ

Following his remarriage, Conan Doyle and his family moved to a new home, Windlesham, on the outskirts of Crowborough in Sussex. Like Undershaw, it was of solid British stock, gable-roofed, and built around a family room that ran the length of the house and included a piano at one end and a billiard table at the other. Houdini would later refer to the interior as "baronial." The chairs were covered with red Moroccan leather, a rich contrast to the dark wood that dominated throughout. On the oak-paneled walls, gleaming under the indirect lighting, hung a variety of Napoleonic sabers, a stag's head, and a Sidney Paget portrait of Doyle. The house offered sweeping views of the Sussex Downs, and as an added bonus was on the edge of a golf course. Two sons, Denis and Adrian, were born in 1909 and 1910 respectively; a daughter, Lena Jean, in 1912. As is so often the case in stepfamilies, Conan Doyle's children from his first marriage occasionally struggled to reconcile themselves to the new arrangement. His daughter Mary, who turned twenty-one in 1910, was devastated to receive a letter informing her that the singing lessons she had embarked on at a Dresden conservatory were "an utter waste" since her voice was flat and she could barely carry a tune. Although written by her father, Mary correctly assumed that this scathing verdict had really been reached by Jean, and that "in future it is [her] and not Daddy whom I shall have to reckon with." Her brother Kingsley, three years younger, left Eton first for the Army Medical Corps and then a commission in the Hampshire Regiment. He too found a somewhat equivocal welcome on his few visits to Windlesham. At one stage, Kingsley was reduced to writing to his father and stepmother pleading with them to provide him with a list of his faults, so that he could attempt to correct them.

At Windlesham, Conan Doyle again relaxed his apparent ban on writing any further Holmes stories, and soon contributed a new series at the tidy rate of £750 each. Lovers of the canon can be grateful that he had bills to pay. A boxing play named *The House of Temperley* opened, appropriately enough, on Monday, December 27, 1909 (Boxing Day), but closed again in the early spring; a stage adaptation of "The Speckled Band" fared better, and the first film versions of Holmes appeared from 1912.* One can hazard a guess at the author's emotions when it became clear

---

*There was some fanciful speculation that Conan Doyle was the hoaxer behind the apparent discovery of an early human fossil said to be the missing link between apes and *homo erectus*—the so-called "Piltdown Man"—found in a gravel pit only six miles from Windlesham in the summer of that year. Like the idea that he was Jack the Ripper, or that he poisoned

that it was his detective fiction, not his "true work," that the public still craved. In October 1912, Conan Doyle published his novel *The Lost World*, an enjoyable if relatively undemanding adventure yarn involving four ill-matched explorers who encounter prehistoric animals on a remote South American plateau, thus bringing dinosaurs back to life three generations before Steven Spielberg did. *The Lost World*'s central character, the irascible Professor Challenger (like Holmes, based on a University of Edinburgh lecturer, William Rutherford) would return in several popular sequels, notably 1926's *The Land of Mist*, which introduced a Spiritualistic theme to the series.

In 1914, twenty-eight years after creating the character, Conan Doyle again revived Sherlock Holmes in the novel *The Valley of Fear*. Like the detective's first appearance in *A Study in Scarlet*, the second half of the book consisted of a lengthy American flashback, which jarred somewhat with the classic Victorian-London milieu associated with the character. Despite any structural flaws, *The Valley of Fear* was a major commercial success, and added a conservatively estimated 70,000 sales to each of the issues of *The Strand* to serialize it.

During the period 1910–14, Conan Doyle was as intent as any British statesman on preparing the nation for war with Germany. In November 1912 he gave a public speech on the need for a Channel tunnel (pre-empting the authorities by seventy years), which he saw as a vital supply route to the continent in the event that the United Kingdom was cut off by enemy naval action. When that initiative failed, he followed up with a cautionary tale called "Danger! Being the Log of Captain John Sirius," a prescient account of Britain being starved into submission by only a small number of submarines. It was a rousing blast of propaganda that found favor with many British naval experts, if not always their civilian masters. Most of Conan Doyle's specific warnings were ignored, at least on the home side. The Germans, on the other hand, were apparently highly impressed. In *The Times* of February 1915, several "well-informed enemy war-planners" were quoted as saying that the idea of a submarine blockade of the British Isles came to them as a direct result of reading Doyle's story. Two years later, the author received another unsolicited testimonial on the floor of the German Reichstag. "The real prophet of the present economic war," announced Admiral Eduard von Capelle, the German navy minister, "was the novelist Sir Arthur Conan Doyle." The idea of Doyle as a

---

Fletcher Robinson, it owes more to an imaginative leap by Doyle's critics than to any solid facts.

Jules Verne–like visionary seemed to gain further ground with the publication of his Professor Challenger novella *The Poison Belt,* in which humanity is threatened with extinction by the release of deadly gas. The end-of-the-world scenario not only foretold the horrific chemical-warfare exchanges of the years ahead, but arguably anticipated the apocalyptic-disaster-movie genre so popular today.

Conan Doyle's other response to the war clouds forming over Europe was to begin attending séances again. In July 1913, he wrote to Hubert Stansbury, the author of a book debunking the idea of man's immortal soul, telling him that he "believed utterly" in a spirit that survived the decomposition of the body. By now he was also in regular correspondence with the physicist Sir Oliver Lodge, whose belief in the paranormal Conan Doyle hoped would be "recognised as a trumpet call for all stragglers" not yet convinced. At the age of fifty-five, Doyle was again beginning to reevaluate the idea of mortality, particularly his own. He seems to have been struck not only by the bellicose noises from Berlin and elsewhere, but by the recent tragedy of the *Titanic* (in which he lost a friend, the Spiritualist writer W. T. Stead), as well as certain intestinal health issues *The Times* had reported as "painful if not grave," but which were enough for Doyle to hurriedly revise his will.

In May 1914, Conan Doyle and his wife set sail on the RMS *Olympic,* sister ship of the *Titanic,* for New York. It was his first Atlantic crossing in twenty years. He had chosen this moment in his country's destiny to accept an invitation from the Canadian government to make a goodwill tour of its national parks. While in North America, Doyle also took the opportunity to visit the notorious Sing Sing penitentiary, where he gingerly sat in the electric chair for a few seconds and allowed himself to be locked into a condemned cell. Unlike Houdini, he was forced to wait for his hosts to release him. On June 28, as the visitors were enjoying the view at Niagara Falls (which Doyle thought might be an appropriate place to drop Holmes), a nineteen-year-old Bosnian Serb nationalist, Gavrilo Princip, succeeded in killing the Austrian Archduke Franz Ferdinand and his wife, setting in motion the reflexive diplomatic steps that led to war. When Conan Doyle arrived home on July 19, the Austro-Hungarian Empire was in the throes of presenting Serbia with an unconditional ultimatum. The outbreak of full-scale hostilities came two weeks later. Within days, Doyle wrote to the War Office offering his services. "I am fifty-five but I am very strong and hardy, and can make my voice audible at great distances, which is useful at drill." What would come through over the next four years was not only Doyle's exemplary concern for the well-being of both the British fighting man and her ordinary citizens (whose increasingly meager food ration he and his family dutifully shared), but also a profound patriotism that would admit of no greater priority than "crushing the Hun aggressor." Although the authorities denied his request for a full army commission, he soon set about organizing a local civil defense unit, marching a group of 120 volunteers up and down the hills around Windlesham, as well as turning out a series of stridently anti-German articles alongside the now, to him, seemingly "minor" Holmes saga *The Valley of Fear.*

"Days of mental anguish" followed as several family members, including Conan Doyle's twenty-two-year-old son Kingsley, awaited their marching orders, made worse by what Doyle called the "far-off throbbing" of the heavy guns in Flanders, which could be clearly heard some 110 miles away at Windlesham. The man who had warned against a German submarine blockade now took up a campaign to issue life belts to British sailors and body armor to her frontline troops, going so far as to have the Crowborough blacksmith rig up a Ned Kelly–like suit for him, in which the author clanked around his garden for the benefit of some invited newspapermen. As in the Boer War, he also set to writing an authoritative account of the conflict which, despite interference from the censor, he published in six volumes between 1916 and 1920. In May 1916, he accepted an official invitation to tour the Italian front, and also managed to visit the British trenches near Ypres, where he was able to train a periscope on the German lines just over 100 yards away. Even in these tense circumstances, Conan Doyle was obliged to field "obtuse [if] well-meaning questions," many of them from an unusually insistent French general, about Holmes. More agreeably, General Douglas Haig, commander-in-chief of the British Expeditionary Force, was able to arrange for Kingsley Conan Doyle to be brought up the line to visit his father, who found him "with his usual jolly grin upon his weather-stained features." Kingsley spoke enthusiastically of the "big push" the British and French troops would soon be making at the Somme. Returning to Windlesham, Conan Doyle published a booklet on his experiences and successfully lobbied the War Office to follow the French example and issue badges of honor to any soldier who suffered a wound. In a subsequent visit to the Australian lines at Saint-Quentin, near the Somme, Doyle wrote of a scene of apocalyptic horror, with a pyre of mangled equipment and dead horses, beside which "a man with his hand blown off was staggering away, the blood gushing from his upturned sleeve."

As the war ground on, Conan Doyle's own family losses mounted. Jean's younger brother Malcolm Leckie had fallen in the first retreat from Mons in August 1914. The Conan Doyles' close friend and resident guest at Windlesham, Lily Loder-Symonds, lost a brother at the battle of Le Cateau and two more in fighting around the Ypres salient in the spring of 1915. She subsequently discovered a gift for automatic writing, which often took the form of channeling messages from her dead siblings. Doyle's nephew Oscar Hornung and Jean's nephew Alec Forbes were each cut down "with bullets through the brain," and another brother-in-law, Leslie Oldham, also fell at Ypres. Even then, the scythe that cut through a generation of young men in the Great War wasn't finished. On July 1, 1916, Kingsley Conan Doyle was wounded in the neck on the opening day of the Somme offensive. Although he was able to return to the front line some two months later, it was an understand-ably "profound jolt" to the family, who by then had begun to hold regular séances at Windlesham under Lily Loder-Symonds's mediumship, until her own death from flu in early 1916. The previous September, the *International Psychic Gazette* had asked Conan Doyle if he had any words of solace for those who had lost loved ones. "I fear I can say nothing worth saying," he wrote back. "Time only is the healer." Later that autumn, however, Lily Loder-Symonds had sat down with her hosts in the darkened parlor at Windlesham, and apparently spoken with Malcolm Leckie. Conan Doyle never revealed precisely what came through from his brother-in-law, but he later wrote of it as "evidential." "I seemed suddenly to see that this subject [Spiritualism] with which I had so long dallied was not merely a study of force outside the rules of science," he added, but that it was "something tremendous, a breaking down of the walls between two worlds, a direct undeniable message from beyond." In the spring of 1916, Conan Doyle contributed two letters to *Light* on the theme, "Where is the Soul during Unconsciousness?" Together, they addressed the inchoate yearning for "meaning" Conan Doyle saw all around him. The strands of theory and experience that he wove together in *Light* would help form the basis for the new Spiritualist movement that emerged in the early 1920s, and led millions of people who had never read a word of his fiction to take serious note of him.

It was no "overnight conversion," as some cynics later claimed, and there were several factors at work in finally transforming Conan Doyle from an "un-committed student of the psychic" into a full-time propagandist on the subject. The continuing losses both of family members and of hundreds of thousands of ordinary troops would have preyed on a far less inquisitive mind than his own. "Where were they?" Doyle later wrote. "What had become of these splendid young lives? They were no longer here. Were they anywhere? The question was [by] far the most pressing in the world." Early death is often seen as a sort of martyrdom, and Lily Loder-Symonds's at the age of forty-two arguably gave her mediumship a sort of sheen for Doyle that it might not otherwise have enjoyed. As we've seen, there was also a connection to be made between Spiritualism and several new scientific philosophies in areas like relativity theory and electromagnetism that combined to suggest man's understanding of the universe was far from complete. This particular link seemed to strengthen when Sir Oliver Lodge's son, Raymond, was lost in the trenches; Lodge's subsequent public conversion to the idea of an afterlife, on which he wrote a best-selling book, lent an intellectual respectability to the topic that was soon being debated on the front pages of both the British and American newspapers.*

Whatever the causes, the result was that in November 1916 Conan Doyle irrevocably came out as an apostle of what he termed the "new revelation." It was now clear to him, he wrote, that this knowledge was not for his own benefit alone, "but that God had placed me in a very special position for conveying it to that world which needed it so badly."

Harry Houdini had reached the age of thirty-five with the same tendency to "talk big" that he had displayed as a precocious teenager, and seemed to be even less troubled by self-doubt as he grew older. He would introduce himself as "The King of all Handcuff Kings" and "The Mighty Potentate of all Jail Breakers." To paraphrase Gore Vidal, it apparently wasn't enough that he succeeded; others had to fail. Houdini wrote of one professional mimic who billed himself as "Oudini" that he was not only a shameless fraud but a cross-dresser to boot. The man in question, he insisted, had once performed as a ballerina, and to prove it he produced an old playbill announcing his rival as "A professor of Legerdemain/Teacher of Fancy Dancing."

With his rare combination of generosity and mean calculation, Houdini would even turn against the man who had done more than anyone else to inspire him. With his "warm, human eye," he recognized the struggles many performers go through on their way up; with his "other, cynical eye," he saw only a parade of "flop magicians" who had preceded him. In 1908, he went on to publish a book called *The Unmasking of Robert-Houdin* which, among other things, accused his namesake of being a third-class conjurer, an egomaniac, and a plagiarist "whose

---

*Sir Oliver Joseph Lodge, FRS (1851–1940), was a prolific inventor, doing pioneering work on the generation and detection of electromagnetic waves, among other subjects, as well as serving as principal of Birmingham University for nineteen years. Although four of his surviving sons successfully went into business using a variety of his patents, Lodge himself was in some ways a classic example of a British scientist who lost out to better-funded rivals, among them Hertz and Marconi, when it came to converting his theories on radio transmission into a practical household wireless set.

autobiography was a tissue of lies written by a hack journalist." When signing copies of his own book, Houdini typically added the flourish, "The First Authentic History of Magic Ever Published." He was at once "so ardent" and "so insincere," the London magic dealer Will Goldston recalled. In May 1911, Goldston invited Houdini to a faction-ridden meeting of some thirty-five performers who were attempting to organize themselves into the Society of British Magicians. "He would tell everyone what he thought they wanted to hear. As a result, you couldn't believe anything he said." Harry Flanders from Whitechapel had been one of those queuing up outside the Alhambra Theatre to see Houdini in June 1900, and had himself gone on to become a stage manager and occasional magician as a result. Approaching Flanders in the new Society's dining room, Houdini promised him his support on the contentious matter of membership fees. "Harry," he said earnestly, "if there's anyone you can believe, it's me." Then he swung across the room and started talking to several members who happened to be opposing Flanders on this very issue. Flanders muttered: "There's that bugger telling them the same thing he just told me."

In January 1908, Houdini debuted a new effect in which he escaped from a galvanized steel can that was filled with water and sealed by six padlocks. "It is a fine looking trick and almost defies detection," he noted. The whole performance was ratcheted up by a typically astute sense of showmanship. Walking on in a bathing suit, Houdini would invite the audience members to time themselves while they held their breaths. Most of them gave up in less than a minute, which added a further touch of drama when he was subsequently battened down into the apparently "impenetrable" urn. Houdini had always made it a point to engage his audience as directly as possible, and even after *The Unmasking* frequently liked to quote Robert-Houdin's dictum that "a magician is but an actor playing the role of a magician." With a mustachioed assistant standing by with an ax to smash the contraption should anything go wrong, the crowds who flocked to the so-called "Miracle milk-can escape" were compelled to wait anxiously as an overhead clock ticked past the minute. After two and a half minutes, there were usually several shouts of alarm to be heard around the theater. At three minutes, it was a scene of pandemonium, complete with attempted stage invasions and fainting cases. Houdini's eventual appearance from behind a small screen at the front of the stage invariably brought the house down; as he took the first of a series of curtain calls, spectators of all ages and classes pummeled their seats, a steady crescendo that often led into a chorus of "For he's a jolly good fellow." According to Will Goldston, Houdini typically escaped from the "impenetrable" can in "ten to fifteen seconds." He didn't bother to emerge until later "sole[ly] so that he could build up the atmosphere in the hall and come back to them almost from the dead."

On a shopping trip to Paris in January 1910, Houdini, who now commanded a fee of up to $2,000 a week for a theater residency, was able to add "seven or eight of the finest" to Bess's already impressive wardrobe of couture dresses and hats. "Her trunks full to overflowing," he noted in his diary. "She has no worries." This was certainly true in the material sense, although several friends, including Goldston, felt that the thirty-four-year-old Bess was "melancholic" or "spent," and apparently "unable to give an heir" to her husband. In time, the destructive pressures created by Houdini's relentless need to outdo the competition found a victim in his own home. Alcohol became Bess's spiritual refuge. On a sea voyage that winter, Houdini noted, his wife had "fainted near me . . . I picked her up and took her to bed. Think she has overexcited herself." There were to be several more similarly euphemistic accounts of Bess's drinking in the times ahead. Some years later, Houdini entered into an affair with the sprightly, forty-five-year-old Charmian London, widow of his friend the novelist Jack London. "Now I know how kings have given kingdoms for a woman," he wrote to her after one New York rendezvous. "You are gorgeous— you are wonderful. I love you." Charmian's diary records that a later, presumably even more effusive "declaration" Houdini made to her by phone "rather shook me up." A subsequent entry refers to him as both "Magic Man" and "Magic Lover." Although both generous and in his way attentive to his wife, the marriage appears to have increasingly become one of affection, and occasional exasperation, rather than passion on his part. A family friend named Dorothy Young remembered an occasion when Bess had smuggled a bottle of gin into the (then "dry") United States following a visit to Canada. Houdini "snapped," and delivered a stinging lecture about his fifty-year-old wife's irresponsibility.

Never one to ignore the latest technology, Houdini took possession of a sixty-horsepower Voisin biplane, essentially a series of rectangular boxes supported by two bicycle wheels, which he piloted for a brief but turbulent maiden flight over Hamburg in November 1909. The following March, he took the plane up to a height of about 30 feet over Diggers Rest, a dusty outpost of Melbourne, where he was appearing for a theatrical season. The exact chronology is hard to establish— there were at least three other local pilots active at the time—but Houdini was characteristically modest about his pioneering achievement. "FIRST REAL FLIGHT IN AUSTRALIA" he wrote in block capitals in his diary. After several more death-defying spins in the Voisin, the nascent Australian Aerial League presented him with a trophy and a plaque depicting him as "The first man to fly on the Continent," an award that "meant more to me—BEING FIRST—than a million bucks." His competitiveness didn't stop there. On the return voyage to North America, Houdini joined in and won several sports contests, including the "Skipping Line" and "Swinging the Monkey" (rope-climbing) events. "I beat Bess out of [one] prize," he noted with unaffected pride. "I am certain I will break all records for being sea sick," he added, further throwing modesty to the wind.

The need to dominate was as evident on the stage as it was on the sea or in the air. In September 1912, Houdini stole a march on the competition by introducing his "Chinese Water Torture" effect. In this escape, which he also called the "Upside Down," Houdini would be locked in stocks and lowered headfirst into an ornate, glass-fronted cell, much like an old-fashioned telephone box, that was filled with water. The occasion would be enlivened by his customary flair for showmanship. Along with the device itself, his deadpan assistant Kukol would be on hand with his ax, as well as several other inscrutable stagehands clad in flowing oriental, or sometimes military, garb. A soaring crescendo from the orchestra marked Houdini's own bustling arrival, and a *Jaws*-like thudding signaled his descent into the cell. As with the milk-can escape, a small screen would then be put in place at the front of the stage. Houdini's panting reappearance anything between one and three minutes later eclipsed even that earlier drama: "To say the applause was deafening is putting it too mildly," *The Times* wrote. "The audience seemingly rose in a body and cannonaded their expressions of approval." In February 1913, Houdini wrote of the Upside Down as "the greatest feat I have ever attempted in a strenuous career . . . literally death-defying," and threatened to sue anyone who imitated it, as he later often did.

Was it really that dangerous? "I damn nearly drowned," the actor Tony Curtis recalled of the time he recreated the trick, under considerably more controlled conditions, for his 1953 biopic of Houdini. "The crew had to smash the cabinet with axes . . . You were squeezed in, unable to move. Every second counts when you're suspended upside down like a rack of meat, and you can't breathe. It's enduring the unendurable."

In July 1913, Houdini was performing in Denmark when he was handed a cable telling him that his mother Cecilia had died at the age of seventy-two. The blow was so great that it made him physically ill, and a doctor had to accompany him on the train taking him to the ship that returned him to New York. On Houdini's instructions, Cecilia's body was preserved for the next eleven days so that he could see her one last time. His mother had been a haven of unconditional love and acceptance, and even if weeks or months passed without him seeing her, while she existed, the possibility of that kind of loving acceptance existed. As Houdini wrote, "something in me also died" that July. The event caused him to reassess his views on Spiritualism, and specifically the matter of whether the dead can communicate with the living, which he had had little to say about for fifteen years. Writing to Bess, he now remarked that his mother had "not pass[ed] away but simply let us say 'gone on ahead.'" In the months that followed, he was said to have often woken in the dead of night and called out, "Mama, are you here?" Houdini not only would go on to hold a series of séances in an attempt to reach Cecilia, but now revived the paranormal side to his stage act. In 1914, he introduced a slate-writing effect, in which messages purportedly sent from the beyond would appear on a blackboard. At the climax of one shipboard performance, he was able to display a few cryptic words allegedly supplied by W. T. Stead, the journalist who had gone down on the *Titanic*. Houdini subsequently "formed a strong impression" that a deep-sea diver who had perished in the waters off Melbourne was speaking to him from the grave, and had even provided him with a detailed sketch of an improved diving suit he wanted to market so that others could avoid his fate. Most or all of these demonstrations may have been mere extensions of the spirit-medium flummery of Houdini's old dime-show days. His real views on the afterlife were more complex, however. In the years ahead, he made a series of midnight visits to his parents' graves on the family plot in New York's Cypress Hills cemetery, and was seen to carry on lengthy discussions there with both parties. Toward the end of his own life, Houdini startled an interviewer from the *Chicago Tribune* by suddenly breaking off from their conversation and looking into the middle distance. "My mother's here," he announced quietly.

Houdini's European tour plans were hurriedly postponed as a result of unfolding world events in 1914. He did, however, take the opportunity to unveil both an effect in which he seemingly walked through a brick wall (the subject of a lively future debate with Conan Doyle), and a series of public escapes that typically saw him wriggle out of a straitjacket while dangling 70 or 80 feet above the street—thanks to the presence of newsreels, still the abiding image of Houdini at work. He also continued to amass his "justly celebrated" library, and rarely passed up a chance to meet a literary figure—though one such encounter ended badly when he fell asleep in the middle of a Columbia University professor's lecture on Shakespeare. Aged forty-three, Houdini registered for military service but, like Conan Doyle, was denied a commission. He did his bit, however, performing at dozens of

Red Cross benefits, and increasing his schedule of outdoor stunts, where associates worked the crowd asking for charitable donations. To stimulate interest, Houdini habitually staged his escapes while hanging upside down from a rope suspended immediately outside the local newspaper office. "I've about reached the limit, it seems to me," he told reporters after one such feat in April 1916. "Hereafter I intend to work entirely with my brain. See these grey hairs? They mean something. I'm not as young as I was. I've had to work hard to keep ahead of the procession. But I'll still be entertaining the public for many years to come."

Despite his personal disappointments with Spiritualism, Houdini would develop his own homegrown brand of that philosophy. He had long been fascinated not only by the possibility of communication with the dead, but by what he called "the mechanics" of death, and kept "seven or eight fat scrap-books" filled with press cuttings of a distinctly macabre flavor. There were several entries, for instance, about the Monte Carlo cemetery reserved exclusively for "plungers" who had lost everything in the nearby casinos and then committed suicide. This particular fate "engrossed" Houdini, he admitted. "Visited the [Monte Carlo] necropolis ... Saw grave of man and wife who committed suicide together . . . Lay down there," he wrote. Then there was the case of Washington Irving Bishop—a thirty-three-year-old New York magician who in 1889 had suffered a cataleptic fit while on stage. Bishop had been pronounced dead and was then autopsied—"all while life remained in him," Houdini noted, adding another morbid entry to his file. A few years earlier, he had found Herman's teeth "in splendid condition" when he had had his half brother exhumed, in order to move him to Cypress Hills. Death clearly also struck him as a suitable theme for his own performances. Although he had failed to raise Cecilia, he had held dozens of "reverent" séances, either by himself or with a professional medium. As a result of his new aquatic escapes, there were now Spiritualists who insisted that Houdini himself possessed some miraculous dematerializing power that allowed him to pass through solid objects and then reassemble himself on the other side. The speculation was "good for trade," he confided to his brother Theo. In time, a combination of moral disenchantment and a typically keen sense of its theatrical potential led Houdini to revive the so-called spookist dimension to his stage act, only now it would be for the purpose of unmasking the "charlatans" and "self-proclaimed miracle mongers" who were preying on a vulnerable public. "Only I can expose these vermin," he would remark, with his usual blunt and impregnable self-assurance. In 1924, Houdini put his views into print in his "weighty" and "great" polemical work *A Magician among the Spirits,* a copy of which he soon presented to Conan Doyle. "A malicious book," the latter scrawled, among other unappreciative remarks, across the title page.

Doyle's attitude was also colored by direct experience, particularly the mounting roll call of both family members and friends lost in the World War. Lingering professional respect initially led him to restrain himself and refuse to be drawn into attacking Houdini publicly, as Oliver Lodge and other prominent Spiritualists would have liked him to. In fact, there was "a real fizz . . . a chemical reaction" between the two men, the illusionist later wrote, while conceding that this had not excluded the potential to explode. In large part because Houdini went out of his way to dissemble his true feelings, he and Doyle remained superficially friendly for at least three of the six and a half years they knew each other. But the real state of affairs was more complicated than either party allowed, and increasingly reflected certain core differences of personality, including the way they expressed themselves. After one "injurious" provocation in 1923, Conan Doyle was obliged to "handle you a little roughly" in the press, he informed Houdini, adding that he "hate[d] sparring with a friend in public." Houdini, for his part, speculated that Doyle's losses and advancing age had driven the author into a state of moral confusion that had resulted in him "going loco."

Christianity had not been in slow decline for 1,900 years, but was "a vital living thing still growing and working," Conan Doyle wrote in his unpublished 1884 novel *The Narrative of John Smith,* the manuscript of which had been lost in the post. In November 1916, Doyle again took up the questions of God and man's relationship to Him in an article published in *Light,* widely reprinted under the headline "Author Says We Can Talk with the Dead." "Are we to satisfy ourselves by observing phenomena with no attention to what the phenomena mean, as a group of savages might stare at a wireless installation with no appreciation of the messages coming through it?" he asked. "Or are we resolutely to set ourselves to define these subtle and elusive utterances from beyond, and to construct from them a religious scheme which shall be founded upon human reason on this side and upon spirit inspiration on the other?" According to Doyle, this emerging data should be the basis of a new religion "in some ways confirmatory" of ancient beliefs and in others a clean break from the past.

Conan Doyle's ideas and ideology had been forged in the crucible of experience. He had, in James Barrie's phrase, "fought very hard for the knowledge and understanding" he had acquired, and he did not surrender his positions easily. Even so, Doyle consistently sought out intellectual support for his beliefs, perhaps reflecting the nagging sense of insecurity and a need for respect that seem to have set in at the time of his father's long and, to some, shameful decline. Early on in his article in *Light*, Doyle cites such men as "Crookes, Wallace, Flammarion, Barrett, Generals Draycott and Turner, Sergeant Ballantyne, W. T. Stead, Judge Edmunds [later to feature in a small museum attached to Doyle's Psychic Bookshop], Vice-Admiral Usborne Moore [and] the late Archdeacon Wilberforce" as corroborating his views. From late 1916, he was to enter into steadily closer correspondence with his "wonderfully distinguished" friend Sir Oliver Lodge. A year earlier, Lodge's son Raymond had apparently spoken to him in a séance, describing his "supremely comfortable" afterlife in a place he called "Summerland." Soon Conan Doyle was writing to Lodge as a man of science to inquire about a Crewe-based "spirit photographer" named William Hope, who claimed to be able to register images on photographic plates simply by holding them in his hands. Doyle appeared eager to believe, noting that Hope was in "very poor circumstances" and a deserving case for subsidy. Even so, the creator of Sherlock Holmes clearly hadn't abandoned his analytical faculties. Writing to Lodge in May 1917, Doyle speaks of having tried to verify the messages given by a medium named Miss Wearne, and that in every case these were "absolutely wrong."

Conan Doyle's life was now "absorbed in advanc[ing]" the Spiritualist cause, and his literary career soon followed suit. Alongside his war history he was to publish works such as *The New Revelation* (1918) and *The Vital Message* (1919) that understandably came as a surprise to those who knew him only as the author of crime fiction and rollicking Napoleonic dramas. "A colossal conceit," one anonymous British reviewer (suspected by some to be George Bernard Shaw) wrote of *The New Revelation*. "The book's enormous load of irrelevant and frequently trivial detail [is] piled on in the hope that it will give the work authority: a more educated future era, if any such will occur, will surely take this common failing as a mark of our current depravity." Another critic accused the author simply of an "incredible naiveté." The *New York Times* was kinder: "With the greatest lucidity and earnestness, Sir Arthur compares the Biblical account of the deeds and words of Christ and His disciples with the accumulated testimony concerning death and the afterward offered by Spiritistic phenomena . . . The truth and importance of these phenomena he considers to 'have been proved up to the hilt for all who care to examine the evidence,' and he recounts briefly the proofs offered by many well-known men."

With *The New Revelation* and *The Vital Message,* Conan Doyle was soon receiving the attention that he had hoped for, but he also took a fair amount of abuse. Over the winter of 1916–17, letters began to arrive at Windlesham addressed to "Chief Devil, Spiritualist Church," among other equally unappreciative titles. The more sane correspondents contented themselves with remarking sadly that Conan Doyle's recent output was more Watson than Holmes—"that great man would never have sat down with spirits," wrote one, a view the author himself evidently shared. As might be expected, both the professional critics and the reading public were mixed in their reaction to Doyle's new revelation; he could live with that. What concerned him rather more were the views of his own family. Conan Doyle's younger sister Ida, a Sussex schoolteacher, was unimpressed and said as much. The eighty-year-old Mam, now almost blind but as plainspoken as ever, apparently worried about her son's public reputation, because he was to write back assuring her that he was hardened to criticism. Back in action in France, Kingsley maintained a relentlessly cheerful correspondence with his father, full of praise for both his commanding officers and fellow soldiers, admitting diplomatically only that he was "interested" by Spiritualism but not personally convinced.

Before *The Vital Message* was even published, Conan Doyle was well aware of the heated debate it would generate. Since he was setting himself up as the harbinger of a new religion, he took full advantage of the controversy. Although some way short of the Houdini class, Doyle was once more the preacher, which at heart he arguably always had been. On October 25, 1917, he gave a widely reported speech to the London Spiritualist Alliance, chaired by Oliver Lodge, in which he spoke unambiguously about his beliefs. A number of well-attended public lectures followed. Meanwhile, readers of the *Strand Magazine* who had long enjoyed a privileged first appearance of Conan Doyle's Sherlock Holmes stories would come to find themselves puzzling over articles entitled "The Absolute Proof" and "The Evidence for Fairies" contributed by the same author. Doyle's sense of mission also took more mundane form. He increasingly spoke out against the perils of alcohol, and fretted about the consequences of thousands of battle-hardened soldiers returning on leave to "harlot-haunted" London.

In September 1918, Conan Doyle paid his brief but indelible visit to the Australian lines. Describing his experiences there to the public was hardly a cheerful task—his image of an incarnadine shambles of men and animals is among his most vivid writing—but at least it appeared that the tide was finally turning in the Allies' favor. But then he learned that Kingsley, who had eventually been posted home both due to his original war wound and to complete his training as a doctor, had been taken to St. Thomas's hospital in London, suffering from influenza. He died there on October 28, just two weeks short of the Armistice and of his own twenty-sixth birthday. His father saw him in the mortuary, "looking his brave steadfast self," and oversaw the arrangements to bury Kingsley next to his mother in the village churchyard near Undershaw. Barely 24 hours after receiving the "stunning" news, Conan Doyle went on stage to deliver a Spiritualist lecture in Nottingham. Composing himself, he told the audience that his oldest son had "survived the grave, and that there was no need to worry." Less than four months later, on February 19, 1919, Doyle's younger brother Innes, organizing relief supplies in Belgium, also succumbed to the influenza epidemic that would eventually account for some 60 million victims worldwide. Innes, who was forty-five at the time of his death, had long ago been his brother's perennially cheerful companion and boy friday in Southsea, making the years of struggle bearable and forging a real-life relationship that foreshadowed that between Holmes and Watson. It was another "terrible, shattering" blow.

If orthodox religion lost ground during the post-war decade, it was perhaps because, as the American writer Walter Lippmann said, "people were not so certain that they were going to meet God when they went to church." This loss of spiritual dynamic was variously ascribed to the wholesale collapse in moral confidence that followed the prolonged shock of the war; and, later in the decade, to prosperity, which encouraged the comfortable belief that it profited a man very considerably if he gained a Morris car and perhaps a round of golf on a Sunday morning. As we've seen, the effect upon traditional religious thinking of scientific doctrines and various scientific discoveries was also deep. There were, too, some specific milestones on Conan Doyle's own path away from the established church. His experiences of both Stonyhurst and some of his more inflexibly Catholic relatives; his father's condition; and then Louisa's long and wrenching decline can only have fueled what was already a marked aversion to accepting most forms of received moral wisdom. But the trigger point for Conan Doyle's full-scale conversion to the Spiritualist cause was clearly the appalling toll taken by the War on his extended family, with eleven members lost to combat or disease, among them his first son and only brother. Even before these last two blows, Doyle had been a "respectful and frequent" visitor to the séance room. From early 1919, it would provide him a near-daily consolation.

Jean Conan Doyle, distraught and desperate for reassurance after her brother Malcolm's death at Mons, had first "sat" with her live-in companion Lily Loder-Symonds, soon to bear a succession of her own family losses. Little is known about the sickly and unmarried Loder-Symonds except that she had once played the harp at competitive level and, like Jean herself, had a superstitious outlook, apparently believing that the Great War had been prophesied to her as long ago as 1901 by a music teacher known for his psychic abilities. At Windlesham, it was remembered that Loder-Symonds knocked on wood, threw salt over her shoulder, and carried a good-luck penny. At a low point in her fortunes, she is said to have begun to read the astrological "word of the week" in a mass-circulation magazine. Increasingly bedridden, she had subsequently revealed her talent as a "sensitive" with the gift of receiving dictation from the spirit world. While acknowledging the possibility of self-deception on the medium's part, Conan Doyle was to say that the number of messages channeled by Loder-Symonds that later proved to be true was "far beyond what any guessing or coincidence could account for."

In time, Jean Conan Doyle also began to perform acts of automatic writing. Initially, she appeared to enjoy only mixed success: in March 1915, Jean had attempted to get in touch with the spirit of Loder-Symonds's brother Bob, who had fallen in France a few days earlier. The dead man apparently reported to her that he was perfectly happy, and insisted that the war would be over in only three months' time. Loder-Symonds herself had died in 1916, and Jean seems to have suspended her own mediumistic efforts for the next few years. By the time she resumed, around 1920, contacting the spirits of the dead had become a popular, often lucrative business (not that, it should be stressed, Jean herself ever charged for her services). Fashionable mediums could fill the Albert Hall with their promises to reunite bereaved audience members with their loved ones. "Madame Sosostris," the "famous clairvoyante" who appears in T. S. Eliot's 1922 poem *The Waste Land*, reflected the contemporary fascination with the occult. Conan Doyle's public advocacy of the movement, even so, divided intellectual opinion. Doyle's sometime literary and cricketing colleague Jerome K. Jerome, author of *Three Men in a Boat*, wrote of the "puerile" antics of the séance room. H. G. Wells went into print describing a "spirit control" Doyle later claimed to have found as "wrought of self-deception, [as] pathetic as a rag doll which some lonely child has made for its own comfort." George Bernard Shaw and James Barrie, among others, were similarly unimpressed. Even Rudyard Kipling, who, like Doyle, lost a son in the war, wrote of the "lamentable" effects of Spiritualism, which he apparently blamed for deranging his younger sister Alice, or "Trix," who became a society medium. On the other hand, no less earthbound a character than P. G. Wodehouse attended several séances, at one of which he reported having been addressed by his late cousin Ernest. Although the episode might seem to have had its comic potential, Wodehouse himself told his friend Bill Townend he saw nothing funny about it. "I think it's the goods," he wrote.

⁓ ⁓

In the summer of 1918, Conan Doyle began to consult a forty-seven-year-old, white-haired medium named Annie Brittain, who practiced at the Longton Spiritualist Church a few miles outside of Stoke-on-Trent. Brittain, the author of a book called *Twixt Earth and Heaven,* had enjoyed some apparent successes with her practice of falling into a trance at the séance table, and then swaying back and forth in her chair, speaking in a low moan that purported to come to her from the spirit world. According to Conan Doyle, she appears to have brought comforting words to a number of bereaved families in this way. Doyle himself paid Brittain a third visit in November 1918, during which she suddenly spoke in his son's voice. Kingsley assured him that he was happy, and also that he was having regular conversations in the beyond with Malcolm Leckie. The following March, Kingsley returned in the same manner and announced that he was "with Innes," although the latter remained mute.

Conan Doyle soon came to find that Spiritualism held a wide variety of practitioners, some good, others less convincing, within its ranks. One public séance he attended promising "Transcendental Spiritistic Enlightenment" ended in disarray when the medium's agent revealed that she had performed nothing more than a magic trick, and that he himself was a sometime seaside conjurer named Percy Tibbles. Doyle nonetheless threw himself into a typically exhausting round of lecturing and writing on the subject. Although now a passionate believer, he retained his characteristic good cheer and unfailing courtesy even when provoked by an opponent. "Mr McCabe has shown that he has no respect for our intellectual position," he told the audience at a debate at the Queen's Hall, London. "But I cannot reciprocate. I have a very deep respect for the honest, earnest materialist, if only because for very many years I was one myself."

On September 7, 1919, Conan Doyle shared a platform at a Spiritualist rally in Portsmouth with a thirty-eight-year-old Welshman, Evan Powell, a colliery clerk who was also a "very powerful" medium. After several spirits had been summoned, the meeting would end among scenes of Houdini-like public tumult. Doyle, his wife, and five friends then went to a private room where they searched Powell, tied him to a chair, and turned off the lights.

"We had strong phenomena from the start," Doyle wrote to Oliver Lodge. "The medium was always groaning, muttering, or talking, so that there was never a doubt where he was. Suddenly I heard a voice.

"'Jean, it is I.'

"My wife cried, 'It is Kingsley.'

"I said, 'Is that you, boy?'

"He said in a very intense whisper and a tone all his own, 'Father!' and then after a pause, 'Forgive me!'"

Conan Doyle, who assumed Kingsley was referring to his earlier doubts about the paranormal, concluded his account by saying that he had then felt a strong hand pressing down on him, followed by a kiss on his forehead. "I am *so* happy," his son assured him.

Relatively little is known of Evan Powell, who was soon to retire from his position at the colliery and take up full-time mediumship in Paignton, Devon, where he frequently addressed clients in the voice of a Cherokee Indian spirit named Black Hawk. The *Scientific American* writer and psychic researcher Malcolm Bird later reported that Powell, even when strapped to a chair, had been able "to ring bells [and] have flowers fly through the air," describing this as "the best séance that I had in England." Others wondered whether, like certain other mediums, Powell might not be above preying on the needs of the bereaved. There were also rare occasions, Doyle acknowledged, when a "truly clairvoyant" individual, not obtaining genuine results, might resort to trickery purely in a well-meaning attempt to bring some comfort to a grieving mother or widow. "We must not argue," he wrote, "that because a man once forges, therefore he never signed an honest cheque in his life."

Conan Doyle was to have five more encounters with his fallen son at roughly monthly intervals between October 1919 and April 1920, at which point he met Harry Houdini.

Across the Atlantic, Houdini's new "mission," as he put it, was increasingly to "walk the thin line" separating his own moral beliefs and public expectations. It sometimes appeared that the thing lying at the heart of American attitudes to life as the country embarked on its extended period of twentieth-century world dominance was the idea of illusion. The nation had bread, but it wanted circuses—and now it got them, in an explosion of music halls and other places of entertainment offering a rich variety of fare whose most common artistic theme was the idea of mystification, legerdemain, or some form of deception. In 1909, there were 427 officially licensed "Mentalists, visual deluders, and [other such] artistes" active in the seven core eastern seaboard states; a decade later, the figure had jumped to 6,390, quite apart from the profusion of "street fakirs, jongleurs, bunco merchants, miracle workers, healers and seers" the *New York World* found at work in that city. One of the striking characteristics of the American post-war era was the unparalleled rapidity and unanimity with which millions of men and women invested time and money in a variety of what the future President Coolidge called "escapist trifles"—whether flocking to the circus, making a national heroine of the so-called "pig woman" Jane Gibson, or raising a series of exotically turbaned mediums to something like modern-day rock star status. It was a "culturally torrid" and "morally fitful" atmosphere, Coolidge complained, in which a peerless showman like Houdini could hardly fail to prosper.

He did prosper. Houdini's paid performances were now a winning mixture of Spiritualist parodies and set-piece extravaganzas such as "Upside Down," judiciously weighted by a few golden greats like "Metamorphosis" or some other simple but effective handcuff escape. Although typically competitive, even toward his own family ("If you want to see my old-time feats performed," he told a friend, "drop in and get acquainted with my brother"), and as keen as ever on a dollar, he was also a selfless champion of the American war effort. A benefit performance Houdini staged in New York on November 11, 1917, raised over $12,000 (roughly $600,000 today) for the families of troops killed in the sinking of the transport ship *Antilles* by a German submarine. He also took a close professional interest in efforts to bring some more ethereal comfort to the bereaved. "Have you read that some of the folks like Conan Doyle . . . are dabbling in Spiritualism again?" Houdini wrote to his fellow illusionist Harry Kellar, adding elsewhere that the paranormal movement had become "a great stampede." He would not be left behind in the rush. Apart from his stage presentations, Houdini now planned to write a book denouncing those who trafficked in "psychic phenomena, Spiritualism, black magic, witchcraft, demonology, hokum, etc.," though it's hard to establish how much of this was motivated by public-mindedness and how much by careerism on his part. By early 1918, he was also speaking of building an "Egyptian-style temple" in New York, where paying customers would enter a darkened chamber and be guided by a mysteriously floating, spectral hand before being addressed by ghostly voices seemingly whispering to them from out of the sky. While the building's architects puzzled over its technical challenges, Houdini introduced his celebrated "vanishing elephant" effect. The 2-ton pachyderm, named Jennie, first lumbered on stage at the suitably vast New York Hippodrome on New Year's Day 1918. She wore a frilly blue ribbon around her neck, and a bridal garter, sometimes switched to a jumbo-sized watch, strapped to her hind leg. After the applause and laughter had died down, Houdini and his assistants wheeled on a cabinet (to show that no trap-doors were being used) to shield Jennie from view; when the cabinet's front door was flung open a few moments later, she was gone. This colossal illusion went on to fill the 6,000-seat Hippodrome eight times a week for nineteen weeks. It was not just "the talk of the town," Houdini shyly admitted, "but the talk of all the show world."*

Meanwhile, a new sort of entertainment was being ushered in by the enormous increase in motion picture production. By 1919, some 40 million Americans bought a ticket to the movies at least once a week, and the cinema's pulp-fiction spinoffs such as *True-Story,* offering a diet of scantily clad starlets, hygiene advice, and behind-the-cameras gossip, weren't far behind: that particular title had 220,000 readers in 1919, 850,000 by 1922, and more than 2 million by 1925, a record of rapid growth probably unparalleled in magazine publishing. Houdini was not slow to respond. In July 1918, he began filming *The Master Mystery,* in which he played an undercover agent named, with heavy-handed irony, Quentin Locke, who successively battles an evil mesmerist, an oriental assassin, a mad strangler, a prototype robot, and a blond vamp named De Luxe Dora over the course of a fifteen-part serial. It was released in January 1919 to capacity audiences. Houdini followed this with pictures called *The Grim Game* and *Terror Island,* both of which similarly shunned introspection in favor of a series of barnstorming aerial stunts and sunken-treasure adventures, respectively. Houdini subsequently formed his own production company—the Houdini Picture Corporation—that soon involved him more as a litigant than an actor. In 1922, he released *The Man from Beyond,* whose plot seemed to suggest that there might be something in the idea of posthumous communication after all. The film opens with a close-up of the Bible and ends with a scene of two former lovers being reunited as spirits while reading from Conan Doyle's *The Vital Message.* Doyle was delighted. "I have seen the Houdini picture," he wrote in an open letter, "and it is difficult to find words to adequately express my

---

*The "vanishing elephant" effect, which Houdini demonstrated to over a million customers, has still never been fully explained. It was actually the climax of a series of public tryouts that had seen him make first a (frequently uncooperative) donkey and then a young woman on a horse similarly evaporate. In all three cases, it may be significant that a black interior curtain, or sometimes a mirror, was discreetly positioned running diagonally from the front corner of the cabinet toward a small door (large enough to admit an animal trainer) at the rear. It remains a peerless feat of showmanship on Houdini's part.

enjoyment and appreciation of it . . . It is punctuated with thrills that fairly make the hair stand on end."

Though personally frugal, and, except on their anniversary, rarely known to join Bess in a glass of champagne, Houdini may have explored other mood-altering substances around the time he went to Hollywood. Will Goldston believed he sometimes partook of "a nip of opium," of the kind widely available in Edwardian music-hall circles, if only for its analgesic properties. The drug may have numbed the pain of a damaged kidney and other health-related issues collected over the years, but, as with Bess's drinking, it didn't always produce a felicitous state. "[Houdini] could become very morbid," Goldston recalled. An ex-convict named Tom Marks was employed around 1920 as a stagehand at the London Palladium. Seven years earlier, he had been convicted of stabbing another man in a pub brawl. Houdini became "immersed" in Marks's crime, and "spent a good deal of his time between performances asking him, 'How did it feel? What was the exact reaction you had just before you committed the deed?'" To Goldston, it seemed that Houdini had a "queer need" to know the smallest details of such acts, "almost as if collect[ing] them for a mental photograph."

Writing home to his brother Theo from London at Christmas 1913, five months after their mother's death, Houdini described a dream in which he had seen Cecilia and Mayer Weiss alive and well, frolicking together in Appleton. Now a five-year-old boy, he had run to fetch a camera to record the scene, wanting to "feast my eyes on both our Parents." Many bereaved children will recognize the general scenario, although it may be less common if, like Houdini, the dreamer is middle-aged. He went on to tell Theo that he had then experienced a moment of panic as the "beautiful illusion" played itself out. "I feared [Cecilia and Mayer] would note by my actions," he wrote, "that I was excited." The lure of the dead was there, but so too, perhaps, was Houdini's own, uniquely haunting obsession with his mother. The dream can be read on various levels, from the oedipal to the Spiritualistic, particularly as Houdini went on to hold a séance later that night in an attempt to reach Cecilia more materially. As he told Theo, he did not want her "highly important" life to end in simple extinction.

When Houdini returned to New York in June 1914, he was able to pass the voyage by performing a few Spiritualistic tricks for his fellow passengers, who included the former president Theodore Roosevelt. "It was a shame the way I had to fool him," he wrote of his distinguished mark. Roosevelt was in good company in apparently believing that Houdini possessed occult powers. The legendary actress Sarah Bernhardt was similarly persuaded after she went to see him perform an outdoor escape in Boston in 1916. Bernhardt returned the compliment by inviting what she called "the world's second greatest entertainer" to watch her on stage later that night. Now aged seventy-one (and with a penchant for sleeping in a coffin), she was still on tour, despite having recently lost her right leg to gangrene. As the two of them were driven off in a limousine, Bernhardt turned to Houdini and with a straight face asked him if he could perform "some form of healing, or miracle" to restore her limb. "She honestly thought I was superhuman," he later informed the press. By this stage, Houdini may have entertained the same thought himself, because not long afterward he announced that he would star in a benefit performance at the Hippodrome, where he would attempt to catch a bullet fired at him from a "real rifle" held by a marksman positioned just a dozen yards away. He was dissuaded only when his friend Chung Ling Soo—Billy Robinson—died when performing the same trick a few days earlier at the Wood Green Empire, London. Someone had reportedly tampered with the barrel of the gun before passing it on to Robinson's stage assistant. Even then, Houdini was ready to go ahead with the stunt until his friend and mentor Harry Kellar sent him an anxious letter. "Now, my dear boy, this is advice from the heart. DON'T TRY THE D—N Bullet Catching trick, no matter how sure you may feel of its success. There is always the biggest kind of risk that some dog will 'job' you." Houdini, well aware that he had "murdering enemies" as well as adoring fans, saw sense and performed "Upside Down" instead.

It was a rare concession by a man consumed by ego, or at least by his ability to appear completely self-confident when he was not. Nor was he apt to downplay his more spectacular achievements. Speaking of his barnstorming epic *The Grim Game,* Houdini would smoothly assure the press that "all the flying stunts [had been] actually performed," and offered a $1,000 prize "to any person who can prove that the collision [shown in] the film was not genuine." In fact, it *was* genuine. It just wasn't performed by Houdini. The audiences who saw a figure jump from the wing of one biplane to another, among other death-defying feats, were actually thrilling to the stunt work of an ex–US Air Service pilot named Robert E. Kennedy. When Houdini later autographed a publicity close-up that showed him clinging for dear life to one of the plane's wings, he added the inscription, "About 4000 feet in the air!" This was a slight overstatement, as the photograph in question had been taken on the ground. In time, Conan Doyle attended a New York screening of *The Grim Game,* and declared himself impressed. The illusionist's whole life was "one long succession" of such "reckless feats of daring," he wrote in his book *The Edge of the Unknown,* which perhaps speaks both of Houdini's gift for relentless self-projection and of Doyle's for consistently thinking the best of people.

When they first met in that spring of 1920, Conan Doyle and Houdini were both past masters of their professions. Doyle was the more obviously couth of the two, though it would be a mistake to underestimate the power of Houdini's mind, and of the mental system that he put together from the material he picked up from his reading and experience. Each man had suffered a family loss—or losses—in recent years, and each had turned to the séance room for solace. But there the similarities ended. Houdini's medicine-show parodies of Spiritualism, undertaken in his early twenties, had set up a lifelong skepticism on the subject that his failure to "reach" his dead mother eventually hardened into a crusade. As with his later embrace of aviation and film, he operated strictly on the basis of giving the public what it wanted, and it had wanted the occult. Doyle's own initial research into the paranormal, which he conducted around the same age, was only slightly more satisfactory. But in his case it was that early experience, painfully reawakened by later events in Flanders, that determined the decision about what was to be "the most important thing in [his] life," a decision not finally made until the autumn of 1916, when he was in his fifty-eighth year.

Now, as the War ended and an era of lost certainties began, a far-reaching debate would get under way about man's whole purpose on earth. It was also a debate about the essence, and permanence, of death.

4

PIERCING THE VEIL

"I n his public performances he seems to do things that cannot be explained by the ordinary laws of nature; in this respect he resembles the men and women who call themselves Spiritualistic mediums," Conan Doyle wrote of Houdini, to whom he also ascribed the "divine" gift of being able to waft in and out of confined spaces. Doyle was soon convinced that the "great self-liberator," as Houdini now called himself, could dematerialize at will. Houdini himself would deny this, of course (as he did), to preserve his double life as a "miracle worker" on the one hand and "the greatest medium-baiter of modern times" on the other.

At first sight, the individual who presented himself for lunch at Windlesham on April 14, 1920, must have seemed somewhat disappointing set against this superhuman ideal. Now aged forty-six, Houdini was a stubby, Chaplinesque figure, thickening around the waist, with patches of receding gray hair rather too prominently dyed black. He was dressed in a typically ill-fitting cream-colored suit and a straw boater, which he courteously removed before ringing the doorbell. As mentioned, he made a striking physical contrast to Conan Doyle, who was a foot taller and some 80 pounds heavier. The two men soon found common ground, however. Doyle and his young family were enchanted by their guest (Bess was "indisposed" that day, and unable to attend), who performed "astounding" conjuring tricks for them. Houdini, in turn, considered Doyle "just as nice and sweet as any mortal I have ever been near." Later that night, he wrote in his diary: "Visited Sir A Conan Doyle at Crowborough. Met Lady Doyle and the three children. Had lunch with them. They believe implicitly in Spiritualism. Sir Arthur told me he had spoken six times to his son. No possible chance for trickery." For all the bonhomie, it's possible that Houdini already had doubts about the author's critical faculties. "[Doyle] saw my performance Friday night," he wrote to Harry Kellar a few days later. "He was so much impressed, that there is little wonder in his believing in Spiritualism so strongly."

It's fairly safe to say that when Houdini arrived for a tour of Britain in early 1920 and sat down to send copies of *The Unmasking of Robert-Houdin* to a cold list of some 200 of the country's leading figures, he did not anticipate that one of the book's recipients would go on to become the "most singular" acquaintance of his life. Conan Doyle soon wrote back to say that he had enjoyed *The Unmasking,* but was irked by Houdini's claim that the Davenport brothers had confessed to "rank trickery" that had allowed them to freely play their musical instruments while apparently tied up in a packing crate. Since the Davenports had given their first performance when they were children, Doyle reasoned, they could hardly have been such practiced hoaxers. Houdini's reply tactfully failed to mention the mid-nineteenth century's other Spiritualistic *cause célèbre,* the Fox sisters, the youngest of whom was just twelve when she first reported hearing "bumps and raps" in her bedroom. A polite exchange followed, and early in April the Conan Doyles traveled to see Houdini on stage at the London Palladium, where he escaped from a series of straitjackets, performed the Upside Down, and told the audience of his "many terrifying close calls" on the set of *The Grim Game,* before finishing on a mildly anticlimactic note with a conjuring trick he called the "Cut and Restored Turban." Although the two men still hadn't met in person, more letters ensued. Later that week, Houdini, evidently hoping to make a friend of this "literary titan [as] justly famous as myself," wrote to assure Conan Doyle that he was "a skeptic, but [also] a seeker after the Truth" in Spiritualistic matters. "I am willing to believe," he added, "if I can find a Medium who, as you suggest, will not resort to 'manipulation' when the Power does not 'arrive.'"

For all their surface courtesy, Conan Doyle and Houdini were beginning to take opposite sides of the Spiritualist barricade. The early exchanges continued in the civil but ambiguous tone adopted by both parties. "I see that you know a great deal about the negative side of Spiritualism," Conan Doyle remarked. "I hope more on the positive side will come your way . . . It wants to be approached not in the spirit of a detective approaching a suspect, but in that of a humble, religious soul, yearning for hope and comfort." For his part, Houdini would admit only that "I can make the positive assertion that the Davenport Brothers never were exposed," and that "regarding my own work, I never claim Spiritualistic or supernatural aid, always informing the public that it is accomplished by natural means, or as you suggest, by 'art and practice.'" He was more than once to return to the subject of the Davenports. Despite the fact that neither Conan Doyle nor Houdini could ever conclusively say how, exactly, the Brothers got their results, this wouldn't stop them taking sides and facing off with all the fury of Lilliput and Blefuscu fighting over whether to break eggs at the big end or small end. "I am seeking Truth," Houdini repeated in another letter touching on the Davenports, before adding the veiled remark: "As a rule, I have found that the greater brain a man has, and the better he is educated, the easier it has been to mystify him." Even at this early stage, there was some spirited intellectual jousting. "When you say there are 96 volumes on your desk," Houdini wrote, "it may interest you to know that I travel with a bookcase containing over one hundred volumes, and recently, in Leeds, I bought two whole collections on Spiritualism." "If you ever index your psychic library, I should like to see the list," Conan Doyle replied. "I have 200 now—and have read them too!"

Doyle, clearly, still saw Houdini as a possible high-profile recruit to the Spiritualist ranks. "I am sending you two little books of my own on psychic matters," he wrote on March 26, "though I fancy in your busy life you have little time for reading." On his side, Houdini was happy to present himself as an impartial seeker of the truth. "I am treating this matter seriously," he stressed, more than once. If, simultaneously, that allowed him to rub shoulders with a "literary titan [and] Analytical Mind" like Conan Doyle, so much the better. To the self-taught illusionist, the creator of Sherlock Holmes represented what he called "the true intellectual giant"—what Houdini himself ached to be and now sensed he might never be. "Am only too delighted to correspond with you," he wrote on April 3, the trigger for Doyle's invitation to lunch. "[I] will avail myself of the opportunity of calling on you Wednesday morning," Houdini instantly replied by telegram. "Mrs Houdini is with me, but will not be able to come at the present time, and wishes to thank you for your kind thought."

Within a week of their first meeting, Houdini was writing to Conan Doyle to ask him to recommend a "really convincing" medium who might be able to show him the "Eternal Truth" once and for all. Doyle suggested he contact Annie Brittain, the woman who had been the first person to speak to him in his son Kingsley's voice. "I met Mrs Brittain," Houdini reported in due course. "She was very interesting to me, and that is all I can say about this medium." He was more forthcoming in his diary. "Mrs B not convincing," he wrote. "Simply kept talking in general.

'Saw' things she heard about. One spirit was to bring me flowers on the stage. All this is ridiculous stuff." Conan Doyle was sufficiently encouraged to invite Houdini and Bess to lunch at the Royal Automobile Club in London. The two men posed for a photograph at the door, Doyle looming over his guest with an air of proconsular authority. "Sir Arthur called attention to the fact that a few days previously [he] had been sitting at the same table with a powerful medium," Houdini wrote. "He told me in a very serious tone, which was corroborated by Lady Doyle, that the table started to move all around the place to the astonishment of the waiter, who was not aware of the close proximity of the medium." The following Sunday, Houdini visited a Mrs. Wriedt of Holland Park, who claimed she could hear the faint whisperings of spirits by pressing the end of a long trumpet to her ear. This, too, proved inconclusive, leaving Mrs. Wriedt to complain that Houdini had been out "to make trouble." Conan Doyle had altogether better results when the same clairvoyant visited him at Windlesham. "She sat in our nursery with my wife and me, and [Doyle's secretary] Major Wood. We sang together. As we sang, and as I clearly heard all four voices, a fifth very beautiful one rose up in our midst. That is surely occult beyond doubt."

In May 1920, the Society for Psychical Research invited a thirty-three-year-old Frenchwoman named Marthe Béraud to give a series of Spiritualist sittings in the upstairs office they rented in an imposingly gothic mansion at 20 Hanover Square in central London. Béraud, who went by the nom-de-séance of Eva C., was said to be able to emit a thick, white, rubbery substance—ectoplasm—from her body. This typically appeared in an amorphous wad, much like an elongated string of chewing gum, but sometimes seemed to take the shape of actual human faces. Both this and the medium's other gifts, including her speaking in tongues, and the "true voices" of departed loved ones, had consistently defied any material explanation. Some years earlier, she had been the subject of a lengthy investigation by a German author and doctor, Von Schrenck-Notzing, who reported that as part of his inquiries he had often "minutely searched" the attractive Mrs. Béraud, before dressing her in a black body-stocking "which permitted for no possible concealment of substances" on her part. The doctor's subsequent best-selling book seemed to endorse Béraud's materializing powers, and was filled with photographs of the ectoplasm oozing from her mouth, ears, nose, and other parts of her body. Conan Doyle considered Schrenck-Notzing's work "the most notable of any investigation which ha[d] ever been recorded" of the occult.

On the evening of June 18, 1920, Houdini walked up the steps of 20 Hanover Square ready to turn a "cold eye" on the "beguiling blonde creature who purports to have psychic abilities" waiting for him in the darkened séance room. There were four other witnesses to the event, including the SPR's thirty-year-old, Cambridge-educated research officer Eric Dingwall, who also happened to be an amateur conjurer, the British Museum's curator of erotica, and the author of the definitive illustrated history of the chastity belt. ("Dingwall and I understand each other," Houdini noted, "not to let ourselves be hoodwinked.") After introductions were made, Eva C., who appeared to be somewhat more heavyset than in her publicity photographs, was taken into an adjoining room, searched by Dingwall's female colleague, and returned wearing her black body-suit. The sitters arranged themselves around the small table, Houdini to the medium's left, and joined hands. Eva C. then appeared to fall into a trance, where she remained for the next three hours. "Nothing happened," Houdini wrote in his diary. "A nail in the chair discommoded Eva. After the séance I went to 5 John Street with [friends]. Had a cup of coffee."

Four days later, Houdini went back to Hanover Square for a second sitting. "This time [Eva] manifested," he wrote to Conan Doyle, bringing up about five inches of a "froth-like substance" into a veil he and Dingwall had placed over the medium's head. There was also "something that looked like a small face, say 4 inches in circumference. Was terra-cotta colored, and Dingwall, who held her hands, had the best look at the 'object.'" Houdini was apparently convinced. "[Eva] asked permission to remove something in her mouth," he told Doyle, "and took out what appeared to be a rubberish substance, which she disengaged and showed us plainly; we held the electric torch, all saw it plainly, when presto! It vanished . . . I found it highly interesting." Houdini's private account of his eight séances with Eva C. told a different story. The medium had "'sleight-of-handed' the [foreign] substances into her mouth," he wrote in his diary, and simply regurgitated them; the alleged human face actually resembled "a colored cartoon, and seemed to have been unrolled." Not surprisingly, Conan Doyle seized on Houdini's more positive public report of the sittings. "I am glad you got some results," he wrote. "It is certainly on the lowest and most mechanical plane of the spiritual world, [but] at least it is beyond our present knowledge."

The illusionist himself remained the more interesting subject. In April 1920, Conan Doyle seems not to have known exactly what to make of Houdini's stage act, and by the latter's account had mostly put it down to "art and practice." Three months later, Doyle became convinced that this "God-given" performer possessed a "dematerialising and reconstructing force [that] could separate the molecules" of any solid object toward which it was directed. "My dear chap," he now wrote to Houdini, "why go around the world seeking a demonstration of the occult when you are giving one all the time? Mrs Guppy [a Victorian mesmerist] could dematerialise, and so could many people in Holy Writ, and I do honestly believe that you can also . . . Such a gift is not given to one man in a hundred million," Doyle said, "that he should amuse the multitude or amass a fortune. Excuse my frank talking, but you know this is all very vital to me."

It was a central fact of Houdini's public life that even some of his most ardent admirers, as well as others who disliked or mistrusted him, so often saw him as a performer, a man not only trying to make an impression but constantly calculating *what* impression he wanted to make—whether of sincerity, candor, open-mindedness, or some other desirable quality. Following the sessions with Eva C., he "eagerly" took up Conan Doyle's suggestion that he investigate the case of a twenty-two-year-old Irish medium named Kathleen Goligher, who also appeared to have the gift of ectoplasm. "The stuff seems to come from the womb," Doyle explained, adding that incredulity seemed to him "a sort of insanity" under the circumstances.

As it turned out, Houdini met neither Goligher nor her similarly mediumistic brother and sisters, but did enter into a correspondence with William J. Crawford, a professor of mechanical engineering at the Belfast Technical Institute who had made a study of the family. In 1918, Crawford had published a book describing how an "ectoplasmic lever" could extend from Kathleen's body and cause the séance table in front of her to levitate. Houdini was publicly tactful, saying that such a device was "a wonderful affair [and] there is no telling how far all this may lead to." Four years later, he was to write in *A Magician among the Spirits,* "Dr Crawford seemed mad to me . . . His credulity [was] limitless." Crawford committed suicide on July 30, 1920, just a week after his last exchange of letters with Houdini, after leaving a note insisting his research into the Golighers was "all done before [my] mental collapse, and is the most perfect work I have done in my life." It was left for Conan Doyle and Houdini to subsequently exchange their own contrasting theories of ectoplasm. "Nothing has crossed my path to make me think that the Great Almighty will allow emanations from a human body of such horrible, revolting, viscous substances," Houdini remarked, in the course of pouring scorn on mediums who "ring bells, move handkerchiefs, wobble tables and do other 'flap-doodle' stunts." Conan Doyle took a more dispassionate academic view of the matter. "Personally," he wrote, "the author is of the opinion that several different forms of plasma with different activities will be discovered, the whole forming a separate science of the future which may well be called Plasmology." Although their occult qualities remain debatable, the use of plasmas today in the production of everything from sanitary gels to supersonic combustion engines goes some way to fulfilling Doyle's prediction.

Skeptics have suggested that there was a sharp role reversal at work when it came to the two men's investigative techniques as a whole. Houdini, having spent twenty years successfully manipulating audiences by a combination of illusion and expertise, now presented himself as the scourge of those who would "willfully dupe the honest observer" such as himself. All that the likes of Eva C. and Mrs. Guppy were offering was "stagecraft" rather than any "supernatural wit," he argued. Much of the "so-called skill known as mentalism," for instance, was merely a question of bombarding the unsuspecting subject with subliminal messages; if you exposed them to enough pictures of black and white parallel lines, as well as mentioning the words "striped" and "animal" several times, you might well find that they subsequently happened to be thinking of a zebra. But while the seasoned illusionist now became a tireless myth buster, the creator of the world's most famous analytical mind seemed to have relaxed his own critical faculties. "Some [manifestation] must come your way if you really persevere and get it out of your mind that you should follow it as a terrier follows a rat," Conan Doyle told Houdini. Some of Doyle's more vociferous critics came to feel that he had actually been driven mad (the word used in the *Daily Express*) by the loss of his son, although Houdini himself was too perceptive for such a sentimental misjudgment. The fact was that there was no true Conan Doyle; several warring personalities struggled for preeminence in the same individual. One was idealistic, thoughtful, generous; another was obstinate, petty, emotional. There was a reflective, philosophical, stoical Doyle; and there was an impetuous, impulsive, and irascible one. Sometimes one set of traits prevailed; sometimes another; occasionally they were in uneasy balance. It would still be wrong to portray the intuitive and street-smart illusionist as invariably right in his psychic methodology and the warm-hearted and sometimes unworldly author as invariably wrong. The gentleman in Conan Doyle may have been reluctant to acknowledge that there were those on the Spiritualist side acting from less pristine motives than he was. But when obvious charlatans did come to his attention, he had no qualms about publicly naming these "human hyenas." Right to the end of his life, Doyle had a remarkable memory, particularly for facts and figures, the dates of significant séances, the specifics of the houses and rooms in which they occurred, which, packaged together with an apt biblical quotation, he often used to confound the critics. Houdini, for his part, never trusted in disinterested rationality, if that can be considered the usual mark of an intellectual, over and above his passionate, or perhaps pathological, need to dominate a crowd. As his wife of thirty-two years was to remark, "the central [relationship] of his life was that between him and the audience."

The portrait of Conan Doyle that most often emerges from the memoirs of former, and often sorely disaffected friends who took issue with him on Spiritualism is of a man who was long on decency and determination and short on practical intelligence. Even some of those who stuck by him throughout the 1920s had their doubts about his intellectual candlepower, at least as he applied it on this subject. To James Barrie, Doyle showed an "almost dissolute" fascination with half-baked scientific data that seemed to lend respectability to his psychic beliefs. Among the newly evolving discoveries that purported to question man's role in the cosmos was Quantum Field Theory—on one hand, a structure designed to analyze the creation and annihilation of minute particles such as electrons and photons and, on another, a contemplation on the "non-observable" material world. It was one of several such "seismic jolts," as Barrie called them, of an era that also saw the belated confirmation of Einstein's general theory of relativity, as well as the rapid availability of the radio, "a dispenser of disembodied voices," Houdini remarked, "to millions of folks around the world." Conan Doyle often made the argument that these were matters that until recently had seemed as outlandish as the idea of spiritual communication, and that future scientific progress might well come to validate the "new revelation."

It seems fair to say that on the whole Houdini was less interested in metaphysical niceties. Eric Dingwall thought his sometime fellow psychic researcher philosophically "untutored," but able to extemporize quickly and correctly on many issues. Dingwall became especially adept at briefing Houdini, whom he discovered lacking in basic knowledge of Spiritualistic terminology and theory. The "little fellow" would go on to become a "tenacious detective," Dingwall remembered, in which capacity his "incurable vulgarity" and "fleetness of mind" stood him in good stead. As a rule, Dingwall would reduce what he had to say to Houdini to simple graphic terms, compressed to five minutes. Often, he had the satisfaction within a few additional minutes of hearing his gifted pupil expound to someone else with emphasis and feeling what he had just learned.

Ample testimony exists, including his own, that Conan Doyle took up the Spiritualist fight fully aware of the fact that it was contrary to his own best commercial interests to do so. It would be wrong, even so, to portray him as completely oblivious to the material world after 1916. When Doyle accepted an invitation to visit Australia and New Zealand in the autumn of 1920, he found that he could do so only if he was paid the sort of speaking fees that would allow him and his entourage of six (his wife, three children, and two servants) to tour the continent in style. With the help of a booking agent, Conan Doyle was eventually able to report that his expenses for the four-month engagement ran to some £3,000, while his net profits topped £3,500 (or, respectively, around £160,000 and £187,000 in 2011 prices). At the same time, he was in protracted negotiations with the Stoll Film Company about bringing a series of Sherlock Holmes adventures to the screen. Together they would go on to adapt some forty-five of the stories into twenty-minute "shorts," topped off by a full-length version of *The Hound of the Baskervilles.* Doyle also relaxed his self-imposed ban on adding to the Holmes canon and wrote twelve new, if only fitfully brilliant stories between 1921 and 1927, each appearance of which was widely reported to be the last. To call the detective the Frank Sinatra of the popular fiction world of the 1920s would be to confer a somewhat flattering sense of consistency on a character who seemed to rest, or retire, and then come back on roughly an annual basis. Of course, it's also fair to say that Conan Doyle had rather more in the way of extracurricular activities than the average author, and that as part of a high-maintenance lifestyle he was consistently generous not only to the Spiritualist cause as a whole but to an impressive list of family members, friends, employees, and even complete strangers, by whom he was regularly "touched" for a pound or two. It's worth dwelling on Conan Doyle's overall financial position for a moment if only to show that, committed as he undoubtedly was to his beliefs, he was also able to indulge them as he might not have been even ten years earlier. By the mid-1920s, Doyle was a seriously rich man; he needed to be, and never felt himself wholly secure, but a combination of talent, perseverance, and sometimes spirited haggling on his part meant that he could now afford to do more or less as he chose with his time. By late 1928, even after ending the Holmes franchise once and for all, Conan Doyle was able to report that he and his wife together were worth £110,000, or over £5 million today.

Houdini, by contrast, clearly still saw Spiritualism as a sideline to his more lucrative career on the stage and screen. Mass-circulation British periodicals like *Boys' Cinema* and *Kinema Comic* now feted him as "The Greatest" or "The Most Dazzling Star in the Sky," and the latter publication put him on its cover for fifty consecutive issues. Houdini later remarked that he attended "100 Spiritualistic sittings" on his 1920 tour of Britain and France, which would have represented some five séances a week during his five-month stay. If so, it was increasingly with a view to exposing what he privately considered "the network of fake mediums, clairvoyants, so-called gravity defiers, etc.," a public service that in no way precluded financial gain on his part. Shortly after returning to New York in July 1920, Houdini commissioned a twenty-nine-year-old Glaswegian magician and firework-maker named Alexander Stewart (who went by the alias DeVega) to investigate a long list of "questionable or crooked practitioners" of the occult. DeVega was soon to report several cases of obvious fraud. "Glad to get the confessions of the mediums," Houdini wrote back. "What I want particularly is Spirit Photos and their methods. I will willingly pay all your expenses, to any sceance [*sic*] you may go to, no matter what it is." By early autumn, DeVega had visited the Crewe-based spirit photographer William Hope and passed on details of Hope's use of "extravagant amounts of thick concealing cloth," which seemed akin to that used in a conjuring trick. "The detailed data you have 'red-inked' was specially interesting," Houdini wrote. "Do you think you could dope out some way to duplicate this stuff, if you had the paraphernalia?"

As it turned out, Hope was only a curtain-raiser to the long, sometimes tragicomic saga that was to occupy Conan Doyle, and to a much lesser extent Houdini, from the midsummer of 1920. The story began one hot Saturday afternoon in July 1917, when sixteen-year-old Elsie Wright and her ten-year-old cousin Frances Griffiths borrowed Elsie's father's new Midg camera and disappeared into the glen behind the Wrights' home in the village of Cottingley, West Yorkshire. The two girls returned about thirty minutes later "in high spirits," it was recalled. Later that evening, Arthur Wright developed the Midg's photographic plate in his home darkroom, where what he called a "curious manifestation" occurred. Looming up at him out of the chemical tray was an image that seemed to show Frances leaning on the side of a small hill on which four fairies were dancing. Knowing of his daughter's artistic sensibility, Mr. Wright dismissed the picture as a girlish prank, and was similarly unmoved when the young cousins returned from a second outing two months later with a picture of Elsie sitting on the back lawn holding out her hand to a winged gnome. The story might have ended there but for Mrs. Wright's growing interest in the Theosophical movement, the westernized version of the Buddhist reincarnation and time-travel theories that had intrigued Conan Doyle in Southsea, and that was active even in the rural Yorkshire of the early 1920s. In time, the local chapter of the Theosophical Society heard of the fairy photographs, which then came into the hands of the society's London-based "Blavatsky Lodge" president, Edward

L. Gardner. The forty-nine-year-old Gardner combined his career as a Harlsden building contractor with an avid belief in leprechauns, goblins, pixies, elves, and other woodland beings. Gardner in turn sent copies of the pictures to the editor of *Light* and to Conan Doyle, who was not slow to pronounce on them as proof of a "primitive missing link" in the evolutionary chain, if not one with a direct bearing on the matter of life after death. "I have something far more precious [than the Goligher photographs]," Doyle wrote to Houdini on June 25, 1920, "—two photos, one of a goblin, the other of four fairies in a Yorkshire wood. A fake! you will say. No, sir, I think not . . . The fairies are about 8 inches high. In one there is a goblin dancing. In the other four beautiful, luminous creatures. Yes, it is a revelation."

So far as is known, Houdini kept his counsel on the matter, at least in public, possibly because he thought the whole thing too ludicrous. Conan Doyle did hear from his friend Oliver Lodge, who raised doubts about the photographs, which he thought might have been faked by using images cut out of a magazine. Meanwhile, partisans of the Wright family contended that the girls did not know enough about photography to produce such convincing results. The Kodak company, to which Conan Doyle took a set of the negatives, found no clear evidence that the original film had been tampered with, but nor were they prepared to rule the possibility out. A Yorkshire photographer named Harold Snelling, whom Gardner consulted, came down firmly in the girls' favor, declaring, "there was no trace whatever of studio work involving card or paper models." It's possible, even so, that there was more to Doyle's own "absolute" and "unstinting" endorsement of the pictures than met the eye. While in his confinement thirty years earlier, his father Charles had grown steadily more preoccupied with fairies and other entities, which had come to monopolize his sketchbook. Charles's brother Richard, the *Punch* illustrator, had shown a similar fascination with the miniature world. Conan Doyle himself had actually been sitting down to write about this "consuming" issue for *The Strand* when the Cottingley photographs first came to his notice. Hurriedly revising his article, which was published that December under the title "The Evidence for Fairies," he included the testimony not only of the young Yorkshire cousins but of several other "witnesses of unimpeachable honesty," among them his own children, who had all encountered the same phenomena.

In late July 1920, as Conan Doyle was preparing to sail to Australia, Gardner went to Cottingley with two Cameo cameras and twenty-four secretly marked photographic plates. The weather was uncongenial for three weeks, but on August 19 Frances and Elsie returned from the woods with two more pictures that appeared to show fairies. A third and final shot, of the diaphanously clad sprites fluttering about the undergrowth, followed two days later. Looking at the first four of the five images today, the central subjects appear to be statically posed and, as Oliver Lodge remarked, "rather too Parisiene" in their clothing and hairstyle than might be expected of such free spirits. However, when Gardner saw the "indisputable" results he sent an ecstatic letter to Conan Doyle, who was by then lecturing in Melbourne. "My heart was gladdened," Doyle wrote back. "When our fairies are admitted other psychic phenomena will find a more ready acceptance . . . We have had continued messages at séances for some time that a visible sign was coming through."

The reaction to Conan Doyle's *Strand* article was mixed. The Sydney newspaper *Truth* expressed a widely held view when, on January 5, 1921, it wrote, "For the real explanation of these fairy photographs what is wanted is not a knowledge of occult phenomena but a knowledge of children." Even that was mild compared to some of the popular jokes that made the rounds, including the one where Doyle was said to have appeared at the climax of his friend Barrie's *Peter Pan* in order to lead the audience in a chorus of "I do believe in fairies!" Other wisecracks were less elevated. It was a credit to Doyle's tenacity that he persevered in his beliefs even when much of the Spiritualist world took issue with him. In March 1922, he published his full-length book *The Coming of the Fairies,* which laid out the story of the photographs, their supposed provenance, and his conclusions about this "subhuman" and "miraculous" life form. It remains his most notorious literary act, not excluding his killing of Sherlock Holmes. In 1983, the then elderly cousins admitted in an article published in the magazine *The Unexplained* that the first four of their pictures had been faked. The girls had cut out illustrations from *Princess Mary's Gift Book,* a 1914 annual (in which Conan Doyle himself had published a story) and propped them up with hat pins to the grassy banks of the stream that ran behind the Wrights' home. Some discrepancy existed, however, about the fifth and final photograph. Elsie maintained it was a fake, just like all the others, but Frances insisted that it was genuine: "I saw these fairies building up in the grasses, and just aimed the camera and took a shot," she said. Prints of the pictures and a first edition of Conan Doyle's book were sold at auction in London for £21,620 in 1997. The "freely adapted" plot of that same year's film *Fairy Tale: A True Story,* showing both Conan Doyle and Houdini tramping around the Wrights' home in Cottingley, truly belongs in fairyland. It's arguable that Doyle's reputation never quite recovered from the original controversy. As Houdini privately noted, "the authority of an evangelist such as [Doyle] is like that of a trainer in a wild-animal act. His mastery depends on never being challenged, [and even if] he survives an assault, his aura of invincibility is gone forever."

Statistically, the Spiritualist movement in Britain continued to steadily gain ground during the post-war decade. According to *The Times,* in late 1920 there were 315 churches formally affiliated to the Spiritualists' National Union, and upward of 800 "individual cells or lodges" catering to the faithful, who were "fast acquir[ing] political influence and might soon hope to wipe out the laws which cramp them in the exercise of their gift"—notably the 1604 Witchcraft Act, which had been reactivated in 1916 after a 300-odd-year lull in order to prosecute mediums like Annie Brittain. The movement was regularly able to pack speaking halls throughout Britain; there were an estimated 640 commercially published Spiritualist books or periodicals in 1920 (up from a total of 27 a decade earlier); and a strenuous nationwide membership drive offered not only the promise of "irrefutably proving man's immortality," as Conan Doyle put it, but also the more secular lure of country-house retreats, open forums, picnics and dances, and muscular good fellowship for the young. Across the Atlantic, where Spiritualists established several self-contained camps that shared some of the broad characteristics of the hippie communes of the 1960s, the movement enjoyed a growing support, and even respectability, due in part to the stated or alleged posthumous interest of men like Abraham Lincoln, Theodore Roosevelt, Woodrow Wilson, and the not much less exalted Houdini. Reporting on a Spiritualist convention at the Waldorf-Astoria hotel in June 1921, the *New York Times* noted, "Whether or not one believes, almost everyone [now takes it] seriously . . . John Slater, the famous medium, who for more than forty years has been giving exhibitions to amazed audiences, made hundreds gasp at sessions at the Waldorf-Astoria by the readiness of his apparent communion with scores and scores of spirits. He performed before a large audience which filled the grand ballroom and made an appearance in matters of dress, behavior, shape of the skull and general characteristics comparing favorably with the average New York audience. Many of the city's most elite and materially well-set citizens were in attendance. Slater was annoyed, however, at the high proportion of silly questions which he said they propounded."

As the movement as a whole grew, so too did attacks on it. Much of the criticism was focused on what Britain's *Daily Herald* called "the half-dozen best known messiahs" of the New Revelation, Conan Doyle prominent among them. "Wherever I go," Doyle remarked, "there are two great types of critics. One is the materialistic gentleman who insists on the right to eternal nothingness. The other is the gentleman with such a deep respect for the Bible that he has never looked into it." It seems possible that Doyle's growing sense of embattlement extended to a press that, up to the fairies episode, had been generally friendly, and a basic contributor to his success. The *Daily Express*, for example, was left to rue that "such a titanic figure [could be] so easily led," while the American wit H. L. Mencken went so far as to call Doyle "an almost fabulous ass." Not untypical of the orthodox ecclesiastical view were the remarks of the Rev. Arnold Pinchard, Secretary of the English Church Union, who in July 1920 wrote to inform Doyle, "You probably do not realise that I speak as a Catholic and that Catholics have certain knowledge upon [spiritual] matters which others like yourselves, more in an atmosphere of doubtful empiricism, lack." Some of his correspondents took a more robust tone than this. Conan Doyle was to remark of one telephone conversation with the perhaps well-named Lord Dunraven (author of an unpublished diary of Spiritualist experiences) that "he was so furious I had to hold the instrument away from my ear." Doyle's primary tactic with his opponents, as with most people he met, was to employ a combination of charm and occasional gentle satire. Though not in Houdini's class as a self-advertiser, nor was he shy of his position. "With all modesty, I am inclined to ask is there any man on this globe who is doing as much psychic research as I?" he later wrote. Why should a Spiritualist heed the words of irresponsible journalists or skeptical scientists, he added, when he had all the proof he wanted? Such critics were "babies in this matter, and should be sitting at his feet."

When Conan Doyle arrived in Australia in September 1920 (having assembled his children on the voyage to explain the purpose of their visit, and assure them, "There is no death"), he found that a group of Presbyterian vicars and their congregations had been praying to prevent him speaking there. Doyle then tactlessly referred to his first port of call, Melbourne, as a "spiritually dead" place in an article that appeared while he was still in the city. A fulsome apology helped quell local dissent for a while, and also to undercut critics demanding that the sixty-one-year-old author be deported, as his "off-the-cuff remarks and writings" represented a threat to Australian morals. The more formal part of the tour was generally a success. Conan Doyle spoke to capacity crowds throughout Australia and New Zealand, and retained his good humor even when confronted on the Christchurch stage by a woman and her allegedly psychic poodle, which eventually failed in a lengthy trial of its telepathic powers. Doyle remarked politely that the dog "clearly had these skills, though age and excitement have now impaired them." He was also to comment favorably on an Australian "manifesting" medium—a "little, ginger-coloured man" named Bailey—who at one séance was able to produce a bird's nest containing a large speckled egg, two baby turtles swimming in a bowl, and fifty-six antique Turkish coins. "The results were far above all possible fraud," Conan Doyle wrote. He later said that he and his family had enjoyed consistent "preternatural help" throughout their travels, though this was unable to prevent an Australian shipping strike that led to the cancellation of the Tasmanian leg of the tour.

On December 30, 1920, as Conan Doyle was returning for a second visit to Melbourne, his mother died at her cottage near West Grinstead in Sussex. She was eighty-three. Although the relationship with her elder son had been a long and warmly affectionate one, the Mam had never quite reconciled to Arthur's psychic beliefs, if only because of the damage she rightly worried they would do to his reputation. Right from the time when she first pleaded for Sherlock Holmes's life in 1891, she had shown a greater concern for her son's popularity with the wider reading public than he had. (As it turned out, Mary's death came in the same month that *The Strand* published Conan Doyle's original article on the Cottingley Fairies.) "For my psychic work she had, I fear, neither sympathy nor understanding," Doyle acknowledged, "but she had an innate faith and spirituality which were so natural to her that she could not conceive the needs of others in that direction. She understands now."

Among the letters awaiting Conan Doyle on his return to Windlesham was one from Houdini, dated March 28, 1921, that reopened their exchange about William and Ira Davenport. Doyle was, if possible, even more convinced about the pair's dematerializing powers. Having visited William's grave in Sydney, he was impressed that Ira had gone to the trouble of engraving an image of a cabinet and ropes on his brother's headstone—evidence, surely, that "their act [was] Spiritual and not a trick." Occasionally, however, Conan Doyle and Houdini seemed to undergo a sort of role-reversal on Spiritualism. Later in the year, the illusionist wrote an excited letter enclosing a photograph that purported to show "something unknown or occult" oozing from a young actress as she embraced Houdini on the set of his latest film. Conan Doyle was unmoved. "The effect is certainly produced by the whisk of the lady's dress as she rushed into your arms," he wrote. "It is certainly not ectoplasm!" A subsequent packet of photographs taken at a Los Angeles séance struck Doyle as similarly "hollow" and "very unconvincing . . . The faces seemed quite absurd."

In September 1920, Houdini had published an article called "Why I am a Skeptic," which concluded that his experiences with British mediums "leave me further than ever from a belief in the genuineness of the manifestations." Most men mature around a central core; Houdini had several. This perhaps explains why only weeks after announcing his doubts about communicating with the dead, he published a promotional booklet for his film *The Man from Beyond* promising, "Audiences everywhere [will] welcome it as evidence that loved ones gone to their Maker are not lost to us here on earth." The same film shows an uneasy mix of swashbuckling thrills and spiritual uplift. Houdini's limited but physically robust acting style carries the first, action-packed half of the story, which otherwise makes the same point—the one about man's surviving the grave—over and over. Some scenes exist only so that this point can be made. Again. When the film was released in April 1922, Houdini gave a public lecture at the Times Square Theater in New York in which he declared that those who believed in Spiritualism were as "good and earnest as anyone else," and that this was a subject "on which I shall concentrate my energies for the rest of my days." In one of those sudden reversals that constitute the basic fabric of Houdini's life, he was back at the same venue just two days later to screen his film, following which he bounded on stage to treat the audience to a "dazzling" hour of escapes and magic tricks, including making an elephant disappear.

Jean Conan Doyle, meanwhile, had recently discovered that she, too, possessed mediumistic powers, with a marked gift for automatic writing. Jean was soon able to channel the spirit of her late mother-in-law. "I ought to have trusted your judgement, my own son," one of the early notes read. Willie Hornung, who died in March 1921, similarly "came through" to offer apologies for having ever doubted Doyle when alive. To produce the messages, Jean herself merely sat poised over a sheaf of paper on a table, and the unseen agency pushed the pencil in her hand over the pages, often at furious speed. Houdini was also corresponding throughout, often to ask for an opinion on a particular séance or medium. "Eglinton was a great man," Doyle wrote of an English clairvoyant popular in the 1890s, "and was long above suspicion. Then one or two cases arose—his power may have declined—which were suspicious. Finally, he married money, forswore the occult, and now lives somewhere up the Thames, and is, I hear, the owner of a rich collection of Oriental bric-à-brac." A lively exchange followed on Daniel Dunglas Home, a Scottish mystic with the reported ability to levitate. In 1868, Home was said to have floated out of the top-story window of one room, and back in through the window of the adjoining room in front of three witnesses. Houdini appears to have kept any doubts he may have had on the subject to himself, just as he never publicly mentioned the Cottingley episode. For his part, Conan Doyle continued to insist, "None of the facts [of Cottingley] have been controverted," and there was "no doubt at all" that the photographs were genuine. On Christmas Day 1921, Doyle entertained a small group at Windlesham by reading out messages from "absent friends." Among the well-wishers, he announced, was the King of the Fairies, who sent "festive good cheer" to all and sundry.

Such "idle fantasy and reveries," as Houdini called them (perhaps missing the humor), were not areas in which he put much stock, any more than self-effacement. Houdini's ambition never slept: even when not performing on stage or screen, he was hard at work writing his magnum opus *Miracle Mongers and Their Methods,* a book he engagingly subtitled *A Complete Exposé of the Modus Operandi of Fire Eaters, Heat Resisters, Venomous Reptile Defiers, Sword Swallowers, Human Ostriches, Strong Men, Etc.* Holing up in the library of his New York brownstone, he spent most of the winter of 1920–21 trying to synthesize a lifetime's experience of the subject into a dozen short chapters. The task would take concentration, he rather brusquely told Bess. She was thus not to disturb or talk to him unless necessary. Trying hard to obey, she dutifully slid trays of snacks inside the door of the room as he wrote.

Later research has shown the autobiographical framework of *Miracle Mongers* to be unreliable. As a necessary next step in mythologizing himself, Houdini had to dramatize his somewhat feckless and desperate early years into a period of diligent professional research and self-education, out of which came his "frankly unrivalled knowledge [and] insights" into the morally shady world of early-twentieth-century vaudeville. The book was a critical and popular success. After praising Houdini's "unsparing exposure of miracle-mongers who claim to be endowed with mysterious powers," the *New York Times* suggested he might profitably turn his attention to "mediumistic frauds," a thought that had already occurred to the author.

Given his fractured command of English and lifelong unease with the written word when compared to the spoken, it's fair to ask whether Houdini possibly enjoyed some uncredited help when it came to producing his book. Could a line such as "The cage of fire has been employed by a number of Rivalli's followers also, and the reader will find a full explanation of the methods employed therein in the chapter devoted to the Arcana of the Fire-eaters, to which we shall come back when we have recorded the work of the master Chabert, the history of some of the heat-resisters featured on magicians' programmes, particularly in our own day, and the interest taken in their art by performers whose chief distinction was won in other fields, as notably Edwin Forrest and the elder Sothern," set in the context of a scholarly account of human salamanders from Greek mythology to the present day, betray the hand of a ghost writer? It's known that in July 1920 Houdini engaged a full-time librarian named Alfred Becks, a "well-bred, courteous Englishman," as he described him, who had served as literary secretary to the Irish dramatist Dion Boucicault. The seventy-five-year-old Becks may have done more than merely type up the successive pages of *Miracle Mongers* as Houdini paced up and down dictating them. Much of the time, however, both men were kept busy cataloging an impressive if chaotic in-house archive. Becks eventually brought some order to bear on a core collection of "18 to 20 thousand" magic books, newspapers, articles, playbills, and autographs crammed into the upper floors of the house. "They seemed to be imprisoned there as in a dungeon," a visitor said of the overflowing boxes of material. "They lined the walls on all sides, pressing against one another for elbow-room and well-nigh touching the ceiling." Becks's only professional regret was that Houdini had "killed" the most precious volumes by his habit of rubber-stamping his name on them.

Houdini's literary ambitions conveyed, in an oddly vulnerable way, a great need to be liked. He cared deeply about the intellectual respect of those he admired. Sending out no fewer than 400 review copies of *Miracle Mongers* was part of this lifelong bid for acceptance by what he called, without irony, "newspapermen, critics and other sages." What struck many people as deceitfulness was often a result of Houdini's attempts to win approval from opposing groups; in "The Houdini Wonder Show of 1922," for example, he would try to convince the Spiritualists among the audience that at heart he was one of them, while simultaneously putting on a demonstration to expose the "so-called soothsayers and clairvoyants" whom he saw as shamelessly fleecing the public. Houdini would go out of his way to curry favor with Conan Doyle and his circle after the author first mildly questioned his sincerity—while at the same time making disparaging comments to his circus-performer friends about the "overeducated [and] credulous boobs" prominent in Spiritualist ranks. Toward the end of his life, Becks, generally an admirer of Houdini, referred to this trait as "his immigrant's desire for approval."

୫୨   ୧୬

Even as Conan Doyle was establishing his reputation as an intrepid psychic researcher, he was becoming the butt of the mild ridicule tinged with regret skeptics showed him throughout his later career. Undaunted by public reaction to the Cottingley Fairies, he now threw himself into the world of spirit photography. Doyle was to take a keen technical interest in the practicalities of capturing a ghost on film, and soon showed an almost Holmes-like obsession in cataloging the various chemicals and dyes—such as the coal-tar derivative dicyanin—

needed to coat the glass plate required for a successful outcome. He had become convinced that there was something to the business of "extras," or ghostly auras, appearing on film after the Crewe photographer William Hope showed him a picture of his son Kingsley that he said came from the beyond. When Hope went on to announce the event, the public had beaten a path to his door ("I am in some demand," Hope noted when declining to meet Houdini in December 1921) to get pictures of their dead loved ones. Doyle was so impressed by the whole process that he agreed to become a vice-president of the Birmingham-based Society for the Study of Supernormal Pictures. It was thus something of a further blow to his reputation when, in February 1922, Houdini's friend Harry Price and a fellow investigator for the Society for Psychical Research seemed to show that Hope produced his results not by "spectral manifestation," as he claimed, but by loading his camera with a plate already prepared with the desired image of a Kingsley Conan Doyle, or whomever the sitter had in mind. When Hope then developed the film, the "extra" would be seen apparently floating in the background. "In this case," Price wrote in the *Journal* of the SPR, "it can, we think, hardly be denied that Mr Hope has been found guilty of deliberately substituting his own plates [for] fraudulent purposes." Conan Doyle refused to be swayed, however, and shot back in a self-published pamphlet that it was Price, and not Hope, who had been guilty of malpractice. "The Hope case is more intricate than any Holmes case I ever invented," Doyle wrote to Houdini in October 1922. "I am sure now that there was trickery [by] the investigators," he insisted, laying out an elaborate tale of espionage and mass conspiracy on the part of the SPR. Houdini, while seemingly sympathetic, immediately wrote to Price to ask whether he had "any reason at all to think that [Hope] was framed," and subsequently devoted several pages of *A Magician among the Spirits* to a largely negative review of the photographer. Conan Doyle went on to endorse many more spirit images, including one taken on Remembrance Sunday that seemed to show the ghostly features of dozens of dead British soldiers looming above the crowd observing the annual two minutes' silence at the London Cenotaph. It was later established that several of the faces were those of professional soccer players torn out of a fan magazine. Doyle's relations with the SPR arguably never quite recovered from their difference of opinion over spirit photography. He spent some years intermittently calling for the Society to censure Price, and later consulted lawyers about the possibility of having him evicted from the room he rented from the London Spiritualist Alliance, of which Doyle was then president. Price wrote in his 1936 memoir *Confessions of a Ghost Hunter,* "Arthur Conan Doyle and his friends abused me for years for exposing Hope," though eventually modifying his opinion to call Doyle "a giant in stature with the heart of a child." Some time later, Price was back in the headlines for testifying against the medium Helen Duncan in her trial for offenses under the Witchcraft Act. Price concluded that Duncan's alleged ectoplasm was no more than regurgitated egg white wrapped in cheesecloth. He died of a heart attack—the result, some said, of a curse placed on him by aggrieved mediums—in 1948, aged sixty-seven.

In the spring of 1921, Conan Doyle began to regularly attend some five or six séances a week at Windlesham, often under his wife's mediumship. His persistence soon bore tangible results. "I have had some great psychic experiences since Australia," he wrote to Houdini. "In a fair light I saw my dead mother, as clearly as ever I saw her in life. I am a cool observer and don't make mistakes." Mary Doyle's spirit continued to assure her son that she and several other of his late relatives approved of his Spiritualist work. In time, Doyle would communicate with many of his intimate family circle, with the notable exception of Touie, his first wife, who seems not to have come through once in fourteen years of séances.

Each time a letter arrived from Conan Doyle, Houdini would have Alfred Becks file it in a special, satin-lined box kept for the purpose. He would "sit back and beam with pride, as if it were his most prized possession," Becks recalled. Whenever a newspaperman called and the interview, as it generally did, touched on literary matters, Houdini would conclude the conversation by inviting the man up to his attic study and announcing, "I think you'll be interested in what my friend the world's greatest author has to say about that."

Such was Houdini's initial attitude to Conan Doyle: pleasure, perhaps a bit of possessiveness, mixed with the sort of ambivalent pride a backward boy might feel when he finds himself showing off a trophy that makes other people respect him. For his part, Doyle evidently still hoped to make a Spiritualist convert of Houdini, while increasingly coming to acknowledge that the professional illusionist sometimes concealed his feelings with a skill in dissimulation "which was his second nature." "You are to me a perpetual mystery," he wrote to Houdini in January 1922. After again rehearsing the saga of the Davenports and their spirit cabinet, Conan Doyle was left to conclude the letter by adding that Houdini seemed to want to appear as the star witness for both the prosecution and the defense of the brothers' psychic powers. "Now how can one reconcile that?" Doyle asked. "It interests me as a problem."

On the frosty morning of March 19, 1922, New Yorkers might have read on the back pages of the paper or heard at the tail end of a bulletin on the radio the news that their hometown's star baseball player, the twenty-seven-year-old "Babe" Ruth (who, the previous season, had inadvertently caused a fan to die of excitement when he saw Ruth smash a ball out of the park), had signed a new three-year contract at an astronomic $45,000 per year. Meanwhile, Ruth's club, the New York Yankees, was spending a barely credible $2.4 million to build him and his teammates a new stadium. Moving backward through the middle part of the papers, column after column shouted the news of nationwide strikes and anti-Bolshevist riots, which had just seen the patriotic citizens of Centralia, Washington, remove from jail a member of the Industrial Workers of the World (the so-called "Wobblies") and lynch him by tying a rope around his neck and throwing him off a bridge; or noted that President Harding had cited as dangerous evidence of radicalism in women's education the fact that the debating society at the all-female Radcliffe College had moved a resolution in support of labor unions, and gone on to express similar reservations about the recently passed Nineteenth Amendment, giving women the right to vote. Along with its innovations in fashion and music, and prohibition of alcohol, it was an era of violent and sometimes murderous defense of law and order, of suspicion and civil conflict—as the historian Frederick Lewis Allen writes, "in a very literal sense, a reign of terror."

On that same March morning, however, the *New York Times* published a prominent story that seemingly had nothing to do with sport, feminism, or the nation's troubled industrial relations. The bold print headline read "CONAN DOYLE TO TELL OF LIFE AFTER DEATH," and went on to report, "The brilliant mystery [writer] is coming to this country for a brief tour to deliver a series of lectures dealing with his investigations of the paranormal." Doyle had "attracted widespread interest by his pronouncements concerning psychical research," the *Times* noted. Like Sir Oliver Lodge and others, "he has become convinced that communication with another plane of existence can be absolutely proved. In agreement with them, he contends that science can no longer afford to ignore occult phenomena . . . Sir Arthur has summed up his views on the subject of spirit communication as follows: 'I was a materialist at one time, and would be one today if it were not for the overwhelming proof of a future existence which has come to me personally. In addition to the evidence put forth by various great leaders of thought, I have spoken face to face with eleven relatives and friends, discussing intimate matters known only to ourselves.'"

Houdini, who saved and copiously underlined the article for his files, had already written to invite Conan Doyle and his family to stay with him during their visit at his New York townhouse. This would not be possible, Doyle replied, as he had to remain "semi-public for my job's sake . . . But I want to see your psychic library and I want still more to see you," he added. For similar reasons, Doyle initially resisted Houdini's latest request that he find time to speak to the Society of American Magicians. "I shall not be available for any meetings until my book is done," he wrote back. "But I shall always be ready to see you."

Conan Doyle and his party left for New York on April 2, 1922, aboard the White Star liner *Baltic*. On the eve of sailing, Houdini sent him a wire: "*Good luck. Best wishes.*" On arrival a week later, Doyle was greeted by the detective William J. Burns—the self-styled "Sherlock Holmes of America"—and an animated crowd of some eighty to one hundred reporters and photographers. Bowing to the inevitable, he agreed to hold an impromptu press conference at the quayside. "I know absolutely what I am going to get after death—happiness," the *New York Times* quoted Doyle as saying. "It is not mere hearsay," he continued. "I have talked with and seen twenty [*sic*] of my dead, including my son, when my wife and other witnesses were present . . . Spiritualism is the one great final antidote to materialism, which is the cause of most of our recent troubles." Taking a less elevated tone, some of the reporters wanted to know whether the spirits could tell fortunes or predict the movements of the Stock Market, and if they had access to sex, alcohol, and cigars in the afterlife. Doyle replied with a convoluted hypothesis suggesting that "certain familiar pleasures" would indeed be available—though he made clear his own moral distaste for liquor—and that "Only the ones we love on this earth [will] be able to meet us in the beyond . . . People who have led selfish, hard lives here will enter that place on a lower plane and gradually descend instead of going higher and higher until the spirit of Christ is reached." Synthesizing these remarks for its readers, the next morning's headline in the *New York World* read: "DOYLE SAYS MARITAL RELATIONS OK IN NEXT WORLD. REAFFIRMS BELIEF IN HELL."

Three days later, Conan Doyle opened his lecture tour with a sold-out performance at New York's 3,500-seat Carnegie Hall. Houdini reportedly sat unrecognized in the back row, did not go backstage, and had nothing public to say about the event afterward. He did, however, promptly open a press-cuttings file in which he eventually collected and annotated over 300 items pertaining to "ACD's American Mission 1922." The illusionist also kept his counsel when he read that Doyle had gone on from Carnegie Hall to attend a séance with an illiterate twenty-three-year-old medium named Nino Pecoraro. After being tied to a chair and placed in a locked cabinet, Pecoraro was able to produce some of the same general effects as the Davenport brothers before him. While Doyle and the other sitters broke into a lusty rendition of "Onward, Christian Soldiers," a counterpoint of high-pitched screams, interspersed with several groans and howls, issued from the cabinet, while a tambourine on the séance table rose up and flew through the air. A warbling voice purporting to be that of the late medium Eusapia Palladino then introduced herself. "I, who used to summon the spirits," she said, speaking through Pecoraro in his cabinet, "now return as one myself." Conan Doyle was apparently satisfied this "startlingly full range" of phenomena, including the channeling of one medium by another, was entirely genuine. "The power is getting stronger, Palladino," he is said to have remarked. "We send you our love and our best encouragement."

Conan Doyle, who was exhausted from his voyage and subsequent events and thus perhaps not at his most astute, continued to believe in the innocence of this "poor Neapolitan lad," much as he had in that of the young cousins at Cottingley. Others demurred. In December 1923, Houdini agreed to help judge a contest sponsored by *Scientific American* magazine to determine if Pecoraro, or any other medium, could exhibit "conclusive psychic manifestations" under test conditions. A prize of up to $5,000 was offered. When it came time for the test, Houdini spent an hour and forty-five minutes tying Pecoraro up. After that, "there were no manifestations," Houdini noted, "with the exception of raps which he managed to make by striking his foot on the side of the cabinet . . . They asked me to rope him up so that he could not move—and he stayed put. Personally, I believe the man is mad and thinks the 'spirits' help him."

On April 30, 1922, Conan Doyle was lecturing in Washington, DC, where he took the opportunity to visit Julius and Ada Zancig, a husband-and-wife sometime vaudeville team who now advertised themselves as "astrologers, tea leaf readers, crystal ball seers, diviners and palmists." As a result of this sitting, Conan Doyle became convinced the couple possessed telepathic powers (although he subsequently modified his view of them). "No word passed at all," Doyle wrote to Houdini, "but Mrs Zancig, standing with her face turned sideways at the far end of the room, was able to repeat names and to duplicate drawings which we made and showed to her husband . . . Possibly it is a real ectoplasmic formation, like the figures of Eva." He went on to affirm his belief in a public letter of endorsement. "I have tested Professor and Mrs Zancig," Doyle wrote, "and I am quite sure that their remarkable performance, as I saw it, is due to psychic causes (through transference) and not to trickery."

Again, Houdini demurred. Having often worked on the same vaudeville stage as Julius Zancig and his previous partner, he wrote in *A Magician among the Spirits* that they struck him as "doing a very clever performance. I had ample opportunity to watch [their] system and codes. They are swift, sure, and silent, and I give [them] credit for being exceptionally adept in their chosen line of mystery. Telepathy does not enter into it." After the first Mrs. Zancig had died, Houdini noted, Julius "took a street-car conductor from Philadelphia and broke him in to the team." Some acrimony had arisen when the young man later defected from Zancig and began offering his own mind-reading routine, using a trained monkey as a foil. He was replaced by a magician known professionally as "Syko the Psychic," who in turn left the act. "At that stage, Professor Zancig came to me for an assistant and I introduced him to an actress," Houdini wrote. "He said he would guarantee to teach her the code inside of a month, but they never came to an agreement on financial matters." In 1917, Julius Zancig married Ada, a Brooklyn schoolteacher, and they continued to perform together until his death in 1929.

ക്ക   ൧൹

On May 9, 1922, Conan Doyle was back at Carnegie Hall to lecture on Spiritualism. He illustrated the performance by projecting a series of "spirit photographs," many of them supplied by William Hope in Crewe. There were gasps in the hall when Doyle showed a picture of W. T. Stead, the journalist who had perished on the *Titanic,* that he said was obtained by psychic means. "It was a very clear portrait of a man," the *New York Times* wrote, "and around the outside was scribbled, in handwriting which Sir Arthur said was undoubtedly Stead's, these words: 'I will try to keep you posted.'"

At 11:00 the next morning, Conan Doyle and his wife took a taxi from the Ambassador Hotel to Houdini's house on West 113th Street in Harlem. The two men briefly posed for a photograph at the front door, once again allowing the press to comment on their physical contrast; side by side, they looked "uncannily like the Lord Kitchener of the 'Your Country Needs You' poster in conversation with a jockey," one journalist wrote. Passing through a long, darkly furnished hallway, the party paused to admire the trophy cabinets containing Houdini's many souvenirs and awards, culminating in a large bronze bust of the illusionist himself. In the chandeliered living room, Conan Doyle proposed an eloquent toast to the couples' friendship, and Jean was to compliment the Houdinis that theirs was the "most home-like home" she had ever seen. Houdini himself took undisguised pride in showing Conan Doyle around his extensive library. At one point, he turned to his guest and remarked that they were both "in the business of the printed word." Houdini returned to the theme over lunch when, untypically fortified by a glass of wine, he leaned toward Doyle and commented that what united them was "very much greater" than what divided them. Any minor differences of opinion, he averred, were now surely in the past.

For once the subtle Houdini touch failed him. Their real issues were just beginning.

5

"SAUL AMONG THE PROPHETS"

In other circumstances, Houdini might have gotten along well with Conan Doyle, being innately well-disposed to artistic figures whom he considered distinguished but unthreatening. In dealing with Hollywood titans like Charlie Chaplin or a range of popular authors from Rudyard Kipling to Jack London, Houdini could ooze charm. The exceptions were those who seemed to him to have knowingly or otherwise made their mark by "taking the work of others before them, or faking it up altogether, and offering it to the public as a new revelation," such as Robert-Houdin in the world of magic. Or Conan Doyle in Spiritualism.

Even as Houdini was clinking glasses with his guest at the lunch table that day, he was planning to give him an object lesson in how easy it was to confuse a mere conjuring trick for a psychic manifestation. After some talk about the phenomenon of "spirit hands"—to Doyle, an irrefutably "miraculous" feat of Spiritualistic intrusion on the material world, and to Houdini a cheap ruse involving some paraffin and a rubber glove—the two men and Houdini's lawyer, Bernard Ernst, again retired upstairs to the library. As Ernst remembered it:

> Houdini produced what appeared to be an ordinary slate, some eighteen inches
> long by fifteen inches high. In two corners of this slate, holes had been bored,
> and through these holes wires had been passed. These wires were several feet in
> length, and hooks had been fastened to the other ends of the wires. The only

other accessories were four small cork balls, a large ink-well filled with white ink, and a table-spoon.

Houdini passed the slate to Sir Arthur for examination. He was then requested to suspend the slate in the middle of the room, by means of the wires and hooks, leaving it free to swing in space, several feet distant from anything . . . The slate was inspected and cleaned.

Houdini now invited Sir Arthur to examine the four cork balls in the saucer. He was told to select any one he liked, and, to show that they were free from preparation, to cut it in two with his knife, thus verifying the fact that they were merely solid cork balls. This was accordingly done. Another ball was then selected, and, by means of the spoon, was placed in the white ink, where it was thoroughly stirred round and round, until its surface was equally coated with the liquid. It was left in the ink to soak up as much of it as possible.

Houdini then asked Conan Doyle to walk out of the house, in any direction he chose, to pause when he was sure he was unobserved, write a phrase on a scrap of paper, put this in his pocket, and return to the house. Doyle did so. Back in the library, Houdini told his guest to fish out the ink-soaked ball and hold it up to the slate hanging in the middle of the room. As Doyle did so, the ball suddenly began to move across the slate, seemingly of its own free will, forming a series of words as it went. When the ball had finished, it just as suddenly dropped to the floor. With his innate sense of showmanship, Houdini then asked Conan Doyle to read out the message on the slate, even though he and Ernst could both plainly see it for themselves. It was the biblical portent of doom, "*Mene, mene, tekel, upharsin*"—the exact line Conan Doyle had written down and put in his pocket.

Neither Doyle nor Ernst could fathom this mystery, which the former was certain had been "contrived by psychic means," and Ernst thought was like a telepathy act Houdini had once done on stage, but later abandoned because it was "too spooky." In any case, both men were stunned. Houdini would remark only that it was "as marvellous a demonstration as you have ever witnessed," but that "I can assure you it was accomplished by trickery and nothing else." As Houdini had purchased the slate and balls from a vaudeville entertainer named Max Berol, they might have been well advised to take him at his word. (Berol's own long-running version of the effect had involved, among other things, a fast exchange of a solid cork ball for one with an iron core, and a strategically placed assistant holding a magnet at the end of a rod.) Nor was the day's entertainment quite over. Houdini was later to remark that his guest had been "flabberghasted" by a "lark" he showed him in the taxi as he accompanied the Conan Doyles back to the Ambassador Hotel. To pass the time at a red light, the illusionist held up his hands, apparently removed the end of his own thumb, and then reattached it. Lady Doyle "nearly fainted," Houdini remarked with some satisfaction. "Never having been taught the artifices of conjuring," he noted of his day with Conan Doyle, "it was the simplest thing in the world for anyone to gain his confidence to hoodwink him."

Over the next six weeks, Conan Doyle was, even so, to hold several large and socially diverse American audiences spellbound with a simple statement of his Spiritualist beliefs that was well delivered, without pathos, and judiciously weighted by William Hope's photographs. "The pictures were of every kind," the *New York Times* wrote of his third sold-out night at Carnegie Hall, "of men, women and children, of landscapes and birds. One was of Sir Arthur's own son, made after he had taken precautions to guard against fraud. Others were of relatives of some of his friends, of men killed in the war, one showing the bullet hole in the temple." In speeches that often lasted two hours or more, Conan Doyle did not make the mistake of haranguing his listeners all the time. He could make them laugh with his mimicry and won their applause by the quick-wittedness with which he answered hecklers. Above all, he seemed like an "eminently sane" and "downright person," according to the *New York Times*. "Sir Arthur does not look like a man who could be easily stampeded. All that solid, suspicious shrewdness is with him. His audience was profoundly attentive. Evidently it was a throng which had its dead."

It would be fair to say that the crowds came to listen to Conan Doyle less for the contents of his speeches, which for the most part consisted of a compact history of the Spiritualist and psychic crusade from the Fox sisters to the present, than for the gift he had of presenting them with a force none of his rivals could equal. The mood of respectful attention in the hall soon gave way to one of near hysteria when Doyle, pointer stick in hand, projected his spirit photographs onto a screen. As well as his own lost relatives and other individuals, these showed several instances of ectoplasm having built up into a human face—"a weird apparition," Doyle agreed, over the gasps, that was "undoubtedly the material projected in quantities from the body of the medium, so much of it that she frequently loses 20 pounds at a sitting." Anyone familiar with the 2006 film *The Illusionist*, with its scenes of audience frenzy when in the presence of paranormal stage phenomena, has only to think of that same charged atmosphere, further inflamed by the rabidly competitive postwar American press, to get some of the flavor. A series of graphic illustrations of ectoplasm seeping from the body of "Eva C." proved so potent at one performance that the wife of New York's mayor vomited at the sight, and several other women had to be helped from the hall. From there, the visual shocks kept coming. Conan Doyle told the story of Kitty King, the 200-year-old spirit apparently summoned by the pioneering Victorian chemist Sir William Crookes. "I will now show you the most remarkable picture in the world," Doyle announced provocatively. "It shows Sir William, at the height of his fame, arm in arm with an angel." An image flashed up of an elderly gentleman apparently in the embrace of a beatifically smiling teen-aged girl in a diaphanous gown. When the applause had died down, Doyle went on to explain that he had "seen things in crystals, also," and he showed a picture seemingly of a crystal ball with the face of a child "so lovely and gentle," one reporter wrote, "that, after a moment's awe, the audience again began to applaud and cheer wildly." Conan Doyle brought the show to a close by stepping forward between two large potted palms on either side of the stage and raising his hand in a quieting gesture. "Now I will show you a picture of a ghost," he announced simply. "A woman was taking a picture in an old English inn. She exposed the plate sixty seconds, and during that time nobody passed in the corridor. But when she developed the plate apparently something had passed, and she brought it to us in perplexity. It was the image of one of those earthbound spirits called ghosts, a coincidence that might not occur again in 100 years." As the picture was shown, there was a steady crescendo of "mingled cheers and sobs of excitement," the *New York World* reported, although a "few scattered remarks of a skeptical nature" were to be heard from the balcony.

From New York, Conan Doyle traveled to Boston (where he visited Oliver Wendell Holmes's grave), and on to such towns as Rochester, Buffalo, Detroit, and Toledo, Ohio. His three school-age children accompanied him and his wife throughout, and soon attracted their own press following. Doyle told the *New York Times* that Denis, thirteen, Adrian, eleven, and Jean, nine, "were all Spiritualists and happy." They often came with him on his psychic investigations and "kn[ew] more of religion than many Bishops," he added. The family was with him when he told a meeting of the American Psychical Institute and Laboratory, "I expect in the next three or four years some definite messages will be received to prove the contentions of Spiritualists. I believe it [*sic*] will come through radio. I think it is along this line that we will get our evidence. They have transmitters in the line of ether, and all we have to have is the receiver." They were together again in Toledo, where a materializing medium named Ada Bessinet was apparently able to conjure the face of Lady Jean's mother Selina, who had died in 1919, and the voice of Kingsley, the latter of which could be heard through a brass trumpet that the sitters passed between them. At another session with Mrs. Bessinet, Conan Doyle said that he saw his own mother. "I swear by all that's holy on earth," he told an audience at Carnegie Hall, "I looked into her eyes."

In giving the American press a *tour d'horizon* of his Spiritualist beliefs, Conan Doyle had dwelled on his theory that the afterlife consisted not so much of a fixed "heaven" or "hell," but of a series of transitory planes. The highest of these he called "paradise," or "summerland," and the lowest "purgatory." The average stay in one of the lower planes was between thirty and forty years, he concluded, at the end of which a spirit rose to the next level in the sequence. There was no physical pain after death, he remarked. There was, however, both marriage and mental suffering. In particular, those who took their own lives would continue to endure their agonies after the spirit left the body. Death was predestined, Doyle declared, and bringing it on before the stated time "will have no good effect upon the suicide." Evidently these remarks were not read by Frank Alexi, a Brooklyn potter who went home from Conan Doyle's first Carnegie Hall lecture and put an ice pick through his wife's skull, convinced, apparently, she was "a demon," before attempting to end his own life. Some days later, a young New Jersey housewife named Maude Fancher poisoned first her two-year-old son Cecil and then herself after listening to Doyle talk on the radio. In her suicide note, Fancher expressed confidence that her child "will live on [and] see no more troubles or suffering. I am going to guide him and also talk to him. Baby can't talk much but he knows everything, so he will talk over there, in heaven." Despite Conan Doyle's clearly stated views on the subject, the *New York Times* soon connected the murder-suicide to his Spiritualist mission, and wrote an editorial rebuke under the headline "She Could Quote Sir Arthur." It was the first discordant note in what had hitherto been a largely effusive press response to the tour.

As well as the secular criticism, Conan Doyle would come to face a stinging backlash from several religious organizations. New York's Presbyterian Synod had already complained about his "unfounded and naive view" of the afterlife, and would not let his illustration of this by photographs of spirits and ghosts go unmentioned. A number of clergy went on to use their Easter Day sermons on April 16 as an opportunity to condemn what Bishop Slattery of Grace Episcopal Church on Broadway called the "unwise prophet" in their midst. Opposition to Doyle's Spiritualist message seems to have united New York's ordained ministry to a degree not seen since their universally stout defense of prohibition in 1919–20. At the city's Seventh-Day Adventist Temple, an overflow audience of 672 heard Rev. Carlyle Haynes speak on the theme of "Can the Dead Come Back? An answer to Sir Arthur Conan Doyle." The vicar of the Community Church of New York was compelled to hurriedly move proceedings to the nearby 800-seat Lyric Theatre in order to accommodate a congregation reportedly "seething" for his own views on the subject. Rabbi Lewis Newman, preaching at the Temple Israel on Central Park West, roundly mocked the idea that "the departed ever bring tidings from the grave," a notion that "could only be visualised by a writer of fiction." Much the same story prevailed at the town's principal Roman Catholic and Lutheran churches. At the Episcopalian Cathedral of St. John the Divine, Bishop William Manning seemed to deliver both a spiritual and artistic rebuke. "We say the world is suffering from the war and this is true," he told a seated crowd of 2,200 and 400 more standing in the aisles. "But the cause of the world's suffering lies deeper than this. Our eyes are blinded by a poor and shallow mysticism which robs us of our divine inheritance and which takes from us the vision of God. This is the reason that we have today no great poets or artists or authors among us."

The following week, a lively secular debate broke out at a political dinner held at the Astor hotel. New York's mayor John Hylan (whose wife had reacted poorly to the sight of Conan Doyle's picture of ectoplasm) stood up to remark, "The creator of Sherlock Holmes [is] in a new line of business, and from all reports the shekels are rolling in to him as fast as when he told how easy it was for the famous detective of fiction to get out of tight places . . . Sir Arthur has told us nothing that has not long since been dismissed as 'wool gathering' [but] the lure of the unknown is always fascinating and there will always be a large audience to listen to airy nothings." The tone particularly jarred, because up until then Conan Doyle had been warmly received by New York society and paid homage by her political leaders. William Prendergast, the city's public service commissioner, was appalled by this breach of civic hospitality. "I have always been an admirer of Sir Arthur," he declared, asking that their "embattled" and now "defamed" guest be treated with respect, "even if here on a singular mission." Conan Doyle himself did not seem to suspect an official conspiracy against him so much as to believe that politicians, in some unspecified but herd-like way, mostly thought and acted as one—against him.

The barbs were not limited to the city elders and the clergy. Writing in the *New York Times*, the author Horace Green reminded his readers that Conan Doyle himself had remarked, "Either Spiritualism is the greatest fraud ever practised on the human race or else it is the greatest revelation." In the course of a closely reasoned article, Green tended toward the former of the two possibilities. On May 21, Doyle wrote back in an open letter offering examples where "some merciful angel" had comforted the bereaved by allowing them to speak to their loved ones. They included the time "when General Doyle, my late brother, came back to me in

Wales, the medium being Evan Powell, an amateur. My brother gave me the name of a healer in Copenhagen, Sigurd Trice, whom he wished his widow to consult. I knew of no such person, but he was proved to exist"—a vision for which Doyle saw "no other explanation save the Spiritual." Meanwhile, the Tombs Court in Lower Manhattan became the scene of a well-publicized trial in which four defendants— among them an Alice Moriarty—were accused of disorderly conduct after holding a series of "mystic events" at a small apartment on the Upper West Side. The four were said to have invited sitters into a darkened room, where they would "twang a piano" and "hymn a lusty version of 'Some One is Waiting for Me, I Know,'" while a "ghostly figure" floated around in a "robe or drape of the most sparing cut." It did not go unnoticed in the press that Doyle himself had attended a séance with the defendants, and apparently seen his late mother materialize in front of him. Three days later, undercover officers from New York's 20th Precinct had gone to the room to request a sitting "like that given to Sir Arthur." One of the detectives had subsequently leaped up from his seat and rugby-tackled a "luminous presence" as it passed by him. This was later established in court as being a twenty-nine-year-old housewife, Eva Thompson, clad in a white sheet, a role she was said to have adopted for "many noted clients."

Conan Doyle, it should be said, consistently denounced the commercial efforts of those, like Thompson and her associates, who tried to "pervert psychic knowledge" by any means. "No punishment is too severe for rogues of this kind," he remarked. "The rotten twigs must come off." It should also be said that Doyle showed notable grace in reaching out to several groups of his most vocal critics. "Far from being antagonistic to religion," he told a meeting of New York clergy, "this psychic movement is destined to vivify it. This new knowledge makes it real and sure, and enables one for the first time to understand the actions and views of the early Christians and of their great founder. Without [the] occult, most of the New Testament is incomprehensible. With it one has renewed assurance of its essential truth." There were words of particular comfort for bereaved mothers. "You have nothing to worry about," Conan Doyle told a standing-room audience at the Academy of Music in Brooklyn. "Children indubitably grow and reach manhood and womanhood in the beyond, are much better off than on earth, and will be waiting there for their mothers." In general, it was a hopeful prospect for all but the most "irredemably corrupt" of society. "It is not the narrow path that leads to heaven and the broad path to destruction," he declared, "but just the reverse." In Doyle's view, "For the moment we are all chained to a clumsy mechanism which is adopted for temporary use in this world of matter. [Our] true habitat is the world of ether. Presently matter will fade away from each of us and we will find ourselves where we really belong." He was even willing to discuss Sherlock Holmes, the mere mention of whom had once been enough to bring interviews to a premature conclusion. Noting that Holmes was "surely too old to interest the present generation," Doyle announced plans to create a "completely fresh kind of hero" who would be a worthy successor to the detective. "I will break new ground," he promised.*

Among the "hundred or so" invitations piled up for Conan Doyle by late May on his desk at the Ambassador Hotel was one from Houdini, asking him to be his guest at the annual Society of American Magicians banquet, a gala affair held in the ballroom of the McAlpin hotel "at which you will meet some notable people . . . city officials and big business men." Doyle was not pleased to learn that there would also be an after-dinner show featuring a variety of spirit exposés. "I fear that the bogus Spiritual phenomena must prevent me from attending . . . I look upon this subject as sacred, and I think that God's gift to man has been intercepted and delayed by the constant pretence that all phenomena are really tricks, which I know they are not," he wrote. After some frantic backpedaling by Houdini, Doyle agreed to come after all, albeit with reservations. "I feel towards faked phenomena as your father would have felt towards a faked Pentecost," he remarked.

In the event, it was Conan Doyle who provided the evening's most memorable entertainment. Rising to his feet, he told the audience—which, in addition to Houdini, included a magician named Heller who made playing cards jump invisibly from one pack to another and a pigtailed "oriental mentalist" who read people's minds—that he would show a motion picture that featured "something remarkable. If I brought here in real existence what I show in these images, it would be a great catastrophe . . . The pictures are not occult," he assured the now silent crowd. "But they are psychic, like everything that emanates from the hu-

---

*For all his geniality and obvious belief in the Spiritualist cause, Conan Doyle may not have been above occasionally adapting the truth to fit the needs of his mission. Previewing his "supernatural photograph" of the journalist W. T. Stead at Carnegie Hall, Doyle spoke at some length about his warm friendship with Stead, a "fine and indomitable fellow-fighter" whom he had first met as long ago as 1890. He did not mention that Stead had later gone on to publish two pamphlets roundly attacking the behavior of the British troops in the Boer War, whose appearance Conan Doyle called an "extraordinary outbreak of defamation" of the fighting man. Doyle's 1902 broadside, *The War in South Africa: Its Causes and Conduct,* was the direct result.

man spirit or human brain." Dimming the lights, Doyle then projected a film of what Houdini called "terrifyingly real" prehistoric monsters fighting and mating in a primeval swamp. The action was "presented without titles or speech of any kind, and the audience was left strictly to its own conclusions," said the *New York Times*, "whether the sober-faced Englishman was making merry with them, or was lifting the veil from mysteries penetrated only by those of his school who know the secret of filming elves and ectoplasm and other things unknown to most minds." Conan Doyle again declined to comment following the presentation, and the magicians' dinner ended on an uncharacteristically subdued note. Doyle revealed in a letter to Houdini the next day that "the purpose of [the film] was simply to provide a little mystification for those who have so often and so successfully mystified others . . . The dinosaurs and other monsters [were] constructed by pure cinema art of the highest kind, and are being used for *The Lost World*, a picture which represents prehistoric life upon a South American plateau. Having such material at hand, and being allowed by the courtesy of Mr. Watterson Rothacker to use it, I could not resist the temptation to surprise your associates and guests. I am sure they will forgive me if, for a few short hours, I had them guessing." Houdini seems to have taken a sort of resentful pleasure in this *coup de théâtre*. "There is one thing positive," he was left to reply, "and that is that the little stunt at the banquet created a great deal more newspaper talk than anything on the program."

The competitiveness underscored Houdini's frustrations with Conan Doyle's press profile, which was "the envy of many a poor boy upon the stage." Privately, he turned hostile, demeaning Doyle's "hogwash" encounter with the "Toledo seer" Ada Bessinet. Houdini soon sent his friend the journalist Fulton Oursler to the medium's home, where he reported that the ghostly wailings to be heard in the séance room were produced by a "not very well concealed" gramophone, and that the spirit hand that touched his face was in fact "Mrs Bessinet's breast, and a pretty hefty one at that." Houdini's accelerating campaign against what he called the "spook racket" had mixed press results. On the one hand, he was able to enjoy several headlines praising him, or sometimes a confederate like Oursler, for their role in exposing what Oursler called "rank dime-hall frauds." On the other hand, his efforts to identify himself publicly with a "fearless" and "unstoppable crusade [on behalf of] the little seeker after truth" often appeared self-indulgent. Thrusting himself into the limelight each time a fake medium fell from grace, Houdini generated criticism that he was using the occasion more to promote himself than to call attention to a "growing national scandal."

Around midday on June 17, 1922, Houdini and Bess joined Conan Doyle and his family for a weekend break at the Ambassador Hotel in Atlantic City, a then-popular family resort some 125 miles down the coast from New York. Four hours later, after a brisk swim in the ocean and a more leisurely one in the hotel pool, Houdini drew up a deck chair next to Doyle, who had removed his shoes for the occasion, but was otherwise dressed "in a neat dark suit, as though attending [a] state event." For most of that late Saturday afternoon, the two men sat on the beach under a cloudless sky and discussed spirit photography. At one point, Doyle reached under his seat and produced a picture of a coffin that he claimed showed several "spirit extras" hovering in the background. He also enthused about a British photographer named Ada Deane and her "many outstanding successes" in the field. Houdini did not mention that the Magic Circle in London had recently caught the same Mrs. Deane using pre-prepared plates. Once again, the illusionist noted "the Britisher's many fine personal qualities . . . His voice and mannerisms are just as nice and sweet as any mortal . . . Lady Doyle told me that he has never spoken a cross word in his life. He is good-natured, very bright, but a monomaniac on the subject of Spiritualism." Though scrupulously polite to Doyle's face, in the privacy of his diary Houdini noted that certain "occult phenomena" his host cited were actually of more material origin: there was the boy who had fractured his skull and "was able to blow wind right through the back of his head," for instance, and "the freak appearing at Huber's Museum who could inflate balloons through his eyes." Houdini was also struck by the three young Doyle children, all of whom shared their parents' Spiritualist philosophy. At one stage, they came running along the sand to Houdini and blurted out to him that they had no fear of death, "since they would still live, and hold conversation in the beyond." It particularly moved him to see thirteen-year-old Denis embrace his mother, telling her he was lonely. "He kissed her caressingly on the mouth," Houdini noted, perhaps recalling his relationship with his own mother. "Then [he] picked up her hand and kissed each finger in as courtly a manner as any prince kissing his queen's hands . . . He adored her," he wrote later. It's possible that Houdini was still mildly in awe of Lady Doyle, a "somewhat regal" figure to whom he had previously sent postage stamps for her collection, "but always exchange[d] only pleasantries."

Some discrepancy exists about the exact sequence of events of Sunday, June 18. In Houdini's account, written later that evening, he and his wife had been sitting on the beach in front of the hotel when Conan Doyle appeared, having been led to them by a small boy. "It seemed that Lady Doyle wanted to hold an automatic writing séance, [to] give me some indication from the spirit world, and she had sent Sir Arthur to find me," Houdini wrote. "Sir Arthur apologised to Mrs Houdini for not inviting her to the séance, saying that two people who were of the same mind, either positive or negative, would possibly hurt, and if this was so Lady Doyle would not be able to get any writing from any of the spirits who would control her. So I followed Sir Arthur, but not until the boy who had found me for him had taken a snapshot of both of us, ere we left." The picture shows the burly Conan Doyle in his three-piece black suit and the compact Houdini in his rumpled white one, each of them wearing a straw hat. On their way to a shadowy paranormal encounter, both men smile politely for the camera, as if merely pausing before a stroll on the beach.

"It was a sudden inspiration of mine to invite [Houdini] up to our room and see if we could get any evidence or consolation for him," Conan Doyle wrote a few weeks later in *Our American Adventure.* "It was done at my suggestion," he added in *The Edge of the Unknown* (1930) before noting two pages further on in the same book: "The method in which Houdini tried to explain away, minimise or contort our attempt at consolation, which was given *entirely at his own urgent request and against my wife's desire,* has left a deplorable shadow in my mind and made some alteration in my feelings for him" (emphasis added). But if Doyle was confused about the timing of events that weekend, so was Houdini. Describing the Atlantic City "miracle" in *A Magician among the Spirits,* he made some play of the fact that "I especially wanted to speak to my late Mother, because that day, *June 17,* was her birthday" (Houdini's emphasis). In fact, the séance took place on the eighteenth of the month. Houdini's professional faculties were still sharp enough, however, because

> before leaving with [Doyle], Mrs Houdini cued me. We did a second sight or mental performance years ago and still use[d] a system or code whereby we could speak silently to each other . . . In that manner Mrs Houdini told me all about the night previous [when] she had gone into detail with Lady Doyle about the great love I bear for my Mother. She related to her a number of instances, such as my returning home from long trips [and] spending months with my Mother and wearing only the clothes that she had given me, because I thought it would please her and give her some happiness. My wife also remarked about my habit of laying my head on my Mother's breast, in order to hear her heart beat. Just little peculiarities that mean so much to a mother and son when they love one another as we did.

This seems to have been a lot of information for Bess to have conveyed merely by blinking her eyes and wiggling her fingers while Doyle turned to walk back to the hotel, but we have Houdini's word for it that he was forewarned "some business was about to occur" that hot Sunday afternoon.

Once in the Conan Doyles' darkened suite, the three took their seats at the round table, bowed their heads, and said a prayer. "I closed my eyes and eliminated from my mind all thoughts but those of a religious order, so that I could help as much as possible," Houdini said.

Lady Doyle took a pencil and, with spasmodic jerks of her right hand, in no gentle way, started to strike the table, explaining that the force had taken hold of her in the most energetic manner that it had ever done at any séance at which she was doing the automatic writing.

For a few moments she seemed to be struggling with it, but then the pencil began to move. She asked of the spirit, "Do you believe in God?" Upon having her hand beat the table three times she said: "Then I will make the sign of the cross." She did so . . . I think that, in her heart of hearts, Lady Doyle is sincere, and I am positive that Sir Arthur is just as religious in his belief as it is possible for any human being to be. From time to time, he would soothe his wife as if admonishing the spirit not to be too forcible with her. These two spoke throughout as if there was someone in reality standing alongside of us.

For some time after the initial affirmation, Lady Conan Doyle again sat with her hand poised over the writing pad in front of her. Then, "with a terrific jolt," Houdini said, "the pencil suddenly began to fly across the page." "Oh, my darling, thank God, at last I'm through—I've tried so often—now I am happy—Why, of course, I want to talk to my boy—my own beloved boy—Friends, thank you, with all my heart for this," she wrote, with Conan Doyle rapidly tearing off the pages and passing them to Houdini.

You have answered the cry of my heart—and of his—God bless him—a thousand fold, for all his life for me—never had a mother such a son—tell him not to grieve, soon he'll get all the evidence he is so anxious for—Yes, we know—tell him I want him to try to write at his own home. It will be far better so.

I will work with him—he is so, so dear to me—I am preparing so sweet a home for him which one day in God's good time he will come to—it is one of my great joys preparing it for our future—

I am so happy in this life—it is so full and joyous—my only shadow has been that my beloved one hasn't known how often I have been with him all the while, all the while—here away from my heart's darling—continuing my work thus in this life of mine.

It is so different over here, so much larger and bigger and more beautiful—so lofty—all sweetness around one—nothing that hurts and we see our beloved ones on earth—that is such a joy and comfort to us—Tell him I love him more than ever—the years only increase it—and his goodness fills my soul with gladness and thankfulness. Oh, just this, it *is* me. I want him only to know that—that—I have bridged the gulf—That is what I wanted, oh so much. Now I can rest in peace.

At that point, Conan Doyle interrupted to ask Houdini whether he would like to speak to the spirit as a test to prove that it really was Cecilia Weiss returning to him after nine years in the grave. Doyle suggested that this might take the form of a question, such as (reflecting both men's interest in telepathy), "Can my mother read my mind?" Houdini duly focused on that, and as soon as he did so Lady Doyle again began to write:

I *always* read my beloved son's mind—his dear mind—there is so much I want to say to him—but I am almost overwhelmed by this joy of talking to him once more—it is almost too much to get through—the joy of it—thank you, thank you, thank you, friend, with all my heart for what you have done for me this day—God bless you, too, Sir Arthur, for what you are doing for us—for us over here—who so need to get in touch with our beloved ones on the earth plane—

"It was a singular scene," Conan Doyle allowed, "my wife with her hand flying wildly, beating the table while she scribbled at a furious rate, I sitting opposite and tearing sheet after sheet from the block as it was filled up, and tossing each across to Houdini, while he sat silent, looking grimmer and paler every moment." By the time the written part of the séance came to an end, Lady Doyle had dashed off fifteen pages in her angular, erratic script. But the proceedings weren't over yet. For a man whose professional energy was fueled by power and recognition, Houdini was ill-suited to the role of being the submissive party at a séance. "When I asked about trying out the automatic writing in my own home," he recalled, "I took a pencil and wrote the name 'Powell.' It was like an electric shock to Sir Arthur, for a friend of his by that name, the editor of the *Financial News* of London, had died about a week previously. 'The Spirits have directed you in writing the name of my dear fighting partner in Spiritualism, Dr Ellis Powell,' Doyle promptly announced. 'I am the person he is most likely to signal to, and here is his name coming through your hands. Truly Saul is among the Prophets. You are a medium!' he declared."

"Houdini had a poker-face and gave nothing away as a rule," Conan Doyle wrote in *The Edge of the Unknown,* "but he seemed to me to be disconcerted by my remark. He muttered something about knowing a man called 'Powell' down in Texas, though he failed to invent any reason why that particular man should come back at that particular moment. Then, gathering up his papers, he hurried from the room."*

Meeting in New York two days later, Houdini gave Conan Doyle the impression that he was "profoundly moved" by the events of Atlantic City. "I have been walking on air ever since," the illusionist remarked. In fact, as he confided to Bess, he could only wonder why Mrs. Weiss, a Jew, would have communicated with her son under the sign of a cross and in fluent English, a language she had never spoken. "I may say that your mother again came back with words of passionate love through Mrs M[etcalfe] of Brooklyn last night," Doyle reported. "She said, 'My son has now told his wife that he is mentally convinced of the truth of this revelation, but he does not see his way and it is dark in front of him. He is seated in his room thinking it over.'"

On June 22, Conan Doyle held an eve-of-departure press conference to announce that he was "hugely pleased over the success of his trip," despite believing there was "more moral courage about psychic matters in England than here." He remarked that he had just had "a particularly instructive conversation" on the subject with William James, the pioneering American psychologist and philosopher who had died twelve years earlier. On a different note, Doyle added that he was "tremendously affected" by what he had seen of prohibition, and predicted "drinking [would] be gradually effaced" in the years ahead. "England will eventually go dry," he declared. "Norway and Sweden are on the verge. Scotland will be dry before Ireland and Italy, and France never, in my opinion."

---

*Houdini later explained that he had been thinking not of the British barrister and journalist Ellis Thomas Powell (1869–1922), but of his friend Frederick Powell, a magician and sometime unit publicist on *The Man from Beyond,* who was then gravely ill and had just written him a letter. Conan Doyle was unmoved. "No, the Powell explanation won't do," he immediately wrote back, noting "there [was] a limit to coincidence." Seven years later, Doyle added, "It is possible that at that moment [in the séance room] I had surprised the master secret of Houdini's life"—that he was psychic.

Later that night, Conan Doyle and his family were guests of the Houdinis at their gala twenty-eighth wedding anniversary party, which began in a restaurant and ended in a box at New York's Carroll Theatre. As at the American Magicians event three weeks earlier, the after-dinner cabaret took an unexpected turn. The notional headliner, a song-and-dance man named Raymond Hitchcock, took the opportunity to press his distinguished audience members into action. The *New York Times* wrote,

> He called the attention of the crowd to the noted author, and then, turning to Sir Arthur himself, inquired of him whether he thought Sherlock Holmes could tell what Margaret Asquith herself wanted. Having made his start, Hitchy kept right on going. He announced the presence of Houdini and asked the arch-mystifier to come to the stage and do a little stunt. Houdini arose and bowed his acknowledgements to the applause that followed, but Hitchy was not satisfied with acknowledgements and insisted that Houdini help him make good his promise. Cries of "The Needle Mystery!" came from the house. Houdini sat down; the audience continued to clamor while Hitchcock pleaded. In his plea he had an able backer in Sir Arthur, who literally pushed the unwilling mystifier upon the stage.

At that Houdini relented and agreed to perform an impromptu version of the "Hindoo Needle" trick. According to most reliable sources, he was not pleased to find himself providing the unpaid entertainment at his own party, and said as much to Hitchcock following the show. When the Houdinis got home to Harlem at around 10 o'clock, they found themselves in the midst of a power cut that affected most of lower New York State, causing Bess to stumble in the gloom and collide with a heavy table holding a jeweled cup in the hallway. Darkness fell on a subdued household.

At 9:00 the next morning, Houdini escorted the Conan Doyles to the RMS *Adriatic* for their return voyage to England. Some 200 reporters and well-wishers were also on hand. The already high-spirited scene at the quayside was further enlivened when eleven-year-old Adrian appeared for embarkation accompanied by a 5-foot king snake, a gift to him from the curator of the Bronx Zoo. Given the precarious nature of Houdini's friendship with Conan Doyle, his sense of having been upstaged at the Magicians' banquet, and Lady Doyle's suspect mediumship at Atlantic City, the innuendo and gossip now doing the rounds in the press that the arch-skeptic had "seen" his dead mother could have done little for his mood. On top of everything else, he had begun lying awake at night, falling asleep only to

dream of what he described as "devils, demons and goblins." But despite their irrec-
oncilable ambitions and conflicting styles, Houdini told reporters that his relationship with Doyle was one of mutual "admiration, fondness and respect." Waiting
for the author in his cabin was a bouquet of flowers and a telegram: "Bon voyage.
May the Decree of Fate send you back here soon for another pleasant visit. Regards.
Houdini."

In public, Houdini's laudatory, even worshipful, tone toward Conan Doyle persisted both in several press interviews and in the "personal" correspondence he
sometimes also copied to the newspapers. "Enclosed you will find two snapshots
taken at the steamer the day you sailed," he wrote to the Doyles while the *Adriatic*
was still in mid-Atlantic. "I am pleased to see that there is a photo of Lady Doyle
smiling. She told me it was very hard to get a good-natured photograph of herself,
but you will agree with me that both of you are beaming with joy." Another long
letter followed a day later: "I have mailed you a number of articles which appeared
in the New York papers, as you might be interested in what they said," the media-
conscious Houdini wrote. "Every big newspaper man I have spoken to compli-
mented you, to me, on the dignity with which you carried on your lecture tour . . .
I hope you had a pleasant trip." From Windlesham, Conan Doyle replied in kind,
sending his "esteem" and "warm regards," while again letting it be known there
"was not the slightest room for doubt" in his beliefs. "I had to write to the *New York
Times* the other day about conjurors," he remarked. "Some fellow, whose name I
have forgotten, had questioned my facts, which is always a dangerous thing to do,
for I have chapter and verse fairly ready."

Day to day, Houdini was careful to calculate every move when dealing with
the man he privately called "perfectly sincere [but] a fanatic, who in my opinion
will do anything to advance his cause." "It may interest you to know that I have obtained a collection of over 100 autographed [pieces] written by your father Charles
A. Doyle," Houdini casually revealed in one letter. But even then, he implied, the
subject matter made a suggestive study of a shared Doyle obsession. "There is one
letter," Houdini continued, "which has two wonderful drawings and is highly interesting. [Your father] writes: 'Here is a design for an historical picture. The subject
is a battle in which the souls of the dead rose into the air and renewed the fight. If
you like it, I think I will do a picture of it as large as life.'"

By the middle of 1922, Houdini's files on the Doyle family were quite voluminous. Along with the folders of closely annotated press cuttings from both sides

of the Atlantic, there were a reported 1,343 items of "correspondence, heirlooms, souvenirs [and] merchandise pertaining to Sherlock Holmes," the last of which the illusionist snapped up, often anonymously, from dealers and auction houses. When Houdini came upon Charles Doyle's portfolio, he immediately recognized its humorous potential, privately remarking to his friend DeVega that it "explained much," and signing his review with a satirical "Ha! ha! ha!," while publicly adopting the persona of an impartial collector of this "and other psychic data that come my way."* The note of scholarly detachment was maintained in an article Houdini contributed to the *New York Times* in August 1922 on the subject of the anonymous 1891 book *Revelations of a Spirit Medium.* "I have personally met all the great clairvoyants and am yet open to be convinced," he wrote. "I want to put on record again that I do not say there is no such thing as Spiritualism, but state that in the 30 years of my investigation nothing has caused me to change my mind."

During the late summer and autumn of 1922, Houdini did, however, engage in an open dispute with a fifty-three-year-old magician named Howard Thurston, who it's possible may have struck him as a proxy for Conan Doyle. The five-times-married Thurston had a colorful pedigree, having variously worked as a pickpocket, snake-oil salesman, and manager of a traveling hoochy-koochy show around the American Midwest before undergoing a religious conversion in his mid-twenties. In time, like Houdini, he became known as the "King of Cards," a role he combined with a critical belief in the occult, on which he published several well-received books and articles. Conan Doyle considered him the "only practicing conjuror who had true knowledge of psychic matters." Thurston's latest wife reportedly also enjoyed the gift of automatic writing. In the course of a heated meeting of the Society of American Magicians, Houdini attacked his rival for such breaches of professional etiquette as "putting pocket tricks in the 'Thurston Box of Candy' he distributed at shows." At the society's autumn banquet that October, the two men gave opposing speeches on Spiritualism. On a personal level, Houdini was evidently jealous of Thurston's glamour (with sour good looks like the actor Ralph Fiennes), fame, and "playboy" lifestyle, viewing him, according to DeVega, as "the Johnny-come-lately who would jump up at a dinner to sing for the folks, and then impishly disappear before the table-clearing and dishwashing began." Perhaps

---

*Houdini clearly spoke more warmly of Charles Doyle's book to a number of other friends and acquaintances. In January 1927, his widow duly forwarded the collection to Conan Doyle, adding that her husband "always intended to present it to you. [It] was the one thing in his huge library that was sacred and marked 'Not to be sold at any price.'"

significantly, Thurston also had his own successful film production company, an aggressive name-licensing business, and a well-developed sense of his market value as a whole. It was enough to lead to an inevitable clash with his main professional competitor. "The great Houdini has been King of Cards," Houdini crowed, "LONG before Thurston ever thought of doing a card act."

In demonstrating how he could duplicate seemingly psychic feats, Houdini made use of not only his own professional skills but also an encyclopedic knowledge of "Spiritualistic humbug down the ages," as he put it in *A Magician among the Spirits*. Sometimes he also appeared to have blind luck on his side. On July 4, 1922, Houdini was enjoying an Independence Day picnic and fireworks display at the suburban New York home of his lawyer and friend Bernard Ernst. When rain threatened to disrupt the proceedings, Ernst's children appealed to their guest for help. Striding confidently into the center of the lawn, Houdini raised his hands and said emphatically, "Rain and storm, I command you to stop"—and "immediately, as if by miracle, the skies became clear," he wrote. When one of the older children later remarked that this struck him as a mere coincidence, Houdini again "walked out, lifted my hands supplicantly toward the heavens and called, 'Listen to my voice and once more let the water flow to earth and allow the flowers and trees to bloom . . . ' A chill came over me, for as if in response to my command or the prayer of my words another downpour then started"—a case, perhaps, of what Conan Doyle called the illusionist's "unacknowledged psychic gift," but to Houdini himself proof only of "the performer's embrace of every accidental occurrence."*

A more controlled demonstration of the magician's art followed later that summer in Houdini's home, in front of an audience that included the journalist and author Walter Lippmann and Joseph Pulitzer, editor of the *New York World*. While Houdini retired to his study upstairs, his guests were invited to think of any subjects they liked, and then to commit these in written or drawn form to pieces of paper that they put in their pockets. In due course, their host returned and was able to repeat the contents of every note and identify every sketch. Houdini's most striking success came when he gave a minutely detailed description of "Buffalo Bill's tomb in Wyoming" (though actually situated in Colorado), just as depicted by one

---

*Although there is no reason to doubt Houdini's story, Ernst himself omits it from his book about his friend. According to the *New York Times*, the local weather that July 4 was "extremely humid," though with no mention of a storm. In that same week, the Brooklyn Bridge was closed to automobile traffic after engineers discovered a slipped suspension cable that had "warped in the drought."

of the group. "Everyone was convinced it was telepathy," he wrote with some pride, although the real explanation was both more simple and ingenious. Unknown to his visitors, Houdini had had the entire house wired with hidden "dictograph" microphones. While they chatted among themselves about their chosen subjects, their host had been sitting at his desk listening to their every word through a speaking tube.

Conan Doyle, his supporters, and a good many independent-minded Spiritualists understood the need to periodically remind themselves that they were a minority group. A sense of embattlement proved an important unifying theme. "Every new thing faces the opposition of ignorant and prejudiced people," Conan Doyle wrote to the *New York Times* on August 4, 1922. "And ectoplasm is no exception." As he noted elsewhere, "reactionary intrigue" and the uniquely malign influence of various "Roman Catholic swindles" had been responsible for everything from persecuting innocent mediums to framing the spirit photographer William Hope, whom Doyle considered to be the victim of an elaborate plate-switching conspiracy that continued to vex him. "We meet again on Tuesday for microscopic examination of Hope's [film]," he wrote to Oliver Lodge. Conan Doyle even saw true believers like himself as under fire from others who allegedly shared their faith. "I should like . . . to say that no one suffers so much from these knaves [false mediums] as Spiritualists do," he remarked, "[and] that no one can be more eager for their suppression." Doyle's claims for his new religion weren't small. "I feel the object is to warn the human race and that sooner or later it should be done," he told Lodge. "I await orders on this subject."

Sometimes Conan Doyle's floating paranoia tended to attach itself to one of his adversaries. "I do not as a rule answer articles which contain personal attacks, for I am indifferent to them," he wrote to the *New York Herald* of Houdini's friend Joseph Rinn. "But I feel that indifference might be mistaken for weakness, and that it is my duty to expose the ignorance and malevolence of the writer." A lengthy salvo followed. Doyle had had nothing to say when Rinn initially attacked him in the press in May 1922 as a "poor credulous old man" who had been made "the dupe of mediums." But a year later the gloves were off. "I wasted a whole day yesterday answering an article of Joseph F. Rinn. I think it takes the record of all the fallacious statements which I have ever had to correct," Doyle fumed to Houdini, apparently unaware that he and Rinn had known one another since working together as fellow necktie cutters in 1889.

Conan Doyle had an opportunity to express his personal philosophy in his correspondence with fellow believers. "So long as I am convinced of the possibility and existence of [occult] powers the particular instance no longer interests me," he told Lodge, adding that he much preferred cases "where my imagination can work." Sometimes these took material form, as when Conan Doyle and twelve other sitters at a London séance were rewarded when they lit a candle and saw "a disc of wood as large as a bread platter [begin] to twitter and twirl in the middle of the table . . . This lasted for several minutes." Increasingly, though, Doyle was exploring the new possibilities opened up by radio, which he thought might prove useful in communicating both with the spirit world and with extraterrestrial life. "You have heard no doubt that Abraham Wallace thinks he is in touch with Mars on a 30,000 metre wireless wave," he remarked blandly in one letter. "He lunches with me today so I shall hear all about it."

Conan Doyle also reaffirmed his belief in the "miraculous stuff"—ectoplasm—that he considered the connecting link between the material and Spiritual worlds. Writing in the *London Chronicle*, he told of his experiences with Eva C. and of subsequent sittings when "I have clearly seen ectoplasm, though in more vaporous form, under the mediumship of Frau von Silbert at the Psychic College . . . Here the room was in darkness, though there was sufficient light to see all that occurred. The ectoplasm, which seemed to cause great pain in its emission, took the form of slightly luminous patches, produced under complete test conditions. They formed on the floor with an inclination to rise and to become more clearly defined. They were quite separate from the medium—in fact they were nearer to me than to her." As a doctor, Conan Doyle was able to speak with authority on how the material was produced. After refuting the "childish" suggestion that it was no more than the medium's saliva or "regurgitation of food," he went on to reveal "it is usually drawn from the mucous surfaces of the body . . . In the case of Eva, the mucous surfaces of the nose and mouth were a common point of origin, though [it] did not always emanate from there." Less refined observers than Doyle were left to note that the principal source of both ectoplasm and other supposedly psychic matériel was often the area least likely to be searched by a predominantly male investigating committee. "This is how she works," Houdini wrote of a Los Angeles medium who began her séances by standing in a bowl of flour so that she was unable to move around without leaving incriminating tracks. "She has a tube for her vagin [*sic*] in which she conceals a pair of silk stockings . . . When the cabinet is closed, as it is impossible to go out of the flour without leaving footprints she reaches and gets the silk stockings, puts them on her feet, steps out of the bowl of flour [and] is able to leave without besmirching the floor or leaving prints. After the materialisation she goes back to the cabinet, conceals her load, takes off her stockings and steps back into the bowl of flour." But for the precise nuances of the trick, it was exactly the sort of classic "locked door" mystery beloved of Sherlock Holmes.

A complex mix of intellectual certainty and personal concerns perhaps inspired Conan Doyle's Spiritualist faith. By the time of his séance with Houdini in Atlantic City, he was sixty-three, already older than the age his father had been at his death. Doyle's correspondence and public writing both frequently touch on his sense of life's transience, and his consequent impatience to make his Spiritual mark. He had wasted too much time, so it seemed to him, before coming to the truth in 1916. Sometimes Conan Doyle's headlong rush to judgment on psychic matters jarred with the more measured, scientific approach. "I by no means wish to uphold the policy of rapid publication of results," Oliver Lodge chided him in December 1922. "I myself am in favour of a longer continued investigation, and the reduction of [all] phenomena to some sort of law and order. Until that is done [they] cannot hope to take their place among scientific facts." The situation became more urgent when Conan Doyle made contact later that month with the spirit guide Pheneas, who began to talk of a global apocalypse. "We are loosening the rivets," Pheneas unambiguously warned after a powerful Asian earthquake. "There will be a terrific convulsion."

In October 1922, Houdini published an article that seemed to take aim at Conan Doyle and his fascination with the technological opportunities for spirit communication. Entitled "Ghosts that Talk—by Radio," it was another superficially polite rebuttal—"I respect such men as Sir Conan Doyle [for] his sincerity," Houdini insisted—that put clear water between their beliefs. Any meaningful reconciliation would be hard to achieve from now on. "Radio at present is the greatest aid to the fraud mediums," Houdini wrote, "and they are sure to take advantage of every new development. I hope that spirits will talk to us through radio instruments some day, but I will prefer to hear such messages in a scientist's laboratory rather than through the presentations of unscrupulous clairvoyants. If there are mediums who are not fraudulent, I have yet to see them."

Strong as this was, it was another article by Houdini, published later that month in the *New York Sun,* that effectively destroyed his friendship with Conan Doyle. "My mind is open," the illusionist again protested. "I am perfectly willing to believe, but in the twenty-five years of my investigation and the hundreds of séances which I have attended, I have never seen or heard anything that could convince me that there is a possibility of communication with the loved ones who have gone beyond." Although Houdini had said much the same thing before, notably in the *New York Times* two months earlier, Doyle considered this to be a "personal affront" to his wife, implying as it did that she had faked the Atlantic City séance. "I felt rather sore about it," he wrote to Houdini on November 19, 1922. "You have all the right in the world to hold your opinion, but when you say that you have had no evidence of survival, you say what I cannot reconcile with what I saw with my own eyes. I know by many examples the purity of my wife's mediumship, and I saw what you got and what the effect was upon you at the time." Houdini's prompt reply signaled his reluctance, even now, to end his relationship with the Doyles. "You write that you are very 'sore' . . . I trust it is not with me, because you, having been truthful and manly all your life, naturally must admire the same traits in other human beings . . . I hold both Lady Doyle and yourself in the highest esteem," Houdini wrote, before coming to the point. "I was heartily in accord and sympathy at the séance, but the letter was written entirely in English, and my sainted mother could not read, write, or speak the language. I did not care to discuss it at the time because my emotions . . . kept me quiet until time passed and I could give it the proper deduction."

As usual, Houdini was considerably more scathing in his private verdict. The automatic writing incident had been "a washout," he told DeVega, though he was unclear whether this had been a case of fraud on Lady Doyle's part or, just as likely, some more subtle form of self-delusion. As he knew full well, the need to succeed "can sometimes get the better of every other faculty." Houdini remarked that he had seen something of this mental state at work when he had accompanied Conan Doyle to a séance in New York. "I noticed that . . . Sir Arthur would ask a question and then change his mind and ask another one. Eventually, when he would get an answer to a question, he had evidently forgotten that he had asked that specific one, and, on receiving a reply to same, would naturally think that he had never spoken on the subject before. All during the séance he was willing to believe."

The new factor that precipitated a rift between Conan Doyle and Houdini was the decision by *Scientific American* magazine to offer a cash prize to the first reader who could produce "conclusive psychic manifestations" under controlled conditions. Doyle was not pleased at this "brazenly commercial" appeal, which he rightly feared would only encourage the fringe entrepreneurs among the psychic community and do little for the cause as a whole. It was a "very dangerous thing," he told the magazine's publisher, as "a large reward will stir up every rascal in the country, while the best type of medium is unworldly and would not be attracted by such a consideration." Underlying these practical concerns was Doyle's own comparative asceticism and complete indifference to any material gain as a result of his Spiritualist mission (as opposed to his literary career)—not factors that applied in the case of Houdini.

Founded in August 1845, *Scientific American* nonetheless had a "venerable history," Doyle conceded, as one of the country's oldest and most resourceful technical publications. Many of its early issues had dwelt on the somewhat dry transactions of the U.S. Patent Office (among them an 1849 sketch of an inflatable device for "Buoying Vessels Over Shoals" submitted by Abraham Lincoln), and it was known to be sparing in its editorial endorsements. Houdini had come to the magazine's attention in July 1912 when he had agreed to be handcuffed and locked inside a heavy pine box which had then been nailed shut, tied with rope, weighed down with 200 pounds of iron dumbbells, and thrown into New York's East River. The illusionist's escape only a minute later was sufficient to break even *Scientific American*'s pose of critical reserve. It was "one of the most remarkable tricks ever performed," the magazine pronounced.

True to form, *Scientific American*'s contest, which it announced in November 1922, came with a number of elaborate rules. As well as a $2,500 prize to the first person to produce a "visible occult manifestation" there was to be a similar award for a "psychic picture" obtained under "the fullest and most objective scrutiny." Would-be mediums and photographers alike were to be subject to search, and not be permitted to operate in full darkness. "Purely mental" phenomena like telepathy, or auditory ones like rappings were specifically excluded from consideration. The publishers would make their decision on the basis of a unanimous vote of the five "incorruptible judges" to be named later, or, failing that, a four-to-one split in the contestant's favor. "Always we have had soothsayers and haruspices, oracles and fortune prophets . . . The medium today is but the same old thing brought up to date," the magazine said in an editorial. "And always we have had a very respectable portion of the community eager to accept the claims of supernatural powers, always a residuum of scoffers unwilling to accept. The thing seeks a scientific basis today simply because the twentieth century medium is living in the twentieth century; approximation to twentieth century methods is as necessary in her case as it would have been out of place in Delphi."

"Of course, it is very satisfactory to see a journal of the standing of *Scientific American* taking an interest in psychic matters," Conan Doyle agreed. "Most newspapers can give pages to sport but refuse to publish a word about the most important phenomena . . . But I don't understand the necessity or wisdom of publicly offering prizes for [manifestations]. That is a direct invitation to the rogues of two continents," he added, in contrast to the "conclusive materialisation which took place a few months ago in Paris, at which casts were taken of a spirit hand." Under the supervision of a medium named Kelusky, the "irreproachable scholars" Professors Geley and Richet had first materialized the spirit and then persuaded it to plunge one of its hands into a bowl of paraffin. "By this means," Doyle wrote, "a perfect cast . . . was obtained and I may mention that the extreme smallness of the wrist proves that it was undoubtedly that of a spirit form."*

That Doyle resented the material incursion into what he called "the temple of faith" was further shown when, in December 1922, he wrote a 1,300-word letter on the subject to the *Scientific American*. Among his numerous reservations was that only "gentle, quiet, courteous, sympathetic" men should serve as the contest's judges, as the "positive, aggressive type" were likely to "inhibit psychic phenomena." The magazine responded the following month by announcing their panel of five names: William McDougall, professor of psychology at Harvard University; Dr. Daniel Comstock, formerly head of the physics department at the Massachusetts Institute of Technology, who went on to patent the Technicolor film process; Rev. Walter Prince of the American Society for Psychical Research; and Hereward Carrington, a researcher and author who had been born (as Hubert Lavington) in Britain, immigrated to Boston, and later founded the American Psychical Institute; a jury of "impeccable journalists and academics" and thus all "good sober men," the magazine said, in something of a non-sequitur.

The fifth member of the investigating body was Houdini.

Conan Doyle was not slow to express his doubts on the selection. "I see that you are on the *Scientific American* committee, but how can it be called an impartial

---

*The French physiologist Charles Richet (1850–1935) was the longtime editor of the *Revue Scientifique,* a prolific writer on animal and human genetics, the author of several works of fiction, and the winner of the 1913 Nobel Prize for medicine. His endorsement of Eva C. and her feats of ectoplasm had made a major impression on Conan Doyle some years earlier. Gustave Geley, a professor at the University of Lyons and a laureate of the French Medical Academy, often sat with the same medium and, trained in obstetrics, sometimes assisted in examining her for foreign substances. "With Eva, I don't merely say, 'There was no trickery,'" he wrote. "There was no possibility of trickery."

committee when you have committed yourself to such statements as that some Spiritualists pass away before they realise they have been deluded, etc.?" he wrote to Houdini in February 1923. "You have every possible right to hold such an opinion, but you can't sit on an impartial committee afterwards. It becomes biased at once. What I wanted was five good, clear-headed men who would stick to it without any prejudice at all—like the Dialectical Society of London, who unanimously endorsed the phenomena. However, it may work out all right." Doyle was less guarded in his remarks elsewhere, fuming at the "capital error" of allowing Houdini to sit in judgment on Spiritual matters. "The Commission is, in my opinion, a farce," he wrote.

Conan Doyle did, however, successfully invite *Scientific American*'s associate editor (and secretary of its prize committee), J. Malcolm Bird, to visit him while in England. The bespectacled, thirty-six-year-old Bird, a former math professor, seemed inclined to a broadly sympathetic view of Spiritualism. In March 1923, Doyle took him to meet Evan Powell, the Welsh medium who had helped convince the author his dead son Kingsley could still talk to him. Bird was impressed: although Powell was "trussed up inside a cabinet," he "had made a bouquet of flowers fly through the air in the séance room, [among] other astonishments." When they later visited the spirit photographer William Hope, Bird was rewarded with a picture of himself in which two "ghost extras" shimmered in the background. "I will say that to me the probabilities seem good that [it] constitutes a genuine psychic phenomenon," he wrote in *Scientific American*. Perhaps unsurprisingly, Bird's working relationship with his committee's most famous member proved to be strained. Houdini was consistently to call Bird's judgment and even his "mental firepower" into question. It seemed to be another case of his jousting with Conan Doyle by proxy. In May 1924, Houdini informed the press that Bird was a "boob" in matters of psychic investigation, and could be "duped by any high class magician." From this point on, their relations began to deteriorate rapidly. Eighteen months later, Houdini jumped up on the stage of a church in Philadelphia where Bird was speaking in order to confront the "little chump" about certain statements included in his recently published memoirs. "You liar, you contemptible liar," Houdini began. "You lied in your book when you said my father was not married to my mother. Ladies and gentlemen, in his book he said Houdini had his hands soiled and said I was unclean . . . Now, do I look like a man like that? If a man would have said that to me I would wipe the floor with him, and so would any other man who loved and respected his mother."

On September 3, 1922, *Lloyd's Sunday News* published the first of twelve weekly installments of Conan Doyle's book *Our American Adventure*. Among other revelations, the serial went into some detail about the events of the previous June in Atlantic City. Before long, Eric Dingwall, the friendly SPR researcher in London, wrote to ask Houdini, "Is there any truth in the story of Doyle that you got an evidential message from your mother through Lady Doyle? Also that people say you have become an automatic writer?"

This was too much. Houdini, who told Dingwall he had no intention of beginning his tenure on the *Scientific American* committee as a "confirmed spookist," swore out a statement and had it notarized on December 19. It began:

THE TRUTH REGARDING SPIRITUALISTIC SÉANCE GIVEN
TO HOUDINI BY LADY DOYLE

Fully realizing the danger of statements made by investigators of psychic phenomena, and knowing full well my reputation earned, after more than thirty years' experience in the realm of mystery, I can truthfully say that I have never seen a mystery, and I have never visited a séance, which I could not fully explain . . . Lady Doyle told me that she was automatically writing a letter which came through her, and was guided by the spirit of my beloved, sainted mother . . . There was not the slightest idea of my having felt my mother's presence, and the letter which followed I cannot possibly accept as having been written or inspired by [her].

Houdini then dealt with his own supposed feat of automatic writing, which he claimed had been a deliberate ruse—"or let us say a kindlier word regarding my thoughts and call it 'coincidence'"—on his part. "I put this on record," he concluded, "so that, in case of my death, no one will say that the spirit of Sir Arthur Conan Doyle's friend Ellis Powell guided my hand."

It seems not to have occurred to Houdini that this public rebuff might in any way harm what he called his "warm and kindly" relations with Conan Doyle. Six months after telling the *New York Sun* that he had never attended a genuine séance, and four months after his notarized statement to that effect, he was to note serenely that the Doyles had "attended and certainly enjoyed" a performance he gave in Denver. "We sent them a bunch of violets and five pounds of candy for little Billy the[ir] tom-boy daughter," he added. Being a pragmatist, Houdini easily overcame his ideological prejudices and continued to speak as if Doyle and he were the "most cordial of friends," and "intellectual piers [*sic*]" at that. The need for respect remained the prime motivating force of his extraordinary life. Associating with "cultural lions [was] pleasurable," he wrote; it was also a means to an end. "I am writing these things in my Day-book," Houdini remarked in an entry of May 1923, "realizing that Sir Arthur is a huge success in the literary world, and a great many things he says or does will be of interest at some future time."

Although Conan Doyle, conversely, felt "sore" about recent developments, other events may have temporarily distracted him from Houdini. On December 10, 1922, he, his wife, and their three young children had sat down to a séance at Windlesham, as they now often did on a winter's evening. Within a few moments, Lady Doyle was violently seized by a new spirit entity, who described himself as "Pheneas," a roughly 10,000-year-old Arab scribe from the ancient Mesopotamian city of Ur. Pheneas would continue to speak at regular intervals throughout the rest of Conan Doyle's life, giving him advice on a wide range of international, political, and even household matters through the agency of his wife's automatic-writing mediumship. On his first appearance, Pheneas had announced that the Doyle family should undertake another tour of North America in 1923, before warning that the world was in imminent danger of destruction. "God has ordained that a great light shall shine into the souls of men through a great external force which is slowly penetrating through into the earth's sphere," he elaborated. "It is something which the most ignorant must see and believe. It will come very soon. The world will be staggered. It is the only thing which can arouse the lethargy of the human race. Such a shock! It is like Sodom and Gomorrah."

A common theme of spirit messages in the past was that they generally offered no more information than that the sender was well and happy. This was something different. Although Pheneas also provided a generous amount of encouragement to Doyle's psychic mission, he spoke in increasingly blunt terms of the coming global apocalypse. In time, Pheneas was to urge the family to buy a house at Bignell Wood, on the edge of the New Forest, as this would provide them a sanctuary in the approaching cataclysm. (Conan Doyle's daughter Jean later remarked that this may have been so, but that the house had also been a birthday gift from her father to her mother.) "God bless you!" the spirit announced in an early séance held at the new home. "I love being with you. Is it not nice round the fire? I am one of the family in the home circle. I will guard over you in this house as long as you sojourn in it.

That is a word the medium [Lady Doyle] never uses. Her tongue could hardly say it. She is very tired tonight."

"You do her good," Conan Doyle remarked.

"We love her," Pheneas replied. "We have chosen her for this work."

Soon Pheneas began to deliver his views in what Conan Doyle called a form of "semi-trance inspirational talking." In practice, this meant that Lady Doyle would sit down at the séance table, cross herself, and close her eyes before speaking in Pheneas's voice. During such sessions, she "never completely lost consciousness, but her hold upon her own organism was slight," her husband wrote. Pheneas would then "manifest" in a low, husky tone, commenting on a variety of Spiritual or more humble, domestic issues. Although some cynics believed that the spirit's more specific messages relating to such matters as house purchases or travel plans were manipulated to give Jean the outcome she wanted, Conan Doyle himself never wavered in his belief in his wife's mediumship. Risking even greater ridicule than had met *The Coming of the Fairies,* in 1927 Doyle went on to publish an anthology he called *Pheneas Speaks,* that, if nothing else, proved him to have been the very model of what one reviewer approvingly called a "stout family man," defending his wife's honor against her "low" critics.

Long before the book was published, however, its subject had turned to another matter of pressing concern to both the Doyles and him. Speaking directly through Lady Doyle, Pheneas remarked acidly on the man then busy investigating the latest, and most promising contender for the *Scientific American* prize. "Houdini is doomed, doomed!" the spirit shouted. "A terrible future awaits him . . . His fate is at hand."

The young Houdini in classic pose. (Library of Congress)

Arthur Conan Doyle just before the outbreak of the First World War, in which he lost eleven family members. It was the final step on his Spiritualist path. (Library of Congress)

After an impoverished spell as the "King of Cards," Houdini went back to the illusion he performed at regular intervals during the rest of his career. The Metamorphosis act—which he actually called his "ghost box"—soon came to resemble the vaudeville stars William and Ira Davenport's pioneering blend of Spiritualism and escapology. (Library of Congress)

Houdini about to execute his milk-can escape. Conan Doyle and others later insisted that he could pass through solid objects and materialize again on the other side. (Library of Congress)

An inveterate performer, Houdini would do almost anything for an audience—including apparently taking a blow from world heavyweight champion Jack Dempsey. (Library of Congress)

Sir Oliver Lodge. (Library of Congress)

Tennison Road, South Norwood, where Conan Doyle apparently killed off Sherlock Holmes in "The Final Problem." "I am weary of his name," he admitted. (C. Sandford)

The author and missionary. (Library of Congress)

Conan Doyle looming over his guest on the steps of the Royal Automobile Club in London. Although scrupulously polite in public, Houdini was less charitable in the privacy of his diary. "All this is ridiculous stuff," he wrote of Doyle's favorite medium. (Mary Evans Picture Library)

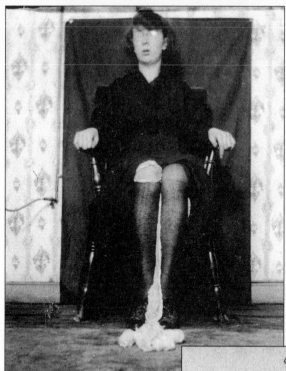

Conan Doyle and Houdini also came to different conclusions about the young Irish medium Kathleen Goligher and her gift of ectoplasm. (Arthur Conan Doyle, courtesy Richard Lancelyn Green Bequest, Portsmouth, UK)

In time, Conan Doyle had a scathing verdict on Houdini's A Magician among the Spirits. "A malicious book, full of every sort of misrepresentation," he scratched across the title page. (The Harry Ransom Center, The University of Texas at Austin)

Sins Conan Doyle

A MAGICIAN AMONG THE SPIRITS

BY

HOUDINI

Illustrated

A malicious book, full of every sort of misrepresentation.

Publishers
HARPER & BROTHERS
New York and London
MCMXXIV

The American Spiritualist crusade of the 1920s and 1930s drew large crowds to its meetings in cities like New York and Los Angeles. Away from these centers, the modest origins of the movement were evident in self-contained communes like this one in Kansas. (Library of Congress)

In later years, Conan Doyle and his family carried on much of their Spiritualist work at Windlesham, their home on the outskirts of Crowborough in Sussex. In April 1920, Doyle met Houdini for the first time here. (C. Sandford)

Although Houdini employed a network of agents to infiltrate séances, he wasn't above donning a blond wig and thick glasses to go undercover himself, disguised as "F. Raud," for "Fraud." (Photo courtesy of the Sydney H. Radner Collection, History Museum at the Castle of Appleton, WI, USA)

(below) Oliver Munn, Malcolm Bird, Margery, and Houdini, with revealing expressions, outside the medium's home in Lime Street, Boston, July 1924. (Library of Congress)

(above) Part of the crowd at Arthur Conan Doyle's memorial service at the Royal Albert Hall. They heard Estelle Roberts, a medium, announce "He is here!" and point to an empty chair on the stage. (Library of Congress)

(right) Bess Houdini with Edward Saint (right, holding handcuffs) at the "final séance" for Houdini on October 31, 1936. Bess later told a reporter that she not only had given up trying to reach her husband but also had her doubts about the existence of a hereafter. "Ten years," she noted, "is long enough to wait for any man." (Library of Congress)

6

THE BLONDE WITCH OF
LIME STREET

On February 19, 1923, Conan Doyle wrote in the *London Evening Standard* that

> Mr Houdini [has] declared of late that he [can] do anything which any medium can do. If I were disposed to put so absurd an assertion to the test I would ask him first to raise up the face of my mother clearly in front of me in the presence of other witnesses who knew her. I should then ask him to allow me to discuss private family matters with my "dead" brother, he mentioning in his own voice a person he was interested in in Copenhagen, whom I had never heard of but whom I found to exist.
>
> I would then ask him for a convincing interview with my own "dead" son, and finally to widen the field I would ask the conjuror to trace out the outline and details of a chapel buried many feet below the ground as has been done at Glastonbury ... I could suggest many other tests, but these would probably suffice.

A month later, Houdini in turn wrote to the New York press to say how pleased he was that "Sir Arthur Conan Doyle pays me many compliments in [his] article," though adding, "I do not claim that I can produce or materialize the three effects he asks."

By now, Conan Doyle had abandoned himself to his Spiritualist crusade. He went at the job the way he went after literary success: aggressively, with an equal emphasis on hard work and an almost childlike inquisitiveness. Just as science had attracted him for its crime-solving potential forty years earlier, so it struck him now as providing "wonderful corroboration" of some of his psychic theories. He was to write to Oliver Lodge, for instance, to share his views on "Major Grey in the USA, who reach[ed] 42,000 feet in a balloon," and to reflect on the state of the ether and heavenly strata at that altitude. Other of Doyle's speculations concerned the nature of planetary rotations and the suitability of radio and eventually television airwaves as means of spirit communication, alongside his "unbreakable" faith in the materializing power—or "apport"—of solid objects at a séance. A more traditional psychic experience came one night at Windlesham, where Doyle suddenly awoke "with the clear consciousness that there was someone in the room, and that the presence was not of this world." After lying seemingly paralyzed for some moments, he heard steps slowly approach his bed, and then a voice murmur, "Doyle, I came to tell you that I am sorry"—another case, he believed, of a formerly skeptical friend who had, in the afterlife, recanted his doubts on Spiritualism.

Given the variety of these phenomena, Conan Doyle's dogged belief in a wide range of occult manifestations, and his tireless dedication to sharing them with as large an audience as possible, he could not have been pleased with the contents of Houdini's latest open letter to him. After listing several mediums who had allegedly materialized Doyle's late family members only to then find themselves exposed, fined, or imprisoned, the illusionist harked back to a "psychic non-event" from the year before. "It is with regret," he wrote in the *New York Times,* "I speak of how Sir Arthur was convinced of [the mind-reading magician] Zancig, yet Zancig in my presence and of many witnesses, denied any supernatural or telepathic powers."

The fuse of controversy had been ignited, and much of the American press actively welcomed the chance to publicize this prototype celebrity feud. The opportunity soon came, when Conan Doyle returned to the country for another lecture tour in the spring of 1923. A headline in the *New York Mail and Express* announced, "Sir Arthur Arriving to Answer Houdini!" while the barker on Manhattan's Radio KDKA melodramatically saw the visit as a "heavyweight title fight" from which "only one man will emerge unbroken." "Our relations are certainly curious," Doyle was forced to admit in a letter to Houdini, "and are likely to become more so, for so long as you attack what I *know* from experience to be true, I have no alternative but to attack you in return. How long a private friendship can survive such an ordeal I do not know—but at least I did not create the situation."

The animosity between the Spiritualists and the materialists—and of their self-confident spokesmen—took another, unexpected turn when, on April 5, George

Herbert, fifth Earl of Carnarvon, died at the age of fifty-six in his Cairo hotel room. Carnarvon had been the principal financial backer of the ultimately successful expedition to excavate King Tutankhamun's tomb. Conan Doyle immediately went into print to suggest that this "mysterious demise" had been caused by "elementals" sent to guard the royal burial site, thus contributing to, if not actually creating, the durable legend of the "Curse of the pharoahs." "There are many tales about the powers of the old Egyptians," Doyle added, "and I know I wouldn't care to go fooling about their tombs and relics. There are many malevolent spirits."

This was perhaps a case where Conan Doyle's Spiritualist zeal got the better of his medical training. The doctors who attended Carnarvon agreed that he had been suffering not from a mummy's curse but from a more mundane case of blood poisoning brought on by a mosquito bite. The exact cause of death was given as erysipelas, a bacterial infection of the sort that might have been treated by penicillin following its discovery by Doyle's fellow Scot Alexander Fleming in 1928. Perhaps predictably, Houdini soon joined in the debate, dismissing as "applesauce" all the "spookist and supernatural theories" involved. "If, as Sir Arthur says, an avenging spirit [was] the cause of the explorer's death, why is it that other Egyptologists have never likewise been slain?" he asked in the *Los Angeles Examiner*. "Conan Doyle has seen fit to call us tricksters . . . Sir Arthur himself has not shown himself a competent judge," the Society of American Magicians added, likely with its president's (Houdini's) encouragement. The war was on. Rather than invite Conan Doyle to its dinner, the Society now challenged him to attend a "gala performance [where] our members will—presto!—produce spirit photos and ghostly hands." Doyle didn't deign to reply.

On April 6, responding to the "pharoah's curse" story, the *New York Times* ran an editorial under the headline "He's Beginning to Strain our Patience." Like the magicians' society, the newspaper seemed to have dropped its pretense of civility over the course of the past year. "Again," it wrote, "Sir Arthur Conan Doyle is placing on many of this country's inhabitants the embarrassing task of trying to strike a balance between their long-established liking for him and their equally well-settled dislike of what he is doing." Three days later, as Conan Doyle began his latest round of public lectures, the paper could hardly contain itself. "It is from one of several illusions into which Doyle has fallen that he gets a pathetically false impression as to the success of his work here as a missionary of Spiritism."

There was no such skepticism in evidence when Conan Doyle returned to the stage at a sold-out Carnegie Hall. He was ecstatically received. "Sir Arthur's manner was stern, his bearing measured and calm, his expression grim—he carried conviction," the *New York World* reported. The sepulchral presentation on the stage contrasted sharply with the mounting hysteria in the auditorium. While Doyle had obvious faults as an orator, including a tendency to be both repetitive and verbose, such shortcomings mattered little beside "the force and immediacy of the passions, the intensity of the key message of hope, redemption and immortality conveyed by the sound of his voice alone." By and large, this was an audience who had come to be consoled, many of them holding up photographs of lost husbands or sons, and Doyle was "brilliantly attuned to the fact," Houdini wrote, after "minutely reading" the transcript he had ordered of the event. "It seemed he spoke to the most profound desires, the sufferings, and the shared grief of a whole nation." Once again, Doyle was able to reduce much of the hall to a state of near-frenzy by calling for the lights to be dimmed and then projecting a series of spirit photographs onto a screen. When he came to the one apparently showing the faces of dead soldiers hovering above the Remembrance Day crowd at the London Cenotaph, several spectators began to sob openly and one woman called out, "Don't you see them? Don't you *see* them?" Even Houdini's paid observer in the hall reported that he had "never witnessed an audience thrown into such a state." The combined effect of the photograph and Doyle's "dry and compelling" explanation of it was to reduce "more than 3,000 souls to transports of both dread and joy . . . There were cries of startled delight when the full import of the picture struck home. It took time for them to recover from the shock." After standing silently at the side of the stage for several moments, Conan Doyle took a step forward to the footlights and announced, "It is no wonder that this moves people's emotions. I think it is the greatest spirit photograph ever taken."

Doyle was so convinced of the fact that he was still arguing the picture's merits several years later, as part of a keen debate, conducted both in private correspondence and through the letter columns of the press, as to its authenticity. "I enclose the Cenotaph photo," he wrote to Oliver Lodge later in 1924. "My son is certainly there and, I think, my nephew." "I examined with interest your 'exposure' [of the picture]," he wrote elsewhere, rebutting the suggestion that the "spirit" faces shown were actually those of several still-living professional soccer players grouped around the popular Senegalese boxing champion Siki. With his twin belief in Spiritualism and science, Doyle eventually "sent the whole thing to [the anatomist] Sir Arthur Keith to take anthropometric measurements . . . So that should settle it. But is it not damnable how our poor mediums are insulted and harried?"

While Conan Doyle was busy lecturing and sparring with his American critics, his wife was becoming increasingly assertive about her own role on the tour. It was she, after all, as he often reminded people, who had the mediumistic gift. After hearing Jean give a late-night radio talk on Spiritualism, Doyle was rhapsodic. "The stars were above, the lights of the huge city below, and as I listened to those great truths ringing out in her beautifully modulated voice it was more like an angel message than anything I could imagine." Lady Doyle took a more earthy line with New York's mayor Hylan, who was "an ass" for once again daring to criticize her husband. If not quite "exploring the male-female dynamic" as one later feminist account of their life together put it, the Doyles were, in their way, a relatively "modern" couple. Conan Doyle "undoubtedly thought that women were the superior sex," his daughter Jean was to remark, reflecting on his belief that "a wife would, in a happy home, influence her husband." The contrast to Houdini, whose own marriage increasingly appeared to be more a matter of fondness and occasional exasperation than of partnership, could not have been more stark.

On April 26, Conan Doyle returned to Toledo to sit with Ada Bessinet, the medium who had supposedly materialized his late mother-in-law and son the year before. He took with him not Houdini but his new friend Malcolm Bird of *Scientific American,* who happened to have sailed back to New York on the same boat. "We were greatly favoured that evening," Doyle wrote, "for we had the full gamut of the medium's powers." This included flashing lights and spectral singing, even when Mrs. Bessinet was bound and gagged, as well as automatic writing, apports, and, finally, the levitation of the heavy séance table 3 feet into the air. "It was a very impressive exhibition," Doyle concluded, "and Mr Bird was as interested as I was." Bird heartily endorsed the whole "tremendous experience" in the *New York Times,* which might have seemed to raise questions about his suitability to serve as the secretary of his magazine's prize committee. Houdini himself was unable to sit with Bessinet, but sent a forty-three-year-old Toledo magician and former medium, Robert Gysel, to investigate on his behalf. Gysel was known for his willingness to disrupt paranormal events by unorthodox means, which over the years included his releasing mice or throwing sneezing powder into the darkened séance room. In the ensuing confusion, he was apparently able to surprise more than one medium in the act of perpetrating a "rank fraud," which he dutifully cataloged for Houdini. In the same spirit, Gysel now flung a brick through Ada Bessinet's parlor window, though whether this led to a similar exposure is not recorded.

The Toledo séance marked the start of a renewed outbreak of shadow boxing. Even as they sparred over the "mummy's curse" and other phenomena, Conan

Doyle evidently still had hopes of bringing Houdini into the Spiritualist fold. Writing to the Chicago medium Bruce Kemp (who performed under an Apache "control"), he noted, "I hope you will give a sitting to Mr and Mrs Houdini, who are deeply interested in psychic phenomena . . . I should much like him to hear 'Redfoot's' voice." One can only speculate as to whether this was evidence of Doyle's credulity or of his faith in Houdini's essential goodwill. In either case, he seems not to have read of the show business news from California, where the "Great Genius of Escape" began a brief lecture tour of his own later that month. According to a full-page advertisement in the *Los Angeles Examiner*, Houdini was set to entertain the crowd at the city's Hill Street Theatre with "a Talk on 'Fraud Mediums and Miracle Mongers,'" as part of a broader "Sensational and Startling Show" by "the world-famous psychic detective."

Conan Doyle, meanwhile, assured audiences in the Midwest that he continued to engage in "friendly" and "productive" discussions with a variety of spirits. According to the *New York Times,* he had had "another recent talk with W. T. Stead, the late editor and writer. Mr Stead's voice was as loud and clear as it was when he was on earth, and he advised Sir Arthur as to the preface of a new book he was writing." Doyle informed a full house at the Orchestra Hall in Chicago, "When bad people die, they go into a gloomy purgatorial waiting room, done in sombre grey, and wait until their names are called for heaven." In Cleveland, this was distilled in the morning press to: "Paradise Postponed, says Author." (It was left to H. L. Mencken to remark archly that Cleveland itself was "surely the model" for this infernal holding area.) Traveling back to lecture in Rochester, New York, Doyle found that he was too busy to visit nearby Hydesville, the small town where Margaret and Kate Fox had launched the modern Spiritualist movement in 1848. The author referred to this in several interviews as "the most important date in 2,000 years." On May 10, Houdini noted in his diary, "Sir Arthur had said that he was liable to go [to Hydesville] at the end of his tour, and that it was agreeable to him that we should both do so, making a special trip to go there so we could make the pilgrimage together." Due to their conflicting lecture schedules, the joint visit was then postponed indefinitely, and Doyle was subsequently forced to cancel his plans to erect a monument to the Fox sisters. "The response to my appeal for some central memorial of our Cause has been so scanty that I cannot bring myself to present it," he wrote in *Light.* "I am, therefore, returning the money to the various subscribers, whom I hereby thank."

But if Doyle was not all that good as a fundraiser, he was "mesmerically effective," Houdini admitted, in his core Spiritualist mission. Speaking to large audiences, he was smooth, professional, solemn, and impressive. Conan Doyle's key message of man's immortality moved even the rougher-hewn crowds he now encountered in the American west. The various spirit photographs invariably made an impact, and he was meticulous in his presentation of them. During one performance, he projected a picture of a Chicago warehouse fire that he said showed the ghosts of some fifteen souls who had died in the blaze. Six days later, he admitted publicly that he had been duped by an "unscrupulous" medium, and that the photo was a fake. Doyle was also good in a small-group situation, so long as that group didn't consist exclusively of medium-baiters or reporters. He had an ability to simplify and generalize that was entirely convincing, at least to an audience who had little idea of the specifics of what he was talking about. Circulating at a party held in his honor in St. Louis or Kansas City, Doyle would react to the most elementary question as if he was hearing it for the first time. He would ponder a bit, congratulate the questioner on his originality, then give the answer he had given hundreds of times before, complete with some figures and a quotation, as his new convert listened in awe.

Conan Doyle continued to believe that much the same mix of charm and reason would ultimately prevail with Houdini. It was merely a question of appealing to the illusionist's better self, rather than to his "enormous vanity and passion for publicity [which] had a great deal to do with his furious campaign against Spiritualism." Doyle was repeatedly to follow up his attempts to match Houdini with a suitable medium. "I wonder if young Bruce Kemp gave you a demonstration of his Indian's powers?" he inquired. And a few days later: "Let me know if you heard from Kemp, the young novice medium . . . If you have Alfred Russel Wallace's *Life* in your library, do me a favour and read Vol II, p. 275 onwards. It is a fine narrative of personal experience from a very great man." Despite everything, Houdini still presented himself to Doyle as an objective researcher, not as the "Sensational Exposer of Clairvoyants and Palm Readers" billed on the Orpheum theater circuit. "In my last letter, I believe I told you that I had two sittings with Mr Alexander Martin of Denver," he wrote. "I will show you the photographs at the first opportunity. I have been invited this evening to a séance of a trumpet medium in the offices of the *Scientific American*. If you will send me your address, I will give you the full facts."

For the most part, Conan Doyle and Houdini felt no immediate need to extend their professional respect into a renewed personal friendship. Even so, the core differences of personality and temperament weren't yet registered in public. Doyle "doesn't hate anybody," Houdini observed to Robert Gysel, with evident surprise. "He disagrees with people, and he takes a strong stand for principle—but . . .

he never allows those arguments to get him emotionally hot. He doesn't think of people who disagree with him as being the enemy." Seeming to illustrate the point, Doyle wrote to once again encourage Houdini to seek "some better psychic evidence . . . I have found the mediums very averse to sitting with you as one who has insulted them," he admitted, "but I do my best to clear away that impression." Conan Doyle's efforts at conciliation had apparently not been entirely successful in his own family circle. "Pray remember us all to your wife," he added. "Mine is, I am afraid, rather angry with you."

Early in May, Conan Doyle and Houdini crossed paths in Denver, where they both found themselves staying at the Brown Palace Hotel for their rival performances in the city. There seems to have been a mutual attempt to extend one another every professional courtesy. Each man attended the other's show, which they duly praised to reporters, and the two families lunched together at the hotel. Unfortunately, the generally benign mood was undermined by the local *Morning Express* of May 8, which led with the front-page headline: "DOYLE IN DENVER DEFIES HOUDINI." According to the paper,

> Sir Arthur Conan Doyle, here to preach his gospel of spiritism, is going to back his
> psychic forces with $5,000 against the skepticism of Harry Houdini, the magician,
> who recently asserted that all séance manifestations were fakes . . . "Houdini and
> I have discussed spiritism before," said Sir Arthur. "I have invited him to attend a
> sitting with me, each of us backing our beliefs with $5,000. I have even offered to
> bring my dead mother before him in physical form and to talk to her. But we have
> never got together on it."

Conan Doyle apologized profusely to Houdini for the piece, claiming he had been misquoted. This frequently happened, Houdini admitted. "Sir Arthur stated positively and emphatically [that] he did not challenge me in any way at all. I told him that I had not seen the challenge, and that anyway it would not m[atter] to me," he noted in his daybook. Somewhat belying this show of indifference, Houdini then visited the offices of the *Morning Express,* where the reporter in question not only stuck by his original story but called in a colleague who had listened in on the interview. Houdini let it pass. "With all [Conan Doyle's] brilliancy and childlike faith, it is almost incredible that he has been so thoroughly convinced . . . Nothing can shake his faith," he wrote.

At the age of forty-nine, Houdini's competitive instinct was as sharp as ever. For public consumption, he was happy to praise the "great success of Sir Arthur's spiritist mission to these shores." He took a different tone in the privacy of his diary. "In the *Denver Post* there was hardly anything about Doyle's lecture at the Ogden Theatre," Houdini wrote. "The theatre was comfortably filled, but I do not think it was a 'turn away.' In my estimation, if this man was circussed he would be turning away thousands." Nor had age dimmed Houdini's nagging sense of insecurity. "Bess goes to Doyle lectures," he noted. "Says mine is more interesting and convincing, but I told her, yes, Doyle is a historical character and his word goes far, in fact much further than mine." The Houdinis went on to pay Doyle the backhanded compliment of remarking that the "great intensity" of his lecture seemed to put "quite a strain" on him, and suggesting that he allow himself a fifteen-minute break in the middle of the show, "let[ting] the audience talk and soft music to play [while] he could have a large armchair, to take the required rest."

The two men's "curious relations" were again on display during an hour-long chauffeured drive they took around the sights of Denver. "Doyle told me about a Dr Wickland who would have people come to him who were possessed with evil spirits. He would lay them down and have the evil spirits go into the body of his wife . . . He then insisted that Mrs Bessinet was genuine in everything she did . . . He said that Zancig was sincere. [I] tried to tell him that Zancig acknowledged to me in front of witnesses that he never claimed telepathy, but all this did not move Sir Arthur," Houdini noted ruefully. There appears to have been some further discussion of the previous year's events in Atlantic City. Conan Doyle later referred to this when he provided Houdini with a detailed account of why, exactly, his Hungarian mother should have communicated with him from beyond the grave in fluent English. After an exchange of views on a local family photographer whose pictures routinely showed images of dead babies, the two men and their wives parted in the hotel lobby.

"Five thousand people last night, and a good, psychic, religious atmosphere," Conan Doyle soon wrote back of his next engagement in Salt Lake City, known for its strict enforcement of the prohibition laws. "It is a really splendid place and fine people. I am very much impressed." But now came another of the misunderstandings that seemed to bedevil the Doyle-Houdini relationship. For once, it had little to do with the supernatural. In June 1922, Doyle had apparently mentioned that he would make his friend a gift of the manuscript of *Our American Adventure,* his work-in-progress about that year's lecture tour. Having heard nothing further on the matter, Houdini now wrote to Salt Lake City to say how much he was still looking forward to receiving this "prized addition to [his] library." Doyle's prompt reply revealed not only surprise, but also a healthy awareness of his commercial worth. "A promise—especially to a friend—is very binding with me," he wrote, "but I wish you could recall more precisely to my mind how I promised you last year to send you the MS. of *Our American Adventure.* I think that you surely confused the book with the manuscript . . . I must say that the value of one of my longer MSS. now, in the open market, is several hundred pounds, but that would not in the least prevent my fulfilling a promise if such a promise was made. But I have no recollection of speaking of anything beyond the printed book. Or was it in a letter?" Houdini in turn wrote back to refresh Doyle's memory. "I am perfectly willing to release you from your promise," he added, "but I want you to feel assured that you had promised to send it to me . . . I assure you the conversation transpired as explained." At that Doyle gracefully acknowledged the debt, and that August Houdini was able to add the manuscript to his collection.

Meanwhile, Conan Doyle's tour took him through the Rockies, on to the Pacific Northwest, and eventually to Los Angeles, where he was feted by movie stars like Douglas Fairbanks and Mary Pickford. While in California, Doyle was not pleased to read an article in the *Oakland Tribune* in which Houdini charged that "this distinguished Britisher" had been duped by several mediums over the years, among them a "society London woman" who performed while veiled and bound to a chair, and whom the press promptly dubbed "the Masked Lady." Doyle sent an energetic rebuttal to the paper. "I have had to handle you a little roughly in the *Tribune,*" he told Houdini, "because they send me a long screed under quotation marks, so it is surely accurate . . . I hate sparring with a friend in public, but what can I do when you say things which are not correct, and which I have to contradict or they go by default?" Still piqued, Doyle wrote Houdini another letter the following day. "I must really ask you to deny over your signature [the] injurious statements which you have made . . . I am very sorry this breach has come, as we have felt very friendly towards Mrs Houdini and yourself, but 'friendly is as friendly does,' and this is not friendly, but on the contrary it is outrageous to make such statements with no atom of truth in them."

Now it was Houdini's turn to act the injured party. "There is quite a stir here about a medium who was detected," he wrote in a deftly evasive letter from New York, "and it seems that the *Times* had one of their reporters at the séance, with the proviso that the manner in which the medium was detected would not be written until the *Scientific American* has been published. A very big misunderstanding has arisen, in which the giving out of the information is placed up to me . . . It is too long to write about it, but will tell it to you in person when you arrive." Although Conan Doyle duly returned to New York early in August before sailing to England, there is no evidence that the two men ever met again.

Back in Windlesham, Pheneas soon resumed dispensing advice on a wide range of Spiritual and material matters. After each session, Conan Doyle would write up a summary of what was said, send the interesting parts to friends like Oliver Lodge, and file the rest, eventually editing the "visionary," if sprawling material into a book. Pheneas appeared ready to comment on almost any issue. On the wider front, there were continued warnings of a future global disaster. "There will shortly occur something which will cause great surprise, and influence the whole world in a Spiritual sense," Pheneas remarked, speaking again through the agency of Lady Doyle. "These alarms are like the sirens which sound in your world to summon the workmen." Pheneas was also willing to take questions, and Doyle used the opportunity to ask him about Houdini shortly after the latter's death. "Remorse is overwhelming him," Pheneas reported. "He was a marked man in the spirit world because he represented darkness, while only those who bring light to humanity gain an entrance into the world where God reigns supreme. His knapsack of results was empty." Sometimes the spirit's remarks were more mundane ("You have a mushroom growing where you should have lovely flowers"), and occasionally they seemed to evoke a mood of lost Edwardian patriotism. "You are better in England," Pheneas told Doyle when he inquired about another overseas tour. "England will always be the centre. If it is right all is right." Once or twice, the spirit guide confined itself to cryptic utterances along the lines of "The Medium draws too many turnips and carrots behind her—soon she will tilt the cart back and shoot them all out." Critics were later to remark that Pheneas seemed particularly drawn to Lady Doyle, and as a rule endorsed her own views on most family issues. When, for example, the Doyles' sometime wayward son Denis joined them at a séance, Pheneas remarked that he saw "a sword hanging over" the teenager's head. It could be argued, too, that this seemingly "omniscient soul" proved itself an only modestly gifted forecaster of events. After reading Conan Doyle's book, several reviewers came to refer to the "Pheneas effect," which involved a tendency to promote a few correct predictions while ignoring a larger number of false ones.

While Conan Doyle communed with his spirit guide in Sussex, across the Atlantic the *Scientific American* contest was beginning in earnest. The prevailing mood was caught by the *New York Times*, with its uncanny flair for blending satire and sincerity. "The greatest spook hunt of modern times will begin here soon," it wrote in April 1923. "Mediums have been invited [to] demonstrate their control over psychic forces, under conditions that will enable infallible scientific deductions to be made."

According to the *Times,* Conan Doyle had overcome his reservations about the material intrusion into the temple of faith by offering to add $1,000 of his own money to the payout for any "conclusive psychic manifestation."

In late May, the *Scientific American* committee began to test a rotund, fifty-year-old Pennsylvania voice-medium named George Valentine. Houdini was present when Valentine was tied to a chair one evening in the darkened *Scientific American* library, where a Native American control named Kokum eventually began shouting unintelligibly, several of the sitters felt their knees being tapped, and a zinc trumpet—allegedly for amplifying the spirits' voices—flew through the air, catching Houdini an "awful clout" on the side of the head. This might have been promising, but for the fact that, unbeknownst to him, Valentine's chair had been rigged so that a light would flash in an adjoining room if he managed to free himself and move around. By comparing the flashes with the various knee-tappings and other phenomena, the committee soon determined that Valentine's "manifestations [had] occurred solely and exactly" at the times he had left his seat. He failed to appear for a further investigation scheduled for the following night. It was left to Houdini to contact the *Times* and denounce Valentine as "an outright fake." At that Malcolm Bird went into print to complain that "the great conjuror" had violated *Scientific American* rules by commenting on an individual case before the official findings could be released. Houdini in turn called Bird an "amateur," and privately pronounced his fellow committee members "a lot of boobs."

"SPIRIT PHENOMENA EXPOSED AS FAKES BY ELECTRICAL TRAP," the *New York Times* headlined its front-page lead, one of a series of stories placing Spiritualism at the forefront of such American preoccupations of the day as the Mah Jong craze and a heated evolution debate that would reach its public climax in the so-called "Scopes Monkey Trial" in July 1925. Mass production in the United States had extended from the factory floor to news and ideas as well; there were fewer newspapers, with larger circulations, than before the war, and they were increasingly the domain of vast networks like the Hearst and Scripps-Howard groups, whose home office provided its local titles with editorials, health talks, horoscopes, entertainment gossip, and Sunday features prepared for a national audience and, as one observer wrote, "guaranteed to tickle the mass mind." Houdini's exploits on behalf of the *Scientific American* were now being devoured with one accord by lumberjacks in Seattle and life-insurance men in Connecticut. His next psychic investigation again made the front pages: it involved a Philadelphia housewife and "healing medium," Sarah Mourer, who claimed among other things that she could cure him of his nearsightedness. As Houdini already enjoyed perfect vision, she, too, was ultimately denied any award. It seems that Mrs. Mourer was only one of several of the marginally qualified applicants to now come to the *Scientific American*'s attention. Later in the summer, a committee investigator spent a day interviewing an elderly woman in Margate, Florida, who had taken a photograph of a "mysterious shape" in her apartment's hallway. It was eventually determined that the woman's dog had walked past a lighting fixture, creating a shadow on the wall—"just as any person with adequate levels of oxygen in the brain might have known," Houdini noted.

In October 1923, the *Scientific American* panel met two more contenders who came forward to claim its grand $5,000 prize. Rev. Josie Stewart, pastor of the First Independent Church of Cleveland, Ohio, whom Houdini described as a "dear little old lady," announced that she could produce "supernormal" writings on ordinary playing cards when these were pressed against the forehead of a "receptive" sitter. One such message, she claimed, bore "spirit tidings" from Conan Doyle's friend W. T. Stead. This latest investigation ended when it was found that the Reverend Stewart was pre-preparing her cards at home, and she deemed it best to withdraw her candidacy. Houdini and his fellow members then sat with an Elizabeth A. Thomson of Chicago, a materializing medium and part of a husband-and-wife act who had left a generally favorable impression on the Doyles. "Sir Arthur believe[s] that the Thomsons are unscrupulous and possess a lack of morality, but they are genuine," Houdini had noted in his diary in Denver. "As Lady Doyle said: 'There are great opera singers who are immoral, but who have a great voice, and may be compared with unscrupulous mediums.'" Houdini himself was unmoved by Mrs. Thomson's ectoplasm, which, far from escaping the body "in a sort of transfiguration," seemed to him to consist of bits of the net curtain-like material she used as a veil. Once again, the *Scientific American* withheld its endorsement.

By late 1923, after some six months of investigation, the growing consensus was that the magazine's money was safe. Even Malcolm Bird, the committee's secretary, was led to remark on October 30 that "exhaustive research into the realm of Spiritism and occult phenomena has not convinced me that any communication exists." Few mediums, it seemed, were willing to subject themselves to the *Scientific American*'s fraud-proof conditions, and those who did were "soon expose[d] as utter humbugs," Houdini wrote.

Across the Atlantic, Conan Doyle faced continuing psychic frustrations of his own. An article he wrote in the magazine *John Bull* seemed to hint how strongly the anti-Spiritualist opposition affected him. "Our progress has been slow but it has been steady," Doyle noted. "We have to fight the conservatism of the old churches and the prepossessions of official science. We suffer also from our own faulty presentment of our case, and from the folly or roguery of many who use us for their own selfish ends . . . Before we can win the human heart must be chastened and made receptive, and chastening comes with trouble. The world war was the first stage. I fear it will not be the last." Added to the "great missionary challenge" facing him were several petty disputes within the Spiritualist camp. Earlier in the year, Conan Doyle had been denied a place on the select inner council of the Society for Psychical Research. Claiming to be "almost alone in the polemical arena," Doyle wrote to Arthur Balfour, the former Conservative prime minister and a founding member of the SPR, asking for a public letter of support. The veteran politician replied only that "my opinions upon this subject are already sufficiently well known." Even Oliver Lodge, whose book of conversations with his dead son had caused such a stir on its appearance in 1916, was left to "rather regret Doyle's decision" to invest in a Spiritualist Church in London. "But that I suppose is part of his missionary activity . . . he regards himself as a sort of Wesley or Whitefield," Lodge wrote, referring to the eighteenth-century evangelical preachers.

In December 1923, a candidate finally came forward as a serious claimant to the *Scientific American* prize. He was Nino Pecoraro, the young Italian who could neither read nor write, but who had impressed Conan Doyle with his materializing powers at a New York séance eighteen months earlier. Over the course of two lengthy sittings for the committee judges (but not yet Houdini), Pecoraro once again channeled the late medium Eusapia Palladino and, despite being tied to a chair, apparently made a bell ring and a bugle toot, among other "rattlings, shrieks and high-pitched sound effects," while, somehow appropriately, dollar bills flew through the air. At one stage, Malcolm Bird leaned forward for a better look at the subject and was "nearly asphyxiated" by the smell, which he later credited, in an apparently serious official minute, to a case of "celestial garlic on Palladino's breath."

On December 18, Houdini broke off from his current lecture tour of the Deep South to attend Pecoraro's third evening session at the *Scientific American* offices on the penthouse floor of the Woolworth Building in New York. He immediately recognized the "burly Eyetie" to be an escape artist like the Davenports and himself, and set about taking the necessary precautions. Over the course of an hour and three-quarters, Houdini first tied Pecoraro's hands into two pairs of gloves, which were folded over his chest and sewn to the arms of his jacket. The jacket in turn was stitched to his trousers. Houdini then bound the crouching subject to his chair using some twenty 8- to 10-foot-long pieces of rope, all connected by a zigzagging series of chains and padlocks, and completed the process by locking him inside a box, which was itself covered with thick curtains that he nailed to the ceiling and the floor. The overall result was said to make Pecoraro look like something between an Egyptian mummy and a contortionist. Other than a faint rapping "produced by striking his foot on the side of the cabinet," Houdini noted, Pecoraro was able to do nothing over the next hour except to complain, in Palladino's voice, that he was uncomfortable. A fourth séance was held a few days later, when Houdini was back on tour, which recorded "limited phenomena" but also revealed that Pecoraro had bloodied his teeth and gums in an attempt to bite through his restraints. The *Scientific American* ruled that the overall test had been "inconclusive," and declined to award its prize. Houdini later wrote to his friend Harry Price that the Italian was "mad," and genuinely under the impression he was possessed. Five years later, Pecoraro returned to claim a cash prize offered for communicating with the spirit of Houdini himself, but was again denied by the supervising committee. He ended his days as a surrealist painter.

"I was surprised and sorry to get your letter," Conan Doyle wrote to Houdini on December 24, only now replying to it some six months later. "You can't bitterly and offensively—often also untruly—attack a subject and yet expect courtesies from those who honour that subject. It is not reasonable. I very much resent some of your press comments and statements, and I wrote you from San Francisco to tell you so . . . At the same time," Doyle concluded, "I wish you personally all good— and your wife most cordially the same."

This was gentlemanly and direct, but it was also one of the last times Conan Doyle bothered to communicate with Houdini. That same week, he published an article in *Light* criticizing the *Scientific American* committee and its "flawed" control methods. "I have slowly and painfully been forced to the conclusion," he wrote, "that none of these newspaper inquiries are honest or useful. They are not carried out to find truth, but they are carried out to disprove truth at any cost." In time, a copy of Doyle's piece joined the capacious file Houdini kept on him at home in New York. Harry Price, for one, regarded the two men as having an "equivocal friendship" because though each basically disliked the other, each also showed an "intense interest" in the other and "maintained an unrelenting scrutiny of the other's activities and attitudes"—a love-hate relationship, in fact, that eventually tilted toward the latter. By 1923, it was no longer possible for Houdini to keep up the pretense of being a dispassionate observer of the occult who needed only the lightest push to declare himself a believer. Doyle suspected (not without reason) that "the conjuror" was regaling his coast-to-coast audiences with tales of his own triumphs in fearlessly exposing apparent charlatans like Nino Pecoraro. It showed nothing like the "humble, enquiring mind" needed to get at the truth, he remarked. Most of what Houdini said on the lecture circuit echoed back, amplified, to stoke Doyle's suspicions even further. In one unguarded moment, the illusionist—generally a stickler for clean speech—told his entourage just before going on stage that he would have to vary his normal routine that night by doing a speech on "all that ghost crap." His chief assistant, a genial Irishman named Jim Collins, remarked that the theater advertising referred to such things as "Spiritual enlightenment." "I don't care," Houdini said irritably. "It *is* crap."

Houdini was not always the utter cynic, however, nor would it be correct to say that everything he did was self-serving. "The sick and downtrodden," as he referred to them, were often the beneficiaries of his sympathy, time, or money. He was famously good with children, and rarely refused a request for a charity performance in a hospital or orphanage. "It was good of you to give those poor invalids a show," Conan Doyle once wrote him, "and you will find yourself in the Third Sphere all right, with your dear wife, world without end, whatever you may believe." Houdini's niece Marie Hinson would remember him presiding over "wonderful family meals [of] Hungarian chicken, spätzels, and custard bread pudding with bing cherries," and the completely natural way in which he then invited the young girl to "help myself to a choice item" from his trophy cabinet. Houdini's professional associates thought similarly highly of him. Jim Collins described him as "a good boss and a fair one . . . Many times, when there was no need for it, as I was on regular salary, he gave me substantial presents and bonuses to show his appreciation . . . as far as I know no magician has ever paid an assistant what Houdini was good enough to pay me." Collins demonstrated his loyalty by remaining on call for sixteen years. There are numerous other instances to suggest that the personally frugal entertainer was conspicuously generous both to the more vulnerable members of society and to his own circle. As Collins said, "For Houdini, doing favours for people was a way of life," at least where those people were no possible threat to him. Others "might not necessarily receive the same courtesy," Collins acknowledged.

Houdini had always been thick skinned, but during the last few years of his life his insensitivity became almost pathological. Apparently unabashed by their most recent exchange, he now wrote to Conan Doyle to ask permission to quote from his book (whose manuscript he already possessed), *Our American Adventure*. Among the excerpts he inquired about "are your [remarks] from page 150—'Houdini is not one of those shallow men who imagine they can explain away Spiritual phenomena as parlour tricks, but that he retains an open—and even, I think, a more receptive—mind towards mysteries which are beyond his art. He understands, I hope, that to get truth in the matter, you have not to sit as a Sanhedrin of Judgment, like the Circle of Conjurors in London, since Spiritual Truth does not come as a culprit to the bar, but you must rather submit in a humble spirit to psychic conditions and so go forth, making most progress when on your knees.'" After larding his request with "thanks," "kindest regards," and "best wishes," Houdini signed off by asking: "Would you be kind enough to cable your reply at my expense?"

Doyle was not pleased. "I am answering you by the first post. I could not make myself clear in a cable," he fired back on February 26, 1924.

> You probably want these extracts in order to twist them in some way against me or my cause, but what I say I say and I do not alter. All the world can quote.
>
> What you quote, however, about your own frame of mind is obviously a back-number . . . I read an interview you gave some American paper the other day, in which you said my wife gave you nothing striking when she wrote for you. When you met us, three [*sic*] days after the writing, in New York, you said: "I have been walking on air ever since," or words to that effect. I wonder how you reconcile your various utterances!
>
> I observe that, in your letter, you put down my starting my world-mission "in a crisis of emotion." I started in 1916. My son died in 1918. My only emotion was impersonal and the reflection of a world in agony. Our regards to Mrs Houdini.

On receiving Conan Doyle's "pleasant line," Houdini promptly wrote back offering to send him a copy of his new book, *A Magician among the Spirits*. This time, Doyle didn't reply.

ᜃᔥ ᔥᜃ

"The times hunger[ed] for something," Houdini remarked, in one of his rare philosophical musings on Spiritualism. "A war memorial had appeared in every town, and many people naturally sought some divine solace for their grief." Unfettered by an established Church, America was particularly rich in alternatives. Among other flourishing sects of the 1920s, there were Holy Jumpers ("pretty much like the Methodists," to the *New York Times*, "except that they are more in the habit of working themselves up to a state of religious frenzy which calls for groans and dancing and laughing and shouts to give it adequate vent"); Holy Rollers, who showed similar Pentecostal enthusiasm; and the estimated 2 million followers of the Protestant evangelist Frank Buchman, whose core gospel of "inclusiveness" eventually led him to attend the 1935 Nuremberg rally in an abortive attempt to convert Hitler. But none of these groups, however well subscribed or devoted to their various causes, compared in size or intensity to the worldwide Spiritualist crusade. By early 1924, there were reported to be more than 14 million "occasionally or frequently" practicing occultists, served by a network of 6,200 individual churches, in North America alone. Barely a week passed without some sensational paranormal claim appearing in the newspapers or over the radio. "'MY FRIENDLY CONTACT WITH DEPARTED SOULS: MESSAGE RECEIVED FROM MURDERED CZAR,' by Grand Duke Alexander of Russia" ran one such headline in the *New York Tribune* of January 1924. Houdini may well have been "heedful of the moral harm," he wrote, arising from some of the excesses and exploitations of the Spiritualist movement, and he soon threw all his authority into support of the thesis that it had become the world's most dangerous cult. But it seems fair to say that the showman in him was equally alive to its commercial potential.

Early that year, Houdini signed up with a speaking agency to undertake a nationwide tour lecturing on "crooked or opportunistic" mediums. The talks themselves would be billed under highbrow titles such as "The Psychology of Mal-Observation of Audiences and Spiritualistic Séances." "Houdini the magician," *Billboard* proclaimed, "has become Houdini the educator!" The tour brought him the most respectful notices of his career, and was said to have struck a telling blow against the excesses of the occult. Houdini's diary suggests there may also have been a more personal motive behind his new mission. "Wait till Sir A. C. Doyle hears of my lectures!" he wrote. "Whew !!!" Three months later, Houdini began contributing a series of gothic-flavored stories to the American pulp magazine *Weird Tales*. With a cast of blundering explorers, sinister oriental avengers, and intrepid detectives, at least one of these—"Imprisoned with the Pharaohs"—owed something in its general outline to *The Sign of Four,* though it perhaps lacked Conan Doyle's limpid prose style. Houdini was to write that he particularly enjoyed the opportunity to "meet the intelligentsa [*sic*]" that his literary activities brought him. It was another milestone down the road to respectability. Houdini's ghostwriter, the future science-horror author H. P. Lovecraft, was less convinced, later curtly dismissing him as a "bimbo." What was more, "he's supremely egotistical, as one can see at a glance." A broadly similar complaint arose when Houdini went on to co-edit a card-trick anthology with a magician named Clinton Burgess. Burgess remarked that he had been credited only as the book's "compiler," and "in type so small as to almost require the use of a magnifying glass to read it, whereas HOUDINI's name was plastered all over it."

Houdini was similarly convinced he had a "socko publishing success" on his hands in *A Magician among the Spirits*. Two months before the book's publication on May 9, 1924, reproductions of its jacket cover began appearing in "specialist and general stores . . . even in many residential windows" and in full-page newspaper advertisements coast-to-coast. From there, the publicity machine went into overdrive with "frequent barked announcements" on the radio, and a mailing including the author's photograph and a detailed list of his accomplishments that went to 400 key critics. "The entire American press," one dissenting journalist was left to remark, "has become a giant band playing but one tune." Perhaps understandably, the book was a commercial success. Although generously acknowledging the work's historical sweep and engaging style, some of the reviewers still felt obliged to point out its numerous factual errors. Houdini deflected such "dopey stuff" and "nit-picking" by blaming his editors at Harper and Brothers for having "mutilated" the text. "The publishing of my book had been so long drawn out that I had a slight premonition that perhaps I would not live to see it in print if I waited much longer," he wrote the author Upton Sinclair. "So I allowed them to rush it, against my judgment, and [made] some very important mistakes they did not think worthy of correction."

For years, even so, Houdini would continue to defend *A Magician among the Spirits* as the "truest" of his public writings. It's a claim that the passage of time seems partly to bear out. The perfunctory nature of some of the research makes it hard to treat Houdini as a bona fide religious scholar, despite the aspirations of his entourage. But the book moves at a lively pace, with some particularly vivid sections on those, like the late Maude Fancher, who "help[ed] their immortality along" by "choosing to swallow arsenic or propel themselves from the roofs of tall buildings." The book also dwells on its author's feelings about Conan Doyle. "There is no doubt that Sir Arthur is sincere in his belief and it is this sincerity which has been one of the fundamentals of our friendship," Houdini wrote. "I have respected everything he has said and *I have always been unbiased*, because at no time have I refused to follow the subject with an open mind. I cannot say the same for him." Although Houdini's offer to send Doyle a copy of the book went unanswered, it seems he did so anyway. In time, the two men diverged significantly in their opinions of it. While Houdini considered *A Magician among the Spirits* "an enduring work . . . part of my monument," Doyle had a less favorable verdict. "A malicious book, full of every sort of misrepresentation," he scratched across the title page.

ಆ೦   ೧ಀ

And yet there were those who felt that Conan Doyle sometimes fell short of being an outspoken Spiritualist. It seemed to them that he had been too ready to compromise by arranging access to mediums for those, like Houdini, who had no real interest in the occult beyond ridiculing it to a large audience. It was either a tribute to the author's undying faith in human nature, or a sign of his childlike innocence, that he continued to be obsessed with converting his enemies long after his own "great revelation." This unabated desire to win approval, a common enough human trait, but one particularly pronounced in Doyle, indicated to them that the attainment of great power and wealth hadn't dispelled the sense of vulnerability that dwelled inside the alcoholic's son from the impoverished household in Edinburgh. If his courtship of Houdini shows nothing else, it was that Doyle remained a mixture of personal insecurity and deep religious zeal for at least the first seven years of his Spiritualist crusade.

But by about the time Conan Doyle read *A Magician among the Spirits,* he seems to have come to a more robust view of his core mission. Now, if anything, he struck many of his fellow devotees as only too keen to advance the cause. "I entirely agree about caution," Doyle wrote to Oliver Lodge, after the physicist had expressed doubts about the latest claimant to come forward for the *Scientific American* prize. "But . . . we members of the SPR are continually being made ridiculous by those who represent us—the Hope case, the Madame Bisson case, and now this case are all scandalous in my opinion and must lead to some explosion of feeling" among the faithful. As Doyle's belief in the paranormal grew, so did the sheer variety of his experiences. In his 1924 autobiography *Memories and Adventures,* he cited among other "irrefutable evidence" of the psychic the fact that he had held spirit hands, spoken to the dead, read entire notebooks of data received by his wife in the séance room, seen solid objects fly through the air, and smelled the unmistakable odor of ectoplasm. To experience such things and not believe now struck him as a form of madness. At one family séance in May 1924, he apparently even made contact with the Russian Bolshevik leader Vladimir Lenin, who had died three months previously. The revolutionary hero parted from the Doyles at their nursery table with the somewhat cryptic advice, "Artists must rouse selfish nations."

Conan Doyle's strategy of linkage, based on trading access to mediums for some helpful article or other endorsement, also now took a more aggressive form.

When the SPR's research officer, Eric Dingwall, asked for an introduction to an American clairvoyant who was said to summon voices, ring bells, and make heavy chairs swim through the air, Doyle replied that Dingwall would first have to withdraw his negative review of the Crewe-based spirit photographer William Hope. This was declined. Conan Doyle later angrily resigned his membership of the SPR, citing the "Dingwall . . . tradition of obtuse negation" as among the reasons for his decision. The Hope inquiry surfaced again when the British researcher Harry Price published an article attacking the magician John Maskelyne, who made a habit of exposing occult tricks. Doyle went on to offer Price a sitting with another medium in exchange for settling the "Crewe controversy" in what he called "some honourable fashion," sufficient for Price to make an at least neutral public statement on the subject. From there the plot thickened considerably. Sensing a potential recruit to the Spiritualist cause, Doyle wrote to Price, "I hear from New York—but this is private—that Houdini is accused of dropping objects into a medium's cabinet in order to discredit her. The facts are very clear as stated and I understand that his own committee is against him. He is a very conceited and self-opinionated man but I should not have thought he would have descended to that." What was more, he added, the illusionist "needs showing up . . . [This] should be the last of him as a psychic researcher, if he could ever have been called one." Price, however, was also courting Houdini himself, whom he considered an "even-handed and eminently qualified" investigator. The feeling was clearly mutual. Houdini's thirst for flattery and Price's penchant for providing it helped to seal a complex relationship in which, like a conjurer's stage effect, nothing was ever quite what it seemed. "Am looking forward with great interest," Houdini confided to Price about his exposure of another medium, "to the alibi the folks interested will make." In his own form of linkage, Price promptly wrote to Conan Doyle criticizing Houdini and asking if he, Doyle, would write an introduction to his new book. This time, it was Doyle's turn to refuse.

As the pace of the Spiritualist debate accelerated and, with the increased press and public focus on the still unclaimed *Scientific American* prize, the stakes grew larger, the frantic quality of Conan Doyle's life intensified. He not only was writing his memoirs and articles, as well as keeping Sherlock Holmes alive through his final adventures, but kept a routine in general that would have taxed a man half his age. An American interviewer would recall traveling to Windlesham to meet Doyle in the spring of 1924. The "hearty but jaded-looking" author led him to his study with the promise of an "uninterrupted hour" of his time, having instructed his secretary that "we weren't to be disturbed, except for calls that simply could not wait." During the hour, there were four such calls, two of them on matters sufficiently complicated so that, as the journalist put it, "I bided my time." By now, Conan Doyle's unpaid commitments ranged from lobbying the Labour government to alter the terms of the 1824 Vagrancy Act, which he saw as a form of religious persecution of mediums, down to interesting himself in the most parochial psychic activity. "I'm [told] that the Spiritualist Sunday schools three years running won the annual competition in Lancashire for smartness and physique in a march past," he wrote to Oliver Lodge.

Houdini, too, was no slouch. In March 1924, when he turned fifty, he was dividing his time between touring America in a series of one-nighters—"a hard grind," he admitted—on the lecture circuit, tirelessly promoting his book and continuing to explore various occult phenomena. Later that month, he took the opportunity to sit with a corpulent young Spanish psychic named Joaquin Argamasilla. Argamasilla was supposed to be blessed with X-ray vision, allowing him to tell the time on a watch or read the writing on a piece of paper when these were locked inside a metal box. As a further safeguard, he allowed himself to be blindfolded with two cotton wads held in place by a white handkerchief. Before coming to Houdini's attention, Argamasilla had already been exhaustively tested and endorsed by the Nobel Prize–winning physiologist Charles Richet. He was also something of a cult figure in the American press, who seem to have taken to his mildly comic appearance (reminding *Billboard* of a "Latin version of Fatty Arbuckle") and exquisitely polite speech, which he communicated through a sombrero-wearing Brazilian manager-interpreter known prosaically as Mister Davis.

On meeting Argamasilla, Houdini immediately saw what the Spaniard's previous investigators had missed. The so-called blindfold was "little more than a joke," he wrote. "I [saw] the man place his left hand to his forehead and by doing so almost imperceptibly raise the handkerchief to improve his downward line of vision." The design of the box also struck him as flawed, so that "a smooth operator could merely glance under the lid at whatever lay inside." Houdini invited Argamasilla to use a specially constructed device, hermetically sealed, padlocked, and wrapped in strands of copper wire, he had brought with him for the occasion, an offer Mr. Davis declined on his protégé's behalf. In a subsequent public exhibition, using his own apparatus, the Spaniard failed to read a single word of a message supplied by Houdini. "When the metal box was opened," the *New York Times* reported, "it was found to contain a real estate advertisement from a newspaper, the type of which was so small that many in the room could not read it without the aid of glasses. Darkness finally stopped the test." Following that, Argamasilla retired to private life in Spain, where he made a living as an occasional author and part-time manufacturer of religious figurines. His "locked box" effect lived on, however. Declaring it "without a doubt a wonderful trick in the hands of a conjuror," Houdini himself used a version of it in various magic performances for the rest of his life.

In July 1924, Houdini and the *Scientific American* committee finally came upon a medium worthy of serious consideration for their prize. She was a thirty-five-year-old Canadian-born woman named Mina Crandon, who went under the *nom de séance* of "Margery" and was popularly known as the "Blonde Witch of Lime Street" in honor of her current address in the fashionable Beacon Hill neighborhood of Boston. Margery, as we'll call her, had come to the United States with her family as a teenager, worked unassumingly as a secretary, liked to sing and play the cello, and was known as an active member of the Congregational church—"a modest and materialistic enough upbringing for anyone," she later said. In 1910, she married the owner of a small Boston grocery store, Earl Rand, with whom she had a son. Tragedy struck the following year, when Margery's elder brother Walter, who worked as a motor-mechanic, died at the age of twenty-eight after being crushed by a derailed train on the Provincetown line. But the "resilient and attractive" young woman had soon "turned her face to God," her husband recalled. With Rand himself prone to swing from excessive enthusiasm to equally unwarranted pessimism, Margery seems to have provided emotional stability. "She was the radar that kept him on track," one Spiritualistic history anachronistically notes. Near the end of his life, Rand alluded to this difference: "My wife [said] that in certain dealings with human beings I was a baby."

In 1917, Margery underwent an abdominal operation at the hands of a Boston surgeon named Le Roi Crandon. Crandon does not always make an immediately congenial figure. "Insufferably pompous, dour and rich," in the account of the *Boston Post,* he was twice divorced, an atheist, and was said to be unusually preoccupied with death for one of his calling, occasionally choosing to spend the night sitting up alone in the local mortuary. Some difficulty had arisen when, in 1914, Crandon removed the appendix of a female patient later discovered to be suffering from an unrelated ailment, and he had subsequently spent the winter on sabbatical, sailing his yacht around the Bahamas. Of the time following his second divorce— the still relatively discreet War years—the doctor sometimes confided to colleagues that he had liked to take a series of young women out to dinner and, as he put it, "let nature take its course." Crandon's activities in this area "appeared prolific," one friend remembered. There is some question of whether he might also have strayed from the strict letter of his wedding vows to one or both of his first two wives. In 1918, Margery divorced Rand and married Crandon; she was twenty-nine and he was forty-eight. Rand relinquished custody of their son, whom Crandon legally adopted, and continued to supply the newlyweds with their groceries.

Early in 1923, the Crandons attended a lecture on Spiritualism by Conan Doyle's friend Oliver Lodge. Meeting privately after the performance, Lodge suggested that the couple read William Crawford's book on the medium Kathleen Goligher, the young Irishwoman whose ectoplasm was apparently so strong it could lift the table in front of her. Shortly afterward, the Crandons began to hold séances of their own in a top-floor room of their elegant Boston home. On the evening of May 27, they retired upstairs with three friends, sat down in a circle, lowered the lights, and joined hands. Margery herself was still unconvinced that their human chain was anything more than an amusing parlor game. "They were all so solemn about it that I couldn't help laughing," she recalled. "They reprimanded me severely, and my husband informed me gravely that 'This is a serious matter.'"

For some time, the five of them had sat motionless, listening to the "mournful strains" of a record playing on the Victrola phonograph in the corner of the room. Then, slowly at first, the table began to move. Recovering his poise, Crandon suggested that each of the group get up and step outside in turn; since the table remained stationary when Margery was absent, and continued to slide to one side, and then "immediately rise up and crash dramatically" on her return, it was determined that she was the medium. At a further sitting on the night of June 9, Margery responded to her husband's advice that she "free [her] vocal chords for the spirit's use" by closing her eyes and beginning to rock back and forth in her seat with increasing violence. At the climax of this frenzy, she suddenly froze in place, paused for a moment, and then remarked in a "loud, gruff, masculine" tone: "I said I could put this through!" It was the voice of her dead brother, Walter, speaking.

If channeling Walter was to be the breakthrough moment for Margery as a medium, it was by no means her only psychic accomplishment. Over the course of the next year, she was able to produce raps and flashes of light; furnish rose petals, dried flowers, and even the occasional small bird apparently at will; and, like Pecoraro before her, make dollar bills fly through the air. Seeming to grow in self-

confidence with her successes, she and her husband went on to host a regular series of well-appointed Spiritualistic events. Margery cut an unmistakable figure on
these occasions, typically greeting her guests for the evening in a froth of pink ball
gown, and presiding over a lavish dinner served by a Japanese footman before donning what were called "garments of severely spare cut" for the night's séance. Sometimes her appearance was even more striking than this; according to the Spiritualist
writer Troy Taylor, "She became well-known for her risqué and sometimes bizarre
sessions. It was not uncommon for [Margery] to hold these in the nude and, some
said, she was especially adept at manifesting ectoplasm from her vagina." The authors William Kalush and Larry Sloman add the further detail that she was in the
habit of sprinkling luminous powder on her breasts, creating a "nice effect" for her
sitters when the lights were extinguished. Perhaps understandably, Margery's many
admirers came to regard an invitation to Lime Street as something akin to a presi-
dential summons, prompting several of Boston's leading citizens to arrange their
schedule around her séances. Inevitably, too, there would later be questions about
the propriety of her relations with at least one of the *Scientific American*'s male investigators. Margery, it should also be said, consistently refused to take money for
her demonstrations, promising she would donate any cash prizes she might win to
charity, and was able to "manifest" abroad just as easily as she was at home in Lime
Street. Before coming to Houdini's attention, she had been tested and endorsed by
Professor Richet in Paris, and had gone to England to sit for a photograph by William Hope, which showed an image of Walter unmistakably standing behind her.
Even the skeptical *Daily Express* was left to conclude, "There must be [a] question
that some supernatural agency was at work" in her case. At a séance held in the
Conan Doyles' new London flat at Buckingham Palace Mansions, near the Houses
of Parliament, she was able to make the table rock up and down and a dried flower
materialize on the floor, all while her feet remained under close observation, nest-
ling on Conan Doyle's lap. Doyle later wrote to Crandon, his fellow doctor, fondly
remembering his charming wife and urging him to enter her as a candidate for the
Scientific American prize.

Writing in the magazine's July 1924 issue, Malcolm Bird duly heralded the arrival of a "serious new contender . . . the initial probability of genuineness [is] much
greater than in any previous case which the Committee has handled." This came as
news to Houdini, who was yet to meet Margery. He was "not pleased," he admitted, to subsequently read headlines such as "Margery, the Boston Medium, Passes
All Psychic Tests" and "Versatile Spook Puzzles Investigators: Houdini the Magician Stumped." Trying to retain an acrobat's balance between his position as an

impartial judge and his role as the relentless hammer of false mediums, he quickly collected Bird and the *Scientific American*'s owner, Orson Munn, and headed to Boston. "Houdini is exceedingly angry and has talked at length about lack of respect to him," Munn acknowledged. "In his estimate, those who prey on the bereaved and vulnerable are about the lowest form of animal life on earth." With Doyle and much of the Spiritualist community praising Margery as lavishly as they did, "the stage," Munn noted, was "set for trouble."

7

DOUBLE EXPOSURE

S hortly before Houdini arrived in Boston, Walter manifested at the Crandons' séance table with an irreverent word of welcome for their distinguished guest. "Harry Houdini, he sure is a Sheeny," the spirit announced
with a chuckle, as part of a generally unappreciative limerick. Dr. Crandon seemed
to broadly echo the sentiment when he later wrote to Conan Doyle expressing his
regret that "this low-minded Jew has any claim on the word American." During the
1920s, the Boston Yacht Club and most of the city's better-heeled medical faculties
were very much a man's world, in which locker-room humor and morals were common; prevailing local attitudes to race were "fundamental" and "pre-Lincolnian,"
the historian Richard Hofstadter has noted. But even some of his closest professional colleagues and acquaintances were startled at Crandon's anti-Semitism. "He
would wrinkle up his nose and do kike jokes," said Felix McGrath, who had known
Crandon at Harvard Medical School and later attended at least one Spiritualist
soiree at Lime Street. "Well, a lot of fellows did that. I did it. But the rest of us
would try and keep it down, where [Crandon] just vented all over town no matter
who was listening." Evidently the doctor restrained himself when Houdini first appeared at Lime Street on July 23, because the visitor was "delighted" by the warmth
of his welcome. "Very nice home, neat taste," he wrote in his diary. "Mrs Crandon
is an attractive woman, which explains Bird's reports."

Repairing to the upstairs séance room, Houdini sat down to Margery's left,
took her hand, and signaled for the lights to be lowered. There were a total of six
sitters present, exclusive of the medium's brother and her eleven-year-old son, who,

though not formally a witness, wandered in from time to time from his bedroom downstairs. After hitching up her skirts above her knees, Margery was apparently soon able to ring a bell that had been placed in a closed wooden box at her feet. This was said to announce Walter's arrival. In fact, Houdini later remarked, "I could distinctly feel [Margery's] ankle slowly and spasmodically sliding as it pressed against mine while she gained space to raise her foot off the floor and touch the top of the box . . . At times she would say: 'Just press hard against my ankle so you can see that my ankle is there,' and as she pressed I could feel her gain another half inch. When she had finally maneuvered her foot around to a point where she could get at the top of the box, the bell ringing began and I positively felt the tendons of her leg flex and tighten as she repeatedly touched the ringing apparatus."

When Malcolm Bird left the room for some minutes, a Chinese screen that had been set up behind Margery promptly fell to the ground. A moment later, Walter was heard drawing the sitters' attention to a megaphone that had been set on the floor. "Have Houdini tell me where to throw it," the voice called out. "Toward me," the illusionist replied, and it clattered to his feet. Houdini remained impassive throughout the rest of the two-hour séance, which also saw a luminous plaque apparently float in the air and the gramophone player stop and start of its own accord. He was less guarded on leaving the house with Bird and Munn to return to his hotel. "I've got her!" Houdini immediately announced. "All fraud." The megaphone was "the *slickest* ruse I ever detected," he admitted, but one he could readily explain; Margery had taken advantage of Bird's departure from the room to swiftly pick up the device in the dark and place it on her head like a witch's cap. When the moment came, "she simply jerked her head, causing the megaphone to fall at my feet," Houdini said.

The next night's séance, held in a Boston hotel suite, followed a broadly similar pattern. Early in the proceedings, Walter's voice ordered everyone to push their chairs back from the table so that he could lift it in the air. This, Houdini later remarked, "was simply another ruse on the medium's part, for when all the rest moved back, she moved back also and this gave her room enough to bend down [and] operate." The "intended feat of spiritual uplift," Houdini added, was rather spoiled by his having groped around under the table until he encountered Margery in the act of pushing it with her head. "I do not think she was more surprised than I," he wrote. The séance ended shortly afterward, with Houdini agreeing to wait for a further sitting in front of the full *Scientific American* committee before exposing Margery in the press. Although satisfied the Crandons were "finished [as] miracle-mongers," he was not pleased at the lack of professionalism of some of his fellow investigators. "Bird is a *traitor*," Houdini noted in his diary while on the train back to New York. "He must have helped [Margery] at séances. He is very intimate with her."

The next storm broke when Bird, who had been the Crandons' guest at Lime Street throughout the tests, wrote a number of articles praising Margery's "divine" abilities. Once again, Houdini was forced to read headlines such as "Experts Vainly Seek Trickery in Spiritualist Demonstrations" and "Psychic Power of Margery 'Definitely Established.'" Both Bird and the *Scientific American* investigator Hereward Carrington were later reported to have enjoyed unusually warm relations with the subject of their inquiries. Carrington is said to have been sufficiently smitten to borrow money from Margery, and eventually to ask her to leave her husband and elope with him to Egypt. This sort of obsessive infatuation, or erotomania, would seem to have been of a piece with what Houdini's biographer calls the "voyeuristic" mood of the occasion. Crandon was not above displaying nude photographs of his wife showing her in the throes of producing ectoplasm or some other occult activity, and inviting sitters to intimately examine her before a session. Houdini, for his part, seems to have resisted the air of sexual possibility that pervaded Lime Street. Like others, he occasionally speculated on the precise nature of Margery's abdominal surgery of some years earlier, reasoning that an "enlarged vagin" might act as a repository for foreign substances that could subsequently be made to "presto! manifest at the [séance] table"; but, to repeat, there is no evidence that he ever saw the "devilishly lovely" medium as anything other than the target of his professional inquiries.

When Houdini finally moved against Conan Doyle, he did so with his customary aggression—going from lavishly praising the author to publicly denouncing him without any apparent intermediate reassessment. On June 29, he had given what the *New York Times* called "an illustrated lecture on fraudulent Spiritualistic exhibitions" at a church near his home in Harlem. Houdini "told of his experience with Sir Arthur Conan Doyle and Lady Doyle," the paper reported, "and concluded with the statement that Doyle, Sir Oliver Lodge and Sir William Crookes were merely laboring under self-delusions regarding their spirit investigations." Such men were "not competent," the illusionist added, when it came to exposing the sort of "tricky and fraudulent" practices of all too many mediums. Houdini would soon go into print calling Doyle "a bit senile" and "easily bamboozled." From there, he went on to lampoon the sixty-five-year-old author from the stage of the New York Hippodrome, where Houdini modestly billed himself as the "World-Famous Writer, Lecturer, and Acknowledged Head of Mystifiers." Conan Doyle responded in a long article in the *Boston Herald* that combined a spirited defense of Margery with an attack on Houdini ("as Oriental," he had once noted, "as our own Disraeli"), a man "with entirely different standards" from the other members of the investigating committee. When the paper asked Houdini to comment, he told them that he felt "very sorry" for Doyle. "It is a pity that a man [should], in his old age, do such really stupid things."

Conan Doyle continued to closely follow the Margery investigation, largely through letters and records sent by Dr. Crandon. These had begun even before the full-scale tests had. "Tonight Houdini and Mr Munn sit with us for the first time and will be here several days," Crandon had written on July 23. "I think Psyche [Margery] is somewhat stirred up over it internally, because of Houdini's general nastiness. She is vomiting merrily this morning." "Dingwall [has] been always the gentleman and has been very considerate of the medium's feelings and her health," Crandon later wrote of the SPR researcher who sat with Margery and excitedly reported seeing a pair of "materialised hands" resting in her lap. "He alone of an audience of fifteen hundred dared to get up and tell Houdini he was a liar," Crandon added—a marked change, if true, to Dingwall's previous position. In what was almost a mirror image of the Crandons' practice, Doyle also reported receiving a "steady flow" of spirit messages channeled to him in his family séances. "How lucky we are in having two help-mates who see the essential thing with the same eyes as ourselves," he told Oliver Lodge. "It was the only thing which divided my wife and me, until the war brought a flood of evidence which convinced her."

Some time later, the Doyles' spirit guide Pheneas gave his verdict on the recent events in Boston. "There is a great deal going on in America at present," he noted. "The evil forces are very strong, but the forces of light are stronger. Truth always prevails. Houdini is going rapidly to his Waterloo. He is exposed. Great will be his downfall before he descends into the darkness of oblivion." A few days later, Pheneas spoke further on Houdini's fate. "A terrible future awaits him," he announced. "He has done untold harm . . . His end is at hand. He, and all who uphold him, will be, as it were, chained together and cast into the sea. Your friends the Crandons will even in this world reap the reward of their brave work. In the fearful crisis which is soon to come, America in her sore need will find that she has here a sure and well tested bridge to that spirit world." (The paradox of how, God being perfectly good and eternal punishment wrong, He would choose to inflict this upon anyone acting in good conscience to expose mediumistic fraud was not examined.) On hearing this, Lady Doyle wrote directly to Margery to tell her, "All you have done is going to have very great results in the future . . . When the upheaval comes [and] America is stricken, as she will be . . . you will be a great centre . . . and they will flock to you as a bridge of knowledge and hope and comfort . . . We are also told that Houdini is *doomed* and that he will soon go down to the black regions which his work against Spiritualism will bring him as his punishment."*

On August 25, Houdini returned to Boston with the full *Scientific American* committee to finally determine the truth about Margery. Around 11:00 that morning, the illusionist and his assistant Jim Collins went by appointment to Lime Street to assemble a large wooden crate in the Crandons' upstairs room. The medium would be locked into this at that night's séance, so that, as Houdini put it, she would be unable to fool "even the imbeciles" among his fellow investigators. With holes bored for Margery's head and arms, the general effect was of someone bolted into a device much like a steam box in a sauna. Dr. Crandon agreed to the arrangement on his wife's behalf, but noted for the record that "while the psychic does not refuse to sit in the cage made by Houdini, [she] knows no precedent where a medium has been so enclosed, [and] believes that it gives little or no regard for the theory and experience of the psychic structure or mechanism."

Ten minutes into the evening's session, the bell-box rang and there was a violent cracking noise from the direction of the medium. Turning on the lights, Houdini found that the top of the restraining crate had been forced open, though whether by some psychic agency or by the medium shoving it from below with her shoulders was unclear. The subsequent debate became so heated that Margery, speaking in Walter's voice, called for a recess. Twenty minutes later, the committee returned. The lights were again dimmed and the sitters joined hands. There was a further disturbance when Malcolm Bird complained that there was no room for

---

*The Conan Doyles' two teenage sons often joined in the family circle and staunchly defended the notion that a 10,000-year-old Arab sage was speaking to them through their mother. They remained their parents' loyal supporters right to the end of their own lives. Away from the séance room, the boys (in contrast to their level-headed sister) were not always so pious. "You came back looking very pale," Doyle wrote to sixteen-year-old Denis, "and [Adrian's] eyes are bloodshot and his nerves so near the surface that he can hardly be polite to his own mother." Before long, Doyle was informing his elder son that his life had taken too much of a "jazzy turn," and suggesting a regimen of more cricket and golf and "less dancing, cinemas and late hours in hot rooms. Please!"

him at the table, but after a hissed exchange he was prevailed upon to wait in a room downstairs. A few minutes later, Walter's gruff voice called, "Houdini, have you got the mark just right? You think you're smart, don't you? How much are they paying you to stop these phenomena?"

"On the contrary," Houdini replied, "it's costing me $2,500 a week to be here."

"Where did you turn down a $2,500 contract in August?"

"In Buffalo," said Houdini, apparently happy to discuss his current theatrical bookings with a spirit. After some more in the same vein, Walter asked for the lights to be turned on. When the committee members examined the bell-box, as he requested, they found a small rubber eraser jammed in the apparatus. Although not completely disabling the bell mechanism, it was enough to render it "nearly mute," Crandon complained, before bitterly accusing Houdini of planting it there. Houdini denied having done so. The séance ended in some acrimony.

Houdini prepared for the next night's session by adding a large padlock ("eight padlocks," in Conan Doyle's later account) to the top of the medium's cabinet, and then by challenging Malcolm Bird's right to attend "since [he was] no longer sane when it [came] to Mrs Crandon." After a brisk exchange, Bird announced that he would resign from the committee. "When do you leave for New York?" Houdini asked. "You go to hell," Bird said. After the administrative squabbles, Margery was searched by a female stenographer and placed in her box, a pillow under her feet. Walter announced himself almost immediately, shouting at Houdini that he and his accomplice Collins had now planted a tool in the cabinet. The spirit then displayed some of the robust manner for which he had been known during his earthly life as a motor-man. "Houdini, you God damned son of a bitch!" Walter roared. "I put a curse on you now that will follow you every day for the rest of your short life. Now get the hell out of here and never come back. If you don't, I will!"

The subsequent discovery of a carpenter's folding ruler under the pillow at Margery's feet—of the kind that could be opened out and made to ring the bell-box in front of her—remains the subject of debate some ninety years later. Who put it there? Houdini blamed the Crandons. The Crandons blamed Houdini, before adding on a note of what he called "warm indignation" that, should he go on to publicly denounce them during his engagement at Keith's Theatre in Boston, "some of our friends will come up on stage and give you a good hiding." Although the eventual response fell short of violence, Dr. Crandon, Houdini remarked with justification, "does not like me." Apart from their Spiritualist differences, it would have been hard to find two men less intended by fate to understand one another than the Boston Brahmin directly descended from the *Mayflower* pilgrims and the

Hungarian-born Jewish entertainer. Houdini chose to appear for their final séance together dressed in a pair of snug-fitting running shorts and a matching vest, to show that he had nothing concealed about his person. Dr. Crandon declined his invitation to medically search him. Walter briefly manifested to shout some more abuse, but otherwise the session proved anticlimactic. Houdini went back to his Boston hotel and drafted his report to the *Scientific American* committee later that night. "I charge Mrs Crandon with practising her feats daily like a professional conjuror," he wrote. "Also that . . . she is not simple and guileless but a shrewd, cunning woman, resourceful in the extreme, and taking advantage of every opportunity to produce a 'manifestation.'"

Conan Doyle transformed Walter's insult of Houdini from "You God damned son of a bitch" to "You unutterable cad" or "You blackguard" when, in turn, writing about the incident, but otherwise pulled no punches. "It is as clear as daylight," he told Malcolm Bird, "that the ruler was put in the box, and the rubber in the apparatus by someone who wished to show that [Margery] was fraudulent. And who could this be save Houdini . . . It is a complete exposure—but not of the medium." Speaking of the Crandons in the *Boston Herald,* Doyle added, "This self-sacrificing couple bore with exemplary patience all the irritations arising from the incursions of these fractious and unreasonable people, while even the gross insult which was inflicted upon them by one member of the committee did not prevent them from continuing the sittings. Personally, I think that they erred upon the side of virtue, and that from the moment Houdini uttered the word 'fraud' the committee should have been compelled either to disown him or cease their visits." Some benefit had accrued from the whole *Scientific American* affair, however. The net result of it would be "very good," Conan Doyle later wrote. "Houdini must know in his own heart that the thing is true and his conscience must gnaw at him. He was terrified, I hear." There had been a number of other, if lesser disappointments on the investigating panel, Doyle felt. William McDougall, who had failed to appear for the final séances, "credit[ed] only the negative," while Walter Prince "was seriously impaired by the fact that he was very deaf" and so could hardly hear Walter's voice. Doyle also had doubts about the SPR's research officer Eric Dingwall, who, though initially impressed by Margery's materializing powers, later wrote only that he "did not succeed in achieving my primary purpose, of coming to a definite conclusion as to the genuineness or otherwise of [the] phenomena." The fickle Dingwall had once sat at Houdini's feet for "magical or sleight-of-hand explanations" of Spiritualism, Conan Doyle noted. "He told me

[Dingwall] was the damndest fool he ever met." However, Doyle allowed, "he may have other sides to him which I have not seen."

Houdini didn't immediately denounce Margery from the stage at Keith's Theatre, as the Crandons had feared. He was similarly discreet during a month-long tour of the western states, where he lectured on the subject "Can the Dead Speak?" On October 15, some seven weeks after their final sitting at Lime Street, the *Scientific American* published a preliminary report that did little more than admit that its committee was divided. While Hereward Carrington felt "Genuine supernormal phenomena frequently occur at Margery's séances," "World-famous magician and author Harry Houdini" demurred. "Everything which took place was a deliberate and conscious fraud," he wrote, "and if the lady possesses any psychic power, at no time was the same proved" in his presence. Houdini went on to add some personal remarks about Conan Doyle, whom he accused of believing "he is a Messiah . . . But instead of that he is misleading the public and his teachings are a menace to sanity and health."

Houdini was now elated by the chance to attack Doyle. All pretense of civility, let alone of psychic cooperation, was gone, and the illusionist remarked it was his "sacred duty" to confront "any such neurotic believer in the occult." Another chance came in December 1924, when Doyle sat on the platform of a 3,000-strong Spiritualist meeting in London where the former *Daily Sketch* gossip columnist Hannen Swaffer spoke of communicating with his old chief Lord Northcliffe, who had died in 1922. Doyle himself went on to write an article that appeared under the headline "Northcliffe Speaks Again!" in the *New York Times*. "Sir Arthur Conan Doyle [has been] hoodwinked from New York to San Francisco and back again," Houdini remarked. "I knew Lord Northcliffe when he was plain Harmsworth, and he came to my dressing room in London. I will write something on a piece of paper and seal it, and I challenge the spirit of His Lordship to tell us the subject matter in question . . . One must be half-witted to believe some of these things," he concluded.

Houdini's official show of neutrality on the Crandons came to an end that month, with a self-published pamphlet he called *Houdini Exposes the Tricks Used by the Boston Medium "Margery."* Its cover photograph showed him locked inside the spirit cabinet, craning his neck forward so he could use his forehead to ring the bell-box on a table in front of him. Although Houdini's specific complaints varied, in years ahead he would cling to his essentially hostile vision of the Crandons as tenaciously as a dog to a trouser leg. Houdini's exposé, which he spent some $3,000 to advertise, freed his fellow *Scientific American* committee members from their own vows of silence. In William McDougall's case, it was the implied insult to the professor's "mental faculties [and] powers of logic" by an "itinerant paid magician" that rankled. "I do not require that man to teach me something about which I probably know more than he does," McDougall harrumphed. A public debate on the respective merits of practical and abstract intelligence followed. "Men like McDougall [and] Conan Doyle are menaces to mankind," Houdini told the press, "because laymen believe them to be as intellectual in all fields as they are in their own particular one." Illustrating his claim that "there [was] more to smarts than academic know-how," he went on to invite McDougall to "demonstrate his great knowledge of psychology" by "consent[ing] to be stripped nude and searched, and then escape from a heavily weighted packing case thrown into the Charles River," a challenge the fifty-five-year-old Harvard dean declined.

After mauling one committee member, Houdini went on to attack two others. Both Hereward Carrington and Malcolm Bird had been sufficiently deluded, he claimed, "to assist Mrs Crandon with little effects at opportune times." This triggered another round of mutual abuse and questioning of intellectual credentials. Carrington called Houdini a "pure publicist" and charged he had "no scientific talent [for] psychic investigation . . . He had himself appointed only because of the fame it would bring him." This gift of self-dramatization surfaced again on the steps of Boston City Hall, where Houdini appeared waving aloft $10,000 in bonds, which he offered to divide equally "between charity and Mrs Crandon" should she agree to join him for a public performance nearby and produce "tricks or manifestations I cannot explain." When Margery failed to materialize on the night in question, Houdini took the opportunity to re-enact the medium's "maneuverings and flim-flams [on] show at her boudoir in Lime Street." These included his ringing a bell and rattling a tambourine, despite having his hands bound and his feet firmly held by a volunteer from the audience. "What convulsed the spectators," the *Boston Post* reported, was that they could see Houdini ease his foot from his shoe and play the instruments with his toes—a "miraculous deceit" that the use of a cloth and subdued lighting concealed from the "astounded rube" sitting across from him. After the physical demonstration, Houdini turned to the "more scholarly part of the presentation," which in practice meant mocking his enemies. "Sir Arthur Conan Doyle states I am a medium," he announced. "That is not so. I am well done." After the guffaws had died down, an audience member stood up to yell, "I will tell you one thing, you can't fill a house like Conan Doyle did twice."

"Well, all right," Houdini shouted back. "If ever I am such a plagiarist as Conan Doyle, who pinched Edgar Allan Poe's plumes, I will fill all houses."

"Do you call him a thief?"

"No, but I say that his story 'Scandal in Bohemia' is only the brilliant letter [*sic*] by Poe . . . I walked into his room at the Ambassador Hotel and I saw twenty books, French, English and German, a paragraph marked out of each one of the detective stories. I don't say he used them . . ." Houdini continued, but the rest of what he said was lost in the ensuing uproar.

Shortly after this, three members of the *Scientific American* committee wrote to the press refuting Houdini's claim of "culpable conduct on the part of [Carrington and Bird] . . . He has indeed made general assertions, but no intelligible specifications, much less proved them in a manner which would be admissible in a court of justice." Nor had he satisfactorily explained "all the phenomena [produced] under conditions of perfect control" by this woman of "personality and charm . . . the wife of a physician of standing."

This was perhaps the heart of Margery's appeal, her ability to create belief, not so much in props like the bell-box, but in herself as a reputable medium, uniquely endowed with superhuman powers to convey the words, and even the distinctive phrasing and idiom, of the dead. The questions remain: did she in fact channel the voice of her brother, or was it all nothing but a form of psychic ventriloquism act? Like a wisecracking wooden dummy, had Walter enabled his sister publicly to berate others in terms she might not have used in her more formal role as Mina Crandon? If so, had the creation eventually come to dominate the creator? Since the Crandons refused to take money from their clients, what could have possessed them to set themselves up in the often bitterly acrimonious world of Spiritualism in the first place? Houdini's friend and lawyer Bernard Ernst (who admired Conan Doyle) suggested the Crandons might have been engaged in a "rare [and] unspoken mental compact" in which each party met some "deep interior need" of the other. According to this theory, Dr. Crandon initially took a paternalistic, if not mildly voyeuristic satisfaction in parading his young wife to strangers, while Margery herself wished only "to oblige the eminent surgeon who appeared to have such hold over her." One can speculate whether, in time, the Crandons came to believe in the utter sincerity of their performance. Might the medium's specific choice of spirit guide equally have been a sort of "closure" of her feelings for the prematurely departed Walter? Were the otherwise impeccably qualified *Scientific American* observers prepared to suspend their disbelief when, after enjoying her lavish hospitality downstairs, they were then confronted by the attractive and scantily clad Margery in a darkened séance room reportedly "perfumed by sex"? They are points worth raising, if only to show that Houdini, while adept at reproducing some of the medium's physical feats, never fully addressed the psychological factors.

"I have written the whole story," Conan Doyle told Oliver Lodge, "which I hope will prick the Houdini bubble for ever. We Spiritualists are too supine [and should] punch back." Doyle's impassioned defense of the Crandons, published in the *Boston Herald* on January 26, 1925, duly seemed to hit its mark. "Houdini Stirred by Article, May Sue Sir Arthur," read one of the next morning's headlines. Doyle was also at work on his definitive, two-volume *History of Spiritualism,* a guide for the lay reader written in his distinctively crisp style, and in establishing the Psychic Bookshop he chose to open, somewhat incongruously, sandwiched between Westminster Abbey and Methodist Central Hall. "You must come to see me for your books," he told a correspondent. "The venture will cost me £1,500 a year but it may in time pay its own way. If not, I don't see how money can be better spent." Pheneas, meanwhile, continued to comment on a range of domestic and international issues, warning, for instance, that Japan was "going under" that month, although, as it turned out, nothing worse seems to have happened there than her decision to withdraw some of her troops from the disputed Pacific island of Sakhalin, and the demise of an Osaka man who for some reason hated the Emperor, slept with a sword under his pillow in case His Imperial Majesty should call, and ultimately chose to disembowel himself in the town square as a show of protest.

"The Margery case will live in history," Conan Doyle predicted in the *Boston Herald,* reviewing the events of the previous summer. "Houdini left Boston a very discredited man," he concluded. "His friends will hope that he will confine himself in future to the art in which he is famous and leave a field in which his strong prejudices and unbalanced judgment entirely unfit him." The same newspaper published an editorial noting that Doyle had "us[ed] the methods of deduction made famous in his Sherlock Holmes stories" in his "minute examination" of the Margery séances—though even Holmes might have hesitated to comment quite as freely without first visiting the scene. Houdini in turn told the press he would "have a retraction or communicate with [his] lawyer." Although he backed off from this particular threat, he kept up a relentless public attack on Doyle, the Crandons, Carrington, and Bird, among others. When Orson Munn defended his magazine's committee, Houdini furiously accused him of "twisting the facts" on Margery, which he wanted known "in case anything should happen to me." The whole affair flared up again when the Crandons hired Boston's 1,200-seat Jordan Hall for what was at first billed as a public séance, but then became an illustrated lecture on Margery's talents. Houdini wasn't present, so he didn't hear the mingled retchings and applause as lantern-slide images of the medium spurting out ectoplasm shaped much like a string of sausages were shown to the audience. This substance often "extended itself to ring bells and flip papers on the floor from a nearby table," Eric Dingwall commented, as Rev. Elwood Worcester, an Episcopalian minister, watched from the platform. According to the *Post,* Dingwall went on "to pay his respects to Houdini by referring to him as an individual 'whose knowledge of the art of self-liberation is as profound as his ignorance of the methods of scientific investigation' . . . This phrase was greeted with prolonged applause," the paper noted.

On February 11, the *Scientific American* committee issued its final verdict on the Margery affair. "We have observed phenomena," it concluded, "the method of production of which we cannot in every case claim to have discovered. But we have observed no phenomena of which we can assert that they could not have been produced by normal means." Although "she belonged to an entirely different class from the usual run of fee-taking Spiritualists," Margery failed to win the prize. Houdini was not pleased at what he considered the "mealy-mouthed" wording of the report, which fell some way short of his own view on this "resourceful and tricky" woman. "This is a very important thing in all of our lives, and I contend that she is fraudulent in all of the manifestations I have witnessed," he wrote. When Malcolm Bird was subsequently appointed chief research officer of the American SPR, Houdini resigned from the society in protest at their promotion of this "nut job." Dr. Crandon wrote to Conan Doyle shrugging off the committee's verdict, though venting his anger at William McDougall, who "took occasion in public print to enlarge on his 'hoax theory'; a cowardly and dishonest statement. In reply I have expressed my opinion of him in today's paper." Doyle in turn proposed that the College of Psychic Science in London award the Crandons a suitably engraved loving cup, "in recognition of their heroic struggle for the truth."

Shortly after the *Scientific American* verdict was announced, Walter returned to the séance room. Banging a megaphone up and down for percussion, he bawled out a song he had composed for the occasion. The first verse ran:

> *Oh Houdini won't talk no more, no more,*
> *He ain't gonna talk no more.*
> *What in hell will the newspapers do?*
> *When Houdini won't talk no more?*

Conan Doyle was sixty-five, and conspicuously lacked Houdini's all-consuming ego and driving energy, of which a Boston reporter noted: "Power just emanated from him . . . There was that look he gave. There was the way he held his head. Even if you didn't know who he was you would know this was a guy to be reckoned with. You would feel: don't cross this guy. He had the bearing of a man on a pedestal." Doyle, by contrast, had largely renounced any material ambitions. Earthly life now seemed to him to be an insignificant way station on an eternal journey. For some years he had scaled back on what he called his worldly activities, not having published a novel since *The Valley of Fear* in 1915. Doyle's memoirs made it clear that this was no oversight on his part. "People ask me," he wrote, "what is it which makes me so perfectly certain that [Spiritualism] is true. That I am perfectly certain is surely demonstrated by the mere fact that I have abandoned my congenial and lucrative work, left my home for long periods at a time, and subjected myself to all sorts of inconveniences, losses and even insults . . . This is the work which will occupy, either by voice or pen, the remainder of my life."

Conan Doyle's Spiritualistic and material interests did find common ground in the Psychic Bookshop he opened in 1925. Doyle and Lady Jean both took turns manning the cash till, and he subsidized the venture even more generously than the £1,500 a year he had estimated.* Giving the shop the telegraphic address "Ectoplasm Sowest London," he eventually expanded it to include a small printing press and a psychic museum. Among other artifacts, the latter boasted

> spirit slate-writing through the medium Eglinton, and the same in English, Latin and French through Slade; writing in Greek with correct accents by an uneducated man, and direct spirit-writing, so small that it can only be read with a magnifying glass, received by Mr Morell Theobald; the painting of a landscape done by Duguid, when in trance and blindfolded; a "precipitated" picture in coloured crayon painted in 17 seconds in the presence of Judge Edmunds . . . finger prints of a ghost taken on smoked glass in a haunted cottage at Inhurst . . . and an ancient Assyrian vase, received among about 2,000 other apports, by an amateur medium, Mrs Maggs of Portsmouth.

While there was generally a healthy-sized crowd of what Conan Doyle called "the committed or the curious" on the premises, some of these would seem to have come less for the opportunity to spend their money than to meet the famous proprietor.

---

*Conan Doyle later calculated that he had given the Spiritualist movement as a whole some £250,000 over ten years—a fortune of about £9.5 million today.

"Yes, this is not a shop only—it is a spirit surgery," Doyle told a reporter. "They bring their psychic experiences, their hopes and their worries. Sometimes we can help them, sometimes we can't. But we do our best." Declaring the whole project a "noble experiment," Doyle ran it at a loss of some £5,000 a year for the rest of his life.

In July 1925, *The Strand* published the first installment of Conan Doyle's novella *The Land of Mist,* in which Professor Challenger returned to engage in a series of Spiritualist debates with his companions. This uneasy mix of Doyle's classic adventure-story style and newfound didacticism failed to impress the critics. "Unfortunately, yet perhaps inevitably," the *New York Times* wrote, "the characters [are] scarcely more than props for Sir Arthur's propaganda." The London *Times* concluded the book was a case of "too much pill, too little sugar-coating." Conan Doyle also published twelve Holmes adventures between 1921 and 1927, bringing the series to a conclusion after forty years. While some of the latter-day stories showed the author's old eye for detail and lapidary description of character, these, too, fell short of his finest work. Doyle acknowledged as much in a letter to Greenhough Smith accompanying Holmes's sixtieth and last appearance, "Shoscombe Old Place." "It is not of the first flight," he wrote, "and Sherlock, like his author, grows a little stiff in the joints, but it is the best I can do."

While Conan Doyle crossed swords with living writers such as George Bernard Shaw and H. G. Wells, both of them skeptics on Spiritualism, he enjoyed warm personal relations with several dead ones. W. T. Stead, for one, continued to appear at séances and to "keenly endorse" his friend's paranormal research. Writing in the SPR *Journal,* Doyle went on to reveal that the spirit of Joseph Conrad had materialized to ask for his help in completing *Suspense,* his unfinished Napoleonic novel, and that Charles Dickens had appeared with a similar commission. When Jerome K. Jerome died in June 1927, Doyle reported that he, too, had emerged and recanted his earthly materialism. "I was wrong," Jerome said. "We never know our greatest mistakes at the time we make them. Make it clear to Doyle that I am not dead."

After "seeing off" the Crandons, as he put it, Houdini's anti-Spiritualist campaign took on an almost missionary zeal. He petitioned President Coolidge and members of Congress for legislation against this "terrible cancer"; wrote to judges, police chiefs, and newspaper editors on the subject; and likened mediums to drug dealers "who peddle stuff to turn ordinary folks crazy." Robert Gysel, the Toledo magician who similarly thought all mediums "fraudulent" and "over-sexed," would say that Houdini was "an emotional man, [and] he would start talking about something and convince himself it was right, and get all worked up, all worked up and emotional, and work all day and all night, and sacrifice, and say, 'Follow me for the cause! Let's do this because it's *right!*'" The process was all-consuming. Soon Houdini was back touring America with a series of lectures and demonstrations, which he enlivened by extending his $10,000 Margery challenge to "any mediums [able] to prove the genuineness of their contentions that they get spirit messages."

A number of confrontations ensued. On stage in Denver, Houdini offered Rev. Josie Stewart (the "dear little old lady" whose claim to produce occult writings on playing cards had collapsed when it was found she was in the habit of marking the cards at home) the house receipts for the night—some $3,000—if she could produce "one word from the beyond." When Rev. Stewart declined, Houdini began to read out the transcript of a recent court case involving Stewart and her husband, the trigger for rival factions in the audience to pelt one another with "assorted light refreshments," the *Denver Post* reported, the scene "fast becoming a bedlam." To assist with his exposures, Houdini enlisted the services of a small, but fanatically loyal group of undercover agents and informants, among them a glamorous New York brunette named Rose Mackenberg. According to Houdini's biographers William Kalush and Larry Sloman, "In two years she attended hundreds of séances and filed detailed field reports that described the premises, the audience, and the medium. She was ordained six separate times as a full-fledged Spiritualistic Reverend with the right to perform marriages, baptize infants, and bury the dead." In 1926, Mackenberg would go on to buy the entire Unity Spiritualist Church of Worcester, Massachusetts, for the bargain sum of $13.50. Houdini also immersed himself in Spiritualist literature, buying complete runs of *Light* and other journals, part of an estimated 50,000 books and pamphlets and 250,000 manuscript pages in his home archive. "I only work five months in a year," he remarked. "The other seven I am in my library." Houdini regularly traveled with two steamer trunks full of papers; if a member of the audience challenged him on his facts, he signaled offstage for an assistant to rapidly sort through the file and bring him the clinching document. "And didn't Houdini love those moments!" a reporter noted. "His bitter wit flowed free, he hurled back challenges, and it took a cast-iron clairvoyant to get out of the house undamaged in mind and soul."

Among Houdini's paid informants was an enigmatic British actor-impresario turned politician named Harry Day. Born Edward Lewis Levy in 1880, he had had a colorful career in the Edwardian music hall before changing his name and going on to serve with distinction in the First World War. Day had first met Houdini in 1902, when he made bookings for him in Europe. In October 1904, the two men had been unsuccessfully sued by the Moss chain of theaters, which claimed they had the exclusive rights to the illusionist's services. Twenty years later, Day was elected as the Labour MP for Southwark Central. As well as his parliamentary duties, he was to regularly turn over to Houdini "boxloads of annotated press cuttings [and] minutes of church meetings, membership lists and other data . . . complete dossiers on the British Spiritist movement."

In August 1925, Le Roi Crandon wrote to Conan Doyle complaining that an "unknown muckraker" had objected to his and his wife's application to adopt an English boy. This party had also spread the "baseless" rumor that the couple had been involved in some form of transatlantic child-trafficking operation. "Our Secret Service Department in Washington received a letter saying that I had first and last 16 boys in my house for ostensible adoption, and that they had all disappeared and advised the Department to look us up. Last week I had a call from the Boston manager of the White Star Line saying that an MP had sent a long questionnaire to their [office] at London concerning the [whereabouts] of a boy. It is quite apparent that there is an enemy here . . . I will try to get the name of the MP. In the meantime, ask Sherlock Holmes to think it over."

When Conan Doyle replied, it was to suggest that it was "the hand of the Roman Catholic Church," and not of a private individual, that lay behind the Crandons' troubles. This conviction would be consistent with his steadily darkening view of Catholicism that had begun at Stonyhurst fifty-five years earlier. Before long, Doyle was able to further report to Crandon that the MP in question was Harry Day. A three-way correspondence ensued. Crandon eventually wrote to Day, explaining that he and his wife had adopted "Horace Newton, an attractive boy [who] did not seem to fit in our household and was sent back . . . In return for this information, I beg you to tell me who was interested to find out these facts. I will give you my word to keep it private and personal." Although Day replied correctly that it would be "a breach of confidence were I to disclose the names of those who called my attention to the original circumstances," Conan Doyle and Crandon soon fixed the blame on Houdini. Some discrepancy existed, however, between their views on whether or not the conspiracy ended there. While Crandon thought the "low-minded Jew" entirely to blame, Doyle persisted in his belief that the Vatican was somehow "using" Houdini through his Roman Catholic wife. One can see too how the author of Sherlock Holmes might have felt a certain concord with a mystery involving an Atlantic crossing, a missing person, and an eminent but elusive villain. The plot thickened considerably when, in June 1927, someone broke into Day's London flat and slashed an oil painting that hung in the living room. A plaque under the work was inscribed, "To Harry Day from his sincere pal, Harry Houdini." *The Times*' account of the "Mysterious Case of the Westminster Art Mutilation" was sent to the Crandons by the SPR researcher Eric Dingwall, who wrote, "This is the man whom Houdini got to ask about your kid. You are revenged!" Crandon himself seemed to agree with this thesis when, on July 6, he cabled Doyle: "Did you notice that the apartment of Harry Day, MP, was robbed and destroyed by vandals? If we were superstitious, we might be inclined to say that old John G. Nemesis was on the job."

The scenario of conspiracy and treachery surrounding the Margery investigation as a whole only intensified following the *Scientific American* report. Houdini was excluded from the medium's latest round of séances, but he successfully infiltrated a spy, a friendly *Boston Herald* reporter named Stewart Griscom, into them. Griscom was soon sending back detailed reports of the Spiritualist goings-on at Lime Street. "Houdini's exploded," Dr. Crandon announced as the party gathered upstairs one night. "He's finished!" A few minutes later, Walter came through to confirm this assessment. "Yes, it's all over with Houdini, that fraud," the spirit voice shouted. "He even tried to plant the kid! But he didn't get away with it, did he?" Griscom, it emerged, wasn't the only mole involved in the increasingly bitter and paranoid power struggle taking place that summer. When Houdini returned to play a season at Keith's Theatre in Boston, Dr. Crandon planted a businessman friend named Carl Dennett in the audience. Following the show, Dennett invited himself into Houdini's dressing room, where he gave his name as "Smith." After some preliminary verbal sparring, a "sharp discussion" ensued about the very real dangers that might befall anyone tempted to criticize or question Margery's abilities. The next morning, Dennett reported to the Crandons that Houdini had been "most anxious to find out who I was and arranged to have men follow me when I left . . . but we were able to throw them off the trail, so that he could not learn my identity."

This was all a dress rehearsal for yet another full-scale Margery investigation, in which Houdini played a key offstage role. It was undertaken by members of the Harvard University psychology department, who reported their findings in an article called "Science and the Medium" in the November 1925 issue of *Atlantic Monthly*. Its author, one Hudson Hoagland, revealed that while "inexplicable manifestations" had taken place at Lime Street, so had "various deceits and subterfuges." Among other things, Margery had been observed guiding a luminous paper disc through the air with her foot, and removing a strand of fake ectoplasm, thought to be butcher's offal, from between her legs. The researchers concluded that the Crandons seemed to have convinced themselves of their own sincerity, and that Margery had slipped into a form of self-hypnosis in order to channel the "Walter" character. Houdini took an active part in the proceedings, whether writing to the president of Harvard with a shopping list of suggestions and requirements for his investigators, or assembling a new and improved spirit cabinet, this one resembling a medieval Iron Maiden, for the occasion. As it turned out, he didn't put his device to use, possibly anticipating the adverse publicity, and preferred to rely on the well-tried system of placing an informant in the room. Houdini was in touch throughout with one of the investigators, a graduate student named Grant Code, with whom he engaged in an almost psychotic (though, at the same time, asexual) exchange on the most clinical details of Margery's anatomy. This confirmed, at least to their mutual satisfaction, that Dr. Crandon had surgically enhanced his wife's reproductive organs. Houdini was characteristically ebullient on reading the *Atlantic Monthly* article, which he copied and sent to some 300 friends and admirers. "A certain group of Professors [has] accomplished in half a year what I did in one night . . . This has been a wonderful vindication for me," he wrote to the author Walter Lippmann. Houdini's satisfaction was compounded by the fact that "the eggheads have now denounced [Margery]," he reported. It was "the highest compliment academia could give [him]." The itinerant paid magician "was right all along."

Houdini saw the apparent exposure of the Crandons as part of a larger defeat being inflicted on the Spiritualist camp as a whole. Never shy about broadcasting his achievements, he now described himself to Lippmann as the "greatest scourge of mediums in history." The popular author and occultist Margaret Deland seemed to confirm Houdini's assessment of the situation when, in July 1925, she wrote to Oliver Lodge, "It seems to be very difficult just now to find American publishers who have any desire to print books on psychic research. The Crandon fiasco has given the subject a black eye among people whose thought does not go further than the obvious, namely the entirely possible fraudulency of the Crandons." For her part, Deland had no doubt whom to blame for this state of affairs. "I am seriously displeased at [William] McDougall's silence in the matter of the [Harvard investigation]," she wrote. "All that would be necessary for him to do would be to good-naturedly caution people not to throw away the baby with the bath . . . But instead [he has] allowed himself to become involved in personal relations with the unspeakable Houdini. He asked the man to dine with him! Houdini is absolutely impossible, and that McDougall, or any other man of cultivation, should have any-thing to do with him, I cannot imagine."

Although Houdini used the likes of Rose Mackenberg to infiltrate séances and carry out a range of covert black ops on his behalf, he wasn't averse to donning a blond wig and thick glasses to go undercover himself. Posing as "F. Raud" (for "Fraud") and looking like a more subdued version of the artist Andy Warhol, he was able to sit with a long-established Cleveland, Ohio, "trumpet medium" named George Renner. In a typical séance, Renner would lower the lights, turn on the gramophone, and ask his clients to direct their attention "upwards, into the be-yond." After a few minutes, a luminous trumpet would sometimes be seen swim-ming through the air. On this occasion, Houdini turned a torch onto the medium, showing his face and hands to be covered in black boot polish. Several moments of profound silence ensued. As Houdini had previously daubed Renner's trumpet with the same distinctive substance, this indicated "some contact had been made between the clairvoyant and his flying horn," in the words of the subsequent crimi-nal indictment, which charged Renner with fraud. Houdini saw this as a "relatively mild" case of a "worldwide infatuation with the occult . . . In America alone, millions of dollars are crookedly obtained each year, homes are wrecked, wills changed." The consequences of this "dangerous and insane" delusion went deeper still. "When a prominent English lecturer was in this country," Houdini wrote, "an aged man and woman killed themselves after hearing lectures on the wonderful life beyond. Suicides are frequent. W. Bonner, 40, of Oran Street, Leicester Square, London, was a Spiritualist and was persecuted by spirit voices. He hanged himself." Houdini saw Spiritualism's hand at work shaping the very fate of nations. "There is no doubt in my mind that Rasputin was the direct cause of the fall of Russia," he told a theater audience. "He was a medium and claimed he could bring back any one of the Bibli-cal characters. He held the Czar and more particularly the Czarina in his clutches, and it was through his mediumistic work that he called down vengeance on his own head." (New reports that the body of the Romanovs' chief oppressor was to be kept in a state of cryonic suspension until such time as science could revive him were "hogwash," Houdini added. "I will be elected Pope ere Comrade Lenin returns to life.")

Curiously, Houdini's assault on this "systematic evil . . . the greatest self-im-posed calamity in human history," as he called Spiritualism, didn't preclude a belief in the theory of communication between the dead and the living. As he readily admitted, there had been "many cases where [he had] escaped from a quite tight spot" only after offering a prayer to his late father. Had Mayer Weiss somehow interceded to let his son swim free of a submerged trunk or wriggle out of a straitjacket while suspended upside down, like an inverted cross, from a skyscraper? Houdini himself always insisted that he was in the business of exposing fraud, not of debunking "the very real prospect of there exist[ing] some form of bridge" to the afterlife. In July 1925, at the height of his campaign against Margery, he wrote to a correspondent named M. M. Soule in Boston, "As you know, I am not a skeptic and mediums who are genuine need have no fear." During his lifetime, Houdini made several elaborate pacts with his family members and friends that whoever among them died should contact him using an agreed code word. None did. When Houdini's older brother Bill succumbed to tuberculosis in January 1925, the illusionist locked himself up in the attic of his home for 48 hours to await a message. Although again disappointed, he retained a "strong sense of communion with worlds unseen." The origins of this outlook may have been the early and intense religious training Houdini received at the hands of his Rabbi father, as well as his own numerous near-death experiences. Whatever the cause, he continued to believe in at least the possibility of Spiritual visitations. In July 1913, Houdini had "many times" woken in the dead of night, apparently convinced he could hear or see his recently departed mother. Not long after that he introduced a paranormal slate-writing effect to his stage act, more than two years before Conan Doyle announced his own Spiritualist conversion.

Conan Doyle frequently characterized himself as a reasonable researcher, whose numerous psychic experiences were "real stepping stones to [a] fixed conclusion," as he said in his memoirs. To some of his critics, the exact opposite was the case; Doyle's mind was remarkable less for its flexibility than for what Houdini half-admiringly called the "granite strength" of his beliefs. Once having arrived at the truth as he saw it, "he [would] never, whatever the arguments to the contrary, abandon his position." According to Houdini, Doyle had "no imaginative skill at all" (a possibly harsh judgment), or any "interest in occult books for their own sake . . . but regarded them solely as a source from which he could extract material that fitted in with views he already held." As we've seen, even Doyle's friend Oliver Lodge sometimes felt his rush to judgment on certain mediums lacking in the necessary scientific rigor. "These physical phenomena in the dark are both difficult and unpleasant," Lodge wrote in May 1925, "and one cannot but regret all that

Mrs Crandon has submitted herself to . . . especially as it seems to be without final and conclusive effect on those who have not previously been convinced [through] other channels. At the present stage of our knowledge, however, each case has to stand on its own merits, since a support with a flaw in it does not really add to the strength of the structure."

If Doyle appeared impetuous by the standards of some psychic researchers, he seemed now to apply the brakes to his cultural life. By his mid-sixties his tastes in literature inclined to the works of Winston Churchill and Thomas Hardy, and he was singularly unimpressed by Radclyffe Hall's lesbian novel *The Well of Loneliness* when it appeared in July 1928. "We do not want to see this country in the same condition as France, which has a great quantity of pornographic [books] in circulation," Doyle noted. "I hate all these sex novels. That sort of stuff is very cheap and very easy." The daughter of a woman who visited Windlesham recalls, "Sir Arthur would sometimes hold court in the music room in the evening and tell rather involved stories while the company struggled to stay awake"; occasionally, he himself would fall asleep while he was talking. All his life, Conan Doyle had been a man of the most extraordinary physical and intellectual energy. Whether dancing across Arctic ice floes, hurling himself down Swiss ski slopes, or abandoning medicine for the vagarious life of an author, he had always been ready for an adventure. For forty years, on a daily basis, he had had to render judgments, make decisions, support an extended family, and ultimately risk everything as the international figurehead of a new cult. The process had left him exhausted.

Conan Doyle continued to communicate, through his wife, with the spirit guide Pheneas, whose warnings about a global apocalypse intensified during 1925. "If you [come] across any prophecies of an impending world catastrophe, please let me know," Doyle wrote Oliver Lodge in July. "I have a drawer full now." This waiting game was agonizing for at least some of those the Doyles took into their confidence. Incapable of averting the crisis themselves, unable to predict exactly what form it might take (there was some talk of a giant meteor, like the one that had struck Siberia in 1908, although others foresaw a biblical-style flood), they could do little more than consult the spirits and pray. The journal of the American SPR referred to this "frequently heard [and] imminent cataclysm" in its Spiritualist *tour d'horizon* that August, while the *British Journal of Astrology* "mapped out the whole thing," Doyle reported. "I have always looked on astrology as pure quackery and yet [this prediction of doom] certainly seemed very wonderful."

Doyle faced a more material challenge when, on September 7, 1925, he arrived at the 800-seat Salle Wagram in Paris to address the International Spiritualist Congress.

His initial appearance turned the scene "into one of almost frenzied celebration," *Le Figaro* reported. Some 4,000 would-be attendees fought with the gendarmes to gain admittance to the auditorium. "The faces of those who found themselves jammed up against one another inside the hall were radiant with relief and pleasure," the paper noted. Following this buildup, the first of the two lectures that followed was to prove something of a disappointment. As Doyle spoke, the theater's projectionist repeatedly put up the wrong images on the large screen at the back of the stage. At a mention of Abraham Lincoln, a picture of the Fox sisters would appear. Doyle, who in general was more tolerant of intellectual disagreement than he was of sloppy workmanship, was not pleased. After struggling to make himself heard over the mounting laughter that greeted each fresh technical error, he brought the lecture to a premature end.

Conan Doyle's second performance evidently went better, because he told a correspondent, "the Spiritualist Congress was a wonderful success . . . the papers and the public seemed equally receptive." But he was still anticipating a "terrible global affliction," remarking that he had made his preparations for the event and wound up his affairs "so as to be free in case I can serve in any way." An article in the *Occult Review* further strengthened Doyle's conviction that "everything now points to a disaster," and that this would likely fall later in September. "Spirit voices have communicated to Lady Conan Doyle a warning to arouse the world to a sense of its responsibility toward a great calamity that is approaching," the *New York Times* announced on the fifteenth of the month. Based on Pheneas's increasingly urgent reports, the end was now thought to be nigh—"it will come within weeks."

Although the deadline passed without a general catastrophe, at least one apparently phenomenal event occurred around this time. Early in the morning of September 15, the day on which the *New York Times* was reporting Pheneas's warning, a crowd of some 2,000 Greek Orthodox worshippers looked up into the sky above the Church of St. John the Theologian in suburban Athens and, in a contemporaneous account, "saw a bright, radiant cross of light . . . It illuminated not only the church and the faithful but, in its rays, the stars of the clear, cloudless sky paled. The form of the cross itself was an especially dense light which could be clearly seen as of Byzantine design, with a crossbar toward the bottom. This heavenly image lasted for half an hour, and then the cross began to rise vertically, as the cross in the hands of the priest does in the ceremony of the elevation of the cross in church. Having come straight up, the cross began gradually to fade away."

Although Conan Doyle is not known to have commented publicly on what became known as the "miracle of the cross," others were convinced this was a foretaste of things to come. In 1927, at a New York banquet celebrating his solo flight across the Atlantic, Charles Lindbergh startled his audience by telling them, over the cigars, "Everything is in place for the battle of Armageddon." One of the portents, he said, was "that great manifestation in the sky above Athens." It was thought particularly significant that the vision had occurred on the Feast of the Cross, the day on which believers commemorate the instrument of Christ's death and of their own salvation. In later years, there were also some who speculated that Pheneas's prophecy had been fulfilled not by celestial auras or global pandemics, but by more insidious forms of cosmic retribution taking place that autumn, such as John Logie Baird's demonstration of the first television, or the birth of Margaret Thatcher.

While awaiting the universal crisis, the Conan Doyles retreated more and more to their six-bedroom cottage at Bignell Wood, near Minstead in the New Forest. The home, which cost £1,800, was described in its prospectus as a "timbered residence [with] stabling and extensive grounds" that ended in a trout stream at the bottom of the garden—an arcadian setting that Pheneas himself had recommended as "more unspoiled than anywhere in England." Among Doyle's neighbors was the seventy-three-year-old Alice Hargreaves, who as a child had inspired Lewis Carroll's *Alice's Adventures in Wonderland.* As A. A. Milne wrote some of his verse collection *When We Were Very Young* (featuring the first appearance of Winnie the Pooh) at the nearby Compton Arms Hotel in Lyndhurst, the area was rich in iconic literary connections. Doyle now restricted his own output largely to Spiritualist pamphleteering and history, as well as to *Pheneas Speaks,* which appeared in 1927. The book's companion piece was the starkly titled essay "A Warning," which the author distributed to friends and fellow believers to prepare them for the worst.

Although Conan Doyle no longer put in a 12- or 14-hour creative writing day as he once had, the determination, self-discipline, and concentration he had to summon to deal with his commitments on the "earthly plane" were still enormous. He never complained about his unpaid duties as the de facto head of a new religion, and apparently enjoyed corresponding with a wide range of believers around the world, replying sympathetically when they wrote to tell him about themselves, their lives, their hopes, and even sometimes their slightly extravagant Spiritualist experiences. Among them was Julian B. Arnold of Chicago, who told Doyle, at some length, about his recently deceased wife "who prompts me in the writing of this letter . . . She lived in both worlds all her life. From childhood she saw the chariots of God and the horsemen thereof. To her eyes, our home (and all places) had intimate visitants from the other side, and with her the sixth sense was absolute in all its phases." Several others wrote from America to speak of such paranormal experiences as poltergeists, wraiths, fairies, premonitions of death, reincarnation, and telepathy. In November 1925, Doyle wrote to one such correspondent to assure him that Margery was genuine and enjoyed a true gift of ectoplasm, arguing convincingly that no woman would emit "this rather horrible stuff" for her own amusement. Doyle's own family séances continued, and yielded a variety of both first-time and returning spirits. "My wife and I alone at the second sitting got the direct voice," he wrote in December 1925. "It was quite loud and said 'Good evening' above our heads—a male voice. We were greatly thrilled." On a subsequent visit to South Africa, Doyle met a local stockbroker and sometime medium named Ashton Jonson, who was able to report that Kingsley had returned to him to offer tips about share prices. Conan Doyle's openness to Spiritualistic experiences of all kinds was based on his fundamental conviction that, no matter what the individual setback or excess along the way, the full truth would eventually emerge and triumph. As he wrote in his memoirs, the movement's key promise was of nothing less than eternal life, since the best available information depicted a heaven "of art, of science, of intellect, of organisation, of combat with evil, of home circles, of flowers, of wide travel, of sports, of the mating of souls, of complete harmony. This is what our 'dead' friends describe."

If Conan Doyle had succeeded in winning a precarious status of respectability for Spiritualism, across the Atlantic Houdini was working with his customary energy and flair to expose its leading practitioners as frauds. As well as attending séances, often in disguise, he again took his campaign on the road. "HOUDINI CHALLENGES LOCAL SOOTHSAYERS! WARNING TO ALL ORGANIZATIONS OF SPIRITUALISTS! . . . OCCULTISTS BEWARE . . . I hereby dare the following individuals to come to the theater tonight to try and take some of my money!" ran a typical billboard, below which he listed the names and addresses of the town's leading mediums. An Indianapolis psychic named Charles Gunsolas had already tangled with Houdini's undercover agent Rose Mackenberg, from whom he had taken a $25 introduction fee to his 800-year-old Hindu guide, along with the suggestion that Mackenberg make the spirit's acquaintance in the nude. Six weeks later, Houdini confronted Gunsolas from the stage of Indianapolis's Loew's Theatre. According to the local *Recorder* newspaper, the illusionist lost no time in "hurling charge after charge" at the "stricken" medium. When Gunsolas stood up to defend himself, Houdini shouted that there was a "large corps of detectives" in the audience, and one by one they duly rose from their seats to relate their own experiences of Gunsolas's "shabby" and "morally libertine" séances. This recitation lasted some 40 minutes. At its conclusion, Gunsolas was heard to mumble that he, too, wished to put an end to fraud, whereupon he left the theater "amid the boos and catcalls of those previously counting themselves among his clients" and promptly announced his retirement from active mediumship. As usual, Houdini conducted the whole performance, which was the highlight of the Indianapolis cultural season, as if it were an all-out war. In the streets and alleys outside the theater, there were "numerous individual skirmishes," the press reported; when a group of Spiritualist advocates gathered at the stage door to confront Houdini and his associates, a flying squad of counter-demonstrators "burst out [to] rough up the hecklers, take down their signs, and silence them."

In Pittsburgh, the failure of the Rev. Alice S. Dooley, pastor of the Church of Divine Healing, "to answer three questions placed before her in sealed envelopes by Harry Houdini, the magician, and a subsequent statement of the artifices practiced by false mediums nearly precipitated a riot in the Alvin Theatre," the *New York Times* reported. "Following the accusation by Houdini that Spiritualism was a fraud, a woman in the first balcony became hysterical and aroused the audience to partiality by her shouts of malediction aimed at the magician . . . The audience took sides for and against and a verbal tilt ensued." It was much the same story in Cleveland, Buffalo, and New York. Uproar was the rule and prolonged periods of scholarly debate the exception throughout the tour, which enjoyed sold-out houses and banner headlines during the autumn of 1925. In Worcester, Massachusetts, the crowd greeted Houdini with a mighty roar, followed by wave after wave of more cheering as he proudly flourished a bright blue handkerchief, the color of the local Normal School (predecessor of Worcester State University). He praised Boston—another roar. Then the local football team. Then the baseball team. Houdini said that the people of Worcester could be proud of their new country club, which would go on to host the inaugural Ryder Cup golf tournament 18 months later. More roars.

Then he got into his theme, which was "the cancer eating into the good folks of Worcester, Massachusetts, and these United States of the so-called Spiritualist enlightenment." The time had come for people of all faiths and beliefs to "recognise that quackery was no substitute for true religion," he said. "Whatever the circumstances . . . No one should suffer the torture of seeing their departed loved ones faked up like a puppet show."

Up in the far reaches of the balcony, a small group of a dozen or so protesters began shouting, "You don't know what you're talking about," "You're a liar," and so forth. When their ringleader identified himself as Armstrong LeVeyne, the husband of a well-known medium, Houdini invited him up on stage. There was more applause.

When the portly LeVeyne appeared, Houdini challenged him on the spot to duplicate "my feat with the locked water tank or any other of my tricks." LeVeyne declined the offer, and instead made an impassioned speech on behalf of his wife and mother, respectively "a psychic endowed by God" and "the famous Australian vaudeville star—the greatest woman who ever lived." Houdini in turn brought Bess and his attractive twenty-one-year-old niece Julia Sawyer onto the stage. Turning to the audience, he bowed and said, "Folks, these are my flesh and blood. Can anyone say anything against their characters?" The crowd, who had been showing increasing signs of annoyance at the hecklers, gave him a long standing ovation.

Encouraged, Houdini raised his voice as he announced, "I drove out the fakes in California and I intend to drive them out of Massachusetts." Another roar of approval erupted. LeVeyne plunged on, struggling to make himself heard above the uproar. "Our Spiritualist church will hold an indignation meeting next Sunday . . . I protect my wife," he cried out. "And I protect the public," Houdini replied. The roar this time was truly deafening; he had clearly struck the most responsive possible chord.

"History repeats itself," LeVeyne shouted. "Christ was persecuted and now we Spiritualists are being persecuted. Some day, the people will see the light!"

"But Christ never robbed people of $2, did he?" said Houdini; and the "truly tumultuous standing ovation that followed," it was reported, "concluded the night's entertainment."

8

PHENEAS SPEAKS

Houdini soon had another, even more prominent forum for his campaign. In February 1926, the US Congress convened a joint Senate and House subcommittee to hear evidence prior to its drafting an anti-fortune-telling bill for the District of Columbia. The proposed legislation called for "those claiming to predict the future [or] unite the separated for reward or compensation" to be classified as "disorderly persons," and subject to a fine or (where "blasphemy and/or lewd conduct" was involved) six months' imprisonment. While the committee's membership was balanced by party, its Spiritualist philosophy was virtually uniform. The bill was sponsored by Sol Bloom, a US Representative from New York who had known Houdini since 1893, when Bloom was one of the ringmasters of the World's Columbian Exposition in Chicago. Serving with him on the panel were William Cicero Hammer, Democrat of North Carolina, whose family-owned *Asheboro Courier* newspaper had editorialized for the criminalization of "hocus-pocus magicians, rain-makers, card sharps [and] pseudo-mediums," among other "itinerant hustlers"; David Reed, Republican of Pennsylvania, the co-author of the 1924 Immigration Act restricting the movement of eastern and southern Europeans into the United States, who was concerned at the influence of "gypsy mystics and other un-American occultists"; and Clarence McLeod, Republican of Michigan, whose primary political goal was to ensure the continued strength of the US military and, as he said on the floor of the House, "allow no deviant sub-culture to imperil these shores." All were critical, in varying degrees, of the concept of mediums and clairvoyants charging for their services; several, like Bloom, were open partisans of Houdini; and most, again like the chairman, had publicly equated séances with witchcraft.

Houdini appeared before the committee for three days in February, and returned to testify briefly when the proceedings concluded the following May. Since the hearings were open to the public, a "lively, vaudeville mood prevailed, not often associated with the US Congress," the *Washington Star* reported. Sometimes the Spiritualist case was put by witnesses on the stand, such as the materializing medium Charles William Myers, who had harsh words apparently directed at Houdini and Bloom. "In the beginning," said Myers, "Judas betrayed Christ. He was a Jew, and I want to say that this bill is being put through by two—well, you can use your opinion." Occasionally, there was a less formal exchange of views, as when Houdini turned to the public gallery, waving $10,000 in cash, and challenged any medium present to tell him what his childhood nickname had been. This was the cue for a woman who identified herself as Madame Marcia to jump up from her seat and scream, "That money belongs to me! I predicted the election of President Harding and his death." The sideshow atmosphere continued with a variety of other ad-hoc public speeches, interjections, and jokes, which Bloom gaveled down with visibly rising irritation. Toward the end of the proceedings, an Ohio fishmonger named John Ferguson, the husband of a medium, lunged at Houdini and reportedly shouted, "I'll break your nose, you kike." As Ferguson approached the witness stand, Representative Hammer leaped down from the platform to separate the two men. After a lengthy delay while the police restored order in the room, Sol Bloom collapsed in the House lobby, apparently suffering from nervous exhaustion.

Before Houdini himself took the stand, his agent Rose Mackenberg made headlines with her testimony about a Spiritualist named Jane Coates. Coates, who was present in the committee room, practiced as a self-described "occult prognosticator" on behalf of Washington, DC's Order of the White Cross Societas. According to Mackenberg, the medium had confided to her that Houdini was "up against a stone wall . . . She said, 'Why try to fight Spiritualism, when most of the Senators are interested in the subject? I have a number of Senators who visit me here, and I know for a fact that there have been Spiritual séances held at the White House with President Coolidge' . . . Then she mentioned the name of Senator Capper, saying his wife had died recently. She also mentioned Senator Watson, Senator Dill and Senator Fletcher, whose wife is a psychic." Mackenberg's remaining remarks were lost in the bedlam that broke out in the hall. For the next few months, Houdini would shock audiences around the country by showing them photographs of the Senate chamber and contending that, instead of being a forum for gentlemanly debate, it was in reality a center for "black magic and mentalism."

On the last day of the hearings, William Hammer called Houdini to the stand. Curiously, the Representative who had campaigned against "hocus-pocus magicians" seemed to be in some doubt as to his star witness's identity. "The original Houdini was a Hindu, was he not?" Hammer asked.

"No," said Houdini.

"You are Houdini the second?"

"No."

"You are the original Houdini?"

"No, the original Houdini was a French clock maker."

"I thought he lived in Allahabab," said Hammer.

"Are you joking?"

"No, I am in earnest . . . Have you ever been in British India?"

"Never in my life, no sir."

"Were both of your parents Hebrews?"

"Yes, sir."

"Is your father living?"

"No, sir. Has this anything to do with the bill?"

To cap the somewhat surrealist performance, Houdini then called Bess to the stand as a character witness. To widespread applause, his wife of thirty-one years testified that he was a "good boy" who was not "brutal or vile." Conan Doyle later approvingly quoted this exchange as evidence of Houdini's "unconventional intimacy . . . He was, like most Jews, estimable in his family relationships," Doyle wrote. As Houdini was leaving the Capitol building following his testimony, Madame Marcia, the woman who had heckled him from the gallery, shouted, "When November comes around, you won't be here."

"How's that?" Houdini asked.

"You'll be dead."

On February 21, 1926, Malcolm Bird, late of the *Scientific American,* addressed a crowded meeting of the Universal Spiritualist Brotherhood Church in Philadelphia. Apparently still smarting from their clash of views on the Crandons, Houdini invited himself to the event. Accompanied by Jim Collins and a female stenographer, he sat in the front row of the auditorium to hear Bird describe Margery as a "true clairvoyant." Both she and her brother had provided "every intellectual proof of a power beyond ourselves," the speaker added. Peering into the footlights, Bird then informed the audience that "the world's number one medium-baiter" was sitting among them and proceeded to describe how the *Scientific American* investigation had been sabotaged by "an infidel [and] his tricks." The details of what followed are unclear, due to conflicting testimony, but it seems fairly certain that Houdini began to heckle Bird and that the two fell into a noisy quarrel. At one point, according to the *Philadelphia Inquirer,* the illusionist leapt onto the stage "like a raging lion" and began a long, impromptu speech denouncing Bird as a "contemptible liar." Although the newspaper report fails to mention it, at least one witness to the scene insisted that the dispute had subsequently turned violent. At a reference to his parents, Houdini apparently grabbed the back of the younger man's neck and invited him outside to settle matters. Bird thereupon took a swing at his opponent, missed, and "fell back into a heavily-laden refreshments table, which collapsed under him." That was at least one account; but the accounts are as various and confused as the scenes they claim to describe, and the only certainty is that the meeting finally broke up after three and a half hours, and only then, the *Inquirer* reported, "when a policeman arrived to cool the overheated emotions of the throng."

Houdini's continued anti-Spiritualist campaign produced a high-maintenance life-style. The $30,000-a-year cost of professional assistants and other operatives was matched by the expense of keeping two lawyers on retainer to fight suits arising from his habit of outing fraud mediums in the press or on the stage; he was currently being sued by three Chicago clairvoyants and their business manager, among others. So it was never very likely that he would retire from performing while there was still an audience willing to pay to see him. Houdini's latest tour began that same month, and consistently earned him some $8,000 to $10,000 a week. A tightly scripted "best of" package, the show was divided into three parts: a magic prelude, followed by a set-piece extravaganza like the Water Torture Cell, which in turn gave way to the climactic section called "Do the Dead Come Back?" Houdini enjoyed a run of eight sold-out weeks at the Princess Theatre in Chicago, where he claimed to have exposed fully seventy-nine crooked professional psychics. In the show's finale, he demonstrated how to produce "so-called occult effects" like a spirit voice or a levitating trumpet, before recalling some of his own Spiritualist adventures. "I caught Margery," he told one Chicago audience. "When I walked into the séance room and saw that beautiful blonde, her applesauce meant nothing to me. I have been through apple orchards . . . There is no deceiving Houdini," he noted. The tour's souvenir program, which he wrote himself, took a similar line: "He is recognized by scientists and mingles with Savants," it assured theatergoers. "Houdini is an omnivorous and miscellaneous reader . . . His home is a Mecca for theologians and writers . . . At one time he taught a Junior Class in his father's college, thereby gaining a knowledge of human nature. It is small wonder that his personality has been developed so when he walks on the stage, immediately he puts himself on a pleasant and friendly footing with the audience." As Houdini acknowledged, not everyone succumbed to this charm offensive. "I get letters from ardent believers in Spiritualism," he told the *Chicago American,* "who prophesy I am going to meet a violent death soon as a fitting punishment for my nefarious work."

There was a striking similarity between Pheneas's warnings of a global apocalypse in 1925 and those he made in 1926. In the first case, the Doyles' harbinger of doom had spoken of a "great calamity . . . Thousands will perish by plagues and incessant floods." A year later, Pheneas sent word that "There will come a great flash of light—no thunder. Then will come a great mist, and people will be terrified. Then will come torrential rains. Then a pause. Then the deluge." In each case, Conan Doyle seized on selected news reports from around the world as proof this "terrific convulsion" had already begun, at least on a regional basis. Quoting the *Morning Post* of January 9, 1926, Doyle wrote to a correspondent of recent events in Venice, where "a curious manifestation occurred . . . There was no thunder, but the heavens opened with a flash of fire, which, seen through the thick sea fog that enveloped the city, had the appearance of a vast furnace, and frightened the people." Pheneas now spoke of a "harvest time" in which non-believers would perish, but the "Elect" would survive by virtue of their Spiritualist beliefs. Over the years, the prophecies of doom regularly issuing from Crowborough would exasperate even some of those broadly sympathetic to the cause. "The cataclysmic disaster with which Doyle has been trying to make our flesh creep still hangs fire," Harry Price wrote in the *Journal* of the American SPR, "and the dawn of 1927 still finds us sleeping serenely in our beds . . . We are now promised a new Armageddon for 1928!"

The avuncular, sixty-seven-year-old Conan Doyle was in some ways an unlikely character to go on record as repeatedly predicting the end of the world. Leaving aside his paranormal activities, he seemed to many to cut a reassuringly old-fashioned, if not mildly fogeyish figure, who liked nothing more than to potter around his garden or get up in plus-fours for a round of golf. At least one American reporter thought Doyle a "prime piece of Merry England . . . He laughed easily, and loudly, with great gusto, usually slapping his knee in exclamation at the same time . . . The emotions were always healthily near the surface. He was blessed with a marvelous expressive face that turned beet-red when he was angry, and lit up when he was pleased." In general, Conan Doyle would seem to have had grounds for satisfaction. Apart from his idyllically happy marriage and the success of his material career, he had been an evangelist for the New Revelation for longer than any other active believer. By mid-1926, Doyle was in the solid position of occupying the broad center ground of the worldwide Spiritualist movement, with its more theatrical practitioners off to one side and its scientific-minded researchers, like Oliver Lodge, off to the other. He remained arguably the best-known author in the world. He might be about to finally retire Sherlock Holmes, but he was an inveterate storyteller who could no more ignore a good plot device than Houdini could ignore a professional challenge. Early that summer, Doyle wrote a note to himself outlining six "real-life" psychic dramas that had caught his attention:

> *Case of another occupying dead body*
> *Queer letter from Australia*
> *Falkland Island seer*
> *Wapping poltergeist*
> *African necklace*
> *Story of suicide's ghost*

—each of which would seem richly promising as a work of gothic fiction. Doyle's twin interest in ripping adventure and spiritual uplift merged in his 1927 novel *The Maracot Deep,* where a gripping, Jules Verne–like tale of underwater exploration is freighted with a subplot involving a small group of religious visionaries "scorned and jeered at by those whom they were trying to save." As a critic remarked, this was not the work of an author "who restrict[ed] himself to one field of endeavour at a time."

Conan Doyle's unwavering public support of the Crandons led to a brisk round of open letters and other shows of disapproval aimed at Margery's critics. The tension that had characterized the Doyle-Houdini relationship since mid-1922 now reached its height. As ever, it centered around differing perceptions of the Spiritualist gospel, and the preponderance of fraud mediums anxious to help this along.

Confirming that the two men were unlikely to find common ground, Doyle now coined the term "Houdinitis" to describe an "abnormal frame of mind" that he believed was based on a pair of grave delusions. "The first is that Spiritualism depends upon physical phenomena for its proofs," he wrote, and the second, "that manual dexterity bears some relation to brain capacity."

Conan Doyle saw their conflict as a moral issue. Although "an honest difference of view [was] quite possible," he said, this was not the case where "lies and deception" were involved. "Houdini has stuffed so many errors of fact into his book *A Magician among the Spirits,*" Doyle wrote, "and has such extraordinary bias on the whole question, that his statement carries no weight." Each man continued to take an intense interest in the other's activities and attitudes. According to Robert Gysel, Houdini was convinced that "Sir Arthur had availed himself over-freely of the works of Edgar Allan Poe [in] forming Sherlock Holmes," and spent "long hours" in his library engaged in a detailed but ultimately fruitless comparison of the respective texts. Doyle for his part spoke of his regret at having called the Crandons to the attention of the *Scientific American* committee. "It was difficult to say which was the more annoying," he wrote. "Houdini the conjurer, with his preposterous and ignorant theories of fraud, or such 'scientific' sitters as Professor McDougall of Harvard, who, after 50 sittings and signing as many papers at the end of each sitting to endorse the wonders recorded, was still unable to give any definite judgement, and contented himself with vague innuendoes."

Another show of the professional and personal disdain at the heart of the relationship surfaced in Houdini's testimony to the Congressional subcommittee early in 1926. Representative McLeod asked why, if Spiritualistic fraud was really so widespread, "it would not be discovered by such men as Conan Doyle, who is an outstanding authority?"

"Conan Doyle is not an outstanding authority," said Houdini.

"He is accepted as one of the best."

"No, he is not accepted as one of the best. He is one of the great dupes . . . Doyle stated that I possess mediumistic powers, which I deny."

"How can you prove it?" asked McLeod.

"I admit that I do not possess mediumistic powers. They claim in a London psychic college I dematerialize my body, and that I ooze through and come out again and put myself together."

"How *do* you do it?"

"I do it like anybody else would do it. There is nothing secret about it. We are all humans. Nobody is supernormal. We are all born alike."

Common sense would win. That was Houdini's message to the Congressmen, as well as to "the many millions who read my words [or] attend the show." His goal was to expose as many as possible of those "who peddle so-called phenomena and thus trifle with the will of the Omnipotent Almighty." He was saddened that Spiritualism had "taken the hold it has on persons of a neurotic temperament, especially those suffering from grief . . . I do not consider Sir Arthur Conan Doyle or Sir Oliver Lodge to be safe judges on this difficult and important subject, in view of their bereavement and unconscious desires. If the wish be father to the thought, it is mother to the hallucination of the senses." Houdini stopped short of saying that Doyle was mentally deranged. He did say, "Even I may be deceived once or twice by a new illusion . . . If my mind, which has been so keenly trained for years, can be deceived, how much more susceptible must the ordinary observer be." Speaking to Robert Gysel, Houdini added that in his opinion, Doyle was "perfectly sincere in his views." Unfortunately, it was this same sincerity that made him prone to a "wide range of mediumistic crooks and frauds, not to mention the wiles of Dr Crandon and his wife." The "Pheneas" spirit had been part of this same morbid pattern. "Doyle believed because he desperately wanted to believe."

The correlative of Doyle's credulity was Houdini's own need for reassurance, as an answer to the doubts and the sense of inferiority that, however much suppressed, Gysel believed "gnawed at him until the day he died." The rich, famous, and fulfilled man whom the world saw still considered himself a "poor immigrant boy from the slums of Budapest." Outwardly, Houdini gave an impression of being completely in control of himself, of an unshakable self-confidence; but beneath the surface passions ran deep—the passion for respectability and acceptance, even for revenge, the intolerance of opposition, and, as ever, the overpowering need for approval. Houdini's public performances were an opportunity for him to project his idealized view of himself as not just a clever magician, but an intellectual peer of the great minds of the day.

Houdini's need for acclaim was a sort of addiction, to be fed from as many sources as possible. He craved recognition not only from artists and writers, but from the "so-called soothsayers, clairvoyants [and] other quacks" he outed as fakes. It wasn't enough that he successfully expose a fraud; often, the disgraced parties were required to sign a statement publicly acknowledging that Houdini had outsmarted them, and even to pose for a photograph with their tormentor, a ritual humiliation with almost an anticipatory touch of Abu Ghraib about it. This twin need for personal vindication and the degradation of his enemies perhaps explains why Houdini's anti-Spiritualist campaign consistently focused more on individuals than it did on less tangible occult phenomena. He had little to say, for instance, about the whole matter of ghosts, such as the one who visited Conan Doyle in his bedroom at night; never really dwelt on the world of out-of-body experiences and premonitions; and managed an only partially convincing explanation of spirit photography. In April 1923, Houdini himself had taken a picture at a Spiritualist church in Los Angeles that showed a vertical streak of light, of about human height, on the negative. He was deeply shocked when he saw the result, and promptly wrote to Conan Doyle suggesting that this was a "genuine psychic effect." (In a marked role reversal, Doyle replied that the whole thing struck him as "absurd.") Where Houdini failed as a paranormal investigator, it was almost always in cases where there was no obvious human protagonist for him to crush. He made little or no pretense to understand the broader Spiritualist movement and, as Doyle complained, instead "dealt exclusively with its physical entities." Houdini was always at his best when confronted by a flesh-and-blood rival rather than grappling with abstract matters such as whether God existed in geographic features like mountains and rivers, as the Animists believed, or commenting authoritatively on the reincarnation debate. Rather, he wrote, his life's work was to "unmask the various hoodwinkers, ventriloquists, soap-bubble merchants [and] other jackals" who exploited the occult for their own ends. To Houdini, spiritually speaking, the medium truly was the message.

The Crandons, whom Houdini believed were "messiahs to half a million or more Americans," remained his principal adversaries. In April 1926, Margery added a new twist to her mediumistic routine by claiming that Walter was now ready to confirm his identity by leaving an impression of his fingerprints in a block of wax. When the lights came up at the end of that night's sitting, "two beautiful indentations" were duly found. Dr. Crandon hired a Boston private detective, the self-styled John "Sherlock" Fife, to test and authenticate the prints, which he soon did. Houdini felt that Fife himself, who appeared to have exaggerated his forensic experience, if any, was the one who should be investigated: "He just materialized out of nowhere . . . Ha! *That's* a good trick." In 1932, a researcher named E. E. Dudley published a report in the bulletin of the Boston Society for Psychic Research claiming that Margery had obtained the spiritual fingerprints not from her dead brother, but from her living dentist, Dr. Frederick Caldwell. The medium's son, John Rand, later gave another version of events. According to him, Le Roi Crandon, accompanied by Conan Doyle, had made a midnight visit to a Boston funeral home in order to lift the fingerprints from a corpse, and these had been provided to Margery for use at a later séance. Although it conjures up a vivid image of the two doctors engaged in this ghoulish nocturnal work, the story should be treated with caution: Doyle "sat" with the Crandons only in London, not in Boston, and the whole idea of him prowling around a morgue, defiling the bodies, perhaps belongs more in an imaginative Hammer horror film than in reality.

In July 1926, Joseph Rhine, a thirty-one-year-old parapsychology professor at North Carolina's Duke University, took the train to Boston to sit with Margery. Rhine, who had been a Spiritualist since attending one of Conan Doyle's New York lectures in 1922, not only claimed to immediately see through the "physical ruses" of the séance, such as the fact that a supposedly levitating bowl was "in reality be[ing] waved aloft on the end of the medium's foot." He also offered a theory of the curious husband-and-wife psychology involved. Over time, "Crandon gradually found out Margery was deceiving him," Rhine wrote in his report the following January. "But he had already begun to enjoy the notoriety it gave him, the groups of admiring society it brought to his home to hear him lecture and to be entertained, the interest and fame aroused in this country and Europe, etc. This was especially appreciated by him in view of decided loss of position and prestige suffered in recent years."

The Crandons were unimpressed by the report. Margery called it "poppycock," and her husband, stung by Rhine's allegation that the medium "wore only the flimsiest robe [and] reached the point of actual kissing and embracing of [her] admirers" at the séance, promised to punch "this perverted little hick" when they next met. As if to demonstrate the strength of their marriage, the Crandons called in the press to proudly show off the engraved loving cup presented to them by Conan Doyle on behalf of the College of Psychic Science. Doyle himself took out a black-bordered advertisement in the *Boston Herald* that read simply, "J.B. Rhine is an Ass."

In March 1926, yet another academic investigation began into the Crandons, and lasted until April 1927. Led by Henry Clay McComas, a professor of psychology at Princeton, who was joined by a psychiatrist, Dr. Knight Dunlap, a physicist, Robert W. Wood, and Margery's friend Malcolm Bird, it got under way with the familiar dinner and drinks downstairs at Lime Street. The hospitality was such that Dunlap woke up in his hotel room at 2:00 the next afternoon with what he called an "ideological hangover," having been "completely won over by the couple's extraordinary personal charm." The softening-up seems not to have applied to Wood, who reported that Margery had sprouted a "teleplasmic rod" at the ensuing séance, and invited him to feel it. "I squeezed it very hard," he wrote, "which produced no ill effect." Wood concluded that the "rod" was really a sack filled with animal intestines that Margery was manipulating with a wire. The committee's final report to the American Society for Psychical Research found that "Mrs Crandon's mediumship is a clever and entertaining performance, but unworthy of any serious consideration by the Society."

Houdini himself hovered in the shadows, like a malevolent spirit, during the first half of the investigation. When McComas invited him to a séance, the illusionist wrote back, "I will be delighted to sit in at 'Margery's,' but have been repeatedly told that my absence was preferable to my presence." In due course, this was confirmed by Dr. Crandon, who wrote Houdini a sulfurous letter effectively banning him from Lime Street. "In as much as the only value which could possibly be attached to your visiting," Crandon concluded, "would be because it would afford some amusement to watch your attempts to duplicate these phenomena, and since this you very wisely decline to do, there seems no other compelling reason for your coming again." Rather than leave it there, Houdini promptly cabled back that he appreciated the "direct challenge," and asked when it might be convenient for him to call in at Lime Street "with a number of witnesses." That concluded the correspondence.

After wrapping up his extended engagement in Chicago, Houdini announced that he would take a four-month sabbatical from the stage. "Am going to lay off [and] do nothing but investigate and look into these fraudulent medium affairs," he wrote. He worked twelve to fourteen hours a day on this project. As well as his standing offer to pay $10,000 (around $420,000 today) to "any Spiritualist [to] present a so-called 'physical' manifestation that I cannot reproduce or explain as being accomplished by natural means," he began each morning by scouring the press for news of any fresh or particularly popular medium working in his area. Houdini was blunt in his evaluation of one New York séance that had apparently summoned the spirit of President Lincoln. "Bosh & Rot!" he scrawled across the published account of "Abe's Apparition."

In July 1926, Houdini went on the radio to denounce Bert Reese, an eighty-five-year-old medium who specialized in billet, or "pellet" divination—the ability to read what a sitter wrote on a folded slip of paper. Reese had enjoyed a long and varied career in Spiritualist circles, having won appreciative reviews from both Conan Doyle and Thomas Edison, and been endorsed by the Nobel laureate Charles Richet as a "cryptesthetic seer." Houdini was less impressed with the "swivel-eyed little hoaxer," whom he had first tested in 1922. Reese's mediumship owed less to Spiritualistic powers, he believed, than it did to his ability to surreptitiously open the slips of paper and memorize their contents while decoying his clients' attention. "I am positive the man resorts to legerdemain," Houdini wrote to Doyle. "That he fooled Edison does not surprise me. He would have surprised me if he did not fool Edison . . . I have no hesitancy in telling you that I set a snare at the séance I had with Reese, and caught him cold-blooded. He was startled when it was over, as he knew that I had bowled him over . . . He claimed I was the only one that had ever detected him."

Four years later, Houdini was still on Reese's case. It wasn't just that this "conniving old man" continued to extract "bucketfuls of shekels" from gullible clients; he had a "holier-than-thou" attitude that Houdini despised. When he read a newspaper report in which Reese claimed to have "cured thousands of folks of their physical ailments," he underlined the sentence and wrote in a separate note, "This man must be *taken apart*." After Houdini's subsequent blistering radio exposé, an "extremely agitated" Reese appeared at the illusionist's house and requested an interview. According to Bernard Ernst, "a frank exchange" ensued. While Houdini was prepared to acknowledge that Reese put on a good act, he was "incensed . . . so mad his teeth clenched" when his guest again claimed he could heal the sick. "People look on me as a holy man," Reese remarked. Houdini went on to remind him of their previous meeting, and suggest that it might be in his interests not to make any further claims of "divine or telepathic" powers. Reese saw the logic of this, and eventually agreed to retire from public performance. He died two years later. Before Reese left his home for the last time, Houdini characteristically asked that he pose for a picture with him.

By mid-1926, Houdini had no illusions about his core reputation with the Spiritualist community and its "armies of sadly deluded" followers. "They hate me," he remarked. The Crandons remained his most vocal critics, but he was also being attacked, vilified, and even directly threatened in a variety of indignation meetings, specialist publications, and séances on both sides of the Atlantic. In the wake of Houdini's testimony on fraudulent mediumship to the US Congress, the Order of the White Cross Societas formally condemned this "mendacious and perjured Oriental" and "crooked perverter of justice" for whom it saw a "sorry future." Other groups and individuals took the opportunity to sue him for a variety of alleged offenses ranging from blasphemy to criminal libel. The Conan Doyles' spirit guide,

Pheneas, also stepped up the tempo of his appearances, predicting imminent tragedy for both the world in general and Houdini in particular. "We had in our family circle several warnings as to his approaching end," Doyle later wrote, "but what could we do, for he would have only mocked at them, and us, if we had sent them on." Some of the more dire forecasts must have reached Houdini, even so, because a reporter from the *Boston Post* asked him what he thought about "Spiritists in this country and England pretty much prophesying your doom." "Well, it isn't exactly a vote of confidence," Houdini replied. "I'm happy to leave them to it," he continued, "so I can get back to the real job of digging out clairvoyants, crime, and corruption." As well as his own speeches and demonstrations, his local operatives were still busy infiltrating and disrupting séances, and Harry Day continued to send reams of damaging anti-Spiritualist material from London. "It was obvious Houdini didn't care whether he was popular in mediumistic circles or not," Ernst confirmed.

If he was intimidated by the increasingly bitter opposition, there was little evidence of it in his public appearances. Houdini bounded on stage to the strains of "Pomp and Circumstance" and typically enjoyed "a lengthy standing ovation prior to his uttering a single word," the *New York World* reported. When he did speak he often had to face raucous heckling, which in turn led to fighting on the floor of the hall. But Houdini invariably mastered the uproar, whipping the crowd up by a mixture of good humor, glowing declarations of love for God and country, and anti-Spiritualist sarcasm. He could make them laugh with his quips and hiss with derision at the mention of a medium's name. If the situation demanded, he thought nothing of jumping down into the auditorium for a face-to-face debate with a particularly vocal opponent. Adding to the drama of the occasion were the two secretaries Houdini employed to sit on either side of the stage and take shorthand notes of everything he said—"to protect myself from my enemies," he confided. More prolonged applause, boos, and scuffles generally followed his announcement. Long before Houdini performed his first illusion, audiences could tell that they were in the presence of someone special.

In June 1926, Houdini read that Hereward Carrington, his rival on the *Scientific American* committee, was touring the United States to promote the Spiritualist claims of a twenty-six-year-old Egyptian fakir named Rahman Bey. Among other feats, Bey could allegedly stop his pulse, force steel needles through his cheeks, and calmly lie down on a bed of swords. Taking his performance to the streets, he then allowed himself to be locked into an airtight coffin, which was paraded down New York's 12th Avenue and lowered into the Hudson River. Within moments of immersion, Bey had begun to frantically ring an emergency bell to alert Carrington and his team to rescue him. It took them almost twenty minutes to retrieve the casket and pry open the lid. When they did so they found Bey "deathly pale but alive," according to the *New York World,* having apparently remained in "self-imposed catalepsy" throughout the ordeal. Carrington told the press that his protégé had cheated death, and that "no other man living today" could possibly duplicate his psychic gifts. A week later, Bey went one better by remaining sealed in his coffin, submerged in the pool of New York's Dalton hotel, for an hour.

His competitive juices not so much flowing as raging, the fifty-two-year-old Houdini immediately announced that he could "remain in any coffin that the fakir does for the same length of time he does, without going into any cataleptic trance." His customary relish for a challenge may have been fortified by his discovery that "Bey" was in fact an Italian-born vaudevillian who was "as much a Hindu mystic as I am." As usual, too, Houdini was careful only to make claims for himself he could support. When he said he could stay underwater for as long as Bey, he had dozens of medically supervised hours of practice in his bathtub to back him up.

On the morning of August 5, Houdini appeared before an invited audience at the pool of the Shelton Hotel, stripped off to a pair of trunks and an undershirt, and lay down in a galvanized iron coffin, specially constructed for the occasion and secured by "32 independently tested nails and bolts." The device also contained a small battery-operated internal phone, allowing Houdini to speak to his associates waiting above. "If I die," he remarked before being sealed up and launched into the water, "it will be the will of God and my own foolishness . . . I am going to prove the copybook wrong, and I shall not pretend to be in a trance either." According to *Variety,* the casket held 34,398 cubic inches of air, "which the attending physician [believed] should have been used up in three or four minutes."

Houdini's primary emotion during the ensuing ordeal was neither fear of drowning, nor the traditional anxiety associated with being effectively buried alive. It was irritation. The warmth of the surrounding water was "oppressive," he later complained, and the six swimmers employed to stand on top of the coffin in order to keep it submerged and level only added to his woes. One of the men soon lost his balance and fell off, causing the coffin to shoot into the air, flip upside down, and bounce back into the pool. "What's the big deal?" Houdini barked into the phone. The strain of speaking left him "gasp[ing] for air," he reported.

"After one hour and twenty-eight minutes I commenced to see yellow lights and carefully watched myself not to go to sleep," Houdini would note. Three minutes later, his support team brought the coffin to the surface and cut off the lid. Houdini emerged "deathly white," according to witnesses, but calmly offered his hand to a waiting doctor to take his pulse; this had been 84 on his arrival at the hotel, and was now 142. He had beaten Bey's record by some half an hour. Houdini went straight from the hotel to his study, where he composed a meticulous account of his day for Dr. W. J. McConnell, a physiologist with the US Bureau of Mines, in the hopes the Bureau might "draw from my not inconsiderable experience in case of any future underground collapse." "At the hour and a half or 1:31, whatever the time was," Houdini wrote, "I had that comfortable feeling when the water pressure was off, not entirely relieving my accordion like movement of lungs, but I was at ease . . . There is no doubt in my mind that had this test been where fresh air could have gotten in the galvanized iron coffin as I was put in same, I could have readily stayed fifteen or thirty minutes longer." The essential thing, he said, was to remain calm. "Fear causes more such deaths than lack of air," he wrote. "No human being can live without air, of course, and I am no block of marble. But by taking shallow breaths and conserving oxygen it is possible to live an hour and a half in such a place . . . Anyone can do it." What strikes one is how serenely he describes the whole experience, which he clearly saw as an interesting scientific experiment rather than a terrifying near-death event. Having duly sent his 1,600-word report, Houdini went off to his local gym to spend the rest of the afternoon playing racquetball and running laps on the indoor track. Despite "a slight metallic taste in the mouth," he reported, he ate "ravenously well" that night. If Houdini paid a price for all his activity, he didn't let it show. "The overriding impression was still one of vitality," *McCall's* wrote. "He [was] an intensely alive human being who went from one herculean task to another." Nevertheless, there were those, like his rival Hereward Carrington, who felt "Houdini appreciably shortened his life by [his] endurance burial," and that the coffin itself assumed a "ghastly significance" just a few weeks later.

Conan Doyle was even more preoccupied with the Spiritualism wars than was Houdini. As well as his existing commitments to the likes of the Psychic Bookshop, and his presidency of both the British College of Psychic Science and the London Spiritualist Alliance, he was always ready to advance the claims of any plausible new medium to appear on the horizon. In early 1926, Doyle heard of a thirty-five-year-old hitherto minor Irish novelist named Geraldine Cummins who, like his own wife, apparently enjoyed the gift of automatic writing. On March 16 of that year, Cummins channeled 1,750 words purporting to come from Cleopas (or "Cleophas"), a figure of early Christianity and one of two disciples said to have encountered the risen Christ on the road to Emmaus. Newspapers on both sides of the Atlantic were soon reporting on the séance. In due course, Cleophas returned to speak, in harshly critical terms, on the biblical teachings of St. Paul and the Acts of the Apostles. Cummins went on to publish this revisionist scriptural account, which gave the New Testament a liberal and feminist twist, in a full-length book called *The Spirits of Cleophas.* Despite the reservations of critics such as the *Catholic Herald,* it soon became a major bestseller. Cummins herself earned a reported £20,000 (or roughly £850,000 today) in its first year of publication, enjoying a degree of recognition denied her earlier literary efforts.

Unfortunately, the worldwide theological debate that ensued was soon eclipsed by a more parochial and material one. When preparing her book for publication, Cummins had had the help of a sixty-two-year-old British biblical scholar and archaeologist named F. Bligh Bond, a great-nephew of Captain Bligh of the *Bounty.* In 1908, the Church of England appointed Bond as director of excavations of Glastonbury Abbey. Some years later, he revealed that he enjoyed "active psychic guidance" in his work, after which his relations with his employers deteriorated and he was sacked. Bond then collaborated with Cummins, but fell out with her when she refused to pay him half the book's royalties as he requested. At that stage Conan Doyle intervened, urging the parties to negotiate the matter through the offices of the Society of Authors. The protracted and increasingly bitter spat that followed soon found its way into the press. British popular-magazine readers were treated to incongruous stories of Cummins commenting on the true nature of the Christian gospel juxtaposed with reports of her threatening to sue her former business partner, and vice versa. Doyle's correspondence, which refers to a "man impossible to deal with" and "that idiot Bond," suggests where his own sympathies lay. Cummins eventually won her case and was awarded punitive damages for what the Society called the "ill-considered and frivolous" complaint against her. Bond, however, absconded to New York, where in time he was ordained, and in 1933 consecrated as a bishop, in the Old Catholic Church of America. Two years later, he published an article in the *Proceedings* of the American SPR claiming that the Crandons had tampered with the notorious "Walter" wax fingerprints. The Society disowned him and he returned to England. Bond died in 1945, leaving an unpublished manuscript containing Spiritual communications from his ancestor Captain Bligh.

If Conan Doyle was exasperated by Bond, he was now growing impatient with Pheneas. Originally a firm believer in the spirit's regular prophecies of doom, Doyle was becoming restive about the timetable. Over the course of three years, this "infallible guide," as his medium called him, had provided more than a hundred warnings about everything from cataclysmic floods and earthquakes to the commercial risks of touring America again. Little, if any, of Pheneas's more apocalyptical view of events had materialized. "I have moments of doubt," Doyle wrote to a fellow Spiritualist, "when I wonder if we have not been victims of some extraordinary prank played upon the human race from the other side . . . I have literally broken my heart in the attempt to give our Spiritual knowledge to the world and to give them something living, instead of the dead and dusty stuff which is served out to them in the name of religion."

For the time being, however, Pheneas continued to appear in the Conan Doyles' family circle.

"*All is going admirably,*" the spirit announced at a séance on October 21, 1926. "*All is according to schedule . . . We thank you for going to help those small people yesterday at the bazaar.*"

"You must help me at Portsmouth," Doyle replied, referring to a speech he was to give in the city.

"*That is a dark place. Evil vibrations from afar concentrate there. It will be destroyed!*"

"Poor people," said Doyle.

"*No, no, there are no poor people. All will be for the best. Those who are even a little good will come into what is a little better. As to those who have misled others and stood in the way of God's light, they shall be removed.*"

"But there will be the terror which they suffer," Doyle fretted.

"*No, there will not be time for terror. It will all be very sudden. You remember years ago how I warned you not to go abroad. You would not be here to-night if you had not taken my warning. I have kept pictures of what would have happened to you. I will show them when you come over. The evil forces had plotted your destruction.*"

"I am greatly obliged to you," said Doyle.

Later that same evening, Houdini went on stage at the Princess Theatre in Montreal. An offended audience member named James P. Clarke later wrote to Conan Doyle to tell him his name had come up in the question-and-answer part of the performance. According to Clarke, "Houdini's [speech] was grossly insolent, insofar that he spoke of you as being just a writer of detective stories, and eaten up with but one subject. Furthermore he said you were no different from the ordinary man—intellectually that you were not a scientist—and acted like a 'big school boy' at a conference in New York. He also stated you would believe anything—and the contemptuous manner in which he passed this remark was exceedingly unfair.

"And now I come to the most important part," Clarke concluded. "As a final retort Houdini said he wished you were there in front of him. He would 'tear you to ribbons.' Obviously he was taking advantage of the distance between London and Montreal. As these remarks were passed publicly, before a large crowd, I think it only right you should know of them. I was shouted down when I indignantly objected—he had the crowd with him."

While in Montreal, Houdini also took the opportunity to address a crowded meeting in the student union building of McGill University. Limping to the stage on a broken left ankle (injured by a twisted cable when being hoisted into the Water Torture Cell), he had some unkind words for Lady Doyle. "She produced for me 23 pages of classical English in a message from my mother . . . who could not speak the language. Don't you ever believe that any medium can take a message for your mother when she has passed to eternal rest." According to the *Montreal Gazette*, Houdini concluded, "If I were to die tomorrow, the Spiritualists would declare an international holiday."

Perhaps even Houdini didn't know how much Lady Doyle, in particular, now deferred to the spirits. When the Doyles went on holiday, Pheneas was summoned to rule on the portents for the trip, once vetoing a planned tour of Scandinavia but promising, instead, to put a "psychic wall" around an alternative destination in Grindelwald, Switzerland. A specific schedule was then typically drawn up by Lady Doyle after a further series of occult consultations. Pheneas's services were also called on to designate favorable and unfavorable days for travel, the preferred times of departure and arrival, and even the ideal route. As a result, Conan Doyle was sometimes presented with a seemingly irrational—and exhausting—itinerary that often required later revision. Although there's no other witness to support the story, a visitor to Windlesham recalled an occasion "around 1925 or 1926" when Conan Doyle's wife rang the stationmaster at Crowborough and asked him to delay the London train by ten minutes because Pheneas thought the scheduled departure time was the "wrong" one for Doyle to be in motion. The man complied. Lady Doyle supposedly then rang back a second time to ensure that her husband would be seated on the left side of the carriage, as this, too, provided the "right vibrations." Again, the necessary arrangements were made. This time, however, the exasperated official is said to have remarked that Lady Doyle was not conspicuously aiding the smooth running of his service. "I know my facts," she replied.

It was easy to make fun of Conan Doyle, and many did. Houdini had no difficulty in raising a laugh when he lampooned this "shambling big schoolboy" on stage. But on another level, Doyle remained the most personally unassuming of men. What impressed the same visitor to Windlesham was the modest style in which her host lived: he started writing before dawn, often working in a small garden hut, and regularly kept going until 9:00 or 10:00 at night. When staying at Bignell Wood, the Conan Doyles' daughter Jean remembered a more relaxed regimen: "People used to just pop in from breakfast time onwards. It was open house . . . My father was very friendly towards the gypsies, and used to go out in the forest and talk with them." Doyle rarely refused a request to speak to a Spiritualist meeting of any size, where his earnestness and sincerity were plain to see. Although he could have retired to a life of well-earned ease, he preferred to use his declining years bringing the psychic message to as wide a circle as possible, even at the cost of his own health and finances. Conan Doyle's first biographer, John Lamond, was moved to tell him, "In less than two centuries, people will be praying to you as the God-man I believe you to be." The simplicity of Doyle's life was not a pose. As even Houdini acknowledged, "Apart from Spiritualism, the man has no other vices. He loves neither money nor pleasure. To him, the mission is all."

Doyle was also staunchly loyal, particularly to those he saw as fellow martyrs to the cause. The negative verdict of successive committees of inquiry had done nothing to shake his faith in the Crandons, any more than they had dented the couple's own self-confidence. By 1926, Margery had added a bondage element to her séances, in an effort to prove that their various levitations and table-tappings took place without her direct help. Houdini himself might not have been disappointed by some of the results. On August 6, "Psyche sat with ankles and wrists lashed, and duly inspected," the minutes reported. "Tightening of screw bolts also inspected . . . Before this was done, Psyche's collar was padlocked [and] its cord fastening to rear of cabinet was firm and adequate. About two inches' freedom of forward motion [remained] to Psyche's head as thus secured." Despite these restraints, Walter soon appeared and "after a little jovial conversation, was able to induce violent bubblings in a beaker of baryta water [barium] placed on the table." A similar demonstration followed three nights later, although on this occasion "Walter had great trouble in getting the apparatus properly arranged. He disliked the small mouthpiece on the barium bottle and asked that a gas tube be substituted. This was done to his satisfaction, and Walter finally blew into the tube with bubbling of moderate intensity. He said, decidedly, 'Tonight I am blowing from the fourth dimension, and there will be no residue in the barium bottle' . . . After a considerable period of bubbling [we] took the phial out in the back room and examined it and found that, contrary to Walter's description, there was a considerable whitish precipitation therein. When this was reported to Walter he was still very emphatic that he had not blown from the third dimension, and was sure that there was some defect in the apparatus." While the Crandons debated the matter of their spirit's respiratory power, Houdini was 200 miles away in New York, calmly relating to reporters how he had just survived an hour and a half in a submerged coffin. Like his fellow spirit Pheneas, Walter now frequently closed his appearances by predicting the imminent doom of skeptics in general and the illusionist in particular. "Houdini will be gone by Halloween," he remarked at the end of one séance.

On August 24, Margery "sat in a lashed cabinet, watched by [her husband] and six other sitters, including Captain Gustafson of the Boston police department . . . Trance came on almost at once and Walter exclaimed, 'Cop! All is lost!' and then proceeded in great good humor," causing a red light to flash on and off while a small wicker basket flew through the air. ("Does this mark an historic moment in the history of psychic science? Is it one of the last rivets?" Dr. Crandon scrawled across the minutes of the séance.) At the next sitting, "Psyche and her clothing [were] thoroughly searched," after which "braided steel picture wire was threaded through rubber tubing tied tightly round each wrist and ankle . . . Strips of surgeon's tape were fixed longitudinally on each forearm," in spite of which "vigorous bubbling" took place of the baryta water. Finally, on October 26, "The Psychic went immediately into trance and Walter came through cheery as ever. He said in effect, 'This is good. Back to the old cow lanes again. I shall have to take a few days to get up steam for the [baryta] experiment. I am not doing much, but my helpers are very busy. You ask why I object to this metal stand holding the pipe to the bottle. Well, it is a little like you putting your hand on a cold brass door-knob in the winter. My teleplasm freezes to it.'" Although, for once, unable to stir up the water, "Walter called for a tin whistle on which notes are played by pulling and pushing a piston at the ends and played on that. He then caressed [one of the sitters] on the shoulder and on the side of his face with a cold, rubbery, sticky touch. The whistling was especially beautiful."

"My experience with Houdini for the last three months of his life was most peculiar," wrote his friend Fulton Oursler. "He would call me at 7 o'clock in the morning and he would be in a quarrelsome mood . . . In all these cases Houdini portrayed to me a clear sense of impending doom. That is not an impression which I have received subsequent to his death. I commented upon it at the time. I believe that Houdini sensed the coming of his death, but did not know that it meant death. He didn't know what it meant, but he hated it and his soul screamed out in indignation."

After committing himself to a new tour in which, among other effects, he would attempt to escape from a coffin lowered into a glass-fronted tank and buried under a ton of sand, Houdini showed understandable signs of concern for his future. Late that August, he made a codicil to his will, which he left with a pile of photographs for Bess to find after his death. The accompanying note was uncharacteristically modest. "I am not important or interesting enough for the world in general," Houdini wrote. His widow was to use the illustrations should she ever write a book about him, "but otherwise destroy all films," he added. "Burn them." One Saturday morning in September, Houdini called Fulton Oursler to tell him "his premonition had [now] taken specific form . . . 'Fraudulent spirit mediums are going to kill me,' he said. 'Every night they are holding séances and praying for my death.'" Early in the morning of October 10, Houdini had a friend named Joe Dunninger meet him at his New York home and drive him downtown to catch a train. Halfway to the station, he suddenly asked that they turn the car around and return to the house. When they got there, Houdini stood in the street for some time staring up at the elegant brownstone where he had lived for the past twenty-two years. "I've seen my house for the last time, Joe," he remarked quietly, when he got back in the car. Adding to Houdini's dark mood, Bess developed a serious case of ptomaine poisoning, sufficiently bad for him to sit up all night in a Providence hotel comforting her. Fatigue may have played a part when he then caught his foot entering the Water Torture Cell in the following night's performance in Albany. After being seen by a doctor backstage, Houdini returned to finish the rest of the program, including his anti-Spiritualist demonstration, on one leg. Although he wasn't concerned about himself, he did worry that "Bess goes through such agony in watching me hobble out on stage every night to deliver the goods."

He did it anyway. Houdini's latest tour began on September 7, in Boston, and was scheduled to run for five months. As well as the live performance—a mixture of death-defying stunts and sharp interplay with the mediums in the house—he was both writing a book called *The Cancer of Superstition* and planning to establish a full-scale College of Magic, which would "issue degrees [and] so compete with the fancy-pants at Harvard, etc." Houdini arrived in Montreal on October 18, and spoke to the students at McGill University the following afternoon. He told the audience the escape artist and the anti-Spiritualist campaigner both needed to condition themselves to simply ignore fear and pain, "and then the miraculous is possible." To illustrate the point, Houdini pulled out a long sewing needle and pushed it through his cheek. After a lively question-and-answer session, he limped out of the room to a prolonged standing ovation. "I spoke for an hour," he wrote in his diary, "my leg broken."

The next night, Houdini packed the ornate Princess Theatre, a pink and black building soaring up in the middle of Montreal like a clumsily iced cake, where he was repeatedly heckled by the Spiritualists in the audience. *The Star* reviewed the show as if it was some kind of religious event, calling it "uplifting" and referring to the headliner as the "messiah" of his trade. Houdini also did a fair Sherlock Holmes impersonation, asking several spectators to stand up so he could astonish, and occasionally mortify them by an apparent bravura display of deduction about the details of their private lives. (His spies had gone around town for the previous two days, digging up the information.) Bess later denied that her husband had gone on to further insult Holmes's creator, as James Clarke claimed. "The very worst Houdini said against you was that you were credulous," she told Conan Doyle. "Mr Clarke's next 'important part' is that Houdini wished you were there, so he could tear you to ribbons! That is too ridiculous for words. What Houdini did say, not only at that performance, but all, [was] 'I can tear all books on Spiritualism to pieces,' meaning he could (as he thought) refute them. Houdini's two secretaries took short-hand notes at every performance (in view of our many law suits) so I can give proof positive re. his speeches."

On the Friday morning of October 22, two McGill students named Sam Smilovitz and Jacques Price called on Houdini backstage at the theater. He told his guests that his ankle was troubling him and that he had gotten through the last week by "force of will." At that, Houdini lay down on a couch in the corner of the dressing room and Smilovitz, a psychology student who dabbled in art, began sketching him. Bess, Julia Sawyer, a nurse, and a secretary were all present. By all accounts, it was one of those slightly dreary scenes of theatrical life, with people standing around, yawning, and complaining about the morning's press notices. After a few minutes there was a knock on the door and Bess ushered in a young man, bringing the total congregating in the small, drab room to eight, all of them crowding around the supine figure who continued to glance through his mail while shifting restively on the couch. Houdini cracked a few sardonic jokes, Price remembered, but otherwise "made no great effort to lighten the atmosphere." After some more in this vein, Bess, Julia Sawyer, and the two assistants excused themselves and returned to their hotel.

Houdini's most recent visitor was another McGill student, Jocelyn Gordon Whitehead. A Divinity postgraduate researcher and keen amateur boxer, he was born in Kelowna, British Columbia, on November 25, 1895, coincidentally the same day on which Houdini performed his first ever public handcuff escape on a stage in New Hampshire. Little else is known of Whitehead except that he eventually took Holy Orders but later fell into obscurity and died of malnutrition, possibly exacerbated by alcohol and drug use, at the age of fifty-eight. According to Smilovitz, he was "powerfully built" and appeared in the dressing room wearing "a blue gabardine suit that was a size too small," announcing that he was there to return a book that Houdini had lent him. Whitehead was then thirty. "His face was ruddy, his hair very thin on top . . . He spoke softly with an exaggerated Oxford accent," Smilovitz said.

According to Jacques Price,

this student then engaged Houdini more or less continually whilst Smilovitz continued to sketch . . . Whitehead was the first to raise the question of Houdini's strength. My friend and I were not so much interested in his strength as we were in his mental acuteness, his skill, his beliefs, and his personal experiences. Houdini stated that he had extraordinary muscles in his forearms, his shoulders and in his back, and he asked all of us present to feel them, which we did. [Whitehead] then asked Houdini whether it was true that punches in the stomach did not hurt him. Houdini remarked rather unenthusiastically that his stomach could resist much, though he did not speak of it in superlative terms. Thereupon he gave Houdini some very hammer-like blows below the belt, first securing Houdini's permission to strike him. Houdini was reclining at the time with his right side nearest Whitehead, and the student was more or less bending over him . . . At the end of the second or third blow I verbally protested against this sudden onslaught, using the words, "Hey there. You must be crazy, what are you doing?" or words to that effect, but Whitehead continued striking Houdini with all his strength.

After the fourth or fifth body blow, Houdini shot out a hand and stopped Whitehead in mid-punch. "That will do," he said firmly. He then lay back on the couch and invited Smilovitz to complete his sketch. Houdini was sufficiently poised to spend some minutes studying the finished work, which he asked the artist to sign and date. "You make me look a little tired in this picture," he remarked. "The truth is, I don't feel so well." As the three students left the room, Houdini courteously thanked them for visiting and promised to write to them in the future. When Julia Sawyer returned to the theater some three hours later, she found Houdini "in pain." He told her that he had invited Whitehead to hit him, but, "possibly because of a misunderstanding of my remarks," the assault had begun "before I could get up and brace myself." After performing for two more nights in Montreal, Houdini and his entourage took the train to Detroit, where he was booked for a week's engagement at the Garrick Theater. During the journey, he began to suffer such severe stomach pains that a still-convalescing Bess sent off a wire asking for a doctor to meet them on arrival. Houdini was a mere parody of himself at the next night's performance, and was so weak he was unable to pull a silk streamer from out of a bowl. The *Detroit News* found him "a little hoarse and more than a little tired." After the show, he was found to have a temperature of 104° and was finally taken to Grace Hospital in the early hours of Monday, October 25. Before the ambulance came for him, Houdini found time to dictate a letter to Fulton Oursler, telling him that he hoped to go over to Toledo the following week for a séance with "that fraudulent woman Ada Bessinet."

Houdini's last seven days must have been torment. On Monday afternoon, surgeons operated to remove his appendix, "a great big affair," Charles Kennedy, the hospital chief of staff, remarked, "which started in the right lower pelvis where it normally should, extended across the midline and lay in his left pelvis, exactly where the fist had landed." (Jacques Price remembered that the punches were actually to the right side of the body.) The likelihood is that Houdini had been suffering from appendicitis even before Whitehead's visit, and that the subsequent blows ruptured his intestine. Peritonitis had set in, virtually a death sentence in the days before penicillin. The doctors privately gave their patient twelve hours to live. On Tuesday and Wednesday, Houdini drifted in and out of consciousness, once rallying to request a bowl of his favorite childhood chop suey. A prostrate Bess was carried in to his bedside. On Thursday, a homoeopath named George LeFevre administered an "experimental serum" that possibly involved no more than dousing Houdini in iced water and rubbing egg whites on the soles of his feet, enough to lower his temperature to 99.4°. Later that night, Jim Collins was able to wire back to New York: "HAS IMPROVED WONDERFULLY DOCTORS PLEASED WITH RESULTS BUT STILL VERY GRAVE." On Friday, Houdini's condition deteriorated again, and surgeons operated for a second time. "Hope for his recovery has not been entirely abandoned," the hospital reported. "His temperature is 103, pulse 130, and respiration 40." Later that night, Houdini was able to hold Bess's hand and tell her to "be prepared if anything happens," which she took as meaning he would try to contact her from beyond the grave. On Saturday afternoon, he dictated a letter to a friend acknowledging, "I feel none too well at the moment," but insisting, "I will get over this waviness in no time." Around 2:00 the next morning, he looked up and told his younger brother Theo, "I guess I'm all through fighting." They were his last words. Bess was again carried in to the room and collapsed on her husband's bed. Houdini died later that afternoon of what the doctors called "Diffuse peritonitis [with] complications." The time of death was given as 1:26 PM on Sunday, October 31—Halloween.

When Houdini had checked in to the hospital, he gave his occupation as "Author and magician." Most of the obituaries, while effusive, fell short of this ideal self-image, and the *New York Times* headline referred to him as the "World's Master Trickster." By a macabre coincidence, Houdini's stage coffin was found to have been left behind when the rest of his props had been shipped out of Detroit. His corpse was now placed in this. The funeral was held at the Elks Clubhouse in New York four days later. A vast wreath of flowers inscribed "Mother Love" lay at the foot of the casket, and a magic wand was broken over it as a token of respect. Just two months earlier, a thirty-one-year-old man named Rudolph Alfonso Raffaele Pierre Filibert Guglielmi di Valentina d'Antonguolla had died, also of peritonitis, and the lying-in-state of Rudolf Valentino (as he had reasonably preferred to call himself) caused riots on the streets of New York. There were no such public lamentations at Houdini's passing, although a procession of fifty cars escorted the deceased to his final resting place at Machpelah cemetery, as Cypress Hills had been renamed. He was buried in a plot immediately next to his mother, as he had requested, with his head resting on a bag containing all her letters to him. A few scraps of newsreel footage exist, and show Houdini's widow and surviving brothers, wearing heavy black overcoats, dropping flowers into the grave. When their fellow mourners began to throw in handfuls of earth, Bess broke down again.

Over the next few days, she recovered sufficiently to summon a parade of Houdini's alleged mistresses to her New York home, where each woman was coldly handed a bundle of her love letters to him. Bess then sold both the house and her husband's books, many of which went to the US Library of Congress. He would likely have been pleased at the intellectual association. Houdini's widow also received a $50,000 life insurance payout, but not without a fight. In 1922, the illusionist had signed a policy with the New York Life company that promised to pay double indemnity in the event of his "murder, manslaughter [or] accidental demise at the hands of a third party," a sound precaution given his activities over the next four years. Bess and Houdini's lawyer Bernard Ernst were forced to provide sworn statements describing Houdini's general health and the dressing room assault on him before the money was eventually paid. Ernst would later tell the press that his client's estate was bankrupt, "show[ing] a $7,110 deficit after settlement of all taxes and arrears." The magician William Frazee added that before selling the New York home, "Bess called in a junk man [who] took several wagon loads of things away. If Houdini knew it he would turn over in his grave. Boxes of handcuffs and thousands of keys, faked mail bag locks, keys from cell locks from all over the world, etc." Houdini willed his brother Theo, or "Hardeen," his larger theatrical props, mysteries, and illusions, which the lawyers valued at $533. Although the will also instructed that the effects be "burnt and scattered" on Hardeen's death, he sold them, instead, to a fellow magician named Sidney Radner. In April 1995, many of the best pieces from the collection were lost in an unexplained fire that destroyed the Houdini Museum in Niagara Falls, Ontario. Radner later sold some of the surviving items for a reported $3 million.

Conan Doyle was characteristically generous when asked to comment on his rival's death. "It is a great shock and mystery to me," he told the *New York Times*. "I greatly admired him, and cannot understand how the end came for one so youthful. We were great friends." This was perhaps to tactfully stretch the truth of their relationship as it had been since October 1922. Doyle had long been convinced that Houdini was a closet medium, and privately believed it was this "central lie" that had sealed his fate. "His death was most certainly decreed from the other side," he wrote Fulton Oursler. "The spirit world might well be incensed against him if he was himself using psychic powers at the very time when he was attacking them." In later years, some commentators felt that Doyle might have played an at least indirect role in helping fulfill the predictions of Houdini's doom. One popular biography has portrayed him as a man "not above using threats to enforce his will," who once warned a skeptic that if he continued "spewing garbage" about phony Spiritualists he would meet the same fate as Houdini. It's known that a number of mediums took it upon themselves to act on Doyle's behalf, and that many of them lacked his self-restraint. One or two of them may even have crossed the line from intensity of belief to full-blown mental derangement. Could one of Doyle's more ardent supporters have interpreted either his or Pheneas's views on Houdini as a call to action?

Most of the conspiracy theories about Houdini's death, it has to be said, perhaps necessarily remain on the hazy side. Subtlety is not a keynote of the debate, though ambiguity is. As always on these occasions, it seems to be easier to ask questions than to provide answers, although there are some intriguing loose ends to the case. The Canadian prime minister at the time of Houdini's death, for instance, was fifty-one-year-old William Mackenzie King, a closet psychic whose diaries reveal his preference for communing with the spirits of Leonardo da Vinci, Theodore Roosevelt, and several of his Irish Terrier dogs. One of King's closest political allies was a McGill University graduate and Liberal MP named Herbert Marler, who in 1929 became Canada's first ambassador to Japan. Marler's wife Beatrice was a prominent Montreal hostess and amateur fortune teller who had befriended Gordon Whitehead, the man who assaulted Houdini in his dressing room. How far the relationship between the statesman's wife and the young student went isn't known; in later years, however, they apparently spent every Sunday afternoon together, possibly engaged in some religious practice. Since Whitehead was a penniless theologian at the time they met, he would seem to have been an unlikely candidate for admission to the Marlers' salon, which centered around a fourteen-bedroom mansion in Montreal's exclusive Mount-Royal district. The question has been asked whether the burly postgraduate student and local boxing champion was somehow put up to the job of attacking Houdini. If so, had he acted on the Marlers', or even King's, instructions? According to one Internet account, a "shadowy network of psychics and mediums reaching the highest ranks of the Canadian government" orchestrated the events of October 22, 1926, as "revenge for Houdini's high-profile debunking of the otherworldly arts as a monumental fraud."

Again, it has to be said that there is no hard and fast evidence that Whitehead was anything more than the unwitting agent of Houdini's death, as both the Montreal police and the New York Life Insurance Company found at the time. The hot-headed lunk may not even have been the only one to hasten the process along. By October 1926, the list of those wishing Houdini ill was an extensive one, and the authors William Kalush and Larry Sloman write of him waiting in the lobby of his Montreal hotel, some forty hours after Whitehead's assault, prior to catching the train for Detroit. "As Houdini sat and read the paper, three young men entered the lobby from the bar and walked up to the magician. One of them, who according to eyewitnesses appeared burly like a football player, without any warning, delivered a crushing blow, right through the newspaper, to Houdini's stomach." (Accepting that a team of muscular goons might have chosen to follow their victim around town repeatedly punching him, the 1878 Canadian Temperance Act makes it unlikely that the door of a Montreal hotel bar would have been open early on a Sunday morning.) This account is a model of journalistic integrity and restraint compared to some of the other published speculation on that week's events. Their general thesis would seem to be that the forces of Spiritualism set out to publicize and justify the message that anyone who expressed opposition to, or even had reservations about, their beliefs put themselves in harm's way. Some of the specific theories of what happened include the psychic underworld having taken out "a hit" on Houdini, administered either by a sinister medical orderly at Grace Hospital in the pay of Dr. Crandon, or by a crew of malevolent circus midgets who surreptitiously entered his hotel room in order to add arsenic to his morning tea, among a host of other colorful scenarios worthy of the most flamboyant Sherlock Holmes story.

At 10:35 on Halloween night 1926, the Crandons and five guests sat down in a circle in the upstairs séance room at Lime Street. According to the minutes,

> The spirit came in and after greetings Dr C said, "Walter, it is apparent that we should not ever take what you say lightly. Houdini passed over at 4pm today . . ." Walter whistled more or less in a minor key and said that Houdini would have a long period of acclimatization, that he would be much confused and resistant to the idea of death, and added, "I am not sure but that I shall have something to do with Houdini and his admission." Asked if we were to understand that when Walter prophesied Houdini's death over 70 times in the past by saying "Give Houdini my love, and tell him I will see him soon," he really saw converging lines that signified Houdini's doom in the near future, the spirit replied, "Look out, don't get superstitious. It isn't that we or your crowd of human wills have anything to do with a human death. But sometimes we can see a little farther ahead than you can."

The next morning, Margery told reporters who descended on Lime Street that neither she nor her spirit guide "had ever damned Houdini [or] put a curse upon him." In fact, she added, "We are sorry to hear of his passing. He was a virile personality of great determination and undoubted physical courage. We have entertained him and our personal relations with him in this house always had been pleasant. At other times and places we have had our differences." Dr. Crandon had less emollient words on the subject when he sent an account of Houdini's death to a colleague named Robin Tillyard. "It is true that a McGill student punched the little man in the abdomen," he wrote. "Walter never said he would 'get' Houdini, but 71 times in our records he has said in the last 13 months: 'Tell Houdini I will see him soon'. Walter was in no way a causal relation. He may see causes converging before we do. That is all."

In the years ahead, the Houdini legend grew in part due to his iconic status as the ultimate self-liberator, a quixotic figure in an era of global economic depression and worsening political tensions, and in part because Bess kept a full-time publicist on her payroll for sixteen years after her husband's death in order to keep the Houdini name alive. "Before Harry passed, he promised to come back to me if he could," his widow told the *New York Evening Journal*, revealing that every Sunday at the hour of his death she sat in a darkened room awaiting word from him. "As I sit star[ing] at his picture, I feel he is guiding me and telling me what to do," she added. "But if only he could speak!" A medium in Attleboro, Massachusetts, soon went one better by announcing that Houdini had returned to her "with a hodgepodge of words, [in] which a few phrases such as 'Tussle with death was agony' and 'Tell my friends I still live' were decipherable." Bess was unmoved, telling the press she had received alleged messages from her husband sent by "dozens" of psychics, but that all of them were "too silly to deserve attention." "Houdini made three compacts before he died: one with me, one with Sir Arthur Conan Doyle and one with a man in Philadelphia," she noted. "I alone have the key to any messages which might be received, a quotation which Houdini used in his work, and which would enable me to recognize anything which really came through." In January 1927, Bess offered a $10,000 reward to any medium who could bring her conclusive news of her husband. The result was a deluge of occult messages that battered the small house she had bought on New York's Payson Avenue like a particularly violent tornado. "*Praise to thee, whose power dominates all creatures, truly thy son Houdini has broken death's shackles and commands me to say . . . A small check to one in need to fight the ignorant skeptics and those who deny the true revelation . . . You won't remember me but I worked backstage with you in the Floral Sisters and I always knew that one day you . . . I enclose your husband's communication to me, which was conveyed in notes played upon a phosphorized trumpet.*" Many other applicants arrived in person at the home, whose front hallway soon teemed with men and women bearing everything from baroque crucifixes and traditional religious artifacts to ventriloquists' dummies. As the first anniversary of Houdini's death approached, Bess went back to the cemetery for the unveiling of his headstone. She again collapsed at the graveside. As the autumn leaves blew at the mourners' feet, Bernard Ernst read out a letter from Conan Doyle. "I should like to send a message of good will," Doyle said. "All differences must be suspended at such a time. [Houdini] was a great master of his profession and, in some ways, the most remarkable man I have ever known."

Houdini's spirit may not have immediately returned, but he did indirectly offer a posthumous gift to Conan Doyle. When clearing her husband's library, Bess came across several Spiritualist volumes that she proposed sending to Windlesham "in view of their intrinsic interest [and] the friendship which for so long existed between you." "I thank you for your kind letter and your offer of books . . . I appreciate it much," Doyle replied the following month. "At the same time it might place me in a delicate position if I were to accept them. I shall probably sooner or later have to write about this remarkable man, and I must do so freely and without any sense of obligation. I am sure you will understand." Doyle concluded by remarking, "I am sure that, with his strength of character (and possibly his desire to make reparation), he will come back. I shall be very glad, if you get a message, if you will tell me. [The telepathist] Zancig writes me that he has had a prearranged test message from his first wife."

Bess immediately replied, expressing her confidence that "surely nothing [Conan Doyle] wrote would be detrimental to Houdini the man, or to yourself." She offered fresh details on her husband's deathbed arrangements for his return.

> Two days before he went to his beloved Mother, he held my hand to his heart and repeated our solemn vow of our compact . . . He repeated the words in formation—"When you hear these words you will know it is Houdini speaking. The same message will go through to Sir Arthur, but in that formation only. Never, despite anything, will I come through otherwise," and with his dying kiss (although he did not know it then) I vowed to wait for that, and only that, message . . . Dear Sir Arthur, Houdini was a level-headed man. He was deeply hurt whenever any journalistic arguments arose between you, and would have been the happiest man in the world had he been able to agree with your views on Spiritism. We never attributed [his escapes] to psychic help. It was Houdini himself that was the secret. His personality, his brilliant mind, carried him through, and perhaps it will be this same Houdini who will come through to you or me. Surely our beloved God will let him bring me the message for which I wait, and not the silly messages I get from various people . . . Please believe me when I say that I have taken an oath to tell the world when I do hear from him.

Conan Doyle in turn replied noting Houdini's "general wild attack upon all that we hold dear," but acknowledging: "Behind all that, I can see quite a different person—a loving husband, a good friend, a man full of sweet impulses. I have never met anyone who left so mixed an impression upon my mind." He agreed "it would be a great day for all of us, and, I believe, for him also, when you could say to the world: 'My doubts are gone. I have most undoubtedly had my message.'"

In January 1927, Bess persevered by offering to send Conan Doyle the portfolio of his father's sketches, "includ[ing] many beautiful forms of angels," from

Houdini's library. This time the gift was accepted. Doyle was gracious in his letter of acknowledgment. "The book has arrived and filled me with surprise . . . It really seems like a series of miracles—first that it should exist still, then that it should cross the Atlantic, and finally that it should come back home. I accept it as a peace-offering from your husband, and thank him as well as you."

In November 1926, Conan Doyle addressed the annual Remembrance Day Spiritualist service at the Royal Albert Hall. "It would have rejoiced your heart to see 8,000 people there," he told Oliver Lodge, fully half of whom had sprung to their feet when asked by Doyle to signify if they had made contact with the dead. He thought it "one of the most remarkable things" that had ever happened in London. Not greatly to his surprise, the press ignored it.

Like Houdini before him, Conan Doyle placed great faith in personal appearances. After ten years of Spiritualist campaigning, he could rightly boast of having spoken to "hundreds of devout groups" in Britain and Europe, as well as on his extensive travels in North America and Australia. Despite declining health, he would go on to arrange lecture tours of South Africa, Holland, and Scandinavia, revealing that it was his ambition "to speak in each non-Catholic capital before I pass." While the cynics variously ridiculed or ignored him, Conan Doyle continued to fill auditoriums, publish front-page articles, and host often dramatic and widely debated séances on four continents. Besides the sheer energy that both Doyle and Houdini brought to their respective work, this underestimate of them by their opponents was another important common factor in their lives.

On December 3, 1926, the same day that Conan Doyle wrote to decline the offer of Houdini's books, the thirty-six-year-old thriller writer Agatha Christie vanished from her home in Sunningdale, Berkshire. She was despondent following her mother's death that spring and the subsequent discovery of her husband's affair with a younger woman. The next morning, Christie's car was found abandoned at the side of a ditch, its headlights still burning. For the next ten days, as police and thousands of civilian volunteers combed the Home Counties, the press teemed with rumors about the disappearance. Had Christie drowned herself in a nearby, supposedly haunted spring called the Silent Pool? Others suggested the incident was a publicity stunt, while some clues seemed to point in the direction of murder at the hands of her unfaithful husband. All the elements of a classic whodunit were there. After a week of "unavailing search," the chief constable of Surrey sought the advice of "the world's foremost detective mind" (and his own county's Deputy

Lieutenant), Arthur Conan Doyle. As we've seen, Doyle took the psychic approach to the problem. After obtaining one of Christie's gloves, he gave it to the medium Horace Leaf. "He never saw it until I laid it on the table at the moment of consultation, and there was nothing to connect either it or me with the Christie business," Doyle wrote. "He at once got the name Agatha." Leaf remarked that the glove's owner was still alive, and that he had "some definite impression of water" in her life.

Two days later, Christie was discovered at a spa hotel in Harrogate, where she was registered as Teresa Neele, the surname of her husband's mistress. She appeared to have suffered some sort of emotional breakdown, possibly accompanied by amnesia. Although Leaf had erred in some of the specifics of the case, Conan Doyle declared it to have been a triumph of psychic divination. "It is, it must be admitted, a power which is elusive and uncertain, but occasionally, it is remarkable in its efficiency," he wrote. "It is often used by the French and German police." Conan Doyle's remarks got short shrift at Scotland Yard, where one official noted, "We do not keep hopeless lunatics in the forces of this country." There were perhaps predictable remarks in the press about Doyle's preference for the occult rather than the logical, Holmes-like approach to the investigation. Neither Agatha Christie nor her husband appears to have acknowledged her fellow author's help in the matter. The couple divorced two years later.

Although not everyone appreciated Conan Doyle's paranormal beliefs or methods, nobody questioned his resilience or dedication to the cause as a whole. "He seemed to take the ill-considered abuse [of the skeptics] as merely the kind of temporary setback bound to occur in life," one American Spiritualist journal reported. "If anything, it redoubled his commitment to the truth." Doyle's unquenchable optimism led him, in March 1927, to pick out the one positive comment in a long letter from Bess Houdini, who was trying to "gently lower any remaining hopes" they might have of her husband's return. The attempt failed. "I am most thankful that you have got so far," Doyle promptly wrote back. "Now the more intimate test should come."

9

"THERE IS NO DEATH"

S
hortly after Houdini's death, among the spate of commemorative articles praising his skill as a magician, Conan Doyle produced something different—a piece claiming him as "the greatest physical medium of modern times." Originally published in the *Strand Magazine* in July 1927, the article turned into the basis of a series of interviews and talks, and was reprinted as the first chapter of what became his final book. Doyle was apparently just as keen to recruit Houdini to the Spiritualist camp now that he was dead as he had been when he was alive. Brushing aside any discouragement on her part, he kept up a steady correspondence with Bess over the next two years, writing as often as once a month (in the days when a letter could take that long to cross the Atlantic), sometimes sending news of his paranormal activities as a whole, but generally enclosing some specific inquiry or detail about Houdini's return. Bess seems to have reacted with much the same combination of deference and evasiveness her husband had initially shown Doyle. "I heard my beloved [say], 'I wish I were as sane as Sir Arthur is,'" she remarked in one letter, adding that she would put a flower on his grave in Doyle's name. Although Houdini had never admitted to occult powers, Bess said in a later exchange, it was possible he might have had them without knowing it. Occasionally, it almost seemed as if the modestly educated former showgirl was toying with the celebrated author. In January 1928, Bess wrote to Doyle revealing that a mirror had broken in her home, for no apparent reason, and that the idea had occurred to her that this might possibly be some "manifestation" by Houdini. Doyle heartily concurred. "I think the mirror incident shows every sign of being a message," he

wrote. "After all, such things don't happen elsewhere. No mirror has ever broken in this house. Why should yours do so? And it is just the sort of energetic thing one could expect from him."

In June 1927, Bess wrote to offer Conan Doyle yet another batch of Spiritualist documents from Houdini's library. Doyle was guarded in his reply, suggesting that she read his article in *The Strand* before making him any more gifts. "But you know that I (I should say 'we') have every respect for you personally, and for [Houdini] also," he added, "so long as he does not stand in the way of the most important thing upon earth, which is to prove immortality." Bess seems to have taken Doyle's reply in her stride, because she sent the documents anyway. "I thank you heartily," he wrote on September 2, 1927. "I hope to have some psychic news for you presently. Mr McKenzie of the College got in touch, as he believes, with Houdini through a trance medium, Mrs. Garrett. I will have a sitting as soon as I can possibly arrange it. According to the McKenzie message, Houdini was still rather clouded in his mind, which is natural enough after the physical change. As he clears, the messages should clear."*

On October 10, 1927, Bess attended a Spiritualist rally at Carnegie Hall, where she met a dapper, thirty-year-old medium named Arthur Ford, of the First Spiritualist Church of Manhattan. Within weeks, Ford announced that he was in touch with both Houdini's mother and Houdini himself. On February 8, Mrs. Weiss was said to have transmitted the message, "*Forgive.*" Fifteen years earlier, she had muttered the same word on her deathbed. Houdini was convinced that his mother had

---

*James Hewat McKenzie (1869–1929) was a Scottish psychologist and hypnotist who went on to found the British College of Psychic Science. His 1916 essay "Spirit Intercourse: Its Theory and Practice" included several firsthand observations of Houdini's alleged occult powers. "A small iron tank filled with water was deposited on the stage, and in it the medium [Houdini] was placed, the water completely covering his body," he wrote. "Over this was placed an iron lid with three hasps and staples, and these were securely locked. The body was then completely dematerialized within the tank in one and a half minutes, while the author stood immediately over it. Without disturbing any of the locks, Houdini was transported from the tank direct to the back of the stage front, dripping with water and attired in the blue jersey-suit in which he entered the tank . . . This startling manifestation of one of Nature's profoundest miracles was probably regarded by most of the audience as a very clever trick." Conan Doyle called McKenzie "one of the greatest psychical researchers in the world." Eileen Garrett (1893–1970) was an Irishwoman who developed psychic abilities shortly after both her parents and an uncle simultaneously committed suicide. All three of her own sons died prematurely. In later years, Garrett was able to summon a fourteenth-century Arab soldier named Uvani to her séances and went on to found *Tomorrow* magazine, specializing in horoscopes and astrology. She died while investigating a case of alleged demonic possession on the French Riviera.

been speaking of the family scandal that had blown up when her son Leopold began an affair with Sadie Weiss, who was married to his brother Nat. "It was indeed the signal for which [Houdini] always secretly hoped," Bess told Ford, "and if it had been given to him while he was still alive, it would I know have changed the entire course of his life. But it came too late ... Aside from this there are one or two trivial inaccuracies—Houdini's mother called him Ehrich—[but] nothing which could be contradicted. I might also say that this is the first message which I have received which has an appearance of truth."

While Bess awaited further developments with Ford, she also announced plans to make a comeback on the vaudeville stage with an effect she called "Freezing a Man in a Cake of Ice." She showed some of her husband's flair for selling a trick, if not his skill at executing it. At a press preview, a Sioux Indian wearing a rubber diving suit was locked into a steel box that was filled with water up to his neck. Using "special scientific apparatus" (carbon dioxide pumped through a bellows), the water was then frozen. At the act's one public performance, a month later, Bess had to be led from the stage after apparently choking on the gas fumes generated by the procedure. A doctor was summoned while "the Indian looked for a hot fire," it was reported. Her plans for a more extensive theatrical tour were shelved following this disappointment, and Bess announced that she would be devoting herself full-time to the "psychic matter."

"I am in for a real good hard winter's work," Conan Doyle wrote Oliver Lodge in September 1927. Doyle had already published his volume of Pheneas's warnings and a long article in *The Graphic* praising the spirit's "broad and beautiful and uplifting views" (among them his prediction of Houdini's doom), all evidence, apparently, of his "entire reliability." The regular family séances also continued. A participant in one sitting who was clasping Lady Doyle's hand at the time felt "a bolt of electricity" run through it at the mention of an "imminent seismic event" somewhere in the world. Several more prophecies followed over the years, although Pheneas increasingly preferred not to put a specific date to them. In time, Doyle was to remark to Lodge that he was considering publishing a sequel to *Pheneas Speaks*, and that this second book would be "much sterner stuff." Later in the autumn, Kingsley Conan Doyle came through to the family and spoke for two hours; he, too, reportedly confirmed that the world was facing a grave crisis. Doyle went on to tell Lodge that he had visited the spirit photographer William Hope in an effort to get a picture of Pheneas—a bearded face had duly appeared, though not of sufficient clarity for it to be used commercially.

The truth was that at sixty-eight, Conan Doyle found it almost impossible to relax while the "great fundamental psychic gospel" remained to be preached, even at the cumulative cost to his reputation and health. Publishing the views of his 10,000-year-old spirit guide was the least of it. Doyle also continued to spread the word in an apparently unstoppable series of lectures and speeches, as well as in what the *Daily Express* mockingly called an "amazing document," "The Ghost of the Moat." In this "real-life story," the author wrote of sitting with some American guests among the roses on the Windlesham veranda, where he witnessed the meta-morphosis of a Mrs. Wickland of Los Angeles into a Sussex stable-boy who had drowned locally over a century earlier. "Have I not said truly that the actual experiences of the Spiritualist, of which this is one in a hundred, are stranger far than what I should dare to invent?" he wrote. Doyle also kept up a voluminous private correspondence on the occult, exchanging views with everyone from Guglielmo Marconi to the "humblest enquiring soul." On December 5, 1926, John Marney of Prusom Street, Wapping, wrote to describe a problem that he thought might appeal on both the "Sherlock Holmes" and Spiritualist levels. "About last June, whilst playing cards, a piece of coal fell on the table from *nowhere*," Mr. Marney reported. "Shortly after a second piece fell on the table. On October 5th, pieces of coal came dropping in different parts of the house and greatly upset my wife. Since then it has been falling almost every day except on two occasions when there was none for four days and again later for six days. After each interval it seemed to get worse."

Conan Doyle's Spiritualist duties left him little time for other literary work, as he made clear to a journalist who wrote inquiring about Sherlock Holmes's prospects. "I fear there is little chance of my doing [any] more," Doyle said. "With a correspondence of 30 or 40 letters a day, dealing often with abstruse cases, and with constant demands to take part in meetings, my time is much broken. I was glad to withdraw Holmes before the public were too weary of him . . . No doubt I shall write upon psychic subjects. My last such book *Pheneas Speaks* has met with considerable success, and I shall be glad if you mentioned the fact. There is a movement to syndicate it in the press of all foreign countries." Doyle did find time to publish his novella *The Maracot Deep,* which *The Strand* serialized over the winter of 1927–28. As we've seen, it balanced science fiction and the occult, describing a group of deep-sea divers who find the lost world of Atlantis, where they ward off a giant crustacean, make use of a thought-projection machine, and eventually confront an evil deity named the Lord of the Dark Face. It's both a ripping yarn and a defiant affirmation of Doyle's belief that humanity was doomed if it continued to ignore the spirit warnings of Pheneas and others. The Atlanteans themselves, we learn, had fallen into a state of "moral degeneracy" that might have been avoided had they listened to "the grave and earnest men, reasoning and pleading with them" about their ways. Although the main plot flowed with Doyle's characteristic style, he brought a more grating, staccato tone to the didactic passages—"like a man honking in a traffic jam," in one critic's phrase.

In March 1927, Conan Doyle again came "vigorously to the defense of Mrs L. R. G. Crandon, better known as 'Margery', who [was] under attack from the academic Dr J. B. Rhine," the *New York Times* reported. Doyle told the paper that Rhine's investigation was a "colossal impertinence." The note of offended propriety was echoed in a letter the following month to Oliver Lodge. The Crandon case had become insufferable, Doyle fumed—"vile charges" had been made against a lady, and Crandon's defense of his wife's honor brushed aside. A number of Doyle's articles and speeches similarly touch on the incivility of his opponents. At times he seemed not just to be speaking about people's Spiritual needs, but also to be addressing the decline of post-war morals.

Although Conan Doyle's chivalrous response to Margery's critics did him credit, he was unaware of the deteriorating domestic situation across the Atlantic at Lime Street. It's unlikely he would have approved. While Dr. Crandon fulminated against Rhine and the other "blockheads" who questioned his wife's mediumship, Margery herself was sinking into alcoholism and depression. A young *Boston Guardian* reporter, John Hamer, would remember calling by appointment at the Crandons' one morning to find the front door ajar and "the lady of the house lying on her back in the hall, drunk, dead to the world." The former beauty "cut a pitiable sight, half-clad, her hair matted like Medusa's, snoring as she breathed." Some time later, Margery is said to have climbed up onto the roof of her house and threatened to jump off. She reportedly changed her mind after hearing Walter recite the Lord's Prayer inside her head. This intervention by the spirits became the basis for many a subsequent séance and many a monologue.

After her failed vaudeville comeback, Bess Houdini also began to take consolation in alcohol and other substances. "Dine at Village Grove—home early, no drink or weed," she told her diary in October 1927. The following year, while celebrating at a Christmas party with Arthur Ford, Bess fell and knocked herself unconscious. Two days later, already heavily sedated, she apparently took a near-fatal overdose of sleeping pills, only to be rescued by Houdini's lawyer Bernard Ernst. A reporter from the *New York Evening Graphic* later called at Payson Avenue and described

Bess as being "semi-delirious," brokenly calling out her husband's name. She was "under constant care of physicians." The house itself appeared "neglected." It seems fair to say that Bess was not, then, at her best when she received Ford and several of his followers at home in the early evening of January 8, 1929. Bess's longtime press agent, Charles Williams, and two reporters were also present. After a year of "preliminary discussions" with the spirits, Ford announced to the gathering, he was finally ready to summon Houdini from the other side.

While a heavily bandaged Bess watched from a sofa, Ford and the others joined hands across the dining table. Candlelight and the mournful strains of a record playing on the Victrola completed the classic elements of the séance. After blindfolding himself and apparently falling into a trance, Ford began to speak in a high, quavering voice he claimed was Houdini's. "Hello, Bess, sweetheart," he said. "I came to impress you that this is of great importance, greater than you ever dreamed. I desire to bring this message before the world . . . *Rosabelle—answer—tell—pray— answer—look—tell—answer—answer—tell,*" Ford, or Houdini, recited. "Now take off your wedding ring and show them what Rosabelle means."

After a moment's pause, Bess removed her ring. Then her lips moved, though just barely, and she began to sing in a voice so soft they had to strain to hear it from a few feet away.

> *Rosabelle, sweet Rosabelle*
> *I love you more than I can tell.*
> *O'er me you cast a spell,*
> *I love you, my sweet Rosabelle.*

It was a song Houdini and his wife had used in their act thirty-five years earlier, and that he had had engraved on her ring. While Bess, on the couch, began sobbing quietly, the medium explained that the other nine words in the message were a code for "*Believe.*" "My words to you before death were '*Rosabelle, believe,*'" he said. "Is that correct?" Bess nodded that it was. "Then tell the whole world that Harry Houdini still lives, and will prove it a thousand times and more," the voice continued, now almost shouting in excitement. "Tell all those who lost faith because of me to lay hold again of hope, and to live with the knowledge that life is continuous. There is no death. That is my message to the world!" Later that evening, Bess issued a press release that perhaps betrayed some sign of having been dictated for her. It read: "Regardless of any statements made to the contrary, I wish to declare that the message, in its entirety, and in the agreed upon sequence, given to me today by

Reverend Arthur Ford, is the correct message prearranged between Mr Houdini and myself."

Amid the next morning's headlines proclaiming that Houdini had spoken from the grave, Conan Doyle was quoted suggesting "this might become *the* classical case of after-death return." In fact, Doyle had had several prior dealings with Ford, whom he met when the medium made a Spiritualist tour of Britain. Some of the press had even come to regard him as Doyle's protégé. "This wonderful new seer," *Psychic News* later reported, was "the next apostle of the age." When the New York papers published their accounts of Ford's breakthrough with Houdini, several of them printed a large photo of Conan Doyle alongside. Even when questions later came to be asked about the "Rosabelle" séance, Doyle stuck to his guns. "If these loving hands can meet through the veil, then ours also can do so," he wrote. "As Houdini is today, you and I will be to-morrow . . . In this case a deliberate test was proposed. If it had not been fulfilled it would have counted a strong argument against survival. But it was fulfilled. Surely it cannot be dismissed as if it never occurred."

Born into a devout Baptist family in Florida, Ford was a hard-drinking ex-soldier who claimed to have had his first psychic vision while serving overseas as a military clerk in 1918. Before long, he was apparently getting premonitions about which of his fellow servicemen would fall in action—or later succumb to the Spanish flu—and took the trouble to advise them accordingly. Ford's comrades on the front lines undoubtedly hoped to avoid catching his eye. After becoming a professional medium in 1923 he went on to run New York's First Spiritualist Church, where he's remembered as a man of considerable personal charm and oratorical skills, in whom piety coexisted with a love of the good things in life. Walking out to conduct one well-attended service, Ford is said to have hurriedly stashed away a large cigar that he had been smoking moments before and absentmindedly brought with him to the pulpit. In the middle of his opening remarks, wisps of smoke began issuing from his robes. Quietly at first, then in some frenzy, Ford had tried to extinguish the inferno raging in his pocket. Some in the crowd apparently interpreted his actions as a sign of Spiritual rapture, and began to applaud enthusiastically. Following Ford's eventual death in 1971, his friend and former supporter William Rauscher discovered that he had kept voluminous books of newspaper cuttings and other biographical material on his clients, disguising these as poetry collections. According to Rauscher, Ford "knew everything" about the principal parties to a séance before he went on to bring them news from the beyond—including, in this case, the fact that the "Rosabelle" code had appeared in Harry Kellock's 1928 Houdini biography that Bess herself had authorized.

Conan Doyle seems to have had a mixed opinion of Ford's mediumship. "I dislike his advertisements very much," Doyle wrote to Bernard Ernst. "At the same time, when I remember Houdini's advertisements, there does seem a rough justice about it." For all his self-promotion, Ford struck him as "a young, clean-shaven, fresh-faced man, carefully dressed, with all the appearance, and indeed the habits of a man of the world, who thoroughly enjoys the things of this life. He is gentle, sympathetic and likely to be popular with the ladies. His manner is silky. His voice is low. He is a man who would be popular in any company." For the most part, these were the same qualities that Ford's detractors believed allowed him to successfully prey on the vulnerable. Some time later, Ernst wrote back with details of Bess's condition. It was a "sorry tale," he confided. "Now about this Houdini test. There is a dangerous snag there and Walter must not run up against it," Doyle in turn wrote Dr. Crandon. "Houdini's lawyer tells me that Mrs Houdini has taken to drink, drugs, and the Lord knows what. [She] is thoroughly unreliable." We know Doyle read Harry Kellock's biography, because in September 1929 he sent the author his 1,500-word review of it. "I think you may take the words 'An unsolved mystery' off your cover," Doyle wrote. "It is I who have solved the mystery of Houdini and I have no more doubt that he used psychic powers than I have that I am dictating this letter."

While Ford's Spiritualist merits were under debate, another contender came forward to claim Bess's $10,000 prize, which, with the help of *Science and Invention* magazine, eventually rose to $31,000—a truly fabulous sum at the time. This was none other than Nino Pecoraro, the illiterate young Italian whose materializing powers had been tested by Houdini in 1923. Once again, Pecoraro was securely bound to a chair, his hands wrapped in gloves that were in turn sewn to his shirt. Houdini's friend Joe Dunninger and two other observers then "drew a curtain around the subject, cranked the gramophone, doused the lights," and awaited developments. Ten minutes later, a high-pitched voice came through, first announcing that it was the spirit of Eusapia Palladino, and then of Houdini. "Both," concluded Dunninger, "sounded as though uttered by Nino." Despite promises that Houdini himself would materialize before them, the test ended inconclusively. Bess and the publishers of *Science and Invention* withheld their prize.

Ford, too, eventually withdrew his claim, after the *New York Graphic* published a front-page article under the headline "HOUDINI MESSAGE A BIG HOAX!

'Séance' Prearranged by 'Medium' and Widow." The contention was that Bess and Ford had scripted the whole "Rosabelle" episode as a way to promote a vaudeville tour they planned to do together. Although the *Graphic* stopped short of saying so, there were those who thought the two parties also enjoyed a personal friendship. Three weeks after the séance, Bess wrote to Ernst, "I am so ill that when anyone speaks to me I want to scream . . . the case against me about the message looks bad. Don't you see I'm mixed up in a sordid affair? I cannot talk yet. This is why I tried to do what I did [in] January . . . Having my friends believe me of deliberately betraying Houdini hurts—and it really hurt me sorely." A year later, in March 1930, Bess and her lawyer told the press she had "now renounced faith in the possibility of communicat[ing] with her husband and denies that any of the mediums presented the clue by which she was to recognize a legitimate message," adding that she was "through [with] psychic affairs" generally. Although temporarily suspended from the United Spiritualist League of New York for "unprofessional conduct," Ford still remained active in paranormal circles forty years later. In September 1967, he appeared in a televised séance with Bishop James Pike of California in an attempt to contact Pike's dead son, an event *Time* magazine dismissed as "theatrical charlatanism."

Bess, too, seems to have reneged on her promise to forgo the occult, because later in the 1930s she took up with a medium who went under the name Edward Saint. A former dime-hall performer then known as "Charlie Myers, the Stone-Faced Man," he had spent the preceding decades touring the country offering to pay $1,000 to anyone who could make him smile. Since his facial muscles had been largely paralyzed since birth, it was a safe bet. Myers, or Saint, rekindled interest in Houdini's return by claiming that he had left behind a secret safety deposit box containing cash and jewels, and that he would try to summon the illusionist so that he could reveal its whereabouts. This attempt, too, ended in disappointment, and Saint ultimately seems only to have added to Bess's problems. "After Ed's death [in 1942], I just collapsed," she told Houdini's brother Theo. "The big Palooka left me with files and files of junk—he took every picture that Harry ever had taken and had hundreds of copies made—hundreds of busts—even photostats of his letters—now who the devil wants all that . . . I never got angry with Ed whilst he lived, but I'm sore at him now for leaving me this mess."

Long before then, Bess had not only lost control of events but had the greatest difficulty in "putting forward a dignified face on Houdini's behalf," as she explained her life's work to the *New York Graphic*. As well as her flirtations with Ford, Saint, and others, there was a public spat with Houdini's voluptuous former assistant

Daisy White, whose duties had sometimes called for her to parade up and down the stage in an overfull dress while the illusionist himself prepared his next trick in the background. Now Daisy, a convert to Spiritualism, threatened to tell the world of her close relationship with "Mr Harry" unless the Houdini camp, in turn, acknowledged the truth of the new revelation. Although Bernard Ernst was able to mediate a solution, leaving Daisy free to open a popular New York speakeasy, Bess's physical and emotional decline continued. Shortly after the Ford episode, she spent a month in the Bronx's West Hill Sanitarium, which specialized in alcoholic cases. Although "Spiritualism was a forbidden subject" there, she told Ernst, she still clung to the possibility of Houdini's return. As well as several semi-public séances, often held on the anniversary of her husband's death, she corresponded with Conan Doyle almost to the end of his own life. "I can report two recent cases of interest," Doyle wrote in his last known letter to her.

> In the first, a friend of mine, Mrs Stobart, had a message from a stranger. The message was that Houdini desired to send a message to Mrs Stobart—that she should go to a medium, and that a bunch of roses would be the sign that it really was Houdini who was speaking. She went accordingly to Mrs Barkel (who had not been specially recommended). When Mrs Barkel went into a trance she said, "There is a spirit here who desires to send a message, and carries a bunch of red flowers as a sign . . ."
>
> In the other case, several messages came through to me, purporting to be from him, but nothing that convinced me. He finally was supposed to say, "I am not developed enough yet over here to get difficult tests through, but I have attracted my wife's attention by sounds and other signs of my presence, but there is an atmosphere of doubt and fear around her which is hard to penetrate." I give this for what it is worth.

Approaching his seventieth birthday, Conan Doyle struck many observers as an acute, opinionated, affable Victorian gentleman not unaffected by the self-indulgent dottiness that flowers in old age. Despite experiencing dizzy spells—the onset of heart disease—Doyle kept up his usual brisk pace as he balanced the demands of being a Spiritualist apostle, popular author, and essayist on everything from the true meaning of life to the correct way to bowl a cricket donkey-drop. Although his reputation had been made nearly forty years earlier, the words just kept on coming. For him, writing was like scratching an endless itch. Doyle opened

1928 by telling *Beckett's Budget* newspaper, "I know just what will happen to you when you die, just as I know what will happen to me. You cannot imagine what a mass of personal evidence we have. There is not the faintest shadow of doubt about it whatever and all the things we have are enormously encouraging. It is better than the wildest dreams we could imagine. And the stupid world! They talk about it as though it were blasphemous." A few days later, Doyle delivered a stinging broadside to H. G. Wells in the *Sunday Express*, after Wells had written unappreciatively of *Pheneas Speaks*. Switching deftly from the spiritual to the material, he went on to publish "The Story of Spedegue's Dropper," in which the eponymous bowler tosses the ball high into the air, over the batsman's head, and onto the top of his wicket, thus winning the Ashes for England.

The appliance of technology was one of the main issues beyond sport and his advocacy of anti-drinking laws that actively engaged Conan Doyle, just as it had forty-one years earlier when he introduced Sherlock Holmes to the world working away among the test tubes in the laboratory at Bart's hospital. In 1924, Doyle had written to *The Times* shortly after George Mallory and his climbing partner disappeared near the summit of Mount Everest, suggesting that a high-powered airplane should circle the peak and if necessary attempt a rescue. (The actual landing and taking off would be "bad," he admitted in a separate letter.) But this essentially scientific view of the world was more than balanced by the spiritual one. In 1928, Doyle brought out a second edition of *The Coming of the Fairies*, in which he reaffirmed his belief that the events at Cottingley were of greater significance to humanity than Columbus's discovery of the New World. Despite several false starts, he also continued to credit the prophecies of both Pheneas and a growing number of other spirit doom mongers. In one letter, Doyle wrote of his interest in a "South African seer, one Goch," a Johannesburg accountant who not only predicted an apocalypse in southern Europe but added a detailed geological account of how it would come about. This boiled down to a complicated formula involving the tilting of the polar axis and the consequent cracking of the earth's crust—another example, perhaps, of Doyle's twinned faith in science and the occult.

On July 24, 1928, Conan Doyle appeared as a witness in Westminster magistrates court on behalf of a Miss Mercy Phillimore and Mrs. Claire Cantlon, respectively the Secretary of the London Spiritualist Alliance and a medium who practiced there, whom the police had charged under the Vagrancy Act. Infuriated at the "medieval" proceedings against the women, Doyle went on to make an appointment with the Home Secretary in an unsuccessful attempt to change the law as it applied to such "honest visionaries" as those in the dock. In short order, he was again writing to *The Times,* advocating the creation of a paranormal political party. "We are a solid body numbering some hundreds of thousands of voters," he noted. Several of the paper's other correspondents raised the issue of how far someone in a Spiritualist coma was liable for his or her actions; what were the courts to make of a "blasphemous" medium, for example, or one who caused wholesale panic by prophesying the end of the world? Doyle plunged into the controversy with the intensity of a nineteenth-century revivalist. "He was mesmerising," a skeptical *Daily Express* journalist admitted, after hearing him speak at the Albert Hall. "I felt that if he wanted to sell us a house with the roof missing, he would achieve his purpose by an eloquent and sustained eulogy of the features that remained."

Conan Doyle seemed to take rejection personally, and he was relentless in his advocacy. Almost no Spiritualist cause, anywhere in the world, was too obscure. In 1928 alone, he was to take up the case of the missing transatlantic pilot Walter Hinchliffe, whose disappearance he speculated had been caused by transportation to a parallel universe, rather than bad weather. He wrote at some length about fairies and spirit photographs, and exchanged views with correspondents as far afield as Alaska and the Falkland Islands. Not untypical was the letter that December from Dr. A. J. Kiser, a Colorado dentist who wrote to tell Doyle, "Under separate cover, postage prepaid, I am sending you a carbon copy of my manuscript, which I regard as a very valuable contribution to the gospel of Spiritualistic phenomena," and which in time apparently received a friendly response. Every day there were more packages purporting to bring proof of man's survival after death, sometimes accompanied by elaborate case-studies of the "fascist-Catholic conspiracy" concealing the truth of Pheneas's predictions, the latter complete with flow-diagrams to Armageddon, typically composed in red ink and apparently written in short bursts of manic energy around the edges of the note, so that one had to turn the page through 360 degrees to read all of it. In October of that year, Doyle received the lengthy transcript of a "fascinating conversation" held between officers of the American SPR and President Woodrow Wilson, who had died in 1924. Dr. Crandon wrote from Boston to report that Walter had again materialized, flirting with one of the lady sitters before "breaking into a vigorous and beautiful whistle[d] version of 'God Save the King,'" while a Chas Stevens of Westbury Furnishing Stores, Southend-on-Sea, commended "Sir Sherlock Holmes" for doing "God's work." On some days more than a hundred pieces of mail went in or out of Windlesham. Although Conan Doyle was unfailingly courteous even to the most testing correspondent, he was also wary of committing himself too far. When a German violinist named Florizel von Denter wrote to suggest that they co-author a "great Spiritualist book," reportedly accompanying the proposal with a picture of himself wearing a ruffled velvet suit with a garland of flowers in his hair, Doyle politely declined the request.

Over time, Conan Doyle's concerns about drinking, rooted in his father's alcoholism, developed into a phobia. Doyle had long had a slightly spinsterish attitude to the subject surprisingly common among writers. "It was done in kindness," he had said of his American hosts' liquid hospitality in 1894, "but it was dangerous for a man who had his work to do." Twenty-four years later, when Doyle watched a man raise a glass in the London street to celebrate the Armistice, he wanted the crowd to lynch "this beast [who] was a blot upon the landscape." Given these views, he might have had reservations about the life Bess Houdini was now leading in New York. In the year between her parting from Arthur Ford and meeting Edward Saint, Bess succumbed further to both the bottle and a succession of young suitors who between them nearly bankrupted her. One visitor to Payson Avenue spoke of encountering a "swollen, prematurely old lady" swigging from a hip-flask of gin while half sitting, half reclining under a glowering portrait of her husband. At one stage, Bess was reduced to running a small, though popular tea shop in a street off Times Square. She then appears to have again suffered some kind of breakdown following an unsuccessful attempt to reach Houdini in October 1929. Bess was "calm and self-assured" when the other sitters arrived, but following the séance "could not restrain herself. She burst out with angry insulting scolding," one of them remembered. "She was led out, stooped over, and the rest of the party then withdrew in silence."

After returning from his South African tour in April 1929, Conan Doyle published a 5,000-word "open letter to all elderly folk" in which he noted matter-of-factly that "you and I are suffering from a wasting and incurable disease called old age, and there is but the one end to it." He turned seventy the following month. Later that summer, Doyle appeared in a Movietone newsreel shot in the garden at Windlesham, where he chatted affably about both Sherlock Holmes and "the psychic matter." On August 15, he and the family were at Bignell Wood when a fire took hold of the cottage's thatched roof. By the time the emergency services eventually arrived from Southampton, most of the house's upper half had been destroyed. Doyle later wrote a letter of thanks to the villagers who had rallied to help drag his furniture onto the lawn, although "one or two, I regret to say, showed a disposition to remove the goods even further." In time, the insurance company determined that the fire had begun in the kitchen chimney, but Doyle wondered whether there might not be a paranormal aspect to it. A few days after the event, Pheneas materialized to announce that there had been a "bad psychic cloud" hovering above the burned part of the building. It had been necessary to remove this, the spirit explained, so that what remained could be used for "high purposes" when the apocalypse finally came.

The following month, Conan Doyle sent a correspondent named Hutchinson a long critique of the latter's self-published "psychic thriller," showing he had lost none of his consummate eye for a good plot. He broadly endorsed the claims of a Mr. Kirkby of Skegness to have invented a device known as "the Reflectograph," a prototype tape recorder that, it was hoped, might capture spirit voices. Later in the year, Doyle contributed an article to the *Daily Mail* called "Have We Lived Before?" in which he speculated that "the misspent life is punished, as it were, by reincarnation, so that the lesson which has not been learnt at once may be taught the second time. Outside this . . . I believe that there is the element of choice and that one may either continue one's development upon the spiritual plane or may descend upon earth in order to complete one's education." Conan Doyle increasingly dwelt on his own death, "as I have broken down badly and have developed Angina Pectoris," he wrote Bernard Ernst. "So there is just a chance that I may talk it all over with Houdini himself before very long. I view the prospect with perfect equanimity. That is one thing that psychic knowledge does. It removes all fear of the future." Doyle's final literary act was to collect a series of essays on the occult into a slim book called *The Edge of the Unknown*. "In a long life which has touched every side of humanity," he wrote in the opening piece, "Houdini is far and away the most curious and intriguing character whom I have ever encountered." The "little magician," though physically courageous, undermined Doyle's belief in discipline, self-effacement, and truth for its own sake. "His favourite argument [against Spiritualism] was this flourishing of dollar-wads."

Although Conan Doyle's book was politely received, there were those, like his editor at the American house Doubleday, who privately thought it "awfully sad" and its subject matter "childish in the extreme." But even if Doyle had arguably outlived his talent as a writer, his skill as a public speaker was undiminished. In October 1929, he set off on a tour of the Low Countries and Scandinavia, part of his continuing mission to take the psychic gospel to the world and, more specifically, to those parts "not suffocated" by the Catholic Church. Curious audiences in Copenhagen and Oslo were thrilled by Conan Doyle's autobiographical account of how the creator of the world's most famous analytical mind had come to believe in fairies and spirits, a process he described for them in his avuncular Scots burr.

Even skeptics who had come to the lectures prepared to scoff were charmed by Doyle's friendly, self-deprecating manner and his homely observations about life. His polished public performances were all the more striking given the fact that his health was now failing so badly. Doyle broke down several times during the tour, privately complaining of acute breathing difficulties, but refused all offers to curtail his schedule. Like Houdini, he battled on, in near-constant pain, determined to fulfill his obligations so long as there was "one single soul willing [to] listen."

On November 7, Conan Doyle's ship returned to Dover, where he had to be carried off by two deckhands. Four days later, he gave back-to-back Armistice Day speeches to packed houses, telling his audiences of a recent séance with Einer Neilsen, a Danish medium, and reminding them there was "no final death." Although Doyle had to postpone a subsequent talk after he had collapsed in a London taxi, he was able to contribute a long, valedictory piece to the *Sunday Graphic*. "I have been pronounced to be suffering from a complaint—angina—which is certainly painful and hardly at my age curable," he wrote, "and yet, owing to my psychic knowledge, I am conscious of a profound inward serenity and a deep peace of mind . . . God does not throw us upon the scrap-heap." Doyle said as much in a letter to Oliver Lodge: he felt "happier and clearer" than he had for years, he insisted, savoring the opportunity to turn from worldly achievements to focus on the future. Reflecting further on his life's work, Doyle later struggled to the desk set up for him in his Windlesham sickroom and drew a sketch, a copy of which today hangs in London's Sherlock Holmes pub. It shows an old workhorse pulling a baggage cart laden with crates, each representing a different aspect of Doyle's career: "Historical Novels," "Poems," "Tales," "The Great War," and "Psychic Research," with perhaps the biggest burden wryly marked "Holmes."

On October 24—Black Thursday—the Dow Jones industrial average lost nearly a quarter of its total value, in a steadily accelerating fall that would continue overnight and at intervals over the next three weeks. As shares dropped vertically with no one buying, traders were sold out as they failed to respond to margin calls, mobs gathered on Broad Street outside the New York stock exchange, and by the end of the day sixteen prominent bankers were known to have committed suicide. The Great Depression had begun. Although the Conan Doyles' spirit guide had long predicted a global crisis that would shake the established order to its core, he seems to have remained uncharacteristically silent as newspapers like the *New York Times* now deployed their boldest "Nation in Panic" headlines. In time, Pheneas issued a fresh warning of doom for September 18, 1931, which would have been the Doyles' twenty-fourth wedding anniversary.

Despite the differences in temperament, the one aggressive, the other composed, there were more points of resemblance between the final period of Houdini's and Doyle's careers. Neither cared to admit he might ever be wrong; neither had any intention of retiring quietly; both were determined to keep up the fight to their dying day, and did so. Although Doyle was so weak he could manage only a bunch of grapes at his final Christmas dinner, he began 1930 with guns blazing, not only taking on the Catholic Church and others whom he saw waging an ever-intensifying anti-Spiritualist conspiracy, but also fighting an internecine war with the Society for Psychical Research, which he accused of being "entirely for evil."

Conan Doyle's specific bone of contention with the SPR was the Society's review of a book by one Ernesto Bozzano, about the Spiritualist activities of an Italian nobleman, Marquis Carlo Scotto, at his Millesimo Castle near Genoa. The Marquis had taken solace in the séance room following the death of his son in a flying accident in 1926. He quickly became an occult *cause célèbre*. At one sitting, he is said to have listened through a brass ear-trumpet to the "unmistakable sound" of an airplane engine, followed by that of the plane falling. Later in 1928 and 1929, he began to communicate with a spirit guide named Cristo d'Angelo, who announced that he had once been a Sicilian shepherd and, like Pheneas, went on to warn of the "terrible events" that lay ahead. Although Bozzano declared both the Marquis and his guide to be "pure . . . Spiritual and mental visionaries for the ages," the SPR took a dim view of the goings-on at Millesimo Castle. "The sittings were held in complete darkness, for the most part without control and without any searching of those present, [despite which] they are described by Sir Arthur as 'on the very highest possible level of psychical research.'" Conan Doyle responded first by lodging a complaint against the SPR's "insolence," and then by ending his thirty-six-year membership in the Society. It was unfortunate, one Sunday newspaper gloated, that the "high priest of Spiritualism [had] come down to the earthly plane to squabble," but Doyle was in no mood to compromise. The whole business "makes one ashamed that such stuff should be issued by a [body] which has any scientific standing," he wrote in his brusque letter of resignation from the SPR, which, rather disarmingly, the Society published in the next issue of its journal.

For all that, Conan Doyle struck many observers as being almost unnaturally cheerful in his final months. He remained self-confident and optimistic, never accepting the notion that his bad health prevented him from living a full life. He enjoyed the chance to "muse on things," he told the journalist Howell Gwynne. "I am still laid by the heels and cannot walk more than 50 yards without getting breathless. However, my mind is clear and I am perfectly happy, for I can assure you from personal experience that there is nothing like psychic knowledge for carrying you through times of difficulty and enabl[ing] you to face death." Doyle's benign mood seems to have been shared elsewhere. The former *New York World* editor, and convicted wife-killer, Charles Chapin, wrote from Sing Sing prison to say that he had been visited by "someone you know—little Beatrice Houdini, widow of my old friend the magician. She told me that while Houdini differed with you about Spiritual manifestations, he always had the highest regard for your great intellect and looked upon you as his friend. Houdini frequently visited me before his tragic death and when he dropped out his widow carried on . . . A hundred magicians came in a body to her little tea room a week ago, and when the supper was finished some of them went into the kitchen and helped wash and dry dishes." Much of Doyle's daily postbag brought him more exotic stuff. "Honourable Sir," one correspondent wrote in the spring of 1930. "Sometimes words are but empty vessels, to give voice to that depth of thought which the soul feeleth at rare moments when our better self climbs to a higher Spiritual chime."

On July 1, Conan Doyle went up to London for the last time, for a meeting with the new Labour home secretary John Clynes. Although Doyle was meant to be at the head of a ten-strong delegation lobbying for changes to the Witchcraft Act, he found himself alone there, but for the journalist Hannen Swaffer; once again, the Spiritualists had fallen out among themselves on a point of principle. Clynes was concerned about his now painfully frail guest, and insisted he sit down to make his presentation. As Doyle spoke, he continually tapped his fingers against his chest as though to coax his breath. Although courteous, Clynes was noncommittal about any change to the law, which, as it turned out, was repealed (to be replaced by the Fraudulent Mediums Act) only twenty-one years later.

After that Conan Doyle returned to his bed at Windlesham. As the end approached, his thoughts were increasingly with his family. One morning, he called in twenty-one-year-old Denis, who had just prematurely come down from Cambridge, and told him he should always heed the advice of his younger sister Jean (or "Billy"), as she knew how to manage money. "And for my sake, continue to avoid alcohol," he told all four of his surviving children. Doyle again reaffirmed the Spiritualist beliefs that had prompted malicious talk among his critics about a complete loss of mind. Early in the morning of Monday, July 7, Denis and his brother Adrian drove off at wild speed to the nearby hospital to bring oxygen back to the house. Conan Doyle was aware that he was dying, and he wanted the end to come soon. Shortly after dawn, he asked to be moved to a favorite armchair placed by the window, where he could look out over the rolling hills to the north. His last words were to his wife. "You are wonderful," he told her. Then he silently looked around at each of his family in turn. At 9:15 he sank back in his chair. His great heart stopped beating.

Conan Doyle's funeral took place at Windlesham on July 11, in a spirit, it was reported, of "no tears, no anguish, and hardly anything that savoured of death." After some breezily optimistic remarks by the Spiritualist minister (and SPR council member) Drayton Thomas, Doyle was laid to rest in a plot at the end of his garden. Six thousand or more people packed the Albert Hall at a memorial service two days later. A vacant chair was set up on the platform alongside those reserved for Lady Jean and the family. A cardboard sign propped up in front of it read, "Sir Arthur Conan Doyle." Once again the mood was determinedly upbeat, with "many gaudy costumes on display," the *Empire News* reported. Rev. George Craze of the Spiritualist Association made the opening remarks, and then asked the audience to stand for two minutes' silence. Following that, a petite, middle-aged medium named Estelle Roberts was invited up on the stage, where she stood for some time, her eyes closed, swaying back and forth in front of a microphone. From time to time, she punctuated the routine by a sudden, birdlike twitch of her head. After what one report called an "interminably suspensful" pause, Mrs. Roberts then looked up toward the ceiling of the hall and announced, "There are vast numbers of spirits here with us. They are pushing me like anything." Working the crowd like a seasoned vaudeville mentalist, she went on to describe the personal characteristics of several apparitions seemingly hovering above the heads of the audience: "You, sir—I see by you the spirit of a young soldier, about 24, who calls you 'Uncle Fred' . . . There is a gentleman on the Other Side, John Martin, looking for his daughter Jane . . . He has got your mother and your sister Mary with him." After some three-quarters of an hour of this, there was a sudden peal of music on the Albert Hall's pipe organ that seemed to galvanize Mrs. Roberts's efforts. "He is here!" she exclaimed, pointing to the empty chair on the stage. "He is here!" At that, she went across to where Lady Conan Doyle was sitting, told her, "I have a message for you from Arthur," and leaned forward to speak in her ear. Just then, a second thunderous chord issued from the organ, making it impossible for the audience to hear what was said. Mrs. Roberts later told the press that she had first seen Doyle during the two minutes' silence. "Then when I was giving my messages, I saw him again. He was wearing evening dress . . . He was behind me, encouraging me while I was doing my work."

Jean Conan Doyle devoted much of the rest of her own life to her efforts to prove that her husband had survived the grave. When Doyle had made out his will the previous May, he left half his annual book royalties to his wife and half to be divided among his three younger children, with a lump sum of £2,000 (£80,000 today) for his forty-one-year-old unwed daughter Mary. While going on to lavish much of their windfall on fast cars and faster women, the boys, in particular, staunchly supported their mother in her Spiritualist activities. The day after the Albert Hall event, a Yorkshire medium, Rev. Charles Tweedale, had a sitting with the spirit photographer William Hope, and forwarded the results to Windlesham. "On the first [photographic] plate were three faces in cloudy banks of ectoplasm," Lady Jean later told the *News Chronicle.* "They are clearly recognisable as pictures of Sir Arthur. The two sitters in the next photograph hoped to get someone belonging to them, but my husband, to their astonishment, appeared to them too." On October 31, Arthur Ford re-emerged from across the Atlantic to hold a candlelit séance for the Doyles. Lady Jean would tell the press that the whole family was "perfectly satisfied" that Conan Doyle had returned to them again, although neither her daughter nor stepdaughter seems to have been present. It also happened to be the fourth anniversary of Houdini's death, and Bess, too, spent the evening with a medium.

On the night of July 7, Dr. Crandon wrote from Boston, "Walter, for the first time ever, failed to come through . . . However, a surrogate named Mark appear[ed], and announced that his friend was busy as part of a reception committee to greet a Great Spirit, recently arrived." In time, Margery would show a talent for automatic writing, and began to receive direct messages from Conan Doyle. "You carry my mantle onward," he once remarked, before encouraging her to write a book with the title *Sherlock Holmes in Heaven.* Margery was only one of several mediums as far afield as Reno, Nevada, and a Spiritualist cell in Australia's Northern Territory to make contact. "Some of these cases are pathetic," Conan Doyle's old antagonist Harry Price confided. "I have heard of a 16-year-old girl in a colliery town who awakened her parents in the small hours and declared that Doyle had visited her. Her hysterical screams brought the neighbours in and morphia was injected to induce sleep. Next morning she was certified as suffering from *dementia praecox.*" (Price soon went on to publish the transcript of his own séance-room talks with Doyle, in which the author assured him he was carrying on doing much the same things he had on earth.) Charles Tweedale proved to be the most persistent of those regularly communing with Doyle's spirit, which once told him, "Well, my dear man, I have arrived here in Paradise. That is not heaven. Oh, no! But what we should call a dumping place, for we all come here as we pass on to rest. Paradise means not heaven, but 'a park'—Persian word." According to *Psychic News,* Doyle then once again returned to his widow and sons through the agency of Estelle Roberts. "Sir Arthur, vigorous, powerful, full of force, very earnest and very grave, came back [and] spoke of the great battle now being waged between Spiritualism and the blundering forces that oppose everything that stands for progress . . . Mrs. Constance Treloar, President of the Marylebone Spiritualist Association, was present, as was George Craze, Lady Carey, and her great friend Lady Hardinge, Maurice Barbanell and Dr. Rust, the brave medical man from Newport, Fifeshire . . . Later, Doyle was heard to say, 'Craze, they [the skeptics] can never stem the tide. We are going to deluge the world. Truth is here at last.'"

For sheer inventiveness, however, none of these could top the activities of the mystical Polaire Brotherhood in France, who in 1931 made contact with the British clairvoyant Grace Cooke to announce that Conan Doyle had chosen her as the medium through whom he wished to speak from the other side. Cooke had previously enjoyed some fame for her channeling of a Native American spirit guide named White Eagle, who believed not so much in the biblical story of Jesus Christ as in a "Cosmic Christ who is both Father and Mother, and the divine spark in all our hearts." The ultimate result of this collaboration was *Arthur Conan Doyle's Book of the Beyond,* which combined a series of posthumous interviews of the author (or "Brighteyes," as he and his guide were interchangeably known) with several chapters of more general New Age philosophizing. Lady Jean and her sons sat in on some of the early séances, although after a sulfurous row in May 1931, "the widow and family withdrew from the joint work," in Mrs. Cooke's measured phrase. "When it came to the messages being published, Lady Doyle was adamant that they should not go out under her husband's name," the medium added. "A letter of 9 December 1933, when Lady Jean had seen this book, set out her upset and her bewilderment." Like Bess Houdini before her, Jean initially seems to have welcomed any possible chance to speak with her dead husband, only to repent later. "When [Conan Doyle] has got anything for the world, he will communicate with us first," she announced. "The messages purporting to come from him already cannot be accepted."

"Experienced Spiritualists look with deep suspicion upon all posthumous productions which have great names attached to them," Conan Doyle himself had written in the *New York Times* in June 1922. "Too much have we suffered from Shakespeares who cannot write and Coleridges who have lost all virility of thought . . . The essence of our creed is that death makes no difference to the personality." It is debatable whether Doyle's own spirit communications bear up to this test. Could his "undoubted and direct" voice really be heard in such messages as, "A delicate balance exists between the celestial, intellectual and institutional, for on this next plane the soul responds to that institutionalised or spiritual light which draws it ever onward, ever higher and nearer to the central focus of its being, the Godhead"? Or, "It is the greatest joy for me to see the little people, the gnomes and fairies, at their work in the gardens of the earth plane, and in the gardens of the astral plane, and on the higher planes, a-weaving their dreams and aspirations (to be some day captured by someone, dexterous with brush and pen), manifesting this cosmic love," as quoted by Grace Cooke? Would Doyle, in fact, have "trilled out" a lengthy paean to the beauty and spiritual acumen of White Eagle, and of Native Americans in general? Or spoken equally effusively of the merits of herbal medicine, Christian Science, and astrology? Similarly, does "Well, Tweedale, I have arrived . . . When I awoke I was astonished and fair surprised beyond measure at finding myself so free and well. Words cannot describe the feeling, and one of the first to greet me was Crookes. I am so bewildered, but I will give you good evidence for your wonderful pen" convey Doyle's known voice? "Now the late Sir Arthur was an admirable writer of English," one critic noted. "If the post-death messages are exact copies of those messages, his knowledge of even the elementary rules of grammar must have suffered woefully since his death."

The messages continued. "We declare that all life can be divided into rays of certain vibration," Conan Doyle supposedly remarked at one séance. "If a healer attempt to treat a man vibrating on, say, no. 7 ray with no. 5 method of treatment he will most certainly fail, and in all probability do harm rather than good. If, however, he treat no. 7 with no. 7, a complete cure will be effected." In 1931, the Italian Nino Pecoraro emerged once more to unsuccessfully claim a reward for having channeled both Doyle and his son Kingsley. On September 18 that year, the "day of doom" predicted by Pheneas passed with nothing more calamitous for humanity than the death of Hitler's young niece Geli Raubal, after a reported lovers' tiff with him, and another of Britain's cyclical currency crises. Doyle apparently manifested again to Mrs. Cooke on May 22, 1932—"my earth birthday," he commented, "and although men may consider this long past and finished, yet indeed the links of earth seem to hold. Be it known that the day of the spirit's incarnation in flesh is a day of power for that spirit, and can be used either for good or evil. Thus on the anniversary of a death, a birth, a murder or a suicide, of any happening tragic or otherwise which vitally affects man's soul, comes a recurrence on the earth plane of psychic vibrations about the scene of the experience."

A month later, Conan Doyle returned to congratulate his old journalist friend Hannen Swaffer on his launch of the weekly *Psychic News*. "'Doyle speaking,' he announced. 'I asked permission just to come for a moment to offer kudos . . . Go forward. Always stand for the truth. Fear no man. Do that which is good always. Do not worry over things. You have much to accomplish yet,'" Swaffer reported him saying. "Hearing [George] Craze's voice, Doyle then added, very dramatically, '*Look after your mediums. You must watch and protect them in the next two months . . . Craze, there is a great force opposing us, but we must go forward . . . Truth is here at last!*'" If Conan Doyle never commented on his post-mortem relations with Houdini, it seems to have been the one subject on which he was silent. "Weird and muffled voices were heard tonight speaking in the darkened interior of a plane soaring high over the city," the *New York Times* reported. "They identified themselves as belonging to the spirits of Arthur Conan Doyle, Wilbur Wright, and Roald Amunsden." Doyle's final remarks to Grace Cooke followed: "Let each man have his due, but all must ultimately recognise and bow to the infinite love of the Creator . . . Truly, truly, every word uttered by the Great Master rings with truth, unsullied by the centuries, eternal and absolute."

Lady Conan Doyle's support of her husband was as constant and extravagant in death as it had been in life. She continued to host family or semi-private séances, if on a gradually more selective basis, and to stoutly defend his reputation in a series of interviews and speeches over the next ten years. At one point she took action against Nino Pecoraro and the *Daily Express* for having suggested that she had come to have doubts about Spiritualism. In later years, Lady Jean traveled the country in a specially equipped van in order to spread the psychic word. She died on June 27, 1940, and was buried next to her husband at Windlesham; when the house was sold in 1955, the couple were disinterred and moved to All Saints churchyard in Minstead, near their home at Bignell Wood.

Oliver Lodge also devoted much of his remaining years to arguing on his friend and colleague's behalf. "No question has ever arisen about the perfect sincerity of Conan Doyle," Lodge told a correspondent in September 1930. "He was consumed with interest in the subject, and sacrificed a great deal for the cause. I should say it is not possible to imagine a more sincere man than he was. Even those who think he was mistaken feel quite assured of that; and no one who knew him can have the smallest doubt." Lodge survived Lady Doyle by just seven weeks, having lived long enough to see the Nazi conquest of France that his spirit guide had "repeatedly" warned him about.

In Boston, Margery continued her séances, many of which came to offer a range of advice and guidance supplied by Conan Doyle from the beyond. He's said to have urged the sitters at one event in the economically strapped days of January 1933 to invest in US Treasury bonds, and to have railed against the lifting of the Prohibition laws later that year. The "indestructible union" of which Margery spoke when describing her marriage to one reporter did not extend to sexual fidelity. "My husband loved people," she later remarked. "It would have been unnatural for him to withhold love from half their number." Dr. Crandon died in December 1939, after falling down a flight of stairs. Following that, Margery moved in with William Button, the president of the American SPR. They and their friends "sat in circles almost every night for the rest of their lives, although Walter himself appeared on a more sparing basis," it was reported. The ASPR later released a confidential letter by Margery's champion Malcolm Bird, in which he spoke of having attended one of the Houdini séances at Lime Street in July 1924. "Psyche sought a private inter-view with me and tried to get me to agree, in the event that nothing occur[red], that I would ring the bell-box myself, or produce something else that might pass as activity by Walter . . . This proposal was clearly the result of Margery's wrought-up state of mind. Nevertheless . . . it shows her, fully conscious and fully normal, in a situation where she thought she might have to choose between fraud and a blank séance; and she was willing to choose fraud." Margery herself told a researcher who visited her bedside in her final days, to ask if she had ever faked phenomena, "You'll all be guessing for the rest of your lives." She died, overnight on Halloween 1941, fifteen years after Houdini; she was fifty-three.

On October 31, 1936, Bess and her companion Edward Saint attempted to reach Houdini via a late-night séance held on the roof of the Knickerbocker Hotel in Hollywood. With several raucous musical fanfares provided by a high school marching band, some 300 spectators accommodated in temporary stands (ser-viced by strolling hot-dog salesmen and gift vendors), and a live radio hookup bringing the event to an estimated 6 million homes, the occasion resembled an American sporting event as much as it did a solemn religious ceremony. This was perhaps the sort of "unbounded self-advertising" Conan Doyle had long dis-paraged, even if Houdini himself could hardly be blamed for it. Saint made a tremulous introduction, speaking of a fabulous diamond pin that he hoped the illusionist's spirit would help him locate. When nothing initially came through, he turned to the audience to ask if any of them had any "psychic information" on the subject. None did. Saint then bowed to the frail, white-haired lady at his side. "Madame Houdini," he said. "The zero hour has passed. The ten years are up. Have you reached a verdict?"

"Yes," said Bess. "Houdini did not appear. My last hope is gone. I do not believe that Houdini can come back to me, or to anyone . . . The shrine has burned for ten years. I now reverently turn out the light. It is finished." At that Bess reached up to extinguish a single red lightbulb that had been placed over a portrait of her husband. "It is finished," she repeated. "Good night, Harry."

Following Edward Saint's death, Bess moved into a modestly furnished Los Angeles nursing home. In January 1943, she was diagnosed with a serious heart condition; although heavily sedated, she had intervals of consciousness, during one of which it became apparent the disease had not dulled her ability to speak her mind. "The nurse came to my room with a wheelchair—what I told her to do with it is still spoken of in the nurses' quarters," she wrote Hardeen. Later that month, Bess told a reporter from *Time* that she not only had given up trying to reach Houdini but had her doubts about the existence of a hereafter. "Ten years," she observed, "is long enough to wait for any man."

Although the formal Houdini séances came to an end in 1936, the attempt to reach him continued. The writer and magician Walter Gibson (1897–1985), author of the pulp fiction character "The Shadow," went on to preside over a series of events at the Magic Towne House in New York. Although Gibson would report some limited successes over the years, he, too, ultimately failed to convincingly manifest or communicate with the risen Houdini. In the 1980s, the torch passed to the television personality Dorothy Dietrich, who continued the annual Halloween tradition at the Houdini Museum in Scranton, Pennsylvania. In 2007, the Canadian media clairvoyant Kim Dennis came to Scranton following a "long discussion with Harry," but was unable to convince Dietrich and others of her psychic powers. According to one report, "Ms. Dennis later did not want to appear for a TV cameraman who came to interview her. She ran away up the stairs to the parking lot and got in her car. She claims on her website, 'I travelled to heaven where I was sometimes taught by a guide,' but did not appear to have their help on this occasion." For some years, there was also a well-subscribed annual sitting in Room 401 of Grace Hospital in Detroit, where Houdini died. This tradition was brought to an end in 1976, when the building was demolished. In 2006, Jon Stetson, a self-styled "internationally acclaimed mind-reading comedian" and "corporate entertainer like no other," organized an eightieth-anniversary séance at the Center for Jewish History in New York. It, too, ended inconclusively. Although three letters of an illuminated sign were seen to flicker mysteriously at the back of the hall, the building manager was left to admit that this "might have been the guy running the lights," rather than an occult presence. Later that year, two Houdini authors, some lawyers, and a PR firm called for the illusionist's body to be exhumed so that an autopsy could belatedly be performed. The suggestion was that Houdini had been "poisoned as part of [a] plot masterminded by Le Roi Crandon" to aggressively defend his wife's honor. Several days of headlines followed about this tabloid equivalent of the unquiet dead. Houdini's closest living relative, a man named Jeff Blood, later revealed that the family was "totally against" exhumation. "It is our firm belief that Bess herself would have never approved," he added. "This is just being done to promote sales of a recent book on Houdini suggesting he may have been murdered."

By early 1943, Bess's thoughts were turning back toward her youth. Visitors to the nursing home noted that she was more inclined to reminisce about her early vaudeville days, or Houdini's experiences as Projea, the Wild Man of Mexico, than she was about Spiritualism or séances. Having beaten the bottle, she appears to have become more like the chirpy and attractive character of old. On February 10, she discharged herself from care and boarded a train for New York, announcing that she wanted to go back to "where it all began." Bess died of a heart attack the following morning; she was sixty-seven. Her body was taken off the train at the small stop of Needles, California. Bess's family would not allow her to be interred with her husband, as she had asked, because she had been raised a Catholic. She was buried instead some twenty miles away at the Gate of Heaven cemetery in upstate New York. Houdini's brother and successor Theo—Hardeen—continued to appear on Broadway until his own death in June 1945. Many of the family's professional secrets went with him. Houdini's last surviving brother Leopold committed suicide in 1962, at the age of eighty-three. He was in poor health and had never quite recovered from losing a fortune in the stock market crash thirty years earlier.

Harry and Bess Houdini were childless. Conan Doyle fathered five children, two with his first wife and three with his second, none of whom had any issue of their own. Doyle's elder daughter Mary continued to run the Psychic Bookshop until its final collapse. A spinster, she died in 1976, aged eighty-seven, with only a small terrace house in Twickenham and little money to her name. Mary's half-sister Jean, Conan

Doyle's youngest child, joined the Women's Royal Air Force in 1938 and retired thirty years later as an Air Commandant, aide-de-camp to the Queen, and a Dame of the British Empire. Along the way, she made a friend and admirer of Lord Dowding, the former head of RAF Fighter Command, who like her became a Spiritualist. Dame Jean died in 1997, aged eighty-four. "'Tidiness' and 'Order' were her catchwords," an obituarist wrote, "and she was known for her hard work and commitment to the job in hand. For many years this stood in the way of close emotional attachments, but in 1965 she married Air Vice-Marshal Sir Geoffrey Bromet, who was 20 years her senior, and they had a happy life together until his death in 1983."

While Conan Doyle would likely have approved of Jean's record of selfless devotion, he might have been less impressed by the activities of her two brothers. Denis, the elder, who married "Princess" Nina Mdivani of Georgia, spent the war years in North America, ran up prodigious bills, and was locked in a dispute with the American tax authorities at the time of his early death in 1955. He told the *New York Times* that he was in "constant" touch with his late father. "I recently had the pleasure of reading some account of your profoundly interesting experiences in the realm of telepathy and thought transference," Denis wrote Conan Doyle's old adversary J. B. Rhine. "My own personal interest in the matter lies in the indirect connection which exists between your realm of research and my own, which is directed towards furthering the studies and experiments into demonstrable survival after death, and especially into the field of Universal Occult Law, and its possible application to mundane affairs, both individual and international." In later years, Princess Nina spent an increasing amount of time apart from her husband, and ended her days as a resident in luxury hotels like the Paris Ritz. A confirmed Spiritualist, Denis was survived only by his pamphlets, interviews, and debts.

Adrian Conan Doyle made his brother's life seem like one of monastic self-denial by comparison. After being dismissed by the Royal Navy for insubordination, Adrian re-launched himself as an amateur race-car driver, big-game hunter, and occasional writer. Following his mother's death in 1940, he took over the running of his father's literary estate, which he managed from a chateau in Switzerland. In short order, there were hotly debated claims of a "lost" Sherlock Holmes story coming to light, followed by a furious row between Adrian and Princess Nina, who had since gone on to marry her late husband's secretary. This involved some $200,000 in disputed book royalties. Adrian then fell foul of his own sister by setting up the Lausanne-based Sir Arthur Conan Doyle Foundation, giving the Canton of Vaud custody of his father's manuscripts in return for $2 million cash and various tax breaks, a move that "gravely concerned" the less materially minded Jean. Nor did

Adrian restrict himself to fighting solely with members of the family. "Dear Sir," he wrote in a typical letter to his solicitor in January 1945. "Last November, the *Daily Sketch* published an article which, in all my experience of journalism, is unequalled in its degree of falsehood against the memory of a famous man, claim[ing] that 'Sir Arthur Conan Doyle would literally credit any fraud if it was practiced by a Spiritualist.' I need hardly add that this monstrous lie aroused strong feelings in many quarters [and] I shall be most grateful for your opinion on the matter." Over the years, in a process that was at once seemingly random as well as bizarre, Adrian would open his father's archive to certain inquiring authors and aggressively deny it to others. (His successors continue the practice today.) He demanded no rigorous biographies, and for years none were published. In the meantime, Adrian left and reconciled with his Danish wife Anna Andersen several times, took a succession of mistresses, and moved around Switzerland and various hotels on the French Riviera, often leaving no forwarding address, continuing to further negotiate the sale of his father's papers as he went. He died in 1970, aged fifty-nine.

Following Adrian's death, Princess Nina was able to establish an offshore company she called Baskerville Investments to manage the Sherlock Holmes part of her father-in-law's estate. When the princess subsequently found herself embarrassed by a pressing hotel bill, she sold out to a Los Angeles–based TV producer named Sheldon Reynolds and his Hungarian wife Andrea (later the mistress of Claus von Bülow at the time of his trial for the attempted murder of his wife). Mrs. Reynolds continues to assert her rights to the Holmes copyright in America, often in the face of spirited opposition from Conan Doyle's indirect descendants and other third parties. Before her death in November 1997, Dame Jean, who suffered from poor eyesight, expressed the hope that as much as possible of her father's archive would go to the Royal Institute of Blind People, where it would be made available to "anyone studying his life." It's yet to happen. Though frequently united in their hostility toward Andrea Reynolds, Dame Jean's and Anna Andersen's heirs would continue to contest ownership of the bulk of Conan Doyle's papers, once or twice marking their dispute by litigation. Dame Jean had wanted her father's letters and unpublished material to remain in Britain; Adrian Conan Doyle's heirs, and other claimants, took the more open-market approach.

In May 2004, Anna Andersen's legally recognized estate put some 3,000 Conan Doyle documents up for auction at Christie's in London, raising around £900,000. Among the choice items to be sold was a handwritten draft of Holmes's first appearance in *A Study in Scarlet* (with the original title, "A Tangled Skein," crossed out) and other Southsea memorabilia such as Conan Doyle's brass nameplate, for which a Hackensack, New Jersey, doctor, Constantine Rossakis, paid £140,000. The British Library bought some 1,200 lesser pieces on behalf of the nation. Meanwhile, a Conan Doyle collector named Richard Lancelyn Green, a flamboyant and well-liked master of ceremonies at meetings of the Sherlock Holmes Society and the self-styled "largest owner of Sherlockiana on earth," had repeatedly tried to stop the sale, expressing the view that Doyle himself would be "literally turning in his grave" both at the squabbling among his heirs and at his property being dispersed across the globe. Shortly before the Christie's auction took place, the fifty-year-old Lancelyn Green was found dead in the locked bedroom of his London flat. He had been garroted. Although the coroner returned an open verdict in the case, there are those convinced Lancelyn Green took his own life in despair at what he had called the "prostitution" of Conan Doyle's work, or even that he was murdered for reasons that may or may not have a Doyle connection. (Lancelyn Green happened to be a wealthy homosexual, and told his last known lover, a nurse named Lawrence Keen, that his flat was "bugged" and that he was being "stalked by unnamed enemies" in the days prior to his death.) As the obituarists pointed out, the world's leading authority on Sherlock Holmes died in a way that could have come from the pages of Holmes's casebook. It's further said that Lancelyn Green had become paranoid about Jon Lellenberg, a policy strategy analyst in the US Defense Department at the time of the second Gulf War, and a respected author of books and articles on Doyle, though it would be fanciful in the extreme to speak, as some appear to, of a Pentagon-sponsored "wet job" in the affair. In his will, Lancelyn Green left the bulk of his collection to Portsmouth City Council. It took a team of ten volunteers two weeks to physically remove the 14,000 books, 3,000 other objects, and 900 boxes of papers involved. The work of cataloging them continues some seven years later, in a room a few minutes' walk away from Conan Doyle's original surgery at Elm Grove. The building itself, where Sherlock Holmes came to life, has been pulled down and replaced by a modern block of flats.

Compared to this, Houdini's estate almost seems a model of cooperation and logical consistency. As noted, the bulk of his archive eventually went to the Library of Congress, which places only modest obstacles in the way of researchers. The fire that largely destroyed the Houdini Museum in Niagara Falls on April 30, 1995, happened to come on the seventieth anniversary of an apparent message from the spirit guide Pheneas that warned of a "terrible" or "fiery" end for the illusionist. The rug salesman and sometime escape artist Sidney Radner, known professionally as Rendar the Magician, put many of the surviving items on display in a combined Houdini archive and gift shop in Appleton, Wisconsin. After a rancorous falling-out between Radner and town officials, the 1,000-piece collection was packed up and sold at an auction held at the Liberace Museum in Las Vegas. The performer David Copperfield paid a reported $300,000 to buy the original Chinese Water Torture Cell—Houdini's celebrated "Upside Down"—which he keeps in his International Museum and Library of the Conjuring Arts, a building entered via a street door operated by pressing a mannequin's nipple outside what's been described as "a mail-order lingerie warehouse" located in a Las Vegas strip mall. Copperfield is the owner of more Houdini apparatus than all other collectors combined. The illusionist's "official" museum in Scranton, Pennsylvania, also houses a number of artifacts, costumes, and props, as well as continuing his researches into the paranormal. The Houdinis' longtime home at 278 West 113th Street in New York is in private hands. There have been occasional reported sightings of a ghost at an estate on Laurel Canyon Boulevard, Los Angeles, where Bess sometimes lived with Edward Saint in the 1930s.

The First World War may have been the starting point of Conan Doyle's Spiritualism, but he was also drawn to the occult by each of the three major strands in his long-held moral code. Doyle's self-reinforcing philosophy was based on his professional interest in the untapped potential of the mind, as seen in his early excursions in mesmerism and telepathy, his unwavering faith that essential human goodness was rewarded by eternal life, and a visionary insistence that what was scoffed at today as "beyond mortal comprehension" (such as radio transmissions had been in his youth) would be accepted tomorrow as commonplace.

Although obviously a catastrophic shock, it would be a mistake to overestimate the effect the loss of Conan Doyle's son Kingsley had on his psychic path. As Doyle himself told Houdini, "I observe that you put down my starting my world-mission 'in a crisis of emotion.' I started in 1916. My son died in 1918." There is ample evidence he turned to the séance room for philosophical reasons more than family circumstances. As well as his predisposition to "find some high[er] truth to the wonderful poise of the universe," Doyle was soon to lose patience with the sort of "corrosive" Roman Catholic dogma he had known at school, and which he eventually came to see as the sinister hand behind a vast anti-Spiritualist conspiracy. It's also possible some of Doyle's specific belief in fairies and other subhuman life forms spoke to his long and apparently forlorn struggle to resolve his feelings about his father, that "sad genius" who had filled up entire notebooks with whimsical and sometimes macabre drawings of little people. Conan Doyle's sense of chivalry similarly led him to doubt the possibility of deception on the part of most female mediums. "Vile charges are made against a lady," Doyle had fumed at the time of J. B. Rhine's sittings with Margery. Time and again, he used words like "impertinence" and "disrespect" when deploring Houdini's activities. Instinct and training also left Doyle ill equipped when it came to detecting fraud by young children, such as the Fox sisters or the two "wonderfully innocent" cousins at Cottingley. The Davenports' "first manifestations seem to have begun when they were quite boys," he once told Houdini, evidence, apparently, of the brothers' occult power. Conan Doyle's critics would say that his good nature made him all too credulous an observer—an "old buffer," in one account, "not to be trusted to expose the obvious crooks and chancers in the darkened séance room . . . They could get away with anything, and routinely did." That the "buffer" view of Doyle is something of a simplification the preceding pages have, perhaps, shown; and there are those on the other side of the coin who prefer to remember him more as the intrepid and all-knowing founder of a world religion, whose fictional writings were a mere sideline to his messianic leadership. This, too, is an inadequate picture of the man.

Houdini was also driven by a small number of basic, unchanging ideas that ultimately led to his clash with Doyle. Chief among these was a genuine aversion to the "human jackals, bunco artists, carnie men and snake-oil types" whom he saw using the bereaved, as well as a characteristic belief in his own professional powers. "It takes a flimflammer to catch a flimflammer," he told the *Los Angeles Times* in October 1924. Nor would Houdini have failed to note the theatrical box-office potential of setting himself up as the world's ranking anti-Spiritualist. Like Conan Doyle, his core philosophy met with a specific shock that went on to help shape his later career; in Doyle's case the death of his son, in Houdini's that of his mother. "Everything changed," the illusionist wrote, after those "desperate days and nights" in the summer of 1913. Houdini himself was never a skeptic, he insisted, but the "complete and miserable failure" of every séance he attended over a thirteen-year period "was simply too much . . . After all the ardent research and endeavor, I declare that nothing has been revealed to convince me that intercommunication has been established between the Spirits of the departed and those still in the flesh."

The most notable characteristic of Houdini's Spiritualist exposés was the extent to which he saw them not only as a public service, but as a way to prolong his career into middle age and beyond as his physical powers declined. The shows were always fascinating, but their dominant theme was the intellectual smartness, and professional shrewdness, of the host: he was not a martyr to false modesty.

To his credit, Houdini also saw through a number ("many hundred," he said) of those whose professed concern for their grieving clients was matched "only by their interest in the contents of their wallets and purses." He had a certain breadth and cultivation rare among early-twentieth-century stage artists, and was more than a match for the subtle feats of autosuggestion, and various trap doors, sliding panels, adjustable fishing rods, painted balloons, air hoses, and other then-standard props of the séance room. Conan Doyle may have been the more susceptible of the two men to the sort of quack mediums who flourished in the 1920s, but it's debatable whether his belief in apports and Arabian spirit guides and the rest tells the full story of his mission. The key idea, Doyle had written in *The Vital Message*, "abolishes that of a grotesque hell and a fantastic heaven, while it substitutes the conception of a gradual rise in the scale of existence without any monstrous change which would turn us in an instant from man to angel or devil." The "new revelation" was more than just Spiritual hocus-pocus, he would have argued, a lot more. It was hope.

SOURCES AND CHAPTER NOTES

The following pages show at least the formal interviews, published works, and/or primary archive material used in the preparation of the book. Please note that I have generally referred to Harry Houdini as "an illusionist" rather than a magician, mystifier, conjurer, or escape artist. Although he was all of these things, and more, illusion surely lay at the heart of his performance, whether it was entertaining his audience or trying to educate them.

CHAPTER 1

A good overview of Harry Houdini's early flirtation with Spiritualism can be found in William Kalush and Larry Sloman's peerless *The Secret Life of Houdini*, cited in the bibliography. Some direct Houdini quotes appearing here are excerpted from his book *A Magician among the Spirits*, also later credited, first published in 1924. Arthur Conan Doyle's "a very clever thing" quote appears in a January 30, 1880, letter to his mother Mary Doyle and reprinted in *Arthur Conan Doyle: A Life in Letters*, edited by Jon Lellenberg, Daniel Stashower, and Charles Foley, as cited in the bibliography. Similarly, Conan Doyle's "a very ghastly Animal Magnetic" quote appears in a letter to his mother ca. July 1882; Conan Doyle's "After weighing the evidence" quote appears in a July 2, 1887, letter to the Spiritualist journal *Light*.

CHAPTER 2

Arthur Conan Doyle's quote "our third prefect has gone . . ." appears in an October 1873 letter to his mother Mary Doyle; Conan Doyle's description of his mother appears in his autobiographical novel *The Stark Munro Letters* (1895); Conan Doyle's description of his first wife Louisa (sometimes named "Louise" by biographers) as "gentle and amiable" recurs in his book *Memories and Adventures*, published first in 1924 and cited in the bibliography; Conan Doyle's "in favour of complete liberty of conscience" quote appears in his October 13, 1900, letter to *The Scotsman*. It's also a pleasure to acknowledge the primary source material made available by Michael Gunton and his colleagues at The Sir Arthur Conan Doyle Collection (Richard Lancelyn Green Bequest) of Portsmouth City Council.

Invaluable assistance on Harry Houdini was provided by The History Museum at the Castle of Appleton, Wisconsin, where I should particularly thank Matt Carpenter; the Houdini Museum of Scranton, Pennsylvania; the US Library of Congress; the Magic Circle; and the archive libraries of the *Boston Daily Advertiser*, the *New York Times*, and the *New York World*, among others. I should also acknowledge Kenneth Silverman's *Houdini!!!: The*

Career of Ehrich Weiss—cited in the bibliography—a thorough and consistently entertaining account of its subject, if one that perhaps dwells on his spectacular early career more than his subsequent obsession with the spiritual.

CHAPTER 3

The "I travelled for two years in Tibet" quote, referring to Sherlock Holmes's "great hiatus," appears in Arthur Conan Doyle's short story "The Adventure of the Empty House," first published in 1903; Conan Doyle's "I like none of them" quote is from his novel *The Parasite* (1894); Conan Doyle's "I seemed suddenly to see" quote is from his book *The New Revelation* (1918); Conan Doyle's "but God had placed me" quote is from his book *Memories and Adventures,* previously cited.

I'm glad to again acknowledge Harry Houdini's book *A Magician among the Spirits* for its gripping account of his evolution as a performer, if not one that labors under any false modesty, as well as the help of Dick Brooks and Dorothy Dietrich at the Houdini Museum of Scranton, Pennsylvania. Frederick Lewis Allen's book *Only Yesterday* (first published by Harper & Brothers, 1931) is the best social and political overview of the 1920s I know of; I'm grateful to my uncle Robert Prins for the gift. I visited Arthur Conan Doyle's surviving homes at South Norwood, Hindhead, and Crowborough, and the scene of as many as possible of Houdini's performances in London, the English provinces, Berlin, and Moscow. Generally reliable accounts of his escapes, if not of his methods, can be found in the archives of *Collier's Weekly,* the *Daily Express,* the *Daily Mirror,* the *Illustrated London News,* the *London Daily Illustrated Mirror,* the *New York Times,* and *The Times.* The librarian at Longton Spiritualist Church kindly provided information on the medium Annie Brittain. Julian Barnes's novel *Arthur and George* (Cape, 2005) deals with Conan Doyle's real-life detective adventure with George Edalji, a case that bears some comparison to the Dreyfus Affair.

CHAPTER 4

Arthur Conan Doyle's quote "For my psychic work the Lord, I fear, neither" appears in his book *The Wanderings of a Spiritualist,* first published in 1921. Harry Houdini's quote "The cage of fire has been employed" is from his *Miracle Mongers and Their Methods,* also first published in 1921; Houdini's quote concerning "[the Zancigs] doing a very clever performance" is from his book *A Magician among the Spirits,* previously cited.

It's a great pleasure to acknowledge the resources provided by the Manuscripts Reading Room of the Cambridge University Library, where I spent rather longer in the course of a week than in my three years as a Cambridge undergraduate, and of the Rare Books Room of the British Library. Again, every effort has been made to comply with the copyright provisions involved. The great majority of excerpts from letters exchanged between Conan Doyle and Houdini are taken from Bernard Ernst and Hereward Carrington's book *Houdini and Conan Doyle: The Story of a Strange Friendship,* cited in the bibliography. Michael Gunton and his team at Portsmouth City Council were also able to supply primary source information on Conan Doyle's dealings with several prominent mediums, among them Kathleen Goligher, and to provide the photograph of her that appears here. Newspaper archives consulted included *Collier's Weekly,* the *Denver Post, International Psychic Gazette, Light, Magic,* the *Morning Post, Nation, New York Sun,* the *New York Times,* the *New York World, Scientific American,* and *The Times.* I visited 20 Hanover Square.

CHAPTER 5

The primary source for the magic demonstration given by Houdini to Conan Doyle at the former's New York home was Bernard Ernst and Hereward Carrington's *Houdini and Conan Doyle: The Story of a Strange Friendship,* previously cited. Houdini's quote "before leaving with [Conan Doyle], Mrs Houdini cued me" is excerpted from his book *A Magician among the Spirits;* his quote "Rain and storm, I command you to stop" (the so-called miracle of July 4, 1922) is from the same source. Houdini's article "Ghosts that Talk—by Radio" was published in *Popular Radio* in October 1922.

Arthur Conan Doyle's comments beginning "Of course, it is very satisfactory" were published in the *New York Times* on November 25, 1922. Conan Doyle's quote "with the clear consciousness that there was someone in the room" is excerpted from his book *The Edge of the Unknown,* previously cited, which also contains an account of the Atlantic City séance of June 18, 1922. I again consulted the archives of the Cambridge University and British Libraries, and of the collection held by Portsmouth City Council. It is also a pleasure to acknowledge both Andrew Lycett's book *The Man Who Created Sherlock Holmes,* and Daniel Stashower's *Teller of Tales: The Life of Arthur Conan Doyle,* cited in the bibliography, which happily combine chronology with searching analysis. The Harry Ransom Center of the University of Texas at Austin was invaluable, and kindly supplied the title page of Houdini's *A Magician among the Spirits,* as annotated by Conan Doyle, which appears here; my thanks to Anna Chen at the Center.

CHAPTER 6

Arthur Conan Doyle's quote "enormous vanity and passion for publicity," in reference to Houdini, is excerpted from his book *The Edge of the Unknown,* as previously cited. Conan Doyle's quote regarding "clasped materialized hands" is from his book *Memories and Adventures.* His comment about "Our progress has been slow but . . ." appeared in *John Bull* of September 29, 1923.

Harry Houdini's quote "There is no doubt that Sir Arthur is sincere . . ." is excerpted from his book *A Magician among the Spirits,* previously noted. The phrase attributed here to Houdini about those like Maude Fancher "choosing to swallow arsenic" is a compound of his remarks to his assistant Jim Collins and an interview he gave the *New York Tribune* on the subject. I consulted Massimo Polidoro's very fine book *Final Séance: The Strange Friendship between Houdini and Conan Doyle,* given in the bibliography, as well as the archives of the *American Weekly,* the *Boston Herald, Chambers's Journal,* the *Daily Express,* the *Illustrated London News, Light, Magic,* the *Morning Post, New York Sun,* the *New York Times,* the *New York World,* the *Saturday Evening Post,* the *Strand,* the *Spiritualist,* the *Sunday Express,* and *The Times.*

CHAPTER 7

Arthur Conan Doyle's quote beginning "People ask me what is it" is excerpted from his *Memories and Adventures,* previously cited; his quote "heaven of art, of science, of intellect" is from the same source. The quote beginning "In two years, she attended hundreds of séances" is from William Kalush and Larry Sloman's book *The Secret Life of Houdini,* as previously cited. Harry Houdini's quote "In America alone, millions of dollars are fraudulently obtained" and selected examples of his medium-baiting are taken from *The Houdini Souvenir Program,* which was supplied by its copyright owners Dick Brooks and Dorothy Dietrich of the Houdini Museum. Houdini's quote "Everything that took place was a deliberate and conscious fraud" appeared in the *New York Times* on October 16, 1924. The case study of the Rev. Alice Dooley and her failure "to answer three questions placed before her" appeared in the *New York Times* on September 18, 1925.

I should again particularly acknowledge the help of the Manuscripts Reading Room of Cambridge University Library, and its indefatigable curator Peter Meadows. As well as the previously cited books, I consulted a variety of journals, magazines, and newspapers, including the *American Weekly,* the *Boston Herald,* the *British Journal of Photography, Chambers's*

Journal, the *Chronicle*, the *Illustrated London News*, *Light*, the *Morning Post*, the *New York Times*, the *New York World*, the *Observer*, *Review of Reviews*, the *Seattle Times*, and *Variety*. I again drew on the resources of the Harry Ransom Center of the University of Texas at Austin, and of the US Library of Congress, which between them house most of Houdini's magic library, as well as his scrapbooks, innumerable newspaper cuttings, and various original photographs, some of them reproduced here.

CHAPTER 8

Arthur Conan Doyle's remarks on Houdini's "unconventional intimacy . . . He was, like most Jews, estimable," very slightly reworded for sense, appear in Conan Doyle's essay "The Riddle of Houdini," from his already cited book *The Edge of the Unknown*. Conan Doyle's quotes "Houdini has stuffed so many errors of fact" and "It was difficult to say which was the more annoying" are both included in his book *The History of Spiritualism* (1926).

The quote "He is recognized by scientists" is taken from *The Houdini Program*, previously cited. Some of the minutes of the séances held by Mina Crandon and of the various remarks of the spirit guide "Pheneas" were again provided by the Cambridge University Library archive. William Kalush and Larry Sloman's previously noted book *The Secret Life of Houdini* gives the most thoroughly researched account of its subject's last days, even if hard evidence for certain details, such as the apparent assault on Houdini in the lobby of his Montreal hotel, appears elusive. The late Surgeon Lieutenant Commander "Johnny" Johnson, RN, gave a unique insight into Houdini's final medical condition, and I'm grateful, too, to the Michigan Department of Community Health, Vital Records Division, for a copy of the death certificate. I also made use of a source, who prefers anonymity, familiar with the unpublished writings of the late Bernard Ernst, who not only could claim to have been Houdini's lawyer and perhaps closest friend, but was also on mutually warm terms with Arthur Conan Doyle. (The reader should be assured that every fact stated in the book has been sourced, and for obvious reasons corroborated to the very fullest extent possible, before publication.) For accounts of Harry Houdini's appearance before the joint US Senate and House subcommittee, of his subsequent theatrical tour, and of his relations with Conan Doyle in the last year of his life, I consulted secondary sources including the *Catholic Herald*, the *Chicago American*, the *Denver Post*, the *Detroit News*, the *Morning Post*, the *New Republic*, the *New York Evening Journal*, the *New York Times*, the *Philadelphia Inquirer*, *Proceedings of the ASPR*, the *Seattle Times*, and the *Toronto Post*. I'm also grateful to the archivists at the British Library, the FBI—Freedom of Information Division, the General Register Office, the Harry Ransom Center of the University of Texas at Austin, the Houdini Museum, Portsmouth City Council, and the UK Public Record Office.

CHAPTER 9

Arthur Conan Doyle's quote on Houdini, "In a long life, which has touched every side" is excerpted from Conan Doyle's essay "The Riddle of Houdini" from *The Edge of the Unknown*, as previously cited. Although critics have been harsh to Conan Doyle's final book, it stands alone as an example of Spiritualist philosophy married to the simple art of storytelling. Several of the posthumous quotes attributed to Conan Doyle in this chapter are excerpted from *Arthur Conan Doyle's Book of the Beyond*, edited by Ivan Cooke—in which the subject allegedly "speaks" through the medium Grace Cooke—as cited in the bibliography.

Harry Houdini's quote "After all the ardent research" is excerpted from his book *A Magician among the Spirits*, as previously cited. The account of Kim Dennis's unsatisfactory attempt to "summon" Harry Houdini at the Houdini Museum in Scranton is taken from "PressReleasePoint" on August 29, 2008. The fullest chronology of the various attempts to raise Houdini from late 1926 until the time of his widow's death in February

1943 appears in William Kalush and Larry Sloman's *The Secret Life of Houdini*, as noted in the bibliography.

Other documentary material was kindly made available by the Cambridge University Library, the British Library, the Library of Congress, the Harry Ransom Center of the University of Texas at Austin, and Portsmouth City Council, all as previously cited. I consulted journals, magazines, and newspapers including the *American Weekly*, *Atlantic Monthly*, *Billboard*, the *Boston Herald*, the *Boston Journal*, the *Evening Graphic*, the *Illustrated London News*, *Light*, *London Society*, the *Morning Post*, *Nation*, the *New Republic*, the *New York Herald*, the *New York Times*, *Pearson's*, *Proceedings of the ASPR*, the *Scientific American*, the *Spectator*, the *Spiritualist*, *Sphinx*, the *Sunday Express*, *The Times*, *Two Worlds*, and *Variety*.

I'm particularly grateful to Matt Carpenter of the History Museum at the Castle of Appleton, Wisconsin, and to the staff of the Harry Ransom Center of the University of Texas at Austin, the US Library of Congress, Portsmouth City Council, and the UK Public Record Office for their help in obtaining photographs or other archive material relating to Arthur Conan Doyle or Harry Houdini.

Although all the above institutions and individuals helped in the preparation of this book, I should again stress that none of them had any editorial control over it. I am solely to blame for the contents.

BIBLIOGRAPHY

Barrie, J. M. *The Greenwood Hat.* London: Peter Davies, 1937.

Booth, Martin. *The Doctor, the Detective and Arthur Conan Doyle.* London: Hodder & Stoughton, 1997.

Brandon, Ruth. *The Spiritualists.* New York: Alfred A. Knopf, 1983.

Brown, Ivor. *Conan Doyle.* London: Hamish Hamilton, 1972.

Carr, John Dickson. *The Life of Sir Arthur Conan Doyle.* London: John Murray, 1949.

Christopher, Milbourne. *Houdini: The Untold Story.* New York: Thomas Y. Crowell, 1969.

Conan Doyle, Adrian. *The True Conan Doyle.* London: John Murray, 1945.

Conan Doyle, Sir Arthur. *The Edge of the Unknown.* New York: G. P. Putnam's Sons, 1930.

———. *Memories and Adventures.* Boston: Little, Brown & Company, 1924.

Cooke, Ivan, ed. *Arthur Conan Doyle's Book of the Beyond.* Liss, Hampshire: White Eagle Publishing Trust, 1994.

Ernst, Bernard M. L., and Hereward Carrington. *Houdini and Conan Doyle: The Story of a Strange Friendship.* New York: Albert & Charles Boni, 1932.

Gresham, William Lindsay. *Houdini: The Man Who Walked through Walls.* New York: Holt Rinehart Winston, 1959.

Higham, Charles. *The Adventures of Conan Doyle.* London: Hamish Hamilton, 1976.

Houdini, Harry. *A Magician among the Spirits.* New York: Harper & Bros., 1924.

Kalush, William, and Larry Sloman. *The Secret Life of Houdini.* New York: Atria Books, 2006.

Kellock, Harold. *Houdini: His Life Story.* New York: Harcourt, Brace, 1928.

Lamond, John. *Arthur Conan Doyle: A Memoir.* London: John Murray, 1931.

Lellenberg, Jon, Daniel Stashower, and Charles Foley, eds. *Arthur Conan Doyle: A Life in Letters.* New York: HarperPress, 2007.

Lodge, Sir Oliver. *Raymond: Or Life and Death.* New York: George H. Doran, 1916.

Lycett, Andrew. *The Man Who Created Sherlock Holmes.* London: Weidenfeld & Nicolson, 2007.

Polidoro, Massimo. *Final Séance: The Strange Friendship between Houdini and Conan Doyle.* Amherst, New York: Prometheus Books, 2001.

Roberts, S. C. *Holmes and Watson: A Miscellany.* Oxford: Oxford University Press, 1953.

Silverman, Kenneth. *Houdini!!!: The Career of Ehrich Weiss.* New York: HarperCollins, 1996.

Stashower, Daniel. *Teller of Tales: The Life of Arthur Conan Doyle.* New York: Henry Holt and Company, 1999.

Tietze, Thomas R. *Margery.* New York: Harper & Row, 1973.

INDEX